MARTHA STEWART Living OMNIMEDIA

MARTHA STEWART
CHAIRMAN
CHIEF EXECUTIVE OFFICER

Dear Stew,

When our family of three moved to Westport, Connecticut, more than 25 years ago, we would buy our half gallons of milk from vending machines conveniently located along the Post Road. The cartons were colorful, the milk was delicious, and we could count on it being fresh and cold.

In 1969, Stew Leonard's opened a Dairy Store on the Post Road in Norwalk, and it became a family habit to shop there once a week, not only for milk, but also for other things for our kitchen.

For the past 26 years we have shopped at Stew's, and marveled at the rapid expansion of the store, from a small, "family" market into a sprawling behemoth of great value, fresh produce, wonderful dairy products and delicious fish and meats and cold cuts and other necessities for the home.

What strikes me most, as a consumer, is the fact that with all this growth, the Leonard family is still closely involved overseeing all aspects of the stores — still concerned with the needs of their customers and still entertaining all of us with amusing displays and clever promotions.

I still love to take one of the oversize carts and stroll leisurely through the store, picking and choosing from the vast array of foodstuffs, and I am always able to fill that basket with good value, great ingredients and useful things for my home.

Now Stew Leonard's is publishing their first cookbook — and I can't wait to try some of the family recipes. The Leonards are not only interested in selling raw ingredients, but also in the way their customers can prepare healthy, nutritious meals.

— Martha Stewart

"A dynamite cookbook from a dynamite store!"

— Tim Zagat, *Zagat Survey*

"What a great cookbook! Of course, the chicken recipes are my favorite!"

— Frank Perdue

"The next best thing to having Stew and Bryan cooking up their magic in your kitchen is owning a copy of their book, which is filled with vibrant and intensely flavored recipes from the farm — as well as great dishes from their great chef friends. Chicken Pot Pie has already become my staple!"

— Sheila Lukins, *best-selling author "The Silver Palate Cookbook" and Food Editor, Parade Magazine*

"Friends thought I was crazy to drive 40 minutes each Saturday to shop and hang around at Stew Leonard's — until they came here with me. There is simply no better food, produce and gardening available. And there is simply no place more fun. With this cookbook, at last, the magic of Stew Leonard's can be available to everyone."

— Sally Jessy Raphael
Television Personality

"Stew Leonard's is a one-of-a-kind experience! They bring fun and excitement to food shopping. I've been waiting for them to write a cookbook!"

— Don Soderquist
Vice Chairman/COO, Wal-Mart

"While visiting my brother in Norwalk, Connecticut, one of the side trips I would make from time to time was to go over and visit this phenomenon of marketing called Stew Leonard's. It was just an amazing experience! We welcome them and are excited about the construction of their new store in New York State!"

— Governor George Pataki

"This cookbook is "Bo-datious!" Grab it, hug it and BUY IT!"

— Bo Dietl
Movie Critic – Imus In The Morning; Producer "One Tough Cop" and Chairman, Beau Dietl & Assoc.

"A cookbook is a natural for Stew Leonard's! I love their stores, their dedication to quality, and their extraordinary customer service philosophy."

— Bill Marriott

"I am sure the recipes in your cookbook will be equal to the exceptional quality of the perishables for which Stew Leonard's has become famous."

— Walter Salmon
Sr. Professor of Retailing, Emeritus Harvard Business School

"When I'm performing in New York, I'm off to Stew Leonard's! When I'm filming 'Mad About You' in LA, I'm still mad about Stew's! So, with this cookbook, I can take a piece of Stew Leonard's with me — it has sensational recipes!"

— Cynthia Harris, *Actress*
A.k.a. Sylvia Buchman, Mad About You

"This cookbook is as eclectic, marvelous, and surprising as the store itself. Just as Stew Leonard has made the chore of shopping a unique experience, Bryan Miller and Stew Jr. have turned cooking into a culinary romp."

— Jay Chiat,
Chairman Chiat/Day Advertising

"The Stew Leonard Cookbook is a class act!"

— Bill Yosses, *Four-star Pastry Chef, Bouley Bakery, New York City*

THE
Stew Leonard's
You Can Do It!
Cookbook

by Stew Leonard, Jr.
Bryan Miller

KIMBERLY PRESS — NORWALK, CONNECTICUT

To my wife Kim and
four beautiful daughters
Blake, Alexandra, Chase
and Madison.

Thanks for your patience
while we wrote this book!
– *Stew, Jr.*

For Lucian
and Dorothy Fletcher
– *Bryan*

Published by Kimberly Press, LLC,
100 Westport Ave., Norwalk, CT 06851.
Visit our Web site at http://stew-leonards.com

Manufactured in the United States of America

ISBN: 0-9668611-0-8

First Printing: November 1998

10 9 8 7 6 5 4 3 2 1

CONTENTS

6. Beef, Pork, Veal, and Lamb

7. Poultry

8. Seafood

9. Vegetables

10. Pasta and Grains

11. Desserts

Stew Leonard's

Dear Friends and Customers,

Why a Stew Leonard's Cookbook? When I'm in the store, there's always one question that I'm sure to be asked, "Stew, any ideas for dinner tonight?" Our customers are always saying that they love to cook but don't have the time. With those folks in mind, we decided to write a cookbook that is easy to follow, uses widely available ingredients, and features terrific recipes.

And there is more. We answered the most commonly asked questions from our customers about buying and storing food. For example, what's the best way to store freshly ground coffee? What is the best apple for baking? Can I freeze milk? What's a "free range" chicken? In this book you will find those answers and hundreds more!

How did we meet Bryan Miller? About 10 years ago, Bryan, then a reporter for *The New York Times*, arrived at Stew Leonard's to write a story. His article was entitled, "Stew Leonard's — The Disneyland of Dairy Stores." At the time, Bryan was living in Westport and we soon became good friends.

About five years ago we began organizing the cookbook. We enlisted the help of a wonderful chef and friend, Priscilla Martel, who developed recipes using products from Stew's. Other recipes came from all over: Chef George Llorens, our executive chef; Bryan Miller; Pierre Franey of *The New York Times*; my mother, my wife, my sisters and other relatives; assorted friends; and some of the most famous chefs in New York and Connecticut.

We then asked focus groups of 25 or more home cooks to prepare the recipes and give us their comments. They would return to the store on following days and we had "cookbook tasting parties." Chef George, Bryan and I joined the groups, and we enjoyed giant buffet lunches. The groups critiqued each dish, and modifications were made when necessary.

The interesting thing about our cookbook writing team is that I have spent my life talking to farmers, buying food, and selling it in the stores. Chef George has spent his life in the kitchen cooking. And Bryan Miller has spent most of his life eating in restaurants! It's an interesting trio of talents, and I know you'll find this book useful and fun.

Your Friend, — Stew Jr.

One night, Bryan, Chef George, and myself dined at the Park Avenue Cafe in NYC. The great chef and author, David Burke, offered us a tour of his kitchen. During the tour I asked him what he thought was the secret of writing a great cookbook. "Test the recipes at home!" he said. David added that, while excellent recipes are important, they could fall flat if they are not tested in a home kitchen.

The following group valiantly took on every recipe in the book, allowing us to make critical adjustments when necessary. We want to thank these cooks for their honest and candid opinions, and for helping us write a book that anyone, novice or professional, can follow.

A Big Thanks to...

Dr. Shams Alam
Laurie & Tom Anrico
Linda Arena
Maria Arizmendi
Candy & Dan Arthur
Beth & Tom Arthur
Theresa Beatty
Gabe Bediako
Josimara Boneto
Elaine Boshell
Barbara Bucknam
Chris Cacciato
Danial Canizalez
Maria Capozzoli
Will Carpenter
Nancy Casey
Bret Cherry
Robert Cherubin
Scott Christiano
Debbie & Andrew Colton
Ivonete Correa
Donna & Mike Derivan
Rich Dibble
Luciana Dimeglio
Liza Donnelly
Mimi Dunn
Martha Elliot
Chaz Fable
Debbie Fabricatore
Rich Falcone
Dorothy & Lucian Fletcher
Dody Forrest
Gina Fox
Rosanne Gagliardi
Bob Gagstetter
Nancy Gendreau
Lori George
Louise Gerson
Ronni & Greg Gibson
Betsy Gilberti
Salnave Gilles
Bob Greene
Erin Greene
Craig Hartman
Betty Holden
Beth Hollis
Floyd Hover
Maria & Mike Hughes
Bernette Johnson
Jodi Kaplan
Diane & Joseph Kaspareck
Jack Kean
Kosta Keramaris
Erika Kovacs
Rosa Libertino
Harry Londono
Karen Mazako
Marie Minck
Doreen Miner
Mark Nedley
Julie Pallotta
Fred Papp
Tracy & Dave Peden
Maryse Philitas
Pierre Philitas
Kathy Piela
Brenda Sachs
Ann & Fred Salvino
Debbie Santolini
Heidi Scott
Zita Sebastian
Allan Simon
Sue & Les Slater
Roy Snider
Patty Somma
Barbara Springer
Jill Tavello
Heather & Josh Taylor
Jackie Topa
Pierre Ulysess
John Visuano
Truda Weaver
Art Weiss
Pam & Dave Zavarelli
Doug Zucker

...and to a special friend,
Marie Garofalo

More Thanks to...

Frederick C. Hart, Jr., *Certified Genealogist* • **Don Stevens**, *National Beef Packers*
Jim McCray, *Perdue Farms* • **Tom J. O'Conner**, *Pennfield Farms* • **Ted Cook**, *Wallace & Cook*
Michael Glenister, *AM Café* • **Murray Bresky and Steve Gold**, *Murray's Free Roaming Chicken*
Peter Heineman, *Homarus Smoked Seafood* • **Daniel Leader**, *Bread Alone*
Anthony Valenti, *Valencambo Seafood* • **Joel Nartel**, *Arthur Stern Meat*
Sheldon Golub, *Glen Ridge Smoked Seafood* • **Doug Stewart**, *Franklin Mushroom Farms*
Jimmy and Greg Belta, *Belta Farms* • **John Chapman**, *Pinecroft Farms*
Gibson Wilkinson, *Wilkinson-Cooper Produce* • **Joy Voita**, *Royal Vista Produce*
Bill, Mark and Joel Fierman, *Fierman Produce* • **Larry Gianatti**, *Quality Sales*
Mike Reed, *BC Hothouse Foods* • **Lola Van Gilst**, *Produce Marketing Association*
Bob Ochsner, *California Avocado Information Bureau* • **John Moody**, *Smithfield Pork*
Barry Hirsch and John Thomas, *Kleiman & Hochberg Produce* • **Steve Katzman**, *Katzman Produce*
Greg Plaskett, *Pacific Valley Produce* • **Frank Tangredi**, *Northeast Apple Sales*
Helena and Kodra Dembroski, *Dembroski Orchards* • **Joe DeFrancisco**, *DeFrancisco Farms*

Richard Lung

Art Director of Stew Leonard's

A lifelong resident of Norwalk, Connecticut, Richard remembers his mom bringing him to Stew's to shop and visiting the "Stew's Little Farm." Richard has worked at Stew's for over 14 years. He is involved with everything from advertising and in-store visuals, to package and store design — and now our cookbook. Richard remarks, "Our cover design was done by our customers! I asked over 1,000 of you for your opinions in store surveys and focus groups. Thank you!"

David Kalman

Cover photography and many of the interior photos

David Kalman's lifelong interest in photography became a consuming passion as he began to explore the challenges intrinsic in medium and large format cameras. He has shown his work at the Westport Arts Center and several combined shows in the area. He lives in Westport with his wife and family.

A Special Thanks to...

Chef Priscilla Martel

for some fabulous recipes

and my assistant

Doreen Miner!

Chef George Llorens

Stew Leonard's Executive Chef

Chef George was born in Barcelona, Spain, and was raised in Paris, where he received his formal culinary training. He came to the United States in 1967 and was the executive chef at *Top of the Park* in New York City for 14 years. He also owned several restaurants in Connecticut. Chef George, who came to Stew Leonard's in 1993, oversees all catering and prepared foods at the stores. He has two children, Margaret and George, Jr. and lives in Westport, Connecticut.

How to Read a Recipe

Before you get further into this book we would like to offer some advice about the proper way to read a recipe. This may sound silly, but in fact there is a method that saves a lot of time and makes cooking more fun.

- Before doing anything, read the recipe carefully from beginning to end so you know what ingredients and skills it requires.
- Read the recipe again to calculate how much time it will take. You don't want to start a stew at 4 p.m. when dinner is at 6 p.m.
- Make sure you have all the proper utensils
- Are there any difficult techniques required?
- Do an ingredient inventory. What recipe ingredients do you have on hand and what do you need to buy?
- What is the recipe's yield? If the yield is four and you are serving six, make adjustments before shopping.

André Soltner Tours Stew's...

Foreword

One day my wife, Simone, and I decided to drive up to Connecticut to visit Stew Leonard's. I had heard about their stores but never had been to one.

When we first entered the store it was a fantasy of the senses. The aroma of freshly baked bread, the scent of freshly roasted coffee, and the perfume of perfectly ripe melons overwhelmed us. What we also found was a sincere dedication to freshness and a special approach to customer service.

All chefs, no matter how talented they are, need quality products to turn out their best work. When you walk through the aisles at Stew's and see the wonderful meats and vegetables, you become inspired to do something special with them. This cookbook is a natural extension of Stew's special connection with its food and its customers. Now you have a road map that points the way to quick and easy family meals as well as fun dishes for entertaining. After all, exciting food makes for excited cooks.

Also, the dozens of questions and answers throughout the book give cooks a unique insider's look at the food business. There are interviews with experts in all fields — produce, meat, fish, coffee, and more — providing valuable information to shoppers.

The excitement and energy of Stew's fuels this cookbook. I wish you all a happy trip.

André Soltner,
Owner/Chef,
Lutèce Restaurant,
New York, for 35 Years.
Currently
Senior Lecturer,
French Culinary Institute,
NYC

Stocking Your Pantry

Cooks are like Boy Scouts — they must always be prepared. Having a well-stocked pantry makes cooking infinitely easier. If you have spices, canned and frozen goods, condiments, cheese, and fruits on hand, all you need to do is shop for the main ingredients. And when you are in a jam you can always toss something together without shopping at all. Following is an inventory of pantry items that you should have on hand.

Dry Goods

- **Coffee** (Regular and Decaffeinated)
- **Cold and hot cereals**
- **Breads** – All breads can be frozen for 6 to 8 months.
- **Dry beans and grains** – Store in airtight containers. White beans (Navy), lentils, red beans, couscous, rice, etc.
- **Herbal and regular teas** – Store in an airtight canister in a cool place.
- **Macaroni and pasta** – These are essential, and life savers when you need to create a quick meal from the pantry.

Dried Herbs, Spices, and Seasonings

It is best to buy dried herbs in small quantities because they lose their potency over time. Also, to get the most flavor from dried herbs, crush them between your fingers before adding them to food.

- **Dried Herbs** – These are indispensable. Use them when you can't get fresh herbs. Among those you should have are basil, bay leaves, dill, marjoram, oregano, rosemary, sage, tarragon, thyme, and parsley. Keep them sealed in a cool place.
- **Salt and pepper** – Table salt, black peppercorns, whole or ground white pepper, and red pepper flakes.

Spices

- Allspice, chili powder, cinnamon, cloves, ground cumin, curry powder, ginger, dry mustard, nutmeg, and paprika.

Bottled and Canned Goods

- Assorted oils (vegetable, olive, peanut).
- **Tomato paste** – This comes in handy for flavoring and thickening stews, soups, and sauces.
- **Wines** – Have on hand a dry red and a dry white for deglazing and flavoring dishes. Fortified wines like Madeira and Port come in handy, too — not to mention being nice to sip after dinner.
- **Anchovies** – For salads, pizzas, and some pasta sauces. Buy anchovies packed in olive oil.
- **Artichoke hearts marinated in olive oil** – Toss in salads, pasta sauces, vegetable plates, and sauces.
- **Beans** – Kidney, garbanzo and baked beans can go in soups, salads, vegetable dishes, and casseroles.
- **Canned broths** – Always have plenty of chicken broth and beef broth for making quick pan sauces…that is, if you don't have homemade broths.
- **Canned clams and clam juice** – You can make a quick pasta with clam sauce. The clam juice can pinch-hit for fish stock.
- **Canned Tuna Fish** – Stock up on this for sandwiches and salads.
- **Capers** – For flavoring sauces, casseroles, and salads.
- **Hot sauce** – There are times when you want to stoke up a sauce or soup. Tabasco is the most famous hot sauce, but there are scores out there to try.
- **Olives** – Green, black and pimiento-stuffed for salads, sandwiches, pasta dishes, and more.
- **Tomatoes (canned)** – These are indispensable when ripe summer tomatoes are not available. Canned tomatoes are picked at the peak of ripeness and always have good flavor. Imported brands tend to be better than domestic. Use in pasta sauces and soups.

Condiments

- **Dijon-style mustard** – It is the basis of vinaigrette, dips, some sauces, and used as a condiment with meats of all kinds.
- **Ketchup** – For hamburgers and as an ingredient in barbecue sauces.
- **Mayonnaise** – This is used all the time, for sandwiches, salad dressings, cold meats, cold sauces, and more.
- **Sundry relishes** – Relishes made with tomatoes, corn, onion and the like are good for sandwiches and roasted meats.
- **Horseradish** – For when you don't have time to grate it fresh. Goes in salad dressings, with all kinds of meats, and sauces.
- **Pasta sauces (in jars)** – When you are really desperate, these come in handy. You may want to jazz them up with garlic, sautéed onions, olives, herbs, or cheese.
- **Soy sauce** – Adds a salty edge to marinades and Oriental-style dishes.
- **Sun-dried tomatoes** – A luxury, but they come in handy for enhancing sauces of all kinds, dressings and salads.

Baking Goods

- **All-purpose flour (5-pound bag)** – Not only is this necessary for baking, you also use flour for dredging meat and fish to give them a crispy crust. It stays for months if you take it out of the bag and store in an airtight container.
- **Baking powder** – An all-purpose leavening agent for cakes, cookies, and quick breads. Baking powder loses its punch over time. To test it: mix 1 teaspoon baking powder with 1/3 cup water. If it fizzes, it's OK.
- **Baking soda** – Another leavening agent, used in batters that contain acid like vinegar or buttermilk. An open box in the refrigerator absorbs odors.
- **Granulated sugar (5-pound bag)** – Used every day. Best stored in a sealed container to keep out bugs.
- **Confectioner's sugar** – Mostly for sprinkling over desserts and for making quick frostings.
- **Brown sugar** – Used in baking, for making barbecue sauce, and for glazing meats like ham.
- **Cornmeal** – A bag of yellow cornmeal comes in handy for quick muffins or for making crunchy toppings for stews and casseroles.
- **Honey** – Used for all kinds of glazes, making syrups and dressings, and for sweetening tea.
- **Vanilla extract** – For flavoring whipped cream and many desserts.
- **Vanilla bean** – More intense than vanilla extract, it also is used in many desserts.

Refrigerated and Frozen Staples

- **Eggs** – You always need eggs, for breakfast, omelets, frittatas (see recipe page 13), sauces, and much more. Eggs can be stored 4 weeks beyond the expiration date.
- **Milk** – Another absolute necessity. Always check the expiration date, for milk lasts only about a week beyond that.
- **Pastas** – It's always a good idea to have fresh pasta on hand as well as quality prepared ravioli on hand so that you can serve it with a quick sauce. Do not defrost it before cooking. Drop it right into boiling water.
- **Cheeses** – You don't want too many cheeses lying around, so store only those that you will use within a few weeks to a month. Parmesan and Romano come in handy as an all-around garnish. Goat cheese makes a nice appetizer with fresh herbs sprinkled on top, or rolled in crushed black pepper. Cover cheese in plastic wrap and refrigerate. Take it out at least an hour before serving.
- **Pie crusts (frozen)** – In a pinch these are great to have. They keep in the freezer up to 8 months. Fill with a quiche mixture, fresh fruits and custards, pie fillings, and much more.

Kitchen equipment is sort of like a pair of shoes — the shoddy stuff will get you there, but with a lot more pain and effort. Make an investment in quality equipment — it will be a joy to work with and last for generations.

How do you know whether equipment is good or not? Pots and pans, for example, should be heavy duty, not thin and tinny. The handle should feel good in your hand, and not get hot. Knives should feel good too, and be well balanced. Among the best knives are Henckels, Wüstof, Chef's Choice, and Sabatier.

When it comes to pots and pans, look for brands like All-Clad, Borgeat, Calphalon, Chantal, Cuisinart, Le Creuset, and Paderno. Copper pans with a stainless steel lining are the best for quick and even heat conduction, but home cooks could do just as well with stainless steel pots that have an aluminum or copper core. Plus, stainless steel is a lot easier to clean.

Here is a rundown of basic kitchen tools.

Knives

Most home cooks can get along quite well with three knives.

Chef's Knife: A 10-inch knife with a well-made handle is used for 90 percent of your kitchen chores. It chops, dices, debones, slices, and much more.

Paring Knife: A 4-inch paring knife performs precision jobs like peeling fruit, trimming shallots, coring berries, and so on.

Serrated Knife: Usually 8-10 inches long, this is your basic bread knife.

Pots and Pans:

Cast-Iron Pan: Inexpensive, indestructible, and versatile, a 10-inch pan can do it all. Cast-iron takes a long time to heat up, but once it is hot it stays that way for a long time. This makes it excellent for browning and searing meats.

10-Inch Omelet Pan: Designed for egg cooking, this compact pan with curved sides can be used for sautéing potatoes and vegetables, too.

Sauté Pan: All home cooks need a 10-inch, slope-sided pan for sautéeing and frying. Non-stick coatings are the best.

12-inch-Rondeau: A rondeau (pronounced ron-DOE) is a straight-sided pan with 2 handles that is great if you have to cook for a mob. It is used for braising, stew-making, poaching, and more.

Basic Saucepan: Usually 8 to 9 inches in diameter, with sloped sides, this is used for all kinds of sauce-making. The sloped sides make it easier to whisk in the corners.

3-Quart Saucepan: This all-around pot is good for pastas, soups, rice, vegetables, and many other things. It has straight sides and a lid.

Stockpot: Aside from making stocks, this 11- to 12-quart pot can be used for steaming (just insert a steamer basket), pasta cooking, soups, and more.

Other Equipment:

Food Processor: Invaluable for chopping and puréeing. It also makes easy work of pastry doughs and breads.

Automatic Chopper (by Zyliss): To me, this is a necessity in the kitchen. It saves me so much time when I'm dicing or chopping garlic, herbs, peppers, or any vegetables. It's especially helpful when you're doing onions because it doesn't hurt your eyes! The chopper has rotating stainless steel blades that cut through food. Zyliss makes a great one, but there are many others as well. They are under $20 and well worth it.

Blender: Aside from drink mixing, blenders are excellent for blending lowfat sauces, the type you see throughout this book; for example, a tomato-and-fresh-herb sauce bound with ricotta (instead of cheese). The blender blade rotates much faster than that of a food processor, making it better suited to sauce making.

Stainless Steel Bowls: You can never have enough of these.

And don't forget...

- Measuring cups (liquid and dry)
- Whisk
- Kitchen scale (preferably one that has a bowl)
- Colander
- Salad spinner
- Grater
- Spatulas
- Wooden spoons
- Kitchen timer
- Potato masher
- Oven thermometer
- Pie plates
- Loaf pans (for meatloaf and breads)
- Springform pans (if you make tarts)
- Ovenproof casserole dishes
- Corkscrew
- Sifter

1864

It All Started in 1864...

Our Family Buys a 207-Acre Farm in 1864

The Stewart family moved from Brooklyn to Bellvale, N.Y. (60 miles north of New York City) where they bought a 207-acre dairy farm. Here is a Courier and Ives print from about the same period.

The First "Dairy Store" Opens in the 1890s.

In the 1890s, Samuel Stewart (they called my great-grandfather, "SJ") and his Dad opened a dairy store at 180 7th Avenue in Brooklyn, selling their fresh products from the Bellvale farm. The 1895-1896 City Directory listed their occupations as "butter" and "milk."

This is a picture of a Hat Factory in Danbury in the 1900s

In 1888, about the same time that the Stewarts were setting up business in Brooklyn, Patrick Leonard (my other great-grandfather), had just settled in Danbury, Connecticut, where he received his American citizenship.

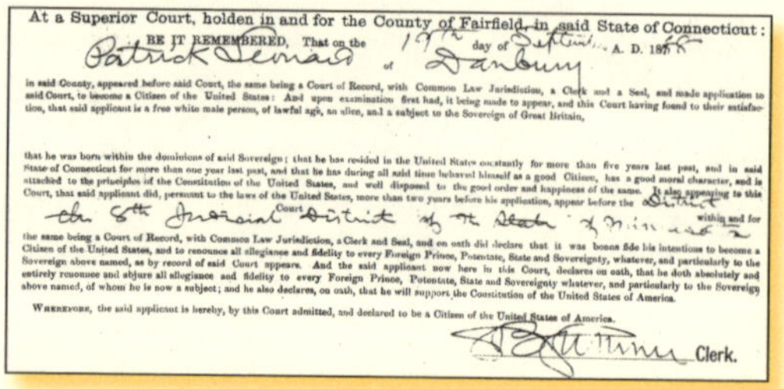

At a Superior Court, holden in and for the County of Fairfield, in said State of Connecticut:

BE IT REMEMBERED, That on the 19th day of Septem... A. D. 188

Patrick Leonard of Danbury

in said County, appeared before said Court, the same being a Court of Record, with Common Law Jurisdiction, a Clerk and a Seal, and made application to said Court, to become a Citizen of the United States: And upon examination first had, it being made to appear, and this Court having found to their satisfaction, that said applicant is a free white male person, of lawful age, an alien, and a subject to the Sovereign of Great Britain,

that he was born within the dominions of said Sovereign; that he has resided in the United States constantly for more than five years last past, and in said State of Connecticut for more than one year last past, and that he has during all said time behaved himself as a good Citizen, has a good moral character, and is attached to the principles of the Constitution of the United States, and well disposed to the good order and happiness of the same. It also appearing to this Court, that said applicant did, persuant to the laws of the United States, more than two years before his application, appear before the District Court within and for

the same being a Court of Record, with Common Law Jurisdiction, a Clerk and Seal, and on oath did declare that it was bona fide his intentions to become a Citizen of the United States, and to renounce all allegiance and fidelity to every Foreign Prince, Potentate, State and Sovereignty, whatever, and particularly to the Sovereign above named, as by record of said Court appears. And the said applicant now here in this Court, declares on oath, that he doth absolutely and entirely renounce and abjure all allegiance and fidelity to every Foreign Prince, Potentate, State and Sovereignty whatever, and particularly to the Sovereign above named, of whom he is now a subject; and he also declares, on oath, that he will support the Constitution of the United States of America.

WHEREFORE, the said applicant is hereby, by this Court admitted, and declared to be a Citizen of the United States of America.

Clerk.

This is a plaque that hangs at the entrance of our Danbury Store in memory of my great-grandfather Patrick Leonard (1863-1920). It documents his official citizenship.

1888

1900 . . . 1920

Samuel Stewart (1871-1935)

SJ Starts a Dairy Business in Westchester County.

In the early 1900s, SJ Stewart became very interested in the new field of milk pasteurization. He then moved to Westchester County.

SJ became a co-proprietor of the White Plains Milk & Cream Company in White Plains, Westchester County.

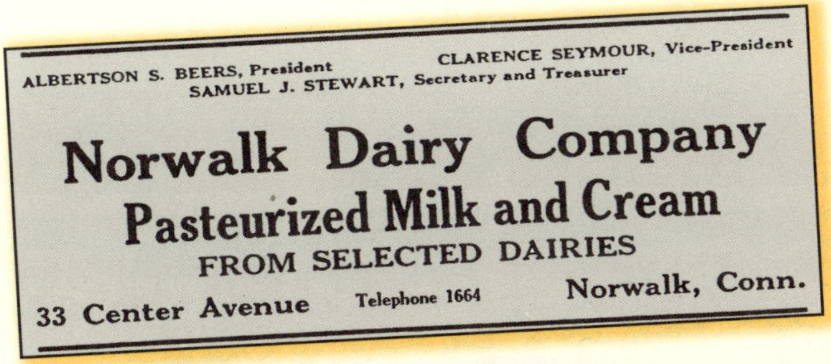

1920 - A New, Modern Dairy Opens in Norwalk, Conn.

In 1920, SJ Stewart was one of the founders of the Norwalk Dairy Company, where he opened a modern pasteurizing and bottling plant. (Pasteurization was not required by law until 1924.) One of his first employees was his son-in-law, Charles Leo Leonard (my grandfather). The company had four home delivery routes, two served by automobiles and two by horse-drawn wagons.

1921

Charles Leo Leonard (1893 - 1951)

1921 - Charles Leo Leonard Ventured Out and Started Clover Farms Dairy, Founded in Norwalk.

Charles Leo Leonard started his own dairy, with the help of SJ Stewart, called Clover Farms, with one milk route. He delivered the milk with a horse and buggy and ran the business out of his garage. "He did it all," my Uncle Leo recalls. "He'd wake up at 3 o'clock in the morning, drive to the farms to get milk, return and bottle it, then deliver it too! His first employee was Ray Flewelynn, who began in 1925 and worked for our family for more than 60 years.

Ray Flewellyn, Sr. (1907 - 1986)

1930 - 1960 Clover Farms Grows; New Generation Takes Over.

Charles Leo Leonard's three sons Leo, Jim, and Stewart ("Stew"), eventually joined him and each worked in the dairy plant and delivered milk.

During World War II, Stew (my Dad), the youngest son, worked with his father every morning before attending junior high school. He also worked after school until dark. He loved the dairy business, and went on to graduate from the University of Connecticut's School of Agriculture in 1950. After returning from the navy, Leo eventually left to form his own land surveying business.

1951

1952 ▼ 1968

In 1952, soon after my father's graduation, my grandfather, Charles Leo Leonard, died. Stew and Jim took over the family dairy business. In 1967, Jim retired and moved to Florida.

My Dad is very proud of the new addition to his fleet. If an employee did a great job, they were allowed to drive this company car to work for a month!

Clover Farms Dairy stared putting milk vending machines around town.

Here are my Dad and his team in the '60s. As a kid, I used to unload the milk trucks and wash the milk cans. We used to live right next door to the dairy. There were ten milk routes at the time.

1969

1970

1969 – My Dad Opens New, "Show Place" Dairy Store.

The construction of Interstate 95 forced Stew to relocate his dairy and rethink the home delivery business. He dreamed of opening a retail dairy store where people could watch their milk being bottled, and do their shopping while having fun.

One of the attractions to the store was a "little farm" with over 40 animals. The kids love it to this day!

The New York Times

"Wendy's, Wal-Mart, Marriott and Union Carbide as well as the United States Postal Service are sending executives to study Stew Leonard's methods."

Our 6,000-pound rock chiseled with our store's policy

My Dad's first lesson in customer service came when a customer wanted to return a half-gallon of eggnog. My Dad tried to convince the customer that it tasted fine, but she insisted it was sour. He finally refunded her $1. She waved the money in his face and said, "I'm never coming back to this store again!" My father was just building his business and couldn't afford to lose any customers. That was the creation of our 6,000-pound inscribed rock, which is the first thing you see when you enter Stew Leonard's!

1970 - 1980s ... From 7 to 700 Items!

During this time we expanded the concept of bottling fresh milk before your eyes into other areas of the food store. My Dad began buying meat directly from Kansas, fresh fish from the Fulton Fish Market, produce from local farms, cheese from Europe, flowers and plants direct from greenhouses. Twenty-four additions were added to the original store!

By cutting out the middle man and going directly to the grower, we are able to save the customer money. At the same time, my sisters Beth and Jill, brother Tom, and I joined our family business.

In 1986, my father, Stew Leonard, Sr., was awarded the Presidential Award for Entrepreneurial Excellence by President Reagan. He said, "If my Dad ever saw me visiting the White House, he wouldn't have believed a milkman could be honored by the President."

Stew's Launches Paul Newman's First Product, "Eats the Whole Thing!"

"Back in 1980 when we were trying to get Newman's Own off the ground, we could not find a bottler who would bottle anything under 5,000 cases. I could see 12 cases going out to delicatessen stores, and the other 4,988 sitting in my garage. And that's what would have happened except Stew Leonard said, "I will eat the whole thing." He did and that was the launch of Newman's Own. We are forever thankful, and for that he will have to take either the credit, or the blame for what we have become."

– Paul Newman

1970 . . . 1980

1990

1990s - The Next Generation Steps In.

A new generation slowly begins taking responsibility for the store. Our philosophy was a simple acronym S.T.E.W. "S"atisying the customer, "T"eamwork, "E"xcellence, and "W"ow, which is making shopping fun.

Beth, Stew, Tom, and Jill in the store

1991 - Danbury Opens In "Hat City".

Just over 100 years after my great-grandfather Patrick became a Danbury resident, we opened our second store there. He wouldn't have believed it! This store is 140,000 square feet, considerably larger than the Norwalk store.

In 1992, the *Guinness Book of World Records* cites Stew Leonard's for "Greatest sales per square foot of $3,470."

People weekly

"Stew Leonard's sells more than 15 regular supermarkets combined, over 100,000 customers flock there each week from as far away as New York City, an hour's commute."

1992

1992 . . . 1999

Ripley's Believe It or Not! included Stew's for selling 11,000,000 quarts of milk each year to 5,200,000 customers! No other store sells more!

My sister Jill, who began Stew Leonard's University at the store, celebrates her 10,000th graduate. *Connecticut Magazine* said, "Stew U draws managers, trainers, human resources personnel from such diverse groups as IBM, Burger King, and Weight Watchers… even foreign businessmen from the U.K. to Japan!"

"Stew Leonard's has the best customer service techniques in the world. It's a once-in-a-lifetime opportunity for anyone who wants to blow the socks off customers!"
— **Danny Cox**, Author of *Leadership When the Heat's On* and *Seize the Day*

1997 - We Buy 50 Acres in Orange, Connecticut for Third Store, But...

The town Planning and Zoning Committee, citing potential traffic problems, turned down our plans for a store in Orange, Conn. The state and the town of Orange are currently engaged in a $25 million road improvement project in the area. We hope this will eliminate the traffic concerns so we can become a member of the Orange community in the future!

1999 - Over 100 Years Later, We Are Returning to Westchester County, N.Y.

We are returning to our "roots" by building our third store in Yonkers, New York. It is scheduled to open in the summer of 1999.

Dairy and Coffee

The heart of Stew Leonard's has always been its dairy. In this chapter we offer a colorful variety of dairy recipes, everything from Stew's popular "Moolatta" drinks to Spanish egg-and-potato tortilla.

Spinach, Romano, and Egg Strata

Italian cuisine is known for its wonderful egg dishes. The recipe here is called "strata" because it is layered like a rock formation. Strata makes a great brunch entree, or a light lunch.

Preparation Time: 20 MINUTES
Cooking Time: ABOUT 1 HOUR

A Clover Farms Dairy truck visits a farm in 1964. The kids in the picture are my brother, sisters, and neighborhood friends. This was taken from our dairy's calendar in the 1960s.

⅓ cup olive oil
1 large onion, thinly sliced, about 1½ cups
1 teaspoon minced garlic
2 potatoes, peeled and thinly sliced
8 eggs
1 cup plus 3 tablespoons grated Romano
Dash cayenne pepper
10 ounces fresh spinach (it usually comes in 1-pound bags), rinsed, drained well, and chopped
½ teaspoon salt
¼ teaspoon freshly ground black pepper
¼ pound sliced mozzarella

1. Preheat the oven to 375 degrees. Grease an 8 x 12-inch casserole (or a 9 x 13) with 1 teaspoon of the olive oil. Cut a piece of aluminum foil to cover the top of the casserole. Grease it on one side with a teaspoon of the olive oil. Set aside.
2. Heat the remaining olive oil in the bottom of a large pan. Add the onions and cook them over medium-high heat for 5 minutes or until wilted. Add the garlic and potatoes and cook until the potatoes begin to soften, about 10 minutes.
3. While the potatoes are cooking, beat the eggs with one cup of Romano cheese in a large bowl. Add the cayenne, spinach, salt and pepper. Add the potato and onion mixture. Pour everything into the greased casserole. (The mixture should come no more than three-quarters up the sides of the casserole.) Layer the slices of mozzarella on top of the casserole then top it with the remaining grated Romano cheese. Cover the casserole with the aluminum foil.
4. Bake the strata for 30 minutes. Remove the foil to make sure the center is set. If it is not, replace the foil and bake for several minutes more, or until set. When the center is set, return it to the oven, uncovered, and bake for an additional 15 to 20 minutes.
5. Cut the strata into 6 4-inch squares and serve with Fresh Tomato Basil Sauce (see recipe page 216) and Stew's Country Hearth Bread.

Yield: 6 servings

Raspberry French Toast

French toast is oddly named, for it is not particularly French. The French have a version of this called pain perdu, or "lost bread," made with stale baguettes. Our French toast is soaked in beaten eggs (sometimes mixed with milk). Topping options are unlimited. We like to use challah, the moist and airy Jewish bread. It soaks up the eggs and milk easily and cooks quickly. If you do not have challah any thickly sliced white bread will do.

Preparation Time: 15 MINUTES
Cooking Time: 15 MINUTES

SUPER FAST

1 small loaf challah or egg bread or enough for 8 to 10 thick slices about ¾-inch thick
1 cup fresh or frozen raspberries
1 tablespoon raspberry preserves
1 tablespoon sugar
2 whole eggs plus 2 egg whites
¼ cup skim milk
1 cup plain lowfat yogurt
Vegetable oil for cooking
Powdered sugar for garnish

1. Preheat the oven to 250 degrees.
2. Cut the challah bread into ¾-inch thick slices. Cut each slice in half crosswise if the loaf is extra wide. You should have 8 to 10 pieces of bread. Set aside.
3. Place the raspberries, preserves and sugar in a food processor or blender. Purée until smooth. Add the eggs and egg whites. Blend to combine. Stir in the milk and the yogurt. Pour this mixture into a shallow bowl.
4. Dip each slice of bread into the raspberry mixture. It will be thick and stick to the bread in lumps. Place the dipped bread on a tray and let it absorb some of the liquid — about 10 minutes.
5. Heat a non-stick pan over high setting. Coat the pan with a teaspoon of vegetable oil. Place two or three pieces of dipped bread in the pan without crowding. Reduce heat to medium and sauté the bread for 3 minutes. Using a spatula, flip the bread and cook it for 3 more minutes. Proceed with the remaining slices of bread, using more vegetable oil as needed. (Keep the cooked slices of bread warm in a warm oven.)
6. To serve, place two slices of French toast on each plate. Garnish with a sprinkling of powdered sugar and serve with syrup or a warm purée of fresh fruit.

Yield: 4 or 5 servings

Stew's TIP

For a twist on French toast, try adding some fresh lemon zest or orange zest to the batter. Garnish the French toast with orange slices. Or, make buttermilk French toast by substituting buttermilk for whole milk in the recipe. Splashes of vanilla extract in the batter add a lovely essence, as does a little cinnamon, nutmeg, or even ginger powder.

Stew's TIP

You can really enhance your cooking repertory by getting to know assorted fresh and dried peppers. Each has its own flavor and heat level. A master of pepper pedagogy is Paul Prudhomme, the famous Cajun chef. We see him every year at the Food Marketing Institute convention in Chicago. Paul has categorized more than a dozen peppers according to various taste sensations and where they ignite on the tongue. He blends hot peppers in his cooking like a chemist.

For starters, the home cook should know the differences among the most common hot peppers.

Black Pepper – This workhorse of the home kitchen should be freshly ground for maximum effect. As soon as black peppercorns are ground they begin to dry out and lose their volatile acids. Black pepper is relatively mild, with a sharp, short-lived heat sensation on the palate.

Scrambled Eggs with Salmon and Scallions

These gently scrambled eggs are rich and creamy, an elegant offering for a brunch. Smoked trout or smoked whitefish may be substituted. This dish may be doubled or tripled. White pepper, made from peppercorns which have had the black hulls removed, complements the taste of smoked fish. White pepper is a little hotter than black.

Preparation Time: 5 MINUTES
Cooking Time: 7 MINUTES

2 ounces smoked salmon, pre-sliced
2 tablespoons unsalted butter
4 eggs
1 teaspoon water
Splash of hot pepper sauce, such as Tabasco
2 whole scallions, trimmed and finely chopped
Freshly ground white pepper

1. Cut the salmon slices widthwise into ¼-inch strips. Set aside.
2. Melt the butter over medium heat in a heavy saucepan. While the butter is melting, beat in a small bowl the eggs, water, and hot pepper sauce. Add the egg mixture and the chopped scallions to the saucepan. Raise the heat to medium high and slowly cook, stirring constantly with a wooden spoon for 5 minutes.
3. Add the smoked salmon and continue stirring until the eggs are cooked, but still creamy — about 2 minutes. Season the eggs with ground white pepper to taste.
4. Divide the eggs between two heated serving plates and accompany each plate with toasted country bread.

Yield: 2 servings

Note: You can double or triple the proportions, except for the butter. Two or three tablespoons of butter is plenty.

Stew's Favorite Egg-White-and-Vegetable Omelet

Just about every morning I start my day with this tasty, lowfat, egg-white-and-vegetable omelet. Use any vegetables in season.

Preparation Time: 15 MINUTES
Cooking Time: 10 MINUTES

SUPER FAST LOW FAT

½ red onion, chopped
1 scallion, chopped (including green part)
½ teaspoon olive oil
1 ripe tomato, chopped
½ sweet red pepper, chopped
4 white mushrooms, trimmed of stems (chop only one of them)
1 egg white
Salt and freshly ground black pepper to taste

1. Coat a large pan (non-stick works best) with the olive oil. Place it over medium-high flame and add the onions and scallions. Place the three whole white mushrooms around the perimeter of the pan to brown, stem side up. Cook, stirring the onions, for 3 minutes. When the mushrooms are browned on top remove and set aside.
2. Add the remaining vegetables to the pan. Cook, stirring, for 5 minutes. Season well with salt and pepper.
3. Remove the vegetables from then pan. Add the egg whites (if not using a non-stick pan, you may need a little more oil) and stir with a plastic spatula. When the egg whites are 70% cooked (still wet), add all of the vegetables back into the pan. Stir vigorously. Taste for seasonings. When the egg whites firm up, empty everything onto a serving platter. With a spatula mold the ingredients into a neat omelet shape. Garnish with the white mushrooms, cap side up.

Yield: Serves 4

White Pepper – This is black peppercorns that are harvested at a riper stage (thus hotter), then soaked in water to loosen and remove the black skin. White peppercorns are slightly more pungent than black. Often they are used in light colored soups and sauces when you don't want to see black specks.

Cayenne Pepper – This earth-toned red powder is made from hot chili peppers (capsicum frutescens) and pack a lot of fire. The name comes from the town of Cayenne in French Guyana, although the peppers are now produced in many other areas of the world. A little cayenne pepper goes a long way so use it sparingly. By the way, it is rich in vitamin C, although you probably will never eat enough to benefit from it.

In the kitchen one morning with Sal and Bernette cooking breakfast. Every holiday, I cook up my secret egg sandwich recipe for over 400 of our team members. They are all starving by 7 a.m. when the store opens.

Stew's TIP

If you are making a recipe with lowfat milk but want to make it richer, thicken it with Stew's Fat Free Plus. This is a Fat Free milk that is fortified with rice flour, beta carotene, and carragenan. The rice flour helps make it thicker. The beta carotene, which is comprised of natural vegetables, is rich in Vitamin A. Carragenan is a natural plant that is used as a thickening agent. Use this milk in your cooking and you can thicken your recipes without any fat!

Horseradish Cream Sauce

This zesty sauce complements boiled or roasted meats and poultry. We also like to use it on sandwiches — but not too much! Lowfat yogurt may be used in place of sour cream, but there is no substitute for fresh horseradish.

Preparation Time: 5 MINUTES
Cooking Time: NONE

½ cup sour cream
1½ tablespoons freshly grated horseradish (skin removed)
½ teaspoon salt
⅛ teaspoon freshly ground pepper

1. Combine all ingredients in a small bowl. Taste for seasonings. You may want to increase salt and pepper.

Yield: ⅔ cup

Note: Before grating fresh horseradish remove the skin with a sharp paring knife. You should cut off the knobs on the surface, too. Run the horseradish flesh over a kitchen grater.

Honey Buttermilk Pancakes

Preparation Time: 15 MINUTES
Cooking Time: 20 MINUTES

LOW FAT

2 cup all-purpose flour
1½ teaspoons baking soda
1 teaspoon baking powder
½ teaspoon salt
2 tablespoons wheat germ
Pinch of cinnamon
2 cups buttermilk
2 tablespoons honey
2 eggs
1 cup fresh peaches, sliced, or blueberries
4 teaspoons vegetable oil
Warm honey, optional

1. Sift together the flour, baking soda, baking powder and salt. Stir in the wheat germ and cinnamon. In a separate bowl, whisk together the buttermilk, honey and eggs. Pour the buttermilk mixture into the flour mixture and stir just until the ingredients are moistened and free of most lumps. Stir in the peaches or blueberries.
2. Place a non-stick skillet or griddle over high heat for about 5 minutes. Reduce heat to medium and pour a teaspoon of vegetable oil onto the skillet. Spread it all over the griddle. Spoon a quarter of a cup of batter onto the skillet. Repeat with as many as you can fit on the skillet. Cook the pancakes for 2 to 3 minutes or until golden brown and set. Flip and finish cooking for 2 minutes.
3. Place the cooked pancakes on a tray and keep warm in the oven while cooking the remaining batter. Use more vegetable oil as needed.
4. Serve the pancakes drizzled with warm honey or maple syrup.

Yield: 12 5-inch pancakes

Here's our fat-free plus. We took skim milk and added all-natural ingredients to make it "taste" like whole milk. It's great for cooking, too!

Can I freeze milk?

Yes, you can freeze all Stew Leonard's milk. Stew's paper half-gallon cartons are ideal containers for freezing. Here's how to defrost our milk:

Water method:

Immerse the carton in warm water. Squeeze it and shake it well every hour. The milk should be thawed after 2 to 3 hours. (You can put it in the refrigerator at any time. It will defrost there, too!)

Microwave method:

- Put a frozen milk carton in a microwave oven for 5 minutes on high.
- Remove, squeeze ice lumps, and shake.
- Return the carton to the microwave for another 5 minutes on high.
- Remove, squeeze, and shake.
- Repeat the steps if necessary — microwaves vary in power.

Farmer's Cheese

The subtle flavor of freshly made cheese is unlike anything you have ever tasted. Farmer's cheese is a soft, pressed cheese made from whole milk. The term goes back to earlier centuries when farm families made their own cheese and butter. Every region of the country had its own special variety. You can serve farmer's cheese with toasted country bread, bagels, or in summer with fresh herbs spread over sliced tomatoes.

Preparation Time: 5 MINUTES
Cooking Time: 5 MINUTES Plus Overnight Draining

LOW FAT · PREPARE IN ADVANCE

2 quarts whole milk
¼ cup cultured buttermilk
¼ cup fresh chopped chives, parsley, dill or chervil (or any combination to your liking)
Salt and freshly ground black pepper to taste

1. Place the milk in a stainless steel pot. Bring to a boil. Remove the milk from the heat and stir in the buttermilk and lemon juice. Pour the milk mixture into a clean stainless steel bowl; cover with plastic wrap and set it aside in a warm place overnight.
2. The next day, pour the mixture through a cheesecloth-lined strainer into a bowl. Let it drain for at least 15 minutes, stirring the curds a few times to remove most of the liquid. If desired, add chopped herbs and adjust the seasonings to taste with salt and pepper.
3. Squeeze the cheesecloth into a tight ball. Place the ball on a plate and cover it with a second plate to weigh it down. Let it sit a few hours in the refrigerator before serving. Serve the cheese whole or cut into ½-inch-thick slices. Farmer's cheese keeps for three days in the refrigerator.

Yield: 1 cup

Brian Trotter and Kathy Zazaridis arrive at 5 a.m. each morning to make sure our customers get fresh, hot bagels. We sell over 60,000 bagels each week.

Labna (Yogurt Cheese)

Popular in the Middle East for centuries, yogurt cheese, called labna, can be used in many dishes as a lowfat substitute for cream cheese. At Stew Leonard's we carry our own brand of yogurt that is all natural and without gelatin as a thickener (gelatin gives the cheese an unpleasant pudding texture). Combine the yogurt cheese with chopped fresh herbs and minced garlic for a lowfat alternative to Alouette or Boursin cheeses; or top it with fresh berries and powdered sugar.

Preparation Time: 5 MINUTES Plus One or Two Days to Drain
Cooking Time: NONE

LOW FAT · PREPARE IN ADVANCE

2 pounds nonfat plain yogurt (4 cups)
Cheesecloth-lined strainer

1. Place a colander or metal strainer over a deep bowl. Line strainer with two layers of cheesecloth. Spoon the yogurt into the cheesecloth, cover with plastic wrap, and refrigerate. Allow yogurt to drain overnight, or up to 48 hours.
2. Discard the liquid and place the yogurt cheese in a covered container. Use in any recipe that calls for cream cheese.

Yield: 2 cups

The Big Cheese

One of the earliest cheese aficionados in this country was the worldly gourmet Thomas Jefferson. His passion for wine is well known, but few realize that his restless mind (and palate) investigated all kinds of foods, including cheeses. He once had Parmesan shipped from Italy to Monticello so he could study its composition. It is not known whether the founding father actually made his own cheeses — although most families of the day did so — but it is certain he sampled and experimented with many. And it was Jefferson the egalitarian who introduced to his fellow citizens that most democratic of dishes: macaroni and cheese.

Here's a master cheese maker we visited in Wisconsin. He just finished making a fresh batch of Gouda cheese. Our trucks pick up cheese directly from these farmers.

Sensational Italian Frittatas

Another great egg dish from Italy is the frittata, which is an omeletlike creation except that the eggs are never stirred in the pan (see recipe page 13). Rather, the beaten eggs brown on the bottom and set loosely on top. All kinds of vegetables, cheeses, and herbs can flavor frittatas. Cooked, sliced potatoes add substance, while sweet red peppers, leeks, asparagus and broccoli rape, among other vegetables, contribute flavor and dazzling colors. Use as few or as many as you like. This is another perfect brunch dish.

Spanish Tortilla

Almost every tavern in Spain has one of these tortillas on the bar for customers to nibble on with their wine. Chef George Llorens, a native of Catalonia, offers this basic recipe for a Spanish tortilla, which can be eaten warm or at room temperature. You may add any other vegetables if you like.

Preparation Time: 15 MINUTES
Cooking Time: 20 MINUTES

PREPARE IN ADVANCE

2 tablespoons plus 1 teaspoon olive oil
½ medium onion, chopped
1 medium zucchini, stem trimmed and washed (leave skin), cut into small cubes
2 medium white potato, peeled and cut into small cubes
2 tablespoons chopped fresh parsley
Salt and freshly ground black pepper to taste
8 eggs

1. In a large pan (preferably non-stick) coated with 1 tablespoon of olive oil, sauté the onions for 2 minutes. Add the zucchini and cook, stirring, for 4 minutes. Remove the vegetables to a plate. Add another tablespoon of oil to the pan and cook the potatoes (in batches if necessary) until they are tender but still slightly firm — about 5 minutes (don't let them get too soft). Season well with salt and pepper. Drain.
2. In a large bowl, beat the eggs. Add the parsley, salt, and pepper. Place the remaining teaspoon of olive oil in the pan and add ½ of the egg mixture. Shake the pan and cook for 1 minute. Add the vegetables and stir. Add remaining eggs and cook for about 3 minutes. Meanwhile, run a wooden or plastic spatula around the edge of the pan so the eggs do not stick. Season with salt and pepper.
3. Take a second pan roughly the size of the first and coat with olive oil (non-stick is best). When the eggs are firm on the bottom but still slightly runny on top, place the empty pan on top of the egg pan. Invert so the eggs transfer. Cook for 1 minute. Slide the tortilla onto a warm serving platter. If desired garnish it with chopped parsley or basil. Serve hot or room temperature.

Yield: Serves 4

Spinach and Prosciutto Frittata

Preparation Time: 15 MINUTES
Cooking Time: 10 MINUTES

SUPER FAST

6 eggs
6 thin slices prosciutto, chopped
12 spinach leaves, chopped
3 ripe tomatoes
1 tablespoon chopped chives
Salt and freshly ground black pepper to taste
1 tablespoon olive oil

1. In a bowl, beat the eggs until blended. Add half the prosciutto, half the spinach leaves, tomatoes, chives and salt and pepper to taste.
2. Heat the oil in a 10-inch non-stick pan over medium-high setting. Pour in the egg mixture, reduce heat to medium, and cook until the frittata is set and lightly brown on the bottom. Take a platter, place it over the pan, and invert the pan. Garnish with the remaining prosciutto, basil and tomatoes.

Yield: Serves 6 as an appetizer

Baked Ciabatta Bread with Melted Cheddar and Tomatoes

Ciabatta bread, a bestseller at Stew Leonard's, is a long, roughly oval shaped flat bread. It is ideal for making all sorts of pizzalike combinations. Just cut the ciabatta lengthwise through the center and add your favorite toppings, then bake or broil. This is a great appetizer for parties.

Preparation Time: 10 MINUTES
Cooking Time: 10 MINUTES

⅓ cup olive oil
1 tablespoon minced garlic
1 loaf Ciabatta bread, sliced in half lengthwise
1½ cup Stew Leonard's Pomodoro Sauce (or your own tomato sauce)
⅓ pound cheddar cheese, grated
2 tomatoes cut into 6 slices
2 tablespoons sliced fresh basil (or 2 teaspoons dried)

1. Preheat oven to 450 degrees.
2. Combine the olive oil and garlic in a bowl. Spoon it evenly over the two halves of bread.
3. Spoon the pomodoro sauce over the bread. Sprinkle the cheddar cheese over everything. Place three tomato slices on each.
4. Place in the oven for 10 minutes or until the cheese is bubbly and beginning to brown. To serve, slice crosswise into serving pieces.

Yield: Serves 6 to 10

Orange Cream Freeze

The secret ingredient in the famed Orange Julius is vanilla. Use it to sweeten this creamy drink, a delightful after-school snack.

Preparation Time: 5 MINUTES
Cooking Time: NONE

¼ cup milk
¼ cup vanilla ice cream or ice milk
1 cup orange juice
¼ teaspoon vanilla extract
2 ice cubes

1. Combine all ingredients in the bowl of a blender. Blend for 60 seconds or until the ice is crushed and a head of foam develops.
2. Pour the mixture into a tall chilled glass.

Yield: 1 serving

Variation: Try using raspberry soda and equal parts raspberry sherbet and vanilla ice cream.

Fresh fruits and vegetables is a cornerstone at Stew's. We like to create a farmers market atmosphere.

Stew's TIP

Anyone who has visited the Caribbean most likely has sampled the wonderful fruit drinks there. Some of these can not be readily replicated in the United States because the ingredients are lacking. But some can be simulated. For instance, try blending a tablespoon of instant coffee or ¾ cup strong coffee with 3½ ounces of coconut cream, which is widely available in stores. Pour this mixture over ice and top off with club soda and, if desired, dark Jamaican rum. (Stew Leonard's roasts and grinds its own coffee daily, with about a dozen types of beans from around the world. The strongest blends are "Stew's Choice," "Café du Jour,"and "French Roast" (see information on coffee pages 20-25).

Stew's TIP

Mango juice also can be the foundation of many titillating summer drinks. You might blend it with equal parts pineapple juice, some coconut milk and club soda. Garnish with mint. An electric blender turns any such concoction into a frothy treat.

Pass the Bubbly

A fun idea for warm-weather brunches is tropical fruit drinks enlivened with Champagne or sparkling wine. A blend of orange juice, bitters, fresh mint, and sparkling wine is a delightful combination. So, too, is our twist on the traditional mimosa, which is made with pineapple and papaya juice, sparkling wine and ice. There is no need to use expensive French Champagne. There are many fine sparkling wines from Spain, France, Italy and California for $15 or less.

Jugo de Frutas (Caribbean Fruit Drink)

This healthful, refreshing drink is so good that it is a great alternative to soft drinks for children. Adults might want to spike it with some rum for a summer cocktail.

Preparation Time: 15 MINUTES
Cooking Time: NONE

SUPER FAST LOW FAT

½ cup chopped banana (about 1 small banana), cut into ½-inch chunks
1 cup orange juice
1 cup hulled strawberries
2 ice cubes
Two sprigs fresh mint

1. Place the banana, orange juice and strawberries in the bowl of a blender or food processor. Blend until smooth (about 40 seconds to 1 minute). Add ice cubes and blend until the ice is crushed.
2. Pour into two chilled stem glasses and garnish with mint.

Yield: 1½ cups

Homestyle Cappuccino

You don't need an expensive cappuccino machine to make delicious foamy cappuccino and hot chocolate. This simple method requires only a blender.

Preparation Time: 15 MINUTES
Cooking Time: NONE

1 cup skim or whole milk
4 cups strong, freshly brewed coffee ground cinnamon or cocoa powder.

1. Place the milk in a saucepan over high heat. Heat the milk just until it begins to boil.
2. Pour the hot milk into a blender or food processor. Blend the milk for 1 minute until it is foamy.
3. Fill four mugs two-thirds full with coffee or hot chocolate. Top each with some milk foam and a pinch of grated cinnamon or cocoa.

Yield: 4 servings

How to be a Pro at the Cappuccino Bar!

What is espresso?

Espresso is often thought of as coffee's pure essence. Hot water is forced, under pressure, through finely ground, dark-roasted coffee to produce a strong, smooth demitasse of espresso.

Does espresso have more caffeine than regular coffee?

No. Actually it has less. In espresso making, water is forced through the coffee at slightly below the boiling point, at high pressure. In this process the water is in contact with the ground coffee for a very short time, extracting less caffeine. That is why many people are able to drink espresso throughout the day and late at night without getting buzzed. A coffee's body and flavor are more pronounced with espresso, but not the caffeine.

The Stew's Coffee Bar bustles every morning with customers stopping in on their way to work. Cappuccinos are one of our best sellers!

How to be a Pro at the Cappuccino Bar!

What is the difference between a Cappuccino and a Caffe Latte?

The difference between a cappuccino and a caffe latte is the amount of milk used. A cappuccino has very little milk and mostly foam. A caffe latte is the opposite, lots of milk and a little foam.

What is the difference between a long and a short espresso?

A short espresso has less water and is stronger than a long espresso.

Hot Mocha Breakfast Drink

Kids love this frothy and creamy drink. The electric blender simulates the texture of cappuccino.

Preparation Time: 15 MINUTES
Cooking Time: NONE

SUPER FAST

1 tablespoon cocoa powder
1 tablespoon sugar
1 cup brewed hot coffee
4 tablespoons light cream

1. In a small saucepan, blend the cocoa, sugar, and coffee with a whisk. Add the cream. Warm over medium heat for 2 minutes.
2. Pour the mixture into a blender. Cover and blend until a light foam forms on top (about one minute).
3. Serve in heated mugs.

Yield: 1 serving of ½ cup

Note: A hand-held immersion blender is a good tool for making this kind of beverage.

It was a great experience to visit the coffee plantations in South America. We buy our beans directly from these farmers and roast the beans fresh in our store. Many of them have come up to visit us, too!

"Stewpendous" Strawberry-Yogurt Smoothie

These frothy and delicious drinks are served at the store. Once you know the technique you can substitute your favorite fruits.

Preparation Time: 5 MINUTES
Cooking Time: NONE

SUPER FAST LOW FAT

6 ounces vanilla frozen yogurt (low fat or no fat)
3 to 4 ripe strawberries, hulled (out of season you can use frozen strawberries)
½ ripe banana
8 ounces skim milk

1. In a blender, combine the frozen yogurt, strawberries and banana.
2. Top off with the skim milk. Blend on high speed for 1 minute.

Yield: one 16-ounce drink

Stew's TIP

Holiday on Ice

If you want to make frozen drinks like a piña colada or Margarita, you do not need an ice crushing machine. Add a few cubes of ice to an electric blender along with the drink ingredients.

The Workhorse Blender

A lot of blenders were relegated to the storage closet in the 1970s when food processors came on the scene. But in recent years they have been rehabilitated as chefs use them to emulsify low-fat sauces, and make soups and drinks. The blender blade rotates much faster than that of a food processor, making it ideal for binding vinaigrette-based sauces and making fruit purées. As you can see with the Homemade Cappuccino recipe, blenders also froth liquids well. Of course, it is unmatched for making all sorts of tropical fruit drinks.

Here Bob Gagstetter, a 20-year veteran at Stew's, makes a "Stewpendous" smoothie. This is the new craze in our ice cream parlor. Frozen yogurt and skim milk make for a tasty, fat-free treat!

How do I know that coffee beans in a store are fresh?

Coffee is as perishable as lettuce! Exposed to air and at room temperature, your coffee will become stale within 10 days. You want to buy freshly roasted coffee. That's why Stew's roasts its own beans throughout the day, 7 days a week. Never buy beans from an "open air" bin unless you can see it being roasted right there. Chances are the coffee was shipped awhile ago and is stale.

Coffee

When you come around the first aisle at Stew Leonard's the heady aroma of fresh roasted coffee hangs in the air like a seaside fog. Stew Leonard's imports coffee directly from the best coffee plantations and estates in the mountainous terrain around the equator. It is then roasted before your eyes in the stores.

What's the real difference between "gourmet" coffee and a can of coffee?

Essentially, commercial coffee sold in cans is a blend of up to a dozen or more beans, usually lower quality beans. The particular blend of the beans often depends more on the world's market prices than quality.

"Gourmet" coffee beans are top-quality Arabica beans with distinctive flavor profiles. Quality is a priority over price.

What is an "Arabica" bean and why is it better?

These are the beans grown at high elevations, and they are famed for their rich, robust flavor, acidity, and body. Coffees grown at lower elevations are called "Robusta," and are not as flavorful.

What are the differences in the types of roasts?

The term "roast" refers to the length of time that coffee beans spend in the roaster. When I explain this to customers I like to equate it to a piece of toast in your toaster. The same bread can be toasted lightly, medium, or dark. It's the same with a coffee bean! The longer the roast, the more body and flavor the coffee. The shorter the roast, the milder the flavor. The same Colombian bean can vary from a mild Colombian roast (brownish looking), to a French roast (darker yet), all the way to espresso (black). Most people are amazed to learn that all come from the same bean!

Our master coffee roaster, Pierre Ulysse, at work.

Here is a rundown of the most common roasts:

Medium – Goes by the names Full City, American, Regular, or Breakfast.

Dark – Continental, New Orleans, Vienna, Stew's Choice, and most Starbucks roasts.

Very Dark – Darkest are French, Italian, and Espresso.

What does Swiss Water Decaf mean?

Swiss Water Decaf was a patented process for extracting the caffeine from coffee without using chemicals. The patent has expired, so any coffee that you see labeled "Water Processed" is using this chemical-free process.

What's the best way to store my coffee?

Keeping the coffee away from air — whether whole beans or ground — is more important than temperature! Remember that air and moisture loss can destroy coffee. The best way to store your coffee is to put the whole beans in a zip lock bag, then squeeze out excess air before putting it in the freezer. Leaving the beans whole and then grinding, as you need them (at room temperature), yields a superior cup of coffee.

Since 90% of our customers grind their coffee in our stores, here's another method. Again, in a zip lock bag, squeeze out all air and store the ground coffee in your refrigerator. Be careful, your refrigerator is full of food aromas and the coffee may absorb these flavors. It's critical that you use an airtight bag.

Each batch of coffee is roasted at over 400 degrees from 12-18 minutes, depending on the roast.

Coffee is very absorbent, like a sponge. All of the moisture is removed from the coffee bean during roasting. "The beans are bone dry," says Pierre Ulysse, Stew's Master Roaster. "It's the customer's job to keep it that way." After using coffee squeeze out all of the air from whatever bag you store it in. We do not recommend storing your coffee in cans with plastic lids. They are not airtight and permit too much air into the coffee can. This makes your coffee stale rapidly and it will pick up other flavors in the refrigerator.

How long can I store my coffee?

The freezer will keep your coffee fresh for about 3 months; in the refrigerator it lasts about 1 month.

What is so special about Jamaica's Blue Mountain coffee?

Jamaica's Blue Mountain coffee has the reputation as being one of the finest coffees in the world. Only a few hundred barrels of these beans are produced each year, causing the price of the beans to escalate. Customers rave about "the smooth taste" of the Jamaican Blue Mountain Blend we sell at Stew's.

We offer more than 40 different roasts, blends, and flavors to choose from. Hazelnut is, by far, the biggest selling flavored coffee.

Frozen drinks have become very popular among our customers. Here are 4 fat-free coffee drinks that you will love. We call them all "moolattas" at Stew's!

Coffee Moolatta

Preparation Time: 5 MINUTES
Cooking Time: NONE

SUPER FAST LOW FAT

3 ounces of strong coffee (French roast or espresso)
2 teaspoons sugar
1½ cups no-fat (or lowfat) frozen vanilla yogurt
1 cup of fat-free milk (or Fat Free Plus from Stew's)
4 ice cubes

1. Combine all ingredients in a blender. Blend until smooth. Pour into a tall glass.

Optional: You can sprinkle cinnamon on top. Cocoa powder and grated chocolate are terrific too, but they are not fat free.

Yield: 2 servings

Daniel Canizalez inspects the quality of the green beans that arrive at Stew's.

Mocha Moolatta

Here's a refreshing drink that we sell at the store. The great thing is that it is also fat free!

Preparation Time: 5 MINUTES
Cooking Time: NONE

SUPER FAST LOW FAT

3 ounces of strong coffee (French roast or espresso)
2 teaspoons sugar
1½ cups of frozen chocolate yogurt (no fat or lowfat)
1 cup of fat-free milk (or Fat Free Plus from Stew's)
4 ice cubes

1. Combine all ingredients in a blender. Blend until smooth. Pour into a tall glass.

Optional: You can sprinkle cinnamon on top. Cocoa powder and grated chocolate are terrific too, but they are not fat free.

Yield: 2 servings

How do I brew a perfect cup of coffee at home?

1. Start with a top-quality, fresh coffee!

Follow the buying, storage and freshness tips discussed for great coffee. You have to start with a great bean!

2. You don't need a fancy coffee machine.

The quality of your beans is more important than an expensive coffee maker. Today there are many great coffee makers on the market. Most of our customers use the automatic drip brewers, which are fine. That's what I use at home. You can also use the French method of pouring hot water over ground coffee and then "plunging it." The only disadvantage with that system is that extra coffee in the pot gets cold in a matter of minutes.

Old-fashioned percolators are okay but not the best method. They boil and recycle coffee through the grinds over and over again, which can produce bitter oils and a burned flavor. As for espresso machines, the key is power — you want a machine that blasts the water and steam through the tightly packed beans.

3. Don't "eyeball it." Know how much coffee to use.

This is a matter of taste. Our Master Roaster, Pierre Ulysse, recommends 1½ tablespoons of ground coffee for each 6 ounces of water. I like my coffee a little stronger and use 2 tablespoons (this is what the Specialty Coffee Association of America recommends). When you buy the valve-lock bags at Stew Leonard's we give you a free "industry standard" coffee scoop that equals one tablespoon.

4. Coffee is 99% water, make sure your water is good.

There are many minerals like chlorine and iron in many tap waters — it varies greatly from town to town. All of these can affect your coffee. Some coffee experts put a filter system on their water at home or use a bottled mineral water. Experiment at home and see if you can tell the difference.

5. Use the right "grind."

As the water in your coffee maker passes through coffee grinds, it "extracts" the coffee oils and flavor. If the grind it too coarse, the water will flow through too fast. Too fine a grind, the water gets backed up. This affects your coffee flavor tremendously.

The type of grind depends on your brewing technique. For the French plunger method you want a coarse grind. With espresso, since the water is in contact with the coffee for a short time, you want a fine grind. Most customers use automatic coffee makers at home, and for this the semicoarse "auto drip" grind is perfect.

6. Don't "cook" your coffee!

Juba's is a coffee shop in Westport, Connecticut, that caters to many local celebrities like Martha Stewart, Michael Bolton and others. Juba's brews an excellent cup of coffee. Julie Pallotta, the owner, says "After the coffee is brewed, if you leave it on the burner, it will continue to cook. Air pots keep the coffee hot without continual cooking." (An air pot is an insulated thermos-like container with a pump attachment on top.)

7. Clean it well!

There are many bitter oils that stick to your filter and brewing area. Take the time to clean these with soap and water after each use.

What's so special about Kona from Hawaii?

The mountains and warm weather of Hawaii are ideal for coffee plantations. The most renowned Hawaiian coffee, Kona, is famous worldwide for its distinctive beans. Many of Hawaii's sugar plantations are being converted to coffee. They produce a sweet, medium-bodied flavor.

My Uncle Don Vucurevich lives on the Hawaiian Island of Kauai. On one of my visits, he introduced me to the Island Coffee Company. During a "cupping," I tasted some of their Kauai #1 and immediately had some shipped directly to our stores. It has the same characteristics as the Kona (a neighboring island) but is much lower in price.

Hazelnut Moolatta

Preparation Time: 5 MINUTES
Cooking Time: NONE

SUPER FAST LOW FAT

3 ounces of strong coffee (French roast or espresso)
2 teaspoons hazelnut flavored syrup (or hazelnut liqueur)
1½ cups no-fat (or lowfat) frozen vanilla yogurt
1 cup of fat-free milk (or Fat Free Plus from Stew's)
4 ice cubes

1. Combine all ingredients in a blender. Blend until smooth. Pour into a tall glass.

Optional: You can sprinkle cinnamon on top. Cocoa powder and grated chocolate are terrific too, but they are not fat free.

Yield: 2 servings

Banana Moolatta

Preparation Time: 5 MINUTES
Cooking Time: NONE

SUPER FAST LOW FAT

3 ounces of strong coffee (French roast or espresso)
1 large ripe banana (if the banana is not ripe, add a little sugar)
1 cup of frozen vanilla yogurt (no fat or lowfat)
1½ cups of fat-free milk (or Fat Free Plus from Stew's)

1. Combine all ingredients in a blender. Blend until smooth. Pour into a tall glass.

Optional: You can sprinkle cinnamon on top. Cocoa powder and grated chocolate are terrific too, but they are not fat free.

Yield: 2 servings

It's breathtaking to see the beautiful Hawaiian coffee plantations. The view of the Pacific Ocean beyond them is gorgeous. Kauai is my Dad and Mom's favorite coffee by far!

Answers to the Most Commonly Asked Coffee Terms

Maria Carreiro tests the coffee in our Danbury store. She developed a Danbury Hatter's Blend, too!

Aroma: The fragrance detected by sniffing coffee — it has been described as everything from sweetly floral (jasmine) to sweetly spicy (orange).

Acidity: Have you ever referred to a cup of coffee as strong? Most people describe acidic coffee that way. Coffee acidity contributes a pleasantly sharp, "snappy," and lively quality that is desirable.

Body: The "mouth-feel" in terms of weight and consistency. This is like the difference between drinking a glass of skim milk versus whole milk. The rich milk would have more "body." It's the same with different kinds of coffee.

Blend: Mixing two or more varieties of roasted coffee or different roasts (light or dark) to produce a balanced, pleasing taste. Many shops feature a "house" blend, like our "Stew's Choice."

Caffeine: The stimulant found in coffee. Many customers mix half-decaffeinated and half-regular beans. They say it eliminates the "buzz!"

Café au lait: French-style coffee made by simultaneously pouring coffee and boiled milk into a cup.

Cappuccino: Espresso coffee and steamed, frothed milk in equal proportions. The frothy "cap" may be garnished with sprinkled chocolate or cocoa, cinnamon, vanilla powders, or sugars crystals.

Espresso: A method of quickly extracting coffee flavor by forcing pressured water through the ground beans. It is made mostly from ground Arabica beans. One-and-one-half ounces of espresso is known as a "shot" and can be the foundation of many delicious coffee drinks.

Flavor: The combination of the aroma and the taste you experience upon sipping coffee. Terms relating to flavor are nutty, earthy, spicy, fruity, smoky, musty, rich, grassy, chocolate, neutral, sweet, and winey.

French or Italian roast: A style of roasting coffee beans that leaves them very dark brown and strong flavored.

Froth/foam: The term given to milk, which has been made thick and foamy by aerating it with hot steam.

Latte: Coffee with steamed milk, usually in a 1-to-3 ratio. It can contain flavored syrup and be topped with a layer of froth.

Mochaccino: A cappuccino made with steamed chocolate milk.

Organic Coffee: Coffee grown without any chemicals or pesticides. This is a loosely defined and unregulated term.

Roasts: Varieties or blends roasted to a specific color, such as Full City Roast, Stew's Choice, and French Roast.

Varietals: A term used for the coffee that comes from a specific geographical region. A Sumatra, Kenya, Costa Rican or a Java are varieties. As in wine, soil, climate and cultivation methods affect the taste of your coffee.

The green coffee beans before harvest.

Appetizers and Finger Food

Finger foods can be great fun to make — and to eat.
This chapter will set you up for all kinds of nibbling situations.
We also give you many quick and easy appetizers, including
the fabulous (and easy) recipe from world-famous chef
André Soltner: Salmon Glazed with Mustard Mousse.

Stew's California Tomato Salsa

Preparation Time: 15 MINUTES
Cooking Time: NONE (although it marinates for 1 to 2 hours)

2 medium tomatoes, skins removed (blanch them in boiling water to make skin removal easier), halved
1 medium onion, peeled and chopped
2 serrano chilies, chopped (or to taste)
⅓ cup chopped fresh cilantro
Salt to taste
3 tablespoons chicken stock or water

LOW FAT

PREPARE IN ADVANCE

1. Place all of the ingredients in a food processor or blender. Purée until blended but still a little chunky. Refrigerate the sauce for 1 to 2 hours before serving. Use as a dip or as a garnish with all kinds of appetizers.

Yield: 4 to 6 servings

My wife, Kim, a California native, picks out some fresh herbs. She introduced me to cilantro. It's now my favorite. (She is, too!)

Stew's Guacamole Dip

Here's another big seller. This makes a terrific dip that everyone gobbles up. It's great with tortilla chips. When I make this I like to leave the avocados chunky.

Preparation Time: 15 MINUTES
Cooking Time: NONE

2 large ripe avocados (the Floridas are bigger than the California Haas variety)
Juice of 1 lime
$\frac{1}{4}$ cup finely minced onion
2 tablespoons minced serrano chilies, canned or fresh (you may use jalapeño but beware of its heat)
$\frac{3}{4}$ cup peeled, seeded, and coarsely chopped tomato
$\frac{1}{4}$ cup chopped fresh cilantro leaves
$\frac{1}{2}$ teaspoon salt (or to taste)
Freshly ground black pepper to taste

1. Halve and peel the avocados. Remove the pits and any brown tissue. Place the avocados and the lime juice in a mixing bowl.
2. Slice the avocado into chunks. With a fork, mash them coarsely. Add the chopped onion, chilies, tomatoes, coriander, salt, and pepper. Mix well.

Yield: 6 servings

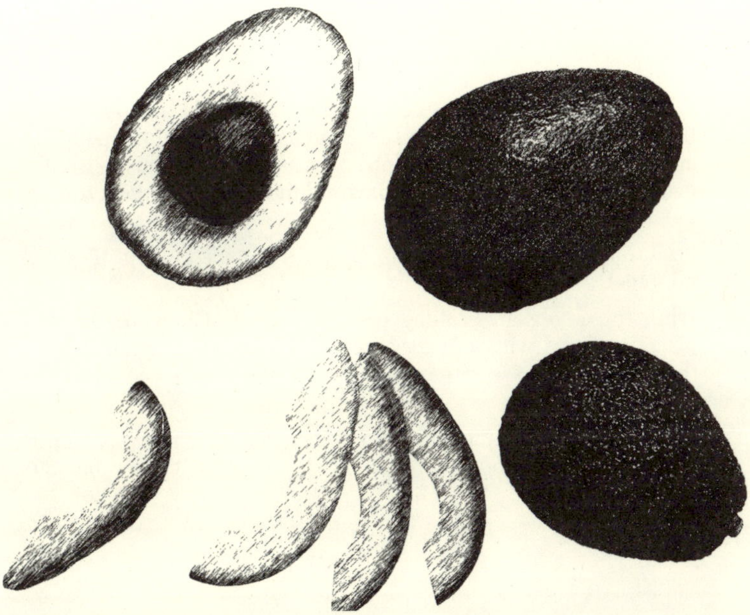

What's the difference between a California avocado and a Florida avocado?

The California or Haas variety is smaller (about the size of your fist) and a bit darker. The Florida (the Booth or Lula varieties) are larger, like a small grapefruit, and usually bright green. The Haas has twice as much fat as the others. However, it's the good monounsaturated fat (like in olives). As far as the flavor, the Haas has a more nutty and rich flavor whereas the Florida is mild.

How do I pick a ripe avocado?
Most of the avocados we sell are a few days from being ripe. It's easy to ripen these at home. Slightly hard avocados will ripen in 2 to 4 days when kept at room temperature in a brown paper bag.

Stew's TIP

Fresh, seasonal dips can be made with ease if you have a blender or food processor. One of our favorites is made with roasted red peppers. First blacken the outside of 2 peppers over a gas flame or under a broiler. Let them cool slightly and place them in a paper bag, closed, to steam for about 15 minutes. When the peppers are cool, peel off the charred skin with your fingers or a paring knife. Halve the peppers and remove the seeds and membrane. Place the peppers in a food processor and, while it is running, add ¾ cup of cream or half-and-half, 1 tablespoon of balsamic vinegar, cayenne pepper to taste, salt to taste, and 3 tablespoons of fresh parsley leaves. This loosely textured dip can also double as a cold sauce for summer vegetable platters.

Roasted Red-Pepper-and-Basil Dip

This is one of our favorite party snacks. It is a robust dip that keeps them coming back. It can be prepared ahead and frozen until needed. Serve with toast wedges, pita bread, croutons, or toasted Mexican tortillas. This recipe is for a party, yielding 10 cups. You can cut it down if desired.

Preparation Time: 20 MINUTES
Cooking Time: ABOUT 1 HOUR

LOW FAT — PREPARE IN ADVANCE

4 large red bell peppers, stems and seeds removed
2 large green bell peppers, stems and seeds removed
2 pounds ripe plum tomatoes (about 12)
1 cup onions, thinly sliced (about 1 medium onion)
1 cup minced garlic (about 12 large cloves)
2 cups fresh basil leaves, finely shredded (about 3 bunches)
1 cup toasted pine nuts (place in a hot pan for about 5 minutes, shaking pan)
1 pound grated Parmesan
1½ pounds goat cheese
1 cup olive oil
2 tablespoons hot pepper sauce (optional)
1 teaspoon salt
½ teaspoon freshly ground black pepper
2 pounds toasted French baguette-style bread (2 to 3 loaves depending on type) cut into ¼-inch slices

1. Preheat the broiler.
2. Broil the peppers on a baking sheet, turning frequently, until the skin is charred on all sides (about 20 minutes). Remove from the oven and place in a paper bag to cool (this makes it easier to remove skins).
3. While the peppers are broiling, cut the tomatoes in half and remove the seeds. Place on a baking sheet, cut side up. When the peppers are done, broil the tomatoes until browned on top. Remove from oven and chop them coarsely. Turn off the broiler and heat the oven to 350 degrees.
4. Broil the onions, stirring frequently, until browned (about 15 minutes).
5. While the onions are broiling, peel the peppers. Chop coarsely and place in a bowl with tomatoes and all remaining ingredients. Mix thoroughly with a wooden spoon. Stir in the onions and adjust seasonings to taste.
6. Spoon the mixture into a 9 x 13 x 3-inch casserole and bake until hot and bubbly (about 10 minutes). Serve with the toasted bread or crudites.

Yield: 10 cups

Herbed Cheese Dip with Stew's Country Hearth Bread

This visually arresting and tasty appetizer is perfect for parties. The herbed cheese is served inside the hollowed-out cavity of the bread.

Preparation Time: 10 MINUTES
Cooking Time: 10 TO 15 MINUTES

SUPER FAST

1-pound loaf of Stew's Country Hearth bread, unsliced
¾ pound herbed goat cheese or other mild white cheese, room temperature
8 ounces cream cheese, room temperature
1 cup minced scallions (about 1 bunch)
1 teaspoon cayenne
½ cup sour cream
2 cups broccoli flowerets (about 1 head)
2 cups of cauliflower flowerets (about ½ cauliflower, or more if you like)
4 plum tomatoes, quartered
2 cups Belgian endive leaves, about 2 endive
1 small head radicchio, leaves separated (or other lettuce)

1. Preheat the oven to 350 degrees.
2. Cut a 5-inch square in the top of the bread. Remove some of the inside to form a cavity in the bread. Reserve the square of crust to decorate the loaf when serving.
3. In the bowl of an electric mixer or food processor, place the goat cheese, cream cheese, scallions, and cayenne. Blend this mixture until it is uniform and creamy. Stir in the sour cream and adjust the seasonings to taste with salt and pepper.
4. Spoon the cheese mixture into the cavity in the bread. Place the bread in the oven and bake for 10 to 15 minutes, until the cheese is warm and the bread is crusty.
5. While the bread is baking, arrange the vegetables around the edge of a large decorative serving tray or platter. Arrange the tomatoes and endive leaves around and on top of the radicchio, and the broccoli next to the cauliflower.
6. When the bread is heated place it in the center of the tray and serve immediately. Lean the reserved lid against the loaf as decoration.

Yield: 8 to 12 servings as an appetizer

What do I need to know when buying fresh goat cheese?

The flavor of goat cheese varies widely according to the way it is made as well as its age. At Stew Leonard's we sell fresh goat cheese, both imported and domestic. The domestic tends to be more moist and mild tasting. The French cheeses have a more pronounced tartness. To judge the freshness of goat cheese, pick it up and squeeze slightly. If it is very soft it is fresh and subtle tasting; if the cheese feels firm and bounces back a little, it is older and more tart. If it is very hard put it back.

Bret Cherry, Rafael Hernando, and my sister, Beth, take some hot bread from the oven. Country Hearth is our best seller.

Stew's TIP

For an instant appetizer, spread some fresh goat cheese over toasted Stew's Country Hearth Bread, then top with Tomato Salsa (see recipe page 28), salt and pepper, and fresh herbs of your choice.

Fresh Tomato-and-Balsamic-Vinegar Relish

Serve this invigorating multi-purpose relish with cold meats, on sandwiches, or in poultry dishes. It can be served hot or cold.

Preparation Time: 10 MINUTES
Cooking Time: 6 TO 8 MINUTES

2 large onions
6 plum tomatoes
3 tablespoons vegetable oil
Salt and pepper to taste
3 tablespoons balsamic vinegar

1. Peel the onions and cut them in half vertically. Slice the onion into thin strips to make about 3 cups. Halve the plum tomatoes, then chop them into 1-inch cubes to make about 3 cups.
2. Cover a pan with the olive oil and sauté the onion until soft, about 5 minutes. Add the tomatoes, salt, and pepper, and cook the relish over medium heat for 6 to 8 minutes. Add the balsamic vinegar and serve.

Yield: 6 servings

A Fourth of July Picnic

Roasted Red-Pepper-and-Basil Dip (see recipe page 30)

Mediterranean Shrimp (see recipe page 38)

Bethy's Tortellini Salad (see recipe page 96)

Grilled Marinated Leg of Lamb (see recipe page 168)

Stew's Silky Cheesecake (see recipe page 314)

Can't-Eat-Just-One Spiced Walnuts

Since we own a food store, when folks drop by the house they expect a large and imaginative selection of munchies. We try not to let them down. These terrific walnuts — exotically aromatic of ginger and cumin — are a perfect nibbler. Make big batches and refrigerate them, because they share the pistachio syndrome: you can't eat just one.

Preparation Time: 5 MINUTES
Cooking Time: ABOUT 20 MINUTES

PREPARE IN ADVANCE

2 cups water
2½ cups walnut sections
2 tablespoons unsalted butter
1 teaspoon powdered ginger
1½ teaspoon ground cumin
¼ teaspoon cayenne
2 tablespoons granulated sugar
1 teaspoon salt
½ teaspoon soy sauce

1. Preheat the oven to 400 degrees.
2. Bring 2 cups of water to a boil. Blanch the walnuts for 2 minutes. Drain and set aside.
3. In a large skillet, melt the butter and add all remaining ingredients. Add the nuts and cook over medium heat, stirring constantly, until warm.
4. Spread the nuts on a baking sheet. Bake for 8 to 10 minutes, turning the nuts frequently to brown them evenly.
5. Allow the nuts to cool, then place in plastic bags. They will keep indefinitely in the refrigerator. Use in salads, put in small bowls on the holiday buffet table, or make little gift bags tied with colorful ribbons.

Yield: 2½ cups

Stew's TIP

Herbes de Provence, an aromatic blend of dried herbs, are a great addition to grilled meat, seafood, salads, and soups. If you do not find the commercial blend (the herbs are sold in little earthenware crocks) you can make a version at home by combining fresh thyme, savory, marjoram, and oregano, and keeping them in an airtight plastic bag.

Before you blend the herbs, first dry them by placing them on a baking sheet, one type at a time, and putting them in a 180-degree oven. Cook until dry, about 15 minutes. In summer you can also dry the herbs by placing them in the shade for a day. You may also add to the mix dried sage, rosemary, lavender flowers, and fennel seeds.

Cajun Spice Mixture

Here is an all-around Cajun spice mixture that you can rub onto chicken or beef. You can even do this with the vegetables before cooking. Calibrate the heat to suit your tastes.

5 teaspoon garlic powder
2 teaspoon dry oregano
2 teaspoon ground black pepper
2 teaspoon paprika
1 teaspoons cayenne (or more to taste)

1. Combine all the ingredients in a small bowl. Use to season meats and vegetables before baking. Store in an airtight jar.

Yield: 1 cup

Cajun-Style Chicken Fingers

Contrary to popular belief, Cajun food is not searingly hot. A few dishes, like these chicken fingers, have a kick, but Cajun dishes generally are known for their richness rather than their BTUs. These mildly spicy chicken fingers are irresistible as appetizers or snacks.

Preparation Time: 10 MINUTES
Cooking Time: 10 MINUTES

SUPER FAST

1 pound boneless, skinless chicken breasts
1 tablespoon soy sauce
Spice mixture (recipe adjacent)
2 tablespoons chopped peanuts
½ cup plain dried breadcrumbs
Vegetable oil for pan
1 lemon cut into 4 wedges

1. Preheat the oven to 375 degrees.
2. Cut the chicken breasts into ¾-inch wide strips that are about the length of a finger. Place them in a bowl with the soy sauce. Stir to coat the chicken pieces with the sauce. Set aside.
3. Place the spice mixture in a small paper bag. Combine the peanuts and bread crumbs in a second paper bag. Place the chicken fingers in the spice bag and shake well. Then transfer them to the bread-crumb bag and shake, pressing the bread crumbs into the chicken strips.
4. Spread the chicken pieces on a baking sheet sprayed with vegetable cooking spray or lightly coated with vegetable oil. Bake the chicken strips for 8 to 10 minutes until crisp. Serve the chicken fingers with lemon wedges.

Yield: 4 servings

Orange-Marinated Mushrooms

The selection of mushrooms at Stew Leonard's varies with the seasons — fall is the best time. Serve these delicious pickled mushrooms on a salad or as a cocktail snack. Their flavor improves the longer they remain in the orange-cumin marinade.

Preparation Time: 5 MINUTES
Cooking Time: 10 MINUTES

LOW FAT · SUPER FAST · PREPARE IN ADVANCE

¼ cup cider or white-wine vinegar
¼ cup orange juice
2 teaspoons minced garlic (2 large cloves)
¼ teaspoon ground cumin
Pinch of salt
⅛ teaspoon freshly ground black pepper
3 cups water
1 teaspoon dried saffron or ½ teaspoon turmeric powder
8 ounces whole fresh button mushrooms

1. Combine the cider, orange juice, garlic, cumin, salt, and pepper in a bowl large enough to hold the mushrooms. Set aside.
2. Bring 3 cups of water to a boil. Add the saffron and mushrooms. Reduce heat to medium and simmer for 5 minutes.
3. Drain the mushrooms and place in the marinade while still warm. Serve cool or chilled. These mushrooms keep for up to 1 week in the refrigerator, covered.

Yield: 4 to 6 appetizer servings

Stew's TIP

Garnish appetizer platters with Greek or Italian kalamata olives, thin slices of proscuitto or dry cured salami, chunks of imported provolone, wedges of ripe tomato, or anchovies. When served with baskets of Stew's Country Hearth Bread, a sampler like this makes a satisfying luncheon.

Mediterranean Antipasto Platter

In Italy, the first course at picnics is often a tantalizing assortment of cold salads, sausages, and olives. When our family has a large picnic or gathering, platters of assorted salads help make the meal festive. Here are some of the salads we love to make for an antipasto platter.

Spanish Tortilla (see recipe page 12)

Orange-Marinated Mushrooms (see recipe page 35)

Lima-Beans-and-Fresh-Fennel Salad (see recipe page 80)

Sweet-and-Sour Fresh Cucumber Pickles (see recipe page 79)

Zarela's Bocaditos de Papa (Potato-Cheese Fritters)

Zarela Martinez from the famous Zarela's in New York City.

Zarela Martinez is an authority on Mexican cooking and the owner of "Zarela," which is our favorite Mexican restaurant in New York. Every night there is a fiesta — and they make mean margaritas! Zarela's most recent cookbook is called *The Food and Life of Oaxaca*, and we highly recommend it to anyone interested in regional Mexican food. Here is how Zarela describes these terrific potato cakes.

"Bocadito or bocadillo means a tidbit, literally a 'little mouthful.' These delicious examples were showing up all over the Isthmian city of Juchitan when I went there one spring to attend the Saint's Day observation. The potato bocaditos are very popular as cocktail appetizers. The cheese adds some salt, so taste before seasoning."

1 pound Idaho potatoes (2 large potatoes), peeled and cut into thick chunks
3 large eggs, lightly beaten
1 cup grated aged ricotta (or other hard, aged cheese)
Freshly ground black pepper
¼-½ teaspoon salt (optional)
Vegetable oil for frying

1. Bring a pot of salted water to a boil and drop in the potatoes. Cook, testing occasionally with a fork, until just done but not too soft, about 12-15 minutes. Drain thoroughly. Transfer the potatoes to a large mixing bowl and mash thoroughly with a fork or a potato masher.
2. With a wooden spoon, beat in the eggs and cheese. Season well with pepper and salt. Shape the mixture between your palms to form 12 compact round cakes about 2½ inches across.
3. Pour the vegetable oil into a medium-size saucepan or deep skillet to a depth of 1 inch. Heat the oil to 375 degrees over medium-high setting — use a deep-frying thermometer, available in any kitchenware shop. As the potato cakes hit the hot oil the oil temperature may dip slightly, so increase the heat to bring it back to 375 degrees. Fry the potato cakes 3 or 4 at a time until golden on both sides. Lift them out onto paper towels to drain as they are done. Serve immediately.

Yield: 12 fritters

"From one of America's most famous chefs ..."

Jacques Pépin's Zucchini-and-Tomato Fans

Chef, author, teacher, and television personality, Jacques Pépin is one of the most recognized names in the food world. We asked Jacques, who lives on the eastern Connecticut shore, if he would contribute to our book a tasty and easy-to-prepare appetizer. It was hard to choose since he has literally hundreds of dishes in his repertory. Here is one of his elegant creations.

Preparation Time: 15 MINUTES
Cooking Time: 30 MINUTES

4 long narrow plum tomatoes (about 12 ounces)
4 small, firm zucchini, about $1\frac{1}{2}$ inches in diameter and 6 inches long
4 large cloves garlic, peeled
2 tablespoons olive oil
$\frac{1}{4}$ teaspoon salt
$\frac{1}{4}$ teaspoon freshly ground black pepper
$\frac{1}{2}$ teaspoon herbes de Provence (see note page 33)

1. Preheat the oven to 400 degrees.
2. Wash the tomatoes and cut each into 4 slices. Wash the zucchini and trim off the stems. Then, starting at the end opposite the stem, cut each zucchini lengthwise into $\frac{1}{4}$-inch-thick slices, leaving the slices attached at the stem so they can be opened like a fan. Each zucchini should have 4 slices.
3. Arrange the zucchini side by side in a large roasting pan, cookie sheet, or large gratin dish. Place the fanned zucchini in the pan and tuck the slices of tomato inside the zucchini slices.
4. Cut each garlic clove lengthwise into eight thin slices. Place the garlic on the tomato slices in the zucchini fan. Brush the entire surface of the fans with the oil and sprinkle on some salt, pepper, and herbes de Provence.
5. Bake for 30 minutes, or until the zucchini are soft and the fans are nicely browned on top. Using a large spatula, transfer the fans to four plates. Serve.

Yield: 4 servings

Stew's TIP

Anchovies are one of those foods that people either love or despise. In fact, many people abhor them without ever having tasted them. That's too bad, for anchovies can make a delicious Mediterranean-style snack. For example, you could make a quick appetizer by sautéeing slices of country style white bread in olive oil until golden on both sides. Then drain them on paper towels. Cut the bread into ½-inch-wide strips. Place 2 anchovy fillets over each slice. Douse with a blend of lemon juice, olive oil, and minced parsley.

In Spain, anchovy bones are eaten like potato chips. They are dredged in seasoned flour and deep-fried until crispy. They are terrific with a frosty glass of beer.

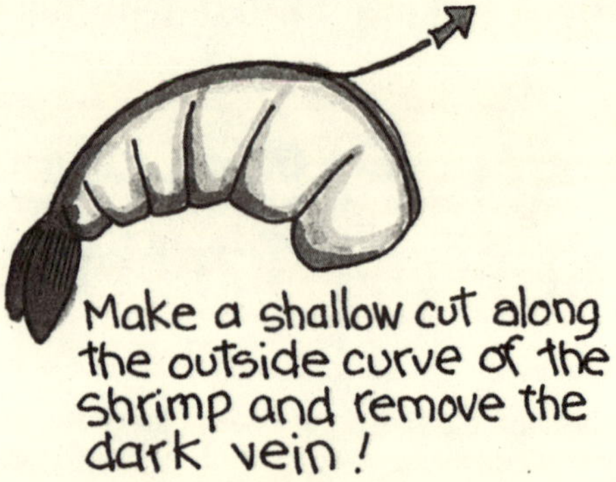

Mediterranean Shrimp

If you are tired of the same old cocktail party appetizers, try this. Shrimp are marinated in a briny anchovy-and-garlic sauce, which gives them a fabulous Mediterranean-style flavor. To serve them as an appetizer, place the shrimp on Melba toast or slices of cucumber.

Preparation Time: 15 MINUTES
Cooking Time: 15 MINUTES

LOW FAT · PREPARE IN ADVANCE

1 quart water
½ teaspoon salt
½ teaspoon hot red pepper flakes
1 teaspoon chopped garlic (about 2 small cloves)
1 small onion, thinly sliced (about ⅔ cup)
Juice of ½ lemon
1 teaspoon mashed anchovy (about 3 fillets — optional)
1 teaspoon olive oil
¾ pound large fresh shrimp (about 24)
Freshly ground black pepper to taste

1. In a pot combine the water, salt, and hot red pepper flakes. Cover and bring to a boil.
2. While the water is heating, combine in a bowl the garlic, onion, lemon juice, anchovy, and olive oil. Set aside.
3. Peel and clean the shrimp. Run a sharp knife along the back (outside) of each shrimp and remove the dark vein that runs down the middle. Cook the shrimp in the boiling water for about a minute or until they are barely pink and firm to the touch.
4. Remove the shrimp from the cooking liquid and place them in the onion mixture. Let the shrimp cool to room temperature or chill them in the refrigerator before serving. Sprinkle with black pepper. The shrimp keep for 5 days refrigerated.

Yield: 4 servings as an appetizer

"From America's Most Famous Restaurant ..."

André Soltner's Salmon Glazed with Mustard Mousse

Bob Greene and Chef George give André Soltner (left) a tour of Stew's kitchen.

The name André Soltner is synonymous with fine dining in America. As the chef-owner of the world-renowned Lutèce for nearly 35 years, Chef Soltner has cooked for kings and connoisseurs, financial barons and faithful fans from far and wide — all of whom praise his genius and amazing consistency.

André Soltner visited Stew Leonard's last summer and the store was abuzz with excitement, as if the Clintons and Michael Jackson had dropped in to pick up a couple of pot pies. We were incredibly honored to get a recipe from him.

André says that for many years this was a favorite dish at Lutèce. There is nothing complicated about it, and it makes a stunning appetizer.

Preparation Time: 15 MINUTES
Cooking Time: ABOUT 10 MINUTES

SUPER FAST

½ pound fillet of salmon, in 1 piece, skin removed
1 tablespoon unsalted butter
Freshly ground black pepper to taste
⅔ cup cream
2 tablespoons whole-grain mustard (sold as Moutarde de Meaux)
1 egg yolk
1 teaspoon lemon juice
¼ teaspoon salt

1. Cut the salmon fillets crosswise into thin pieces. Place the slices between sheets of plastic wrap and tap them with the bottom of a pan to about ¼-inch thickness.
2. Butter the center portions of a sheet tray or baking tray. Sprinkle the buttered portions with ground pepper, and arrange the slices of salmon over them.
3. Preheat a broiler. Preheat the oven to 400 degrees.
4. To prepare the mousse of mustard: In a bowl, whip the cream — do not over-whip; the cream should not be stiff, just fluffy. In another bowl, combine the mustard: egg yolk, lemon juice, salt, and pepper. With a spatula gently fold the whipped cream into this mixture.
5. Cover the salmon with the mousse — the salmon should be completely hidden under it. Put the fish under the broiler until the mousse is golden brown — about 4 to 5 minutes — keep an eye on it! Transfer the salmon to the preheated oven for 2 to 3 minutes, until the mousse gets a little firm. Serve immediately.

Yield: 6 servings

Stew's Smoked Salmon

Having stores so close to New York City, we are able to buy some of the best smoked salmon — and we sell about one ton each week. We buy from two smokehouses, each with its own unique flavor. One smokes their salmon in New York and the other smokes it in the Faroe Islands between Norway and Scotland.

Here's a fresh salmon from Fundy Bay in northern Maine.

What's the difference between "Nova" and "Lox?"

Lox is a method used by the older traditional Europeans. It is heavily salted salmon but is not smoked. The word actually translates as "salmon" in most European languages. "Nova" is a salmon that is cured with less salt and is cold-smoked. As the owner of Homarus Smoked Seafood Peter Heineman says, "For every 1,000 pounds of Nova sold in the U.S., less than 2% is Lox."

How do you pick the best smoked salmon?

To some extent it is a matter of taste. Do you prefer a heavily smoked salmon? A lightly smoked one? Do you like a buttery texture, or a leaner texture? That is determined by tasting. In general though, look for salmon that has a nice reddish-pink color. If smoked salmon has been mishandled it will lose its color and begin to turn whitish. Also, pick a fatty fish (don't worry, it's the good kind of fat with Omega 3 oils). These fish are the prizes of great smokehouses. If you see some white lines running through the fish, that is a good sign.

Is all smoked salmon the same?

There is one variety of Atlantic Salmon called the "Salmo Salar." There are also 6 varieties of Pacific Salmon. The only two that are any good when smoked are the King (called Chinook) salmon and the Coho Salmon. Again, these are fatty fishes too.

Every smokehouse uses salt. Some use salt and brown sugar. Others will spray some scotch on the fish before curing (hence "scotch style" smoked salmon). The "Irish cured" salmon is smoked with peat moss and Irish Whiskey is added after smoking.

All of these recipes affect the taste of the fish. The last thing to determine the flavor of the salmon is the smoking process. This is where the fish sits for up to 24 hours at about 70-75 degrees with some type of hardwood smoke burning. The time it is smoked and the type of wood give you different flavors. At Stew's, we find our customers like a lighter salt and a milder smoke.

How long will my smoked salmon last and can I freeze it?

The smoked salmon that we sell at Stew's is vacuum packed and will last for 14 days in your refrigerator. You can also freeze it. The high oil content in salmon makes it a terrific fish to freeze. It will last for 3 months in your freezer. To defrost, just put in the refrigerator overnight or put the vacuum-packed salmon in lukewarm water for 20 minutes.

Holiday Colors of Red, White & Green

Smoked-Salmon-and-Melted-Brie Wheel

If you are wondering what to bring to a party, here's an idea. This is guaranteed to go fast, but it isn't lowfat!

Preparation Time: 5 MINUTES
Cooking Time: 5 MINUTES

SUPER FAST

1 kilogram (2.2 pounds) wheel of Brie
8 ounces of smoked salmon
½ handful of fresh dill
½ handful of fresh parsley

1. Put wheel of Brie in freezer for 1 hour (this hardens the Brie and makes it easier to cut).
2. Slice it in thirds (you'll end up with 3 pizza-shaped pieces).
3. Lay the salmon in the middle layers to form a club sandwich.
4. Chop up the dill and parsley and spread over the salmon.
5. Put in oven for 5 minutes at 350 degrees. Slice and serve.

Smoked Salmon Tartar with Sliced New Potatoes

All you have to do is put some sour cream on a sliced potato, add some smoked salmon, scallions, dill and viola!

Preparation Time: 10 MINUTES
Cooking Time: 10 MINUTES

LOW FAT
SUPER FAST
PREPARE IN ADVANCE

6 red potatoes, 1½ to 2 inches in diameter (about ¾ pound)
¼ pound smoked salmon, minced
1½ tablespoons (approximately) chopped dill
1 tablespoon chopped scallions
1 tablespoon fresh lemon juice
Salt and freshly ground black pepper to taste
¼ cup sour cream

1. Slice the potatoes into ¼-inch-thick rounds (about 24). Steam them for about 8 minutes — they should be cooked through but still firm and not falling apart. Set aside to cool.
2. In a bowl, combine all of the tartar ingredients except salt, pepper, and the sour cream.
3. Arrange the potato slices on a serving platter. Season with salt and pepper. Top each slice with a bite-sized mound of tartar and garnish with a little sour cream.

Yield: 4 servings

Smoked Salmon with Horseradish Cream Sauce

Preparation Time: 5 MINUTES
Cooking Time: NONE

½ cup freshly grated horseradish, or ¼ cup bottled horseradish, well drained
¾ cup sour cream or plain yogurt
Salt to taste
¼ to ½ pound smoked salmon (depending on number of guests)

1. In a mixing bowl, stir together the horseradish, sour cream or yogurt, and salt. Taste for seasonings.

Yield: About 1 cup

Stew's TIP

To avoid getting seeds on your food when sprinkling with fresh lemons, wrap the lemon half in cheesecloth. Or, squeeze the juice through a fine-mesh sieve.

Lobster on the Half Shell with Basil Mayonnaise

Preparation Time: 15 MINUTES (plus overnight chilling)
Cooking Time: ABOUT 15 MINUTES FOR 1½-POUND LOBSTERS

PREPARE IN ADVANCE

2 tablespoons salt
3 bay leaves
2 lemons, halved
2 1½-pound or 2-pound live lobsters (see lobster information page 237)

1. Pour about 3 inches of salted water into a large pot over high heat. Bring to a boil and add the bay leaves and lemons. Drop the lobsters into the pot, cover, and cook for 12 to 15 minutes for 1½-pounders or about 18 minutes for 2-pounders. (For instructions on how to kill lobsters instantly before cooking see page 237.)
2. Remove the lobsters from the kettle using a long fork or tongs. Place the cooked lobsters on their backs in cool water in a large bowl or high-sided roasting pan in cool water. Let the lobsters cool for 30 minutes. Drain the lobsters, and then put them in the refrigerator to chill completely.
3. Place a lobster upside down on a cutting board. Insert a large knife into the point where the tail meets the body and split the entire tail in half lengthwise. Reverse the lobster, place the knife at the spot where you began, and cut through in the other direction, toward the head. Repeat with the second lobster.

4. Scrape out and discard the dark green liver and red roe. Pick out the intestinal tract that runs along the tail meat. With a teaspoon remove and discard the white lung sacs in the upper cavity and any membrane in the head cavity. Clean out the rest of the cavity.
5. Place 1 half lobster on each of 4 serving plates. Spoon a ½ cup of Warm Red Potato Salad (see recipe page 92) into the head cavity of each lobster. Serve the lobster with a mixed green salad and Basil Mayonnaise (see recipe below).

Yield: 4 servings

Basil Mayonnaise

Preparation Time: 5 TO 10 MINUTES
Cooking Time: NONE

1 cup prepared mayonnaise
3 tablespoons lemon juice (about 1 lemon)
⅛ teaspoon cayenne
Salt to taste
3 tablespoons extra virgin olive oil
½ cup fresh basil leaves (about 1 small bunch) finely shredded

1. Combine the mayonnaise, lemon juice and cayenne in a small bowl. Stir well. Stir in the olive oil and the shredded basil. Adjust seasonings to taste.

Yield: 1⅓ cups

Fred Papp, from our Fish Department, selects a few perfect lobsters.

How do I judge the quality of a lobster?

As a rule, the colder the water the better the lobster — hence the cachet for Maine and Canadian lobsters. When you buy a lobster, touch the shell (make sure the pincers are tied). It should be hard and thick. Soft shells indicate one of two things: that the lobster has recently shed its shell and is growing into a new one (in which case the meat would be skimpy), or that the lobster comes from warm waters.

When buying from tanks in fish stores, choose a lobster that is lively. This indicates cold temperatures and, in general, good conditions. If a lobster is inactive in the tank, try something else for dinner! (See more on lobsters page 237.)

Soups and Stews

We had a lot of fun putting together this diverse chapter, which contains everything from cold fruit soups to Stew's Award-Winning Clam Chowder. Let us know what you think!

Stew's Summer Vegetable Soup

Preparation Time: 20 MINUTES
Cooking Time: 20 MINUTES

LOW FAT

PREPARE IN ADVANCE

2 tablespoons butter
2 tablespoons olive oil
3 cups diced leeks (split leeks lengthwise and rinse well), white section and a little of the green
3 cups diced zucchini, with skins
3 cups diced yellow squash, with skins
2 cups diced onions
6 quarts vegetable stock or chicken stock (see vegetable stock recipe page 174; chicken stock recipe page 63)
3 cups diced red potatoes, with skins
3 cups thinly sliced carrots, washed and trimmed
Salt and freshly ground black pepper to taste

1. In a large pan melt the butter with the olive oil over medium-high flame. Sauté the leeks, zucchini, yellow squash, and onions for 3 minutes, stirring. Add the stock. Add the diced potatoes and carrots and bring to a boil. Reduce to simmer and cook for 15 minutes, or until the potatoes are tender.

2. In batches, add the soup to a blender or food processor and purée well. Add the salt and freshly ground black pepper to taste. Serve with croutons.

Yield: 8 to 10 servings

I love visiting old-fashioned farmers markets throughout Europe. Everything is so fresh and colorful!

Red Bell Pepper Soup

Feel free to substitute any of your favorite seasonal vegetables to this soup.

Preparation Time: 15 MINUTES
Cooking Time: 25 MINUTES

LOW FAT

PREPARE IN ADVANCE

3 red bell peppers
2 cups sliced onion (about 1 large onion)
¾ cup fresh basil leaves, stems removed (or 1 teaspoon dried basil)
3 cups chicken stock, homemade or canned
½ cup peeled and diced carrots (about 1 carrot)
½ cup diced zucchini (about 1 zucchini)
Pinch of ground cumin seed
1 teaspoon salt, or more to taste
Freshly ground black pepper to taste
¼ cup sour cream
2 teaspoons chopped parsley or cilantro

Les Slater, our Produce Director, inspects the red peppers that are imported from Canada.

1. Seed, core, and coarsely chop the red peppers. Place the pepper slices in a deep pot with the onion and the chicken stock. Bring the mixture to a boil, cover, and simmer for about 10 minutes, or until the peppers are tender.
2. Scoop the peppers and onions from the pot and place them in a blender or food processor, along with the basil leaves. Purée until smooth, adding some cooking liquid as needed to make a creamy texture. Return to the pot.
3. Add the carrots and zucchini to the pot. Bring to a boil, cover, and simmer until all the vegetables are tender. Add cumin and adjust seasonings to taste.
4. Spoon the soup into heated bowls. Garnish with a spoon of sour cream and a pinch of parsley or cilantro.

Yield: 4 cups

Stew's TIP

Cajun and Creole Cooking

The terms Creole and Cajun are often misused in cooking, or considered synonymous. In fact, both represent distinct cultures and very different culinary styles. The Cajuns of south-central Louisiana are of French Canadian descent and are largely agrarian (although today many work on offshore oil rigs). Their cuisine has French roots, based on a browned roux (butter and flour cooked together until darkened), and leans toward heavy stews and casseroles. It can be hot, but in most cases it is not searing.

Creole food, which originated in New Orleans, is a blend of French, Spanish, Italian, African, and Native American cooking. Seven different nations ruled New Orleans in its early days, and each left behind distinct spices in the regional stockpot. Creole cooks use more tomato than Cajuns, and the food's presentation is more citified. In general, Creole cooking, based on seafood, is slightly lighter than Cajun fare.

Creole Lentil Soup

Lentils are the symbol of luck and prosperity in many European countries, and a staple of New Year's Eve meals. This soup has the texture of a stew. It is a meal in itself when served with grilled sausages (Stew's sells pork sausage, turkey sausage and chicken sausage), and hearty bread.

Preparation Time: 20 MINUTES
Cooking Time: ABOUT 45 MINUTES

PREPARE IN ADVANCE

8 ounces spicy Cajun or Italian sausage
1 tablespoon olive oil
2 cups diced onions (about 2 medium onions)
1 cup finely diced carrots (about 3 medium carrots)
1 cup finely diced celery (about 2 stalks)
1 cup finely diced red bell pepper (about 1 large pepper)
1 cup finely diced green bell pepper (about 1 large pepper)
1 pound lentils, washed and inspected for small stones
1 teaspoon hot pepper sauce
½ teaspoon dried oregano
2 bay leaves
1 teaspoon salt
1 28-ounce can crushed tomatoes
32 ounces cold water

1. With a sharp knife, remove the sausage casings. Crumble the sausage meat and cook it in a heavy pan over medium-high heat until the fat is rendered (about 4 minutes). Remove from the pan and set aside.
2. Drain the fat from the pan and add the olive oil, onions, carrots, celery, and peppers. Cook until the vegetables begin to soften (about 7 minutes). Add the lentils and remaining ingredients. Bring the mixture to a boil, reduce heat, cover, and simmer for 30 minutes.
3. Check the soup. If it seems too thick add up to 3 additional cups of cold water. Let it simmer for another 30 minutes until the lentils are tender. Adjust the seasonings to taste.
4. Serve in warm bowls with toasted country bread.

Yield: 8 to 10 servings

Purée of Vegetable Soup

This soup is very easy to prepare. All the vegetables are covered with water, boiled until tender, and puréed — voila! If you have more leeks than onions, that's fine. If you have some extra green beans, spinach, or peas on hand, toss them in, too!

Preparation Time: 20 MINUTES
Cooking Time: 45 MINUTES

LOW FAT · PREPARE IN ADVANCE

½ cup chopped carrots (about 1 large carrot)
½ cup chopped celery (about 1 stalk)
1 cup cubed potato, peeled (about 1 large potato)
1 leek, split lengthwise and rinsed well (chopped)
3 cups water or broth
2 cups chopped onion (1 medium onion)
6 ounces diced ham (optional)
2 tablespoons minced garlic
½ teaspoon chopped fresh thyme, or ¼ teaspoon dried
½ teaspoon salt
Freshly ground black pepper to taste
¼ cup sour cream or yogurt (optional)

1. Combine in a large pot all of the ingredients except the salt, pepper, and sour cream. Bring to a boil, cover, and reduce heat. Simmer for 45 minutes or until all the vegetables are tender.
2. Purée the mixture until smooth in a food processor, food mill, or blender. Adjust seasonings to taste.
3. Serve in heated bowls. Garnish with a tablespoon of sour cream and serve with Stew's Country Hearth Bread Croutons (see recipe page 84).

Yield: 4 to 6 servings

New Year's Brunch

Gina's Blue-Ribbon Herbed Biscuits (see recipe page 160)

Homestyle Cappuccino (see recipe page 17)

Creole Lentil Soup (see recipe page 48)

Spinach, Romano, and Egg Strata (see recipe page 4)

Winter Fruit Compote (see recipe page 315)

Stew's TIP

Many of the recipes in this book call for fresh herbs — or dried herbs as a substitute. Keep in mind that dried herbs are more concentrated than fresh; that is why we specify ½ as much dried herbs as fresh. Of course, the real test is in the tasting, so always sample your food for seasonings before serving it.

Stew's TIP

Instant Soup

Almost every ethnic cuisine has its version of vegetable soup. The Italians have minestrone, the Americans have their own variations, the Spanish have gazpacho, and the Mexicans have various dried-bean soups.

With the help of food processors and blenders today, home cooks can create all kinds of healthful vegetable soups at the push of a button.

To make a quick, summery soup, try combining in a pot ¼ cup olive oil, 1 chopped onion, 2 cups chopped sweet red peppers, 2 cups peeled tomatoes, (cored and chopped), 1 bay leaf, 2 sprigs fresh thyme. Sauté for 10 minutes. Add 3 cups of homemade chicken stock, and 1 cup dry white wine. Bring to a simmer. When the vegetables are soft transfer the soup, in batches, to a blender or food processor. Purée until smooth. Taste for seasonings. Serve the soup with a dollop of sour cream for garnish.

Pistou (Southern French Vegetable Soup)

Pistou, the French minestrone, is the harvest soup of southern France. All the bounty of late summer is combined in a rich, thick soup based on tomato purée, garlic, and basil.

This version blends the sweet taste of ripe tomatoes with red peppers, and has a little kick from hot sauce. Three starches — pasta, chickpeas, and potatoes — give the soup a creamy texture.

Preparation Time: 25 MINUTES
Cooking Time: 30 MINUTES

LOW FAT

PREPARE IN ADVANCE

½ cup chopped carrots (1 large carrot, peeled)
½ cup chopped onion (1 medium onion)
1 teaspoon minced garlic (about 2 small cloves)
1 cup chopped tomato (1 medium tomato)
1 15-ounce can chickpeas, with liquid
2 cups chicken stock (see recipe page 63) or vegetable stock (see recipe page 174)
2 to 3 cups water
½ cup chopped potato (1 medium peeled potato)
¼ cup hot cherry pepper, seeded and chopped (or jalapeños)
½ cup shredded fresh cabbage
Salt and freshly ground black pepper to taste
2 ounces pasta or noodles of choice (if long, like spaghetti, break into small pieces)
⅓ cup fresh basil, finely chopped (or 2 teaspoons dried)
⅓ cup fresh parsley, minced
Hot-pepper sauce to taste, like Tabasco (about 1 teaspoon)
¼ cup finely chopped scallions (about 2 scallions)
Grated Parmesan

1. Combine in a pot the carrots, onions, garlic, and tomato. Cook over high heat for 5 minutes, or until the onions are soft.
2. Add the chickpeas, stock, water, potato, cherry pepper, and cabbage. Season with the salt and freshly ground black pepper. Cook over high heat for 15 minutes, or until the vegetables are tender.
3. Add the pasta, basil, parsley, scallions, and hot-pepper sauce, and cook for 10 to 12 minutes over high heat, adding more water as needed.
4. Add salt and freshly ground black pepper to taste. Serve with a teaspoon of grated Parmesan.

Yield: 4 to 6 servings

Winter Vegetable Chowder

Here is one of our favorite midwinter lunches, all vegetables with a little lean Canadian bacon or smoked turkey added for extra flavor.

Preparation Time: 15 MINUTES
Cooking Time: 25 MINUTES

LOW FAT
PREPARE IN ADVANCE

1 tablespoon vegetable oil
½ cup minced Canadian bacon or Stew Leonard's Smoked Turkey
1 cup minced onion (about 2 small onions)
½ teaspoon minced fresh thyme (or ¼ teaspoon dried)
3 tablespoons all-purpose flour
1½ cups peeled, diced new potatoes (about 4 medium potatoes)
½ cup cubed carrots (about 2 carrots)
1½ cups diced sweet potato (about 1 medium sweet potato)
2 cups chicken stock (see recipe page 63) or water
½ teaspoon salt
¼ teaspoon pepper
1 cup corn kernels, fresh or frozen
2 cups milk, lowfat or regular
Several sprigs of fresh parsley, chopped

1. In a large pot over medium-high setting, heat the oil and cook the Canadian bacon, onion, and thyme for 3 minutes, or until the onion is softened.
2. Sprinkle in the flour while stirring. Continue stirring until the flour mixture turns golden. Add the potatoes, carrots, sweet potato, chicken stock, salt, and pepper. Bring the soup to a boil, then reduce heat and cover. Simmer until the vegetables are tender (about 15 minutes).
3. Add the corn and simmer for 5 more minutes. Add the milk and stir until the mixture is creamy and smooth. Correct seasonings. Heat the soup to serve but do not let it boil.
4. Serve in heated soup bowls. Garnish each serving with chopped parsley.

Yield: 6 to 8 servings

Our customers have been buying more and more fresh vegetables.

Carrot Soup with Dill

Preparation Time: 10 MINUTES
Cooking Time: 30 MINUTES

LOW FAT

PREPARE IN ADVANCE

2 pounds of carrots, peeled and chopped
1 tablespoon chopped dill (or $\frac{1}{2}$ tablespoon dried)
$\frac{1}{2}$ tablespoon chopped fresh ginger (or $\frac{1}{4}$ tablespoon dried ginger)
1 cup chopped onions
$\frac{1}{2}$ tablespoon butter
$1\frac{1}{2}$ quarts of vegetable stock or chicken stock (or water) (See recipe for vegetable stock page 174; for chicken stock page 63.)
Salt and pepper to taste
Pinch of sugar (optional)

1. In a soup pot over medium heat, melt the butter and sauté the onions until golden. Add the carrots and half of the dill and cook for 2 minutes, stirring.
2. Add the stock and cook over high heat until it boils, then reduce to medium and cook until the carrots are tender.
3. Transfer the contents of the pan to a blender. Purée until smooth. Taste for seasoning. Serve with the remaining dill as garnish.

Yield: 6 servings

The Cohen brothers grow our pumpkins on their farms in Ellington, Connecticut. We've become good friends, and we visit them regularly to check the crop. We sell more than 120 trailer loads every year!

Halloween Pumpkin-Sage Soup

For a festive fall presentation, this soup can be served in hollowed-out baby pumpkins.

Preparation Time: 10 MINUTES
Cooking Time: 35 MINUTES

LOW FAT · PREPARE IN ADVANCE

3 tablespoons unsalted butter
6 sage leaves, slightly crushed
1 cup finely chopped onion
2 pounds canned pumpkin chunks (not pumpkin purée)
2 cups fresh or canned chicken broth
1 cup water
Salt and freshly ground pepper to taste
1 cup milk
1 cup half-and-half or heavy cream
¼ teaspoon grated fresh nutmeg
⅛ teaspoon cayenne

1. Heat the butter in a pot and add the crushed sage leaves and onion. Cook over medium heat, stirring, for 1 minute. Add the pumpkin chunks, chicken broth, salt, and freshly ground black pepper.
2. Bring the liquid to a boil, reduce to a simmer, and cook for about 20 minutes. Transfer the liquid to the bowl of an electric blender or food processor and purée until smooth. Return the mixture to the pot.
3. Add the milk and half-and-half, nutmeg, cayenne, salt, and freshly ground black pepper. Stir well and simmer for 5 to 10 minutes. Taste for seasonings.

Yield: 6 to 8 servings

How to Prepare Pumpkin-Sage Soup

Stew's Mexican-Style Black Bean Soup

This recipe is for classic American black bean soup, using salt pork and smoked pork hocks (both available at Stew Leonard's meat department). These two ingredients give the soup its lusty flavor.

Preparation Time: 15 MINUTES, plus overnight soaking of black beans
Cooking Time: 2½ HOURS

LOW FAT

PREPARE IN ADVANCE

1 pound black beans
2 tablespoons olive oil
¼ pound lean salt pork, cut into small cubes
2 cups chopped onion
1 tablespoon minced garlic
1½ cups finely diced green pepper
8 cups canned beef broth
1 bay leaf
½ cup minced cilantro (optional)
1 teaspoon dried oregano
1½ pounds smoked pork hocks
Salt and freshly ground black pepper to taste
2 dried hot peppers, chopped (or 2 teaspoons hot red pepper flakes)
2 tablespoons red wine vinegar
¼ cup sherry (optional)

Tom Arthur has become a master at listening and reacting to our customer ideas. He is running our new store in Yonkers.

1. Put the beans in a large bowl and add cold water to cover by about 2 inches. Soak overnight.
2. The next day, heat the oil in a large pan and add the salt pork. Cook, stirring often, until it renders its fat. Add the onion, garlic, and green pepper. Cook until the vegetables are wilted.
3. Drain the beans and add them to the pan. Add the beef broth. Add the bay leaf, the cilantro, oregano, pork hocks, salt, pepper, and the hot red pepper. Bring to a boil and reduce heat to simmer. Cook for about 2 hours, or until the beans are soft.
4. Remove the pork hocks. When they are cool enough to handle, tear off the meat from the hocks and chop it well. Return the meat to the pot and stir.
5. Pour half of the bean mixture into the container of a food processor or blender. Blend to a fine texture. Return this to the soup and stir to blend. Add the vinegar and sherry. Heat thoroughly. Serve, if desired, with chopped onions, chopped scallions, or lime slices.

Yield: About 12 servings

Stew's Navy Bean Soup

This hearty winter soup is built on the rich, smoky flavor of ham hocks. It gets better after sitting a day or two in the refrigerator.

Preparation Time: 20 MINUTES
Cooking Time: 3½ HOURS

PREPARE IN ADVANCE

1 smoked ham hock
1 neck bone (beef or pork)
1 bay leaf
5 quarts chicken stock
1 cup diced onions
2 teaspoon minced garlic
2 tablespoons olive oil
1 pound navy beans (soaked overnight)
½ cup chopped plum tomatoes
½ teaspoon dried thyme
2 bay leaves
Salt and freshly ground black pepper to taste
2 carrots, peeled, trimmed and diced
2 medium potatoes, washed and cut into little cubes
2 tablespoons cornstarch

1. Place the ham hock, neck bone and bay leaf in 6 quarts of water. Bring to a boil. Reduce heat and simmer until the ham hock is tender and the meat comes off easily — about 2½ hours. Remove the ham hock and set aside to cool. Strain the liquid and reserve.
2. When the ham hock is cool enough to handle, tear the meat off. Chop the meat and set aside. Add the chicken stock to the pot. In a pan, sauté the diced onions and the garlic in the olive oil until golden. Add to the pot. Add the navy beans, tomato, thyme, and bay leaves. Cook, skimming, until the beans are very soft — about 45 minutes. Add the carrots and potatoes.
3. If the soup has a thick consistency, leave it; if not, in a small bowl mix the cornstarch with 2 tablespoons of cold water. Add to the soup, stir, and cook another 5 minutes. Taste for seasonings. Serve.

Yield: 8 to 10 servings

Kids love the costume characters roaming the store. My dad and I sometimes have fun and dress as Wow the Cow. It's a blast!

Stew's TIP

Chowders

More than 200 years ago, when fishing fleets returned to ports in the south of France, fishermen used to toss some of their catch into a huge communal pot called "la chaudière." A giant fish stew was made as a celebration for the fishermen's safe journey. This tradition later found its way to maritime Canada, and eventually to the coast of New England, where the seafood soup was called "chowder."

The best known chowders today are clam chowders, either red (Manhattan style) or white (New England style). A debate has raged through the years about which is the real chowder. In Maine the controversy once got so heated that the state legislature introduced a bill to outlaw forever the blending of clams with tomatoes. (It didn't pass.)

Stew's Manhattan Clam Chowder

This chunky, tomato-tinged soup takes little time to prepare, but will win raves! If you want to give it a boost, add a few shakes of Tabasco sauce.

Preparation Time: 25 MINUTES
Cooking Time: 30 MINUTES

PREPARE IN ADVANCE

6 slices chopped bacon
2 cups diced onions
1 cup diced celery
1 cup diced carrots
1 cup diced potatoes
28-ounce can of chopped clams
1 cup clam juice
2 cups diced tomatoes
2 cups tomato juice
1 teaspoon dried thyme
1 bay leaf
Salt and freshly ground black pepper to taste

1. In a pan over medium-high heat, cook the bacon until it is crisp. Reserve the fat.
2. In another pan over medium-high heat, add the bacon fat and cook the onions until golden. Add all of the other ingredients except the clams and the potatoes and cook for 15 minutes.
3. Add the potatoes and clams and simmer for 10 minutes, or until the potatoes are tender. Add salt and freshly ground black pepper and taste.

Yield: 8 servings

We entered the Newport Chowderfest last summer. There was tough competition, but we were proud to get a third place.

Stew's Award-Winning New England Clam Chowder

Here's our pride and joy. In summer our family always went digging for clams on Long Island Sound, right behind our house. We brought the fresh clams back home and made "Grandma's Clam Chowder." She used heavy cream and butter from our dairy — and there was never a drop of that chowder left. Now we make it at the store and sell hundreds of gallons a week! This summer we entered our New England Style Clam Chowder in the Newport Chowder Fest, and it was voted one of the top three in New England! The secret? Twice the clams and half the potatoes!

For convenience sake, we offer a recipe made with chopped clams in a can, which are very good. Of course, you could use fresh clams.

Preparation Time: 10 MINUTES
Cooking Time: 25 MINUTES

PREPARE IN ADVANCE

1 stick butter
1½ cups diced onion
Salt and freshly ground black pepper to taste
1 14-ounce can or jar clam juice
1 cup milk
½ cup heavy cream
2 cups cubed potatoes (skinned)
1 cup flour
1 28-ounce can of chopped clams

1. In a soup pot over medium heat, melt the butter. Add the onions and the black pepper. Sauté until translucent. Add the flour and mix well.
2. Add the clam juice and mix well. Add the milk and cream and bring to a boil.
3. Add the potatoes and cook over medium-high heat until they start to soften — don't cook them too much or they will become mushy by the time you eat them. Add the clams and simmer for 5 minutes. Season to taste — very important!

Yield: 4 to 6 servings

My grandmother, Anna Stewart Leonard. She loved the dairy business, and was a master in the kitchen!

Stew's TIP

How do I cook leeks?

Many recipes in this book call for leeks. Resembling giant scallions, leeks have bulbous white roots and long green leaves — the white section and a few inches of the green are cooked, the rest can be used in stocks. Leeks can be very sandy, so split them vertically down the center and hold them under running tap water until the sand washes away. Choose leeks that have firm white bulbs and bright green leaves without dark spots. In general, the smaller the leek the more tender. Leeks are delicious braised in vegetable or chicken stock, or chopped and added to soups and salads.

Fishermen's Seafood Stew with Garlic Mayonnaise

Stew's is always bringing in different fresh seafood, so customers have a wide selection from which to choose. Here's an easy recipe that gives you a lot of options — you can make it with any of your favorite fish. Refer to the fish chart on pages 204-205.

The garlic mayonnaise, added just before serving, lends a great Mediterranean zest. It also makes the broth creamy and rich.

Preparation Time: 30 MINUTES
Cooking Time: ABOUT 30 MINUTES

LOW FAT

PREPARE IN ADVANCE

3 potatoes, peeled and diced
2 leeks (white part only), cut into ½-inch-thick rings
3 carrots, peeled and sliced widthwise into ¼-inch pieces
1 stalk celery, minced
½ bulb fresh fennel, minced, or 1 teaspoon fennel seed
1 tablespoon grated orange zest
1 large clove garlic, minced
2 cups dry white wine
2 cups water
1 sprig fresh thyme (or ½ teaspoon dried)
Salt and freshly ground black pepper to taste
3 pounds of assorted fish fillets (monkfish, scallops, cod, haddock), cut into 2-inch pieces
12 littleneck clams
1 cup Garlic Mayonnaise (see recipe page 59)

1. In a large pan, combine the potatoes, leeks, carrots, celery, fennel, orange zest, garlic, white wine, and water. Bring to a boil, add thyme, salt and pepper, cover, and simmer for 25 minutes or until the vegetables are tender.
2. Add the fish and clams. Cover and simmer another 5 to 8 minutes.
3. Serve in heated bowls and garnish with a large dollop (about 2 tablespoons) of Garlic Mayonnaise.

Yield: 6 to 8 servings

Butch stocking leeks.

Garlic Mayonnaise

Preparation Time: 5 MINUTES
Cooking Time: 10 MINUTES

SUPER FAST

PREPARE IN ADVANCE

1 egg
1 egg yolk
2 cloves garlic, peeled
1 tablespoon
Fresh lemon juice
¼ teaspoon salt
⅛ teaspoon paprika
¼ teaspoon Dijon-style mustard
1 cup olive oil
Freshly ground black pepper to taste

1. Combine in the bowl of a food processor or blender the egg, egg yolk, and garlic. Blend until the mixture is light and frothy. Blend in all the remaining ingredients except the olive oil.
2. With the processor running, drizzle in the oil. Stop the machine, scrape the sides of the bowl, and blend again. Adjust the seasonings to taste. This mayonnaise keeps for up to a week if covered and refrigerated.

Yield: 2 cups

Instant Variation: Combine 2 cups of homemade or prepared mayonnaise with 2 teaspoons minced garlic, ⅛ teaspoon Hungarian paprika, and ¼ teaspoon Dijon mustard.

Stew's TIP

If you make mayonnaise at home you can season it in many ways for different dishes. For example, add some Dijon mustard and you have mustard mayonnaise for fish or cold meats; add some curry powder for an Indian flavor; add chopped tarragon or basil for an herb mayonnaise; or a little tomato purée and some hot sauce to serve with cold shellfish.

A busy day at Stew's. High turnover keeps the products fresh.

I'm concerned about making mayonnaise with raw eggs. What can I do?

While the risk of using raw eggs is slight — the classic recipe has been made for centuries — many cooks today prefer to use commercial mayonnaise or make it with cooked eggs. Dr. Shams Alam, Stew Leonard's Quality Director, says that if you have vinegar or lemon juice in a raw egg mayonnaise, it will kill any bacteria present.

If you want to try a cooked egg mayonnaise, here is a recipe from The American Egg Board.

Cooked Egg Mayonnaise

2 egg yolks
2 tablespoons vinegar or lemon juice
2 tablespoons water
1 teaspoon water
1 teaspoon dry mustard
½ teaspoon salt
Dash of white pepper (or freshly ground black pepper)
1 cup olive oil (or vegetable oil)

1. In a saucepan over very low heat, whisk together the egg yolks, vinegar, water, sugar, mustard, salt, and pepper until thoroughly blended. Continue cooking, whisking constantly, until the mixture begins to bubble — no more! Remove from the heat immediately. Let stand for 4 minutes.
2. Pour the egg mixture into a blender container. Cover and mix at high speed. While blending, very slowly drizzle in the oil. Blend until the mixture is thick and smooth. Occasionally turn off the blender and scrape down the sides of the container with a rubber spatula. Transfer to a bowl, cover, and chill.

Yield: 1¼ cup

How to Clean Mussels

1. Using a clam knife or a scouring pad, scrape any barnacles off the shells.
2. Pull off the beardlike strands that stick out through the crack. (This kills the mussels, so cook them immediately.)
3. Place the mussels in a large pot and cover with cool, fresh water by about 2 inches. Agitate the mussels with your hand in a washing machine motion.
4. Drain and discard the water.
5. Repeat steps 3 and 4 until the water is clear.
6. Drain and cook.

Shellfish Stew with Spicy Sausage

If you ever have had the good fortune to visit Portugal you would recognize this soup. The Portugese make all kinds of shellfish dishes, often anchored by spicy sausage to give them zip. Lots of garlic is another characteristic of their cooking.

Preparation Time: 25 MINUTES
Cooking Time: 40 MINUTES

LOW FAT

PREPARE IN ADVANCE

1 tablespoon olive oil
1 pound hot pork sausage, cut into 1-inch pieces
3 cups white onion, peeled and chopped
1 tablespoon minced garlic
1 hot cherry pepper, seeded and minced (or jalapeño)
2 cups canned crushed tomato
1 teaspoon paprika
1 cup white wine
2 pounds mussels, cleaned (about 25)
(see instructions for cleaning mussels page 60)
20 littleneck clams, rinsed

1. In a heavy pan, heat the olive oil over medium-high setting. Add the sausage and cook it until lightly browned and some of the fat has rendered, about 8 minutes. Add the chopped onion, garlic, cherry pepper, tomato, paprika, and wine. Bring the sauce to a boil. Reduce the heat to simmer, cover the pan, and cook for 15 minutes.
2. Add the cleaned shellfish, cover, and cook 10 minutes longer, until the mussels and clams open.
3. To serve, divide the shellfish evenly among 6 heated soup bowls. Spoon some of the sausage and broth into each bowl. Serve with crusty Stew's Country Hearth Bread.

Yield: 6 servings

Stew's TIP

Fresh Mussels

Fresh mussels can come to the rescue as a quick, economical, and healthful appetizer. First make sure that all the mussels close firmly when you pinch them — if not, discard. Clean any barnacles clinging to their shells (see instructions page 60). Remove the small "beard" at the narrow end of each mussel. Then steam them in a little white wine, tarragon, and shallots. Remove the empty half of the shells and arrange the other half, holding the meat, around a serving platter. Garnish with fresh parsley or chervil and moisten with an herb vinaigrette of your choice. You also could spoon over them some Fresh Tomato-and-Balsamic-Vinegar Relish (see recipe page 32) or Stew's California Tomato Salsa (see recipe page 28).

What does Provençal mean?

The term Provençal means "in the style of the south of France," — usually incorporating fresh herbs, garlic, tomatoes, and other summer vegetables. This wonderful Provençal fish soup calls for a fish stock (see quick recipe page 211). Prepare a large batch of fish stock and freeze it.

Fish Stew Provençal

Preparation Time: 25 MINUTES
Cooking Time: ABOUT 25 MINUTES

LOW FAT

PREPARE IN ADVANCE

2 tablespoons olive oil
½ cup finely chopped onion
1 leek, cleaned (see instructions page 58), white section chopped — reserve green portion for stocks
½ cup finely chopped celery
1 tablespoon finely chopped garlic
1 teaspoon fennel seeds
2 cups fresh tomatoes cut into ½-inch cubes, or 2 cups canned whole tomatoes, chopped
1 cup dry white wine
½ teaspoon Tabasco sauce
3 cups fish stock (see recipe page 211), or water
2 sprigs fresh thyme (or ½ teaspoon dried thyme)
Salt and freshly ground black pepper to taste
1¼ pounds skinless, boneless fish fillets (like monkfish, tilefish, or red snapper), cut into 1-inch cubes
1 pound mussels, well scrubbed, "beards" removed (see instructions page 60)
2 teaspoons Ricard or other anise-flavored liqueur (like Pernod)
¼ cup chopped fresh parsley

1. Heat the oil in a pot. Add the onion, leek, celery, garlic, and fennel seeds. Cook, stirring, until wilted — do not brown. Add the tomatoes, wine, Tabasco sauce, fish broth, thyme, salt, and freshly ground black pepper. Stir and cook over medium heat for 15 minutes.
2. Add the fish to the pot along with the mussels. Cook over medium heat for about 5 minutes or until the mussels open (discard any that do not open). Stir in the Ricard and add the parsley. Serve hot with croutons (see recipe page 84).

Yield: 4 to 6 servings

Homemade Chicken Stock

Homemade chicken stock is easy to make and is vastly superior to the commercial variety. Freeze all leftover chicken wings, necks, and carcasses for stock making. Make a big batch of stock and freeze it in ice cube trays so you can pull out just the amount you need.

Preparation Time: 10 MINUTES
Cooking Time: 1 HOUR

1 pound chicken bones (backs, necks, wings, and carcasses)
2 cups chopped carrots (about 5 medium carrots)
2 cups chopped celery (about 2 stalks)
1 cup chopped onion (1 medium onion)
3 cloves of unpeeled garlic, halved
½ teaspoon dried thyme
6 black peppercorns
6 cups cold water

1. Place all the ingredients in a deep pot and bring to a boil. Reduce the heat to low and simmer for 1 hour. Skim the surface 2 or 3 times while cooking.
2. Let the stock cool, then strain. Discard the bones and vegetables. Refrigerate the liquid.
3. When the stock is completely chilled, skim the fat from the surface. Use the stock for soups and sauces. It freezes well.

Yield: 1 quart

Stew's TIP

Stew's sells all kinds of fresh ravioli and tortellini that you can use to make an instant meal! Just simmer the pasta in homemade chicken stock, add some chopped parsley or other fresh herbs, and season with salt and pepper — you have a wholesome and tasty meal. You might want to grate some Parmesan cheese over the soup.

Stew's TIP

You can reduce the fat in soups and stews by preparing them a day ahead and chilling overnight. The fat rises to the top and solidifies, making removal easy. Cooking soups and stews the day before also enhances the flavor. Soups freeze well for up to six months.

Spicy Chicken-Sausage-and-Lentil Soup

This wholesome treat is enlivened by the peppery, and low fat, turkey sausage sold at Stew's. Or, if you prefer, use our equally zesty chicken sausage.

Preparation Time: 20 MINUTES
Cooking Time: 40 MINUTES

LOW FAT · PREPARE IN ADVANCE

1 acorn squash
1 tablespoon vegetable oil
8 ounces veal sausage or any spicy Italian-style sausage, cut into 1-inch pieces
1 cup onions, cut into ¼-inch cubes (about 1 medium onion)
1 cup celery, cut into ¼-inch cubes (2 stalks)
1 teaspoon chopped garlic
8 cups chicken stock (see recipe page 63), or water
1 large clove
1 pound lentils (2 cups), washed, rinsed, and inspected for small stones
½ teaspoon dried thyme
1 teaspoon salt
½ teaspoon freshly ground black pepper
Stew's Country Hearth Bread Croutons (see recipe page 84) or feta cheese, for garnish

1. Cut the acorn squash in half through the stem. Scrape out the seeds. Cut the squash into segments following its natural ridge lines. With a sharp paring knife, peel the skin off each segment then cut the peeled squash into ½-inch cubes (you should have about 2½ cups). Set aside.
2. Place a pot over high heat. Add the vegetable oil and sausage. Cook the sausage for 5 minutes, turning it, until it browns lightly.
3. Remove the sausage from the pan, set it aside, then add the cubed squash, onions, celery, garlic, and chicken stock. Cook for 5 minutes. Add to the pot the reserved sausage, lentils, thyme, salt, and freshly ground black pepper. Bring the liquid to a boil then reduce the heat and simmer for 35 minutes, or until the lentils are tender.
4. Remove 3 or 4 cups of the soup and purée it in a food processor or blender. Return the purée to the pot. Adjust the seasonings to taste.
5. To serve, ladle the soup into warm bowls and garnish with Country Bread Croutons (see recipe page 84) or crumbled feta cheese.

Yield: 6 to 8 servings

Tortellini in Brodo (Cheese-Filled Pasta in Broth)

One of the most popular sections of our store is the pasta counter, where you find both dried and fresh products. Tortellini are little ring-shaped, stuffed pastas. They can be filled with sausage, vegetables, herbed cheeses, and much more. All you need to make a meal is a tasty broth or a light sauce. Stew's sells its own marinara sauce, which is perfect with tortellini.

Preparation Time: 10 MINUTES
Cooking Time: 30 MINUTES

1 cup minced carrot (1 large carrot)
½ cup chopped celery (1 large stalk)
1 medium onion, sliced
1 teaspoon minced garlic (about 2 small cloves)
3 cups water or chicken broth
12 ounces Stew Leonard's cheese tortellini
Salt and freshly ground black pepper to taste
2 tablespoons chopped flat-leaf parsley
Grated Parmesan

1. Place the carrot, celery, onion, garlic, and water in a pot over high heat. Bring to a boil, reduce heat, and let the soup simmer for 15 minutes or until the vegetables are tender.
2. Add the tortellini and cook for about 8 to 10 minutes. Season the broth with salt (if necessary) and freshly ground black pepper to taste, then add the chopped parsley. Serve the soup garnished with grated Parmesan.

Yield: 4 servings

Stew's TIP

When a recipe calls for "mincing" or "dicing" a vegetable, that means cutting it into little pieces about ½ the size of a dime. This is done so all vegetables (soft and hard) are cooked at the same time.

Here are four of our chefs at a training class at the Culinary Institute of America in Hyde Park, New York.

Curried Lentil Soup with Smoked Ham

This curried lentil soup has a little smoked ham in it for extra flavor. Serve with a salad and country style bread.

Preparation Time: 10 MINUTES
Cooking Time: 35 MINUTES

$\frac{1}{2}$ pound lean country smoked ham (optional)
3 medium carrots
$\frac{1}{2}$ pound green lentils
1 tablespoon butter
1 cup finely chopped onions
1 tablespoon finely chopped garlic
$1\frac{1}{2}$ tablespoons curry powder (or more to taste)
5 cups fresh chicken broth (or canned)
2 cups water
1 bay leaf
3 sprigs fresh thyme or 1 teaspoon dried
Salt to taste
1 tablespoon red wine vinegar

1. Remove most of the fat from the ham and cut into $\frac{1}{2}$-inch cubes.
2. Trim and scrape the carrots and cut them into $\frac{1}{4}$-inch-thick cubes.
3. Wash the lentils in a colander.
4. Heat the butter in a pot. Add the ham, carrots, onions, garlic, and curry powder. Cook briefly over medium heat, stirring, until the onions are wilted.
5. Add the lentils, 4 cups of the chicken broth, water, bay leaf, thyme and salt. Bring to a boil, reduce heat, and simmer for about 30 minutes, stirring occasionally. With a slotted spoon remove the bay leaf and thyme sprigs.
6. Add the remaining cup of chicken broth, and the vinegar. Check for seasoning and serve.

Yield: 4 servings

A group of our managers shows a school tour how bread is made from scratch.

Hearty Beef Stew with Red Wine and Olives

Our family loves to make stews in winter — the long-cooked chunks of beef shoulder or other sinewy meats have so much flavor. This stew is suitable for any occasion. Notice how it is sweetened with parsnips and made slightly salty from the green olives.

Preparation Time: 15 MINUTES (plus overnight marination)
Cooking Time: ABOUT 1 HOUR AND 50 MINUTES

2 cups red wine
3 teaspoons minced garlic (about 3 large cloves)
1½ cups coarsely chopped onion (about 1 large onion)
1 cup carrots sliced into ¼-inch-thick rings (about 3 small carrots)
1 bay leaf
1½ pounds beef stew meat, like shoulder (cubed)
2 tablespoons vegetable oil
2 cups potatoes cut into 2-inch cubes (about 4 small potatoes)
½ cup pitted green olives
Salt and freshly ground black pepper to taste

1. The night before, combine the red wine, 2 teaspoons of garlic, onions, carrots, and bay leaf in a large stainless steel or ceramic bowl. Add the beef and stir until the meat is thoroughly moistened by the marinade. Cover and refrigerate for 12 to 24 hours.
2. Remove the meat from the marinade. Reserve the marinade. Let the beef drain in a colander for 10 minutes or more.
3. When the beef is drained, heat the oil over medium-high setting in a heavy pan or cast-iron skillet. Add ⅓ of the beef to the pan and brown it thoroughly on all sides. Remove the cooked meat and brown the remaining beef in two batches. Set aside.
4. Remove the carrots and onions from the marinade with a slotted spoon and cook them in the same pan. Cook for 5 minutes until they soften slightly. Return the beef to the pan, and add the remaining garlic. Add the marinade and bring the mixture to a boil, then reduce the heat. Cover and simmer the stew for 35 minutes.
5. Add the potatoes and olives and continue simmering for another 30 to 45 minutes, or until the meat and vegetables are tender.
6. Before serving, adjust salt and freshly ground black pepper to taste.

Yield: 4 servings

Stew's TIP

The basic cooking technique for this lamb stew applies to all kinds of stews. First you brown your meat well, then take it out of the pot. Then you add your vegetables and cook until they start to wilt, about 5 to 10 minutes. After that you return the meat to the pot and add the liquids and seasonings. Simmer until tender. That's it!

Lamb-and-Carrot Stew with Orange

Look in Stew Leonard's vast meat department for shoulder of lamb, which makes a fantastic stew. If you don't see it ask one of the butchers. In this dish the shoulder is cut into fairly large chunks because the meat shrinks while cooking. The orange essence is super!

Preparation Time: 15 MINUTES
Cooking Time: ABOUT 2 HOURS AND 20 MINUTES

PREPARE IN ADVANCE

4 to 5 pounds lamb shoulder or stew meat, cut into 3-inch cubes
Salt and freshly ground black pepper to taste
½ cup olive oil
3 cups chopped onions (about 2 medium onions)
3 tablespoons minced garlic
½ cup white wine
1 quart fresh or canned beef stock plus 2 cups water
½ teaspoon dried thyme
2 tablespoons orange juice concentrate
Peel of one orange, cut into very thin strips
1 pound of carrots, peeled and cut into 2-inch-thick chunks
Chopped fresh parsley

1. Season the lamb chunks generously with salt and freshly ground black pepper. Place ¼ of the lamb in a deep pot over high heat. Add ¼ cup of the olive oil. Reduce the heat to medium-high and brown the meat on all sides. Transfer the lamb to a plate. Add more oil to the pot if necessary, and brown the next batch. Do this until all of the lamb has been browned and transferred to a plate.
2. Add the onions and garlic to the pot. Cook for 5 minutes or until the onions have begun to soften. Add the white wine and scrape the bottom of the pan with a wooden spatula.
3. Return the lamb to the pot and cover it with the stock, water, thyme, orange juice concentrate and orange peel. Bring the stew to a boil and reduce the heat to simmer. Cover, and cook for an hour. Add the carrots and cook another 30 minutes, or until the meat is tender.
4. Remove the lamb and carrots from the pot. Cook the sauce over high heat until it is reduced by nearly half. Adjust seasonings. Return the meat to the pot and reheat the ingredients for 4 to 5 minutes. Adjust seasonings. Serve the stew garnished with chopped parsley and accompanied by roasted or boiled potatoes.

Yield: 8 to 10 servings

Stew's Split Pea Soup

Preparation Time: 15 MINUTES
Cooking Time: 90 MINUTES

PREPARE IN ADVANCE

6 quarts water
1 neck bone, beef or pork (ask your butcher)
1 smoked ham hock
6 quarts chicken stock (see recipe page 63)
1 pound split peas
½ teaspoon diced garlic
1 medium onion pierced with a clove
1 bay leaf
Salt and freshly ground black pepper to taste
2 carrots, trimmed, peeled, and diced
2 medium potatoes, washed and cut into small cubes
2 cups chopped onions
1 tablespoon butter
½ pound kielbasa, cut into bite-sized pieces (or other type of sausage)
3 tablespoons cornstarch (optional)

1. In a large pot filled with 6 quarts of water, boil the neck bone and ham hock for 1 hour, skimming the froth on the surface as it cooks. Strain and set aside the neck bone and ham hock.
2. To another pot add the chicken stock, split peas, garlic, onion pierced with a clove, bay leaf, and black pepper. Cook over medium-high heat until it reaches a boil — skim well. Reduce to simmer and cook until the split peas are tender.
3. In a pan, cook the chopped onions in a tablespoon of butter until golden. Add to the vegetable pot and skim the surface again. Add to the pot the carrots, potatoes, and meat from the neck and hocks. Dice the kielbasa and add to the pot. Cook for 10 to 15 minutes or until the vegetables are tender.
4. If the soup has a thick consistency, leave it; if not, in a small bowl mix the cornstarch with 2 tablespoons cold water. Add to the soup, bring to a boil, stir, and cook another 5 minutes.
5. Turn off the heat. Taste for seasonings.

Yield: 8 to 10 servings

Baba's California "Quick Blender" Gazpacho

There are as many "authentic" recipes for gazpacho as there are trees along the Merritt Parkway. This cold vegetable soup originated in northern Spain, but it has become associated with California, where fresh vegetables are available year-round. When we started looking around for a great gazpacho recipe we talked with chefs, friends and family, including my wife Kim's grandmother "Baba." After lots of experimentation we came up with this version, which is full of ripe vegetable flavors (you can spike it up with as much black pepper and Tabasco sauce as you like). The cilantro gives you that real garden-fresh vegetable taste too. A dollop of sour cream or plain yogurt provides the crowning touch! Our customers love it!

Preparation Time: 20 MINUTES
Cooking Time: NONE (chill for 45 minutes)

LOW FAT · PREPARE IN ADVANCE

4 cups diced ripe tomatoes, about 4 medium tomatoes (use canned if fresh tomatoes are not ripe)
1½ cups diced cucumber (about 1 medium cucumber, seeds removed)
1 cup diced scallions (about 8 scallions)
½ cup diced green bell pepper (about 1 small pepper)
½ cup diced red bell pepper (about 1 small pepper)
1 cup chopped red onion (about 1 small onion)
1 tablespoon chopped garlic (about 3 cloves)
Salt and freshly ground black pepper to taste
2 tablespoons olive oil
¼ cup sour cream or plain yogurt
2 tablespoons chopped cilantro (about 4 sprigs), optional
Hot pepper sauce (like Tabasco sauce), optional

Here's my wife's grandparents in Los Angeles. Milla (a.k.a. Baba) and Milan Vucurevich. Baba does more than 70 push-ups every day. Her gazpacho must be good!

1 Place the tomatoes, cucumber, scallions, peppers, onion, and garlic in the bowl of a blender or food processor. Blend for 2 to 3 minutes. Adjust the seasonings to taste with the salt and freshly ground black pepper. With the machine running, add the oil and blend until the soup is smooth.

2. Chill the soup for at least 45 minutes before serving. To serve, pour the soup into chilled bowls. Garnish each portion with a few tablespoons of sour cream or yogurt, topped with a teaspoon of fresh chopped cilantro. Place a bottle of hot pepper sauce on the table.

Yield: 6 servings

Cold Cucumber-and-Yogurt Soup with Fresh Mint

This is a refreshing and lowfat summer soup. You can make it in advance and refrigerate it.

Preparation Time: 15 MINUTES
Cooking Time: 10 MINUTES

SUPER FAST

LOW FAT

PREPARE IN ADVANCE

1 tablespoon butter
1 cup chopped onions
1 teaspoon minced garlic
3 medium cucumbers, seeded and sliced crosswise into ¼-inch-thick pieces
1 teaspoon curry powder
2 cups fresh or canned chicken stock
Salt and freshly ground black pepper to taste
2 cups plain yogurt
2 medium cucumbers, peeled, seeded, and cut into ¼-inch cubes (for garnish)
2 tablespoons chopped fresh mint

1. Heat the butter in a 4-quart pot and add the onions and garlic. Cook, stirring, over medium heat until wilted — do not brown the garlic! Add the sliced cucumbers, curry powder, chicken stock, salt, and freshly ground black pepper. Bring to a simmer and cook for 5 minutes, stirring occasionally.
2. Put the mixture in a food processor and pulse to reach a fine texture (you could also use a blender). Pour the mixture into a large bowl. Chill thoroughly.
3. Stir in the yogurt, cucumber cubes, and mint. Taste for seasonings. Blend well and serve in chilled bowls.

Yield: 4 servings

Chilled Cantaloupe Soup with Ginger

Preparation Time:
10 MINUTES
Cooking Time: NONE

4 cups cubed, ripe cantaloupe (about 2 medium cantaloupe — you will have some leftover melon)
1 tablespoon lemon juice
¾ cup plain yogurt
1 teaspoon honey
2 teaspoons grated fresh ginger

1. In a blender or food processor, purée the cantaloupe with the lemon juice. Remove to a bowl. Add the yogurt and honey and mix just to blend, no more. Serve in chilled bowls garnished with grated ginger.

Yield: 4 servings

There is nothing like a ripe cantaloupe. Look on page 319 for tips on picking a perfect melon.

Salads and Dressings

We foraged through the garden in this chapter, creating all kinds of bright and colorful salads. Some are substantial enough to be served as main courses, like our Rotisserie-Roasted Chicken Salad and the Grilled Flank Steak Salad with Orange Vinaigrette.

Baked Sesame-Coated Goat Cheese on Mixed Greens

Just 10 years ago, trying to sell goat cheese to Stew Leonard's customers would have been very difficult. Since then many of our customers have traveled to Europe where wonderfully tart goat cheese is served on toasted bread with olive oil and herbs, and in salads. Not only is fresh goat cheese versatile and delicious, but it also is much lower in fat and calories than most cows' cheeses. Stew's carries three varieties, both domestic and imported. Two of our customers' favorites are the goat cheese rolled in fresh herbs, and another encrusted with black pepper.

Preparation Time: 15 MINUTES
Cooking Time: 20 MINUTES

LOW FAT SUPER FAST

8 slices Stew's Country Hearth Bread, without crust
2 cloves garlic, peeled
¼-cup sesame seeds
2 4-ounce logs fresh goat cheese
8 cups mixed salad greens: red leaf, escarole, radicchio, endive, Romaine (or Stew's premixed "Gourmet" greens)
Lemon-Garlic Dressing (see recipe page 75)

1. Preheat oven to 375 degrees.
2. Toast the crustless slices of country bread. When the bread is toasted, rub each slice with a garlic clove. Cut each toast slice in half. Set aside.
3. Place the sesame seeds on a flat plate. Cut each log of goat cheese into four 2-inch-thick pieces (if it crumbles, as it is cut, press it back into shape). Roll each piece of cheese in the sesame seeds, pressing the seeds into the cheese with your hand. Each piece should be evenly coated.
4. Place the sesame-coated cheese rolls on a baking tray. Bake until they begin to soften and brown (about 8 to 10 minutes).
5. While the cheese is baking, toss the salad greens in a large bowl with the Lemon-Garlic dressing. Place equal amounts of salad on 8 salad plates. Put two pieces of garlic toast on the side of each plate.
6. Place a piece of the baked goat cheese in the center of each salad.

Yield: 8 servings

Rich Falcone displays some goat cheese imported from Denmark. "Customers are buying more and more goat cheese, it's an up-and-coming product," Rich says.

Lemon-Garlic Dressing

This lively dressing is every bit as good as it sounds. Lemon juice in place of vinegar adds a fresh citric flavor. It goes with everything — you could also drizzle it over grilled fish.

Preparation Time: 10 MINUTES
Cooking Time: NONE

LOW FAT · PREPARE IN ADVANCE · SUPER FAST

1/3 cup lemon juice (1 1/2 lemons)
1/4 teaspoon salt
1/8 teaspoon freshly ground pepper
1 teaspoon minced garlic
1/2 cup olive oil

1. Place all ingredients in a blender or food processor. Blend until well mixed.

Yield: 1 1/4 cups

Basic French Vinaigrette

3/4 teaspoon Dijon-style mustard
3/4 teaspoon red wine vinegar
3/4 cup olive oil
Salt and freshly ground black pepper to taste
1/4 teaspoon dried herb of choice (optional)

1. In a bowl, whisk together vigorously the mustard and vinegar. Drizzle in the olive oil while whisking. Season to taste with salt and pepper. You may want to adjust the vinegar level.

Yield: 3/4 cup

Herbed Mayonnaise Dressing

Preparation Time: 5 MINUTES
Cooking Time: NONE

PREPARE IN ADVANCE · SUPER FAST

1/3 cup mayonnaise
3 tablespoons sour cream
2 tablespoons minced fresh chives
2 tablespoons minced fresh parsley
1 1/2 tablespoons fresh lemon juice (about half a lemon)
Salt and freshly ground white pepper to taste (or black pepper)

1. Combine all ingredients in a bowl and whisk well. Taste for seasonings.

Yield: About 1/2 cup

Stew's TIP

How do I make a good salad dressing at home?

It is surprising how many customers ask about how to make a good basic vinaigrette for salads. At my house we make a big batch of it and store it in an empty wine bottle.

On this page is a great all-around vinaigrette.

Fresh Herbs

Basil – Highly aromatic when fresh, basil is related to mint. It was used as far back as Roman times. Cooks today use sweet basil in all kinds of sauces. It is also tasty in soups. Aside from sweet basil, the most common other varieties include purple basil, lemon basil, cinnamon basil, and anise basil.

Bay Leaf – This is the unglamorous workhorse of the kitchen, frequently recruited but rarely given any credit. Integral to the bouquet garni (parsley, thyme and bay leaf tied in cheesecloth), bay leaves are used widely in soups, stocks, and sauces to impart an earthy flavor.

Chives – A member of the onion family, chives are milder than most of their relatives. They make a sprightly addition to salads, soups, and vegetable dishes. Use the thinnest, youngest chives you can find. The older and thicker they are, the sharper the flavor.

Cilantro – The frail leaves of this aromatic herb have a sweet-spicy flavor, and they are used extensively in the cuisines of India, Mexico, the Caribbean, and all over the Orient. Cilantro can be added to soups or sauces at the last minute for maximum effect. Beware, however, for it can easily overpower a dish.

Coriander – These are the seeds of the cilantro plant, and they are traditionally found in Mexican, Thai, and Middle Eastern cooking. After the seeds are ground they are dried to extract their flavor. Some liken the pungent flavor to lemon and caraway.

Dill – A perennial favorite, dill has a fresh, cooling sensation — with a hint of anise flavor — that is ideal for summer cooking. It is often used in marinades for fish, and in salads and cold soups.

Marjoram – Often confused with oregano, marjoram is a Mediterranean herb. It has a delicate but somewhat spicy fragrance and is most often used in stocks, soups, and sauces.

Mint – Mint can be baffling because there are so many varieties: lemon mint, spearmint, and peppermint just to name a few. Almost all varieties of mint are potent, so very little goes a long way in cooking. If you are adding it to a cold soup, taste frequently so as not to overdo it. Mint makes a lovely aromatic garnish to many summer platters.

Then there are mint juleps, but that's another recipe.

Oregano – Probably most recognized as the pizza herb, oregano is difficult to distinguish from marjoram. The two are used in soups like minestrone, as well as in omelets, salad dressings, Greek-style marinades, meatloaf, chili, and stuffings.

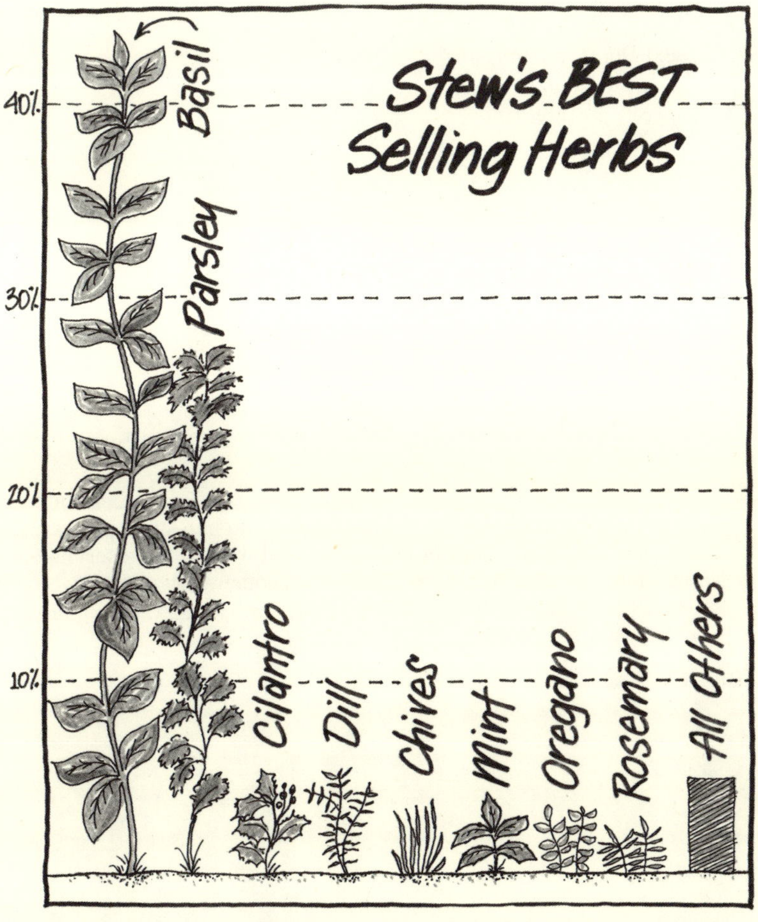

Parsley

Perhaps the most widely used fresh herb, parsley comes in several forms. Flat-leaf (also known as Italian) parsley is usually preferred for cooking, while the curly variety is used for garnish. Both kinds of parsley are powerhouses of vitamins and minerals, especially vitamins C and E.

Rosemary

One of the most versatile cooking herbs, rosemary has a natural bond with chicken and pork. It also complements tomato-based sauces. Rosemary is also wonderful placed under grilled meats. As the rosemary burns it infuses the meats with flavor.

Sage

A staple of northern Italian cooking, sage has a distinctive flowery and earthy aroma. It is often used with ravioli, and sometimes cooked in brown butter as part of a sauce. It is also splendid in any kind of bread stuffing. Sage can be added to roast pork, chicken, or veal with great success.

Nutritious Beet-and-Broccoli-Rabe Salad

Who said that salads have to be green? In winter, certain salad greens are available, but it is still fun to use nutrition-packed root vegetables and other off-season produce to create unusual combinations. The pairing of sweet baked beets with broccoli rabe is an occasional cold-weather starter around the Leonard home.

By the way, save the extra beet greens for Sautéed Beet Greens and Oyster Mushrooms (see recipe page 261).

Preparation Time: 15 MINUTES
Cooking Time: ABOUT 90 MINUTES (for roasting the beets)

LOW FAT

PREPARE IN ADVANCE

3 beets, trimmed of greens
3 cups water
1 teaspoon salt
1 bunch broccoli rabe, trimmed of hard stems (½ pound)
1 teaspoon minced garlic (about 2 small cloves)
1 teaspoon mashed anchovies, about 2 fillets (optional)
1 teaspoon Dijon-style mustard
1 tablespoon red wine vinegar
2 tablespoons olive oil
½ cup finely chopped scallions (about 4 scallions)
Freshly ground black pepper to taste

1. Preheat the oven to 350 degrees.
2. Wrap the beets in aluminum foil and bake for about 1 to 1¼ hours, or until tender.
3. Bring 3 cups of water to a boil. Add the salt and broccoli rabe. Simmer, covered, for 20 minutes, or until tender.
4. While the broccoli rabe is cooking, combine the garlic, anchovies, mustard, and vinegar in a salad bowl. Blend to make a smooth paste. Stir in the oil.
5. When cool to the touch, peel the cooked beets and slice them into ½-inch-thick rounds. Cut the broccoli rabe into bite-sized pieces. Combine the sliced beets, broccoli rabe, and dressing in a serving bowl. Toss the mix to coat each slice with some of the dressing. Garnish the salad with the scallions and a generous grating of black pepper. Add salt to taste.

Yield: 4 to 6 servings

Savory

This Mediterranean herb is a little milder than sage. It can be used in many of the same ways. Europeans often add savory to cold bean dishes. It is also a fine addition to grilled vegetables.

Tarragon

This is the king of cooking herbs, at least in classic French cuisine, where it anchors the famous sauce Béarnaise and so many other sauces. It has a faint anise flavor, and is wonderful with seafood. Always seek the delicate French tarragon, not the rougher and bland Russian variety.

Thyme

More than 100 varieties of thyme are edible. Just remember that the upright thyme is for eating, and the "spreading" thyme is ground cover. Part of the hallowed bouquet garni in French cooking (along with parsley and bay leaf), thyme is a cornerstone of many sauces and casseroles. Thyme is particularly effective with slow-cooked roasts.

"Your Own" Sweet-and-Sour Pickles

Making your own pickles allows you to experiment with all kinds of flavors like sweet, sour and spicy. The pickles here are wonderful with sandwiches, hamburgers and sliced cold meats.

Preparation Time: 10 MINUTES
Cooking Time: 10 MINUTES

LOW FAT · PREPARE IN ADVANCE · SUPER FAST

1 cup red onion, thinly sliced (about 1 medium onion)
1 pound cucumber, peeled, seeded, and thinly sliced (1 large or 2 medium cucumbers)
½ cup apple cider or rice-wine vinegar
½ cup water
1 teaspoon sugar
½ teaspoon salt
1 teaspoon hot red pepper flakes

1. Toss the sliced onion and cucumber in a stainless steel or glass bowl.
2. Combine all the remaining ingredients in a non-aluminum metal pot and bring to a boil. Remove from heat and pour over the onion-cucumber mixture.
3. Serve at room temperature, or chilled. These pickles keep for several weeks in the refrigerator.

Yield: 3 cups

Stew discusses the quality of lettuce with Michael Hirsch early one morning at the Hunts Point Terminal Market.

Stew's TIP

Dried Beans

The variety of dried beans on the market today can be confusing. Most dried beans are excellent sources of iron, B vitamins, and protein. They are also loaded with fiber. Here are some of the more common varieties.

Black Beans – Used often in Latin American and South American soups and stews, black beans are soft inside with a thin durable skin.

Black-Eyed Peas – The name comes from the flavor, which is similar to field peas in the South. For centuries they have been a staple of Southern soul food.

Chickpeas – Also called garbanzos, these fat, round, nutty beans are found in Moroccan and Mediterranean cooking. They are excellent in cold salads and soups.

Fava Beans – Resembling giant lima beans, but thinner, these mild flavored beans are a favorite among Italian cooks, who add them to soups, casseroles, and even pasta.

Lima Beans-and-Fresh-Fennel Salad

The combination of earthy lima beans and refreshing fennel in this salad is terrific. Sage and thyme add another invigorating flavor sensation.

Preparation Time: 15 MINUTES
Cooking Time: ABOUT 1½ HOURS

LOW FAT · PREPARE IN ADVANCE

1 cup dry white lima beans (or green lima beans)
3½ cups cold water
½ cup chopped white or Bermuda onion (about 1 medium onion)
1 bay leaf
1 dried sage leaf
¼ teaspoon dried thyme (for cooking the beans)
½ cup thinly sliced red onion
½ cup red wine vinegar
½ teaspoon fresh thyme
1 cup minced fresh fennel (about 1 small bulb)
Salt and freshly ground pepper to taste

1. Rinse the lima beans under cold running water. Place them in a pot with 1½ cups of cold water. Bring to a boil and remove from the heat. Cover and let the beans to sit for at least 1 hour, or overnight.
2. Add 2 more cups of water to the beans, then the chopped onion, bay leaf, sage, and thyme. Bring to a boil, reduce heat, and simmer for 30 to 35 minutes or until the beans are tender. Drain and set aside to cool.
3. In a salad bowl, combine the cooled beans, thinly sliced red onion, vinegar, fresh thyme, and fennel. Adjust seasonings to taste. Serve cold or warm.

Yield: 4 to 6 servings

White Beans and Onion Salad

Dried beans are more popular than ever among both home cooks and restaurant chefs. Part of the reason is their versatility and low cost. In addition, dried beans are excellent sources of lowfat protein.

Preparation Time: 15 MINUTES
Cooking Time: 60 MINUTES

LOW FAT

PREPARE IN ADVANCE

2 cups Great Northern white beans
½ cup thinly sliced red onions (about 1 medium onion)
½ cup red wine vinegar
½ teaspoon salt
½ teaspoon minced fresh thyme (or ¼ teaspoon dried)
1 cup minced fresh fennel
1 cup cooked green beans cut into 2-inch lengths
2 tablespoons olive oil

1. Rinse the beans under cold running water. Place them in a pot with 3 cups cold water. Bring them to a boil and remove from heat. Cover and allow to sit in the water for at least 1 hour, or overnight.
2. Place the cooked beans in a salad bowl with 1 cup of their cooking liquid. Add the sliced onion, vinegar, salt, and thyme. Stir, and season well with salt and pepper.
3. Stir in the fennel and green beans. Drizzle salad with the oil.

Yield: 4 cups

Les Slater, our Produce Manager, inspects greenhouse-grown tomatoes in British Columbia.

Stew's TIP

Dried Beans

Flageolets – Found mostly dried or canned in America, these delicate little French beans are the most tender part of the fresh string bean.

Kidney Beans – Reddish-brown, kidney-shaped, and starchy, these are among the most common of American dried beans. Kidney beans are found in chili, all kinds of Mexican dishes, and cold salads.

Lima Beans – These small, pale, green beans are high in starch, distinctively flavored, and suitable for soups, stews and salads.

Pinto Beans – These are a variety of the kidney bean. They are reddish pink with little brown spots. Mostly used in soups.

Red Beans – Most often associated with Louisiana-style cooking, this variety of kidney bean has a medium starch content and neutral flavor that blends well with spicy food.

White Beans – These versatile beans come in three sizes: Marrowfat, the biggest; Great Northern, medium; and the smaller Yankee, also called Navy.

Arugula and Red Onion Salad

We sell a lot of fresh arugula in the store. It's good on its own or mixed with red leaf lettuce or Romaine. The red onion in this salad introduces a little sweetness.

Preparation Time: 10 MINUTES
Cooking Time: NONE

LOW FAT · SUPER FAST

¾ pound arugula leaves (about 6 cups)
1 cup chopped red onion
½ cup finely chopped parsley, preferably flat-leaf Italian style
1½ teaspoons red wine vinegar
Salt and freshly ground black pepper to taste
¼ cup olive oil

1. Pick over the arugula leaves and remove any tough stems. Rinse and drain the leaves well. Pat them dry or put them in a salad spinner. There should be about 6 cups, loosely packed. Put the leaves in a salad bowl and add the onion and parsley.
2. Put the vinegar in a bowl and add salt and pepper. Start whisking while gradually adding the oil. Taste for balance and seasonings. Pour the vinaigrette over the lettuce and toss well.

Yield: Serves 4

Our friends, the Sclafani family, have been importing olive oil and other products from Italy for more than 100 years.

Stew's TIP

Olive Oil

We carry several types of olive oil at Stew Leonard's, each with different flavors. When buying olive oil the most important thing to look for is its grading, which is printed on the front of the container. In ascending order of quality are pure, virgin, and extra virgin.

The grade refers to the acidity of an oil, with the finest oils having the least acidity. Extra virgin and virgin come entirely from the first pressing of the olives. Extra virgin oil, which is made from premium olives, has the richest aroma, the lowest acidity, and the richest flavor. Virgin is slightly less flavorful. Pure olive oil can come from both the first and second pressings of the olives and may be blended with 5% to 10% virgin olive oil to enrich its flavor. It is usually sold in big square cans. Extra virgin olive oil is best used for salad dressings, sauces, and the like; less expensive virgin olive oil is fine for cooking. Don't be fooled by the term "light" olive oil. The "light" refers to its pale color — and it is usually bland. One tablespoon of so-called light olive oil contains 120 calories, the same as extra virgin.

"Our Customers' Favorite" Caesar Salad

Caesar salad, the most popular salad in America (at least in restaurants), is said to have been created by Caesar Cardini, who owned a restaurant in Tijuana, Mexico.

Caesar salad is a huge seller at the store. Here is the recipe. If you don't have both types of cheeses, just use one.

Preparation Time: 10 MINUTES
Cooking Time: NONE (except croutons, see following recipe)

SUPER FAST

¼ teaspoon dry mustard
2 garlic cloves, chopped
½ teaspoon Worcestershire Sauce
½ teaspoon Tabasco sauce
Salt and freshly ground black pepper to taste
½ anchovy fillet (optional)
2 tablespoons Parmesan cheese
2 tablespoons Pecorino-Romano cheese
Juice of 1 lemon
½ cup olive oil
1 large head Romaine cut into 2 inch lengths
1 cup Stew's Country Bread Croutons (see recipe page 84)

1. Place 1 tablespoon of the Parmesan cheese and 1 tablespoon of Pecorino-Romano in a food processor or blender, along with all the other ingredients (except the olive oil). Purée until combined, and still a little chunky. Drizzle in the olive oil while continuing to mix.
2. Pour the dressing over the salad greens, sprinkle with the remaining cheeses, and toss very well. Add the croutons, season with salt and pepper, and toss again.

Yield: 4 servings

Stew's TIP

Dressing

When making a salad, remember that it is best to add just a little dressing and toss the salad extremely well. If you add too much dressing the salad will quickly become soggy.

John Talento stocks fresh romaine lettuce at our Norwalk store.

Stew's Country Hearth Bread Croutons

Stew's crusty Country Hearth Bread and its baguettes makes the best croutons for Caesar Salad or any other salad that needs a bit of crunch.

Preparation Time: 5 MINUTES
Cooking Time: NONE

LOW FAT · PREPARE IN ADVANCE · SUPER FAST

1 tablespoon olive oil
1 clove of garlic, halved
2 cups cubed bread, about ½-inch cubes

1. Warm a non-stick skillet over medium heat. Add the oil and garlic and cook for 1 minute.
2. Add the bread cubes. Toss to coat with oil. Cook over medium heat, stirring frequently until golden brown on all sides.
3. Discard the garlic. When croutons are cool, place them in a plastic bag and refrigerate. They will keep for a month.

Variations: Italian Croutons – Toss cooked croutons with ½ teaspoon of chopped dried oregano or basil and 2 tablespoons grated Parmesan cheese.

Cajun Croutons – Toss cooked croutons with ⅛ teaspoon cayenne pepper, ¼ teaspoon finely ground black pepper, and ½ teaspoon paprika.

Nancy Campagna has been with Stew's for 12 years. "I get here early and make sure our customers get fresh bread — just like in my hometown of Sicily!"

Greek Feta Cheese and Vegetable Salad

This refreshing salad, with the tart flavor of feta cheese, is served in tavernas all over Greece. Ideal as a first course, it is also a good filling for a pita bread sandwich.

Preparation Time: 15 MINUTES
Cooking Time: NONE

LOW FAT SUPER FAST

2 whole cucumbers, peeled, seeded and chopped (about 3 cups)
½ cup minced red or white onion (1 medium onion)
2 cups chopped tomatoes (about 2 tomatoes)
½ cup diced feta cheese
¼ cup minced fresh oregano or parsley
½ cup Lemon-Garlic Dressing (see recipe page 75)
3 cups pita bread croutons (see recipe page 86)

1. In a salad bowl, combine the cucumbers, onions, tomatoes, cheese, and oregano or parsley. Add the dressing, cover, and refrigerate overnight before serving.
2. Top each serving with Pita Bread Croutons.

Yield: 6 appetizer salads

Stew's TIP

Andy Rooney, the "60 Minutes" commentator, lives a short distance from the store. In a local newspaper interview a few years ago he talked about food, and specifically how he makes croutons at home.

Here is his recipe: He cuts bread into ¾-inch cubes and puts them on a cookie sheet or a sheet pan. He sets the oven to 450 degrees, puts the bread cubes inside, and then turns the oven off! He says that turning off the heat keeps the croutons from burning. When they are hard and nicely browned, he warms them in a sauté pan with olive oil and garlic. Andy says that he eats them as a snack like peanuts or potato chips!

Pita Bread Croutons

Make these croutons when you have a few leftover slices of pita bread. They are a delicious topping for the Greek Feta Cheese and Vegetable Salad (see recipe page 85), soups, or a delightful snack.

Preparation Time: 5 MINUTES
Cooking Time: 5 MINUTES

LOW FAT · PREPARE IN ADVANCE · SUPER FAST

4 pita breads
2 tablespoons olive oil
¼ teaspoon salt
⅛ teaspoon freshly ground black pepper

1. Preheat oven to 375 degrees.
2. Cut each pita bread into small cubes. Place the pieces in a bowl, toss with oil, and season with salt and pepper.
3. Place the croutons on a cookie sheet and bake for 3 minutes. Shake to turn them, and bake for another 3 minutes or until croutons are dry and lightly browned.
4. Store croutons in a plastic bag. They will keep in a cool place for 3 weeks.

Yield: 3 cups

"We have the friendliest cashiers anywhere," says Dan Arthur, who runs our Danbury store. Here he is with Nicole Petrellese and Kathy Piela.

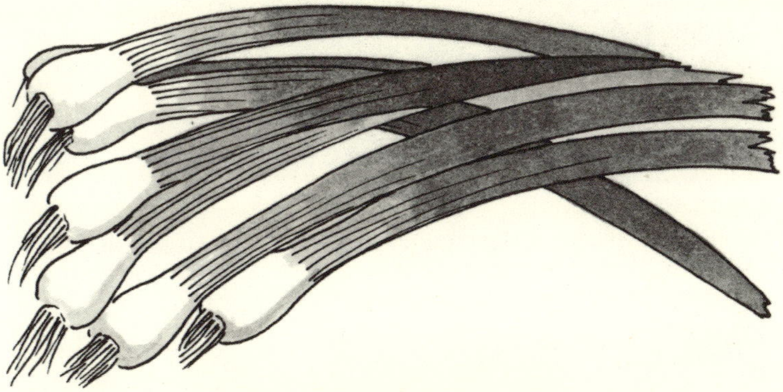

Spinach-and-Scallion Salad with Mustard Vinaigrette

When we have beautiful, leafy fresh spinach in the store our family likes to make this healthful salad. It's great with sandwiches or soups.

Preparation Time: 10 MINUTES
Cooking Time: NONE

LOW FAT SUPER FAST

6 cups fresh spinach, washed (about 10 ounces)
9 whole scallions (1 bunch)
2 medium tomatoes
1 tablespoon Dijon-style mustard
¼ cup red wine vinegar
½ teaspoon salt
¼ teaspoon freshly ground black pepper
½ cup vegetable oil
¼ cup olive oil

1. Wash and dry the spinach leaves and remove the stems. Trim the scallions of half their green part and discard, then cut the rest in half lengthwise. Chop the scallions crosswise into 3-inch pieces. Slice the tomatoes into wedges. Combine the spinach, scallions, and tomato wedges in a large salad bowl. Set aside.
2. In a small glass jar or blender, combine the mustard, vinegar, salt, and pepper. Shake or blend well. Add the oils and shake or blend. Adjust seasonings to taste.
3. Pour the dressing over the salad, and toss.

Yield: 6 servings

Stew's TIP

Mustard

There was a time, not long ago, when Americans had essentially two types of mustard: bright yellow and not-so-bright yellow. Today, the assortment is amazing. Stew Leonard's carries several types. English style is made with mustard flour and is an eye-opener. The most recognized brand is Coleman's. Dijon, the French-style mustard, is more subtle and only mildly sharp. That is what our customers prefer. Its creamy texture makes it superior for sauces and vinaigrettes.

American-style mustard is still bright yellow (from the yellow mustard seeds used in processing) and has a sharp vinegar taste.

Marinated Carrot-and-Red-Onion Salad

This sprightly salad can be served as a light appetizer. It is also terrific for picnics.

Preparation Time: 5 MINUTES
Cooking Time: 10 MINUTES

LOW FAT · PREPARE IN ADVANCE · SUPER FAST

3 whole medium carrots
Salt for cooking water
½ cup chopped red onion
2 tablespoons Lemon-Herb Vinaigrette (see recipe this page)

1. Peel the carrots and slice them into ¼-inch-thick rounds (about 1¼ cups).
2. Bring a medium size pot of salted water to a boil. Add the carrots and cook for 6 to 8 minutes, or until the carrots are tender. Drain.
3. Place the cooked carrots in a bowl with the chopped onion and the Lemon-Herb Vinaigrette. Toss, and let the carrots cool in the dressing before serving.

Yield: 3 or 4 appetizer servings

Lemon-Herb Vinaigrette

This refreshing vinaigrette takes advantage of many fresh herbs available at Stew Leonard's.

Preparation Time: 5 MINUTES
Cooking Time: NONE

LOW FAT · PREPARE IN ADVANCE · SUPER FAST

¼ cup lemon juice
½ teaspoon salt
¼ teaspoon freshly ground pepper
¾ cup olive oil
4 tablespoons chopped fresh herbs: tarragon, chives, thyme, parsley, basil or any combination

1. In a bowl combine the lemon juice, salt, and pepper. Whisk in the olive oil. Stir in the chopped herbs.
2. Serve this as a salad dressing or over grilled fish or poultry.

Yield: 1 cup

"Garden Fresh" Cucumber and Fennel Salad

Here is another salad that uses the crisp, refreshing sensation of fennel to enliven the mix.

Preparation Time: 10 MINUTES
Cooking Time: NONE

LOW FAT SUPER FAST

1 cucumber
2 teaspoons chopped fresh dill (dried dill does not work)
1 tablespoon white wine vinegar
¼ teaspoon sugar
1 teaspoon olive oil
1 tablespoon sour cream
Salt and freshly ground black pepper to taste

1. Peel the cucumber and cut it in half lengthwise. Scoop out the seeds with a teaspoon, and then cut the cucumber into ¼-inch-thick slices (to make about 1 cup).
2. Combine the sliced cucumber with the fennel, vinegar, sugar, oil, and sour cream. Add seasonings to taste.

Yield: 1 cup

What is fennel?

Ten years ago Stew's did not carry fennel because few customers knew what to do with it. Today it is widespread in both home and restaurant cooking. Its fresh, snappy flavor, suggesting anise, adds vibrancy to all sorts of dishes. The anise flavor of raw fennel diminishes in cooking. Fennel bulbs can be sliced and added raw to salads (our favorite), sautéed with other vegetables, baked, stuffed or puréed.

Our Norwalk store.

Tender Asparagus Salad

The first tender stalks of asparagus from a spring garden usually have not reached peak flavor, but they can still make a lovely salad. A little lemon juice, capers, and parsley can help. Be careful not to overcook the asparagus.

Preparation Time: 10 MINUTES
Cooking Time: 5 TO 7 MINUTES

2 pounds asparagus
4 quarts water combined with 2 tablespoons salt
3 tablespoons lemon juice
2 teaspoons capers
2 tablespoons chopped parsley
Salt and freshly ground black pepper to taste
¼ cup olive oil
1 cup diced tomato (about 1 medium tomato)
2 hard-boiled eggs, coarsely chopped

1. Trim the asparagus by bending each spear 2 or 3 inches from the bottom. The tough white end of each stalk will snap off where the stem begins to get tender. Cook the asparagus in rapidly boiling salted water for 5 to 7 minutes, or until tender. Remove the asparagus from the boiling water and plunge them into ice water to prevent continued cooking.
2. While the asparagus are cooking, combine the lemon juice, capers, and parsley in a small bowl. Season with salt and pepper then whisk in the olive oil. Adjust the seasonings with salt and pepper, then stir in the chopped tomatoes and hard-boiled egg.
3. Divide the cooked asparagus among 4 to 6 serving plates. Spoon some of the dressing in a neat line across each row of spears.

Yield: 4 to 6 servings

"Great for Picnics!"

Chicory, Pear, and Gorgonzola Salad

The combination of sweet pears and intense Gorgonzola is sublime in this attractive salad. Our customers love Gorgonzola, based on sales of this salad.

Preparation Time: 15 MINUTES
Cooking Time: NONE

2 small heads of chicory, washed and dried
¼ cup olive oil
3 tablespoons red wine vinegar
1 teaspoon chopped garlic (about 1 large clove)
3 ounces Gorgonzola cheese, crumbled
Salt and freshly ground black pepper to taste
3 large ripe pears, halved, cored, and thinly sliced
2 Belgian endive, leaves separated and washed
½ cup toasted walnuts

1. Place the walnuts on a baking sheet in a 375-degree oven. Cook, stirring them until they are golden brown.
2. Tear the chicory into small pieces. Set aside.
3. In another bowl, combine the oil, vinegar, garlic, and Gorgonzola. Blend with a spoon. Adjust the seasonings with salt and pepper. Add the pear slices to the mixture. Taste for seasonings (you may want to add more vinegar). Let it sit about 15 minutes before serving. (The pear slices can stay in this mixture overnight without discoloring.)
4. Divide the endive evenly among 4 plates, forming a flower pattern on each. Make nests of chicory in the center of each plate. Spoon the pear mixture over each nest. Garnish with the toasted walnuts.

Yield: 4 servings

A Fourth of July Picnic

Fresh Fruit Platter
Roasted Red-Pepper-and-Basil Dip (see recipe page 30)
Stew's Country Hearth Bread
Bethy's Tortellini Salad (see recipe page 96)
Smoky Black-Pepper Burgers (see recipe page 147)
Aunt Bernetta's Rhubarb Pie (see recipe page 337)

Lowfat Mustard-Yogurt Dressing

This creamy, yet low-calorie dressing could go with any mix of greens.

Preparation Time:
15 MINUTES
Cooking Time: NONE

¼ cup Dijon-style mustard
2 tablespoons course mustard with seeds
3 tablespoons minced shallots (about 1 large shallot)
1 teaspoon minced garlic (about 1 large clove)
3 tablespoons lemon juice (about 1 lemon)
⅔ cup plain lowfat yogurt
3 tablespoons chopped fresh dill or parsley
½ teaspoon salt
Freshly ground black pepper (use generously)

1. Place all the ingredients in a bowl. Whisk to combine. Adjust the seasonings to taste with salt and pepper. Toss with the Romaine. You can also use this on the Spinach-and-Scallion Salad instead of the Mustard Vinaigrette (see recipe page 87). Store the dressing in a tightly covered container. It will keep for 3 weeks in the refrigerator.

Yield: 1¼ cups

Warm Red Potato Salad

This zesty salad contains no mayonnaise so it is well-suited for picnics.

Preparation Time: 15 MINUTES
Cooking Time: ABOUT 20 MINUTES

LOW FAT

PREPARE IN ADVANCE

3 pounds red potatoes (about 8 potatoes)
1 bay leaf
1 tablespoon salt
Freshly ground black pepper to taste
½ cup red wine vinegar mixed with ½ cup balsamic vinegar
1 cup minced Bermuda onion (about 1 onion)
1 cup chopped scallions
⅓ cup minced parsley
2 teaspoons Dijon-style mustard
½ teaspoon salt
2 tablespoons olive oil

1. Place the unpeeled potatoes in a pot, cover with water, and bring to a boil. Add the bay leaf, salt, and pepper. Cover, reduce heat, and simmer until tender (about 20 minutes, or until a fork can be easily inserted into the center).

2. While the potatoes are cooking, combine the vinegar, onion, scallions, parsley, mustard, salt, and pepper in a large stainless steel or glass bowl (not aluminum — it will discolor the sauce). Whisk in the oil. When the potatoes are cooked but cool enough to handle, cut them widthwise into ⅓-inch-thick slices. Combine well with the dressing and marinate for at least 30 minutes. (This salad tastes best when prepared several hours in advance.)

3. To serve hot, reheat gently in a pan. Spoon the potatoes onto small plates (or, if you like, into little cups of lettuce) as an accompaniment to grilled meats or fish. This salad can also be served at room temperature as part of a picnic.

Yield: Serves 4 to 6

Irene proudly keeps the produce department stocked with fresh fruits and vegetables.

Fiesta Pasta Salad

This combination of nutty barley and fusilli pasta turns a standard picnic salad into an unusual and healthful side dish. Coating the grains and pasta with the dressing while they are still warm helps them absorb the flavors.

Preparation Time: 10 MINUTES
Cooking Time: 1 HOUR AND FIVE MINUTES

LOW FAT

PREPARE IN ADVANCE

1 cup pearl barley
1 pound uncooked fusilli
½ cup prepared mayonnaise
2 tablespoons tomato paste
¼ cup red wine vinegar
1 teaspoon honey
2 red bell peppers, seeded and minced
2 green bell peppers, seeded and minced
3 minced scallions
Salt and freshly ground black pepper to taste

1. Cook the barley, covered, in 3 cups of salted boiling water for about 40 minutes. Check to see if more liquid is needed. If necessary, add up to ½ cup more water and cook for another 10 minutes or until the barley is tender.
2. While the barley is cooking, boil the pasta until al dente in a large pot of salted water.
3. Meanwhile, combine the mayonnaise, tomato paste, vinegar, honey, peppers, and scallions. Stir and add seasonings to taste.
4. Drain the cooked barley and pasta in a colander. Rinse briefly under cold water. While they are still warm, add them to the dressing and toss to coat. Adjust seasonings to taste — it may need a good dose of salt and pepper. Serve at room temperature or slightly chilled.

Yield: 6 to 8 servings

Grilled Chicken Breast Salad

Preparation Time: 15 MINUTES
Cooking Time: 6 TO 10 MINUTES

LOW FAT SUPER FAST

2 whole chicken breasts, skinless, split down the middle to make 4 fillets

The Marinade:
2 garlic cloves, chopped
Juice of 1 lemon
3 tablespoons white wine
3 tablespoons olive oil
2 teaspoons fresh thyme or 1 teaspoon dried
1 teaspoon fresh tarragon, chopped (or $\frac{1}{2}$ teaspoon dried)
Salt and freshly ground black pepper to taste

The Dressing:
$\frac{1}{2}$ teaspoon dry mustard
2 garlic cloves, chopped
$\frac{1}{2}$ teaspoon Worcestershire Sauce
$\frac{1}{2}$ teaspoon Tabasco sauce
Salt and freshly ground black pepper to taste
Juice of lemon
Garlic croutons (see instructions)
1 raw garlic clove
1 medium head of Romaine lettuce
$\frac{3}{4}$ cup olive oil
6 tablespoons grated Parmesan cheese

1. In a shallow dish combine all of the ingredients for the marinade. Marinate the chicken breasts, refrigerated, for 1 to 2 hours. Flip the breasts occasionally.
2. Preheat a charcoal or gas grill to high.
3. In a food processor or blender, combine all the ingredients for the dressing except 2 tablespoons of the Parmesan cheese and the olive oil. Process until well blended (in a blender that takes only seconds) and then drizzle in the remaining olive oil with the machine on. Transfer to a bowl.
4. To make the croutons, toast 2 slices of bread and let them sit out to harden — or put them in a 350-degree oven for 15 minutes. Rub the bread with a raw garlic clove. Sprinkle with salt and pepper. Cut into little croutons. Reserve.
5. Place the chicken pieces on the grill or on a rack under the broiler (about 4 to 6 inches from the heating coils). Cover the grill or close the door to the broiler. Cook about 2 to 3 minutes and turn the pieces. Continue cooking until done, about 2 to 3 more minutes on the grill, possibly a little longer under the broiler. Check by slicing open a chicken fillet at its thickest point — it should be white all the way through.
6. Slice the chicken into $\frac{1}{4}$-inch strips. Place the greens in a salad bowl and toss well with the dressing. Add the croutons and toss. Add the chicken strips and toss. Salt and pepper generously. Taste for seasonings. Drizzle the remaining olive oil over the salad and sprinkle over it the Parmesan cheese. Toss well.

Yield: 4 servings

Rotisserie-Roasted Chicken Salad

My mother makes the best balsamic vinaigrette. It is so good we bottled it.

All Stew Leonard's stores have juicy, crisp-skinned rotisserie-roasted chickens for takeout. They are perfect for making a quick chicken salad. To make it even easier, use "Mrs. Leonard's Balsamic Vinaigrette."

Preparation Time: 15 MINUTES
Cooking Time: NONE

LOW FAT SUPER FAST

1 Stew Leonard's rotisserie-roasted chicken, between 2½ and 3 pounds
1 head of Romaine lettuce, cleaned, and hard core trimmed
1 head green leaf lettuce or a bag (2 cups) of Stew Leonard's Gourmet Salad Mix
Mrs. Leonard's Balsamic vinaigrette (or homemade vinaigrette)
Salt and freshly ground black pepper to taste

1. With your hands, remove the meat from the legs and breast of the chicken (discard the skin). Slice the meat into ¼-inch strips. Place in a mixing bowl.
2. Tear the lettuce into bite-sized pieces and place it in a large salad bowl. Add the chicken. Moisten the chicken and the greens with the vinaigrette. Season well with salt and pepper. Toss well.

Yield: 4 to 6 servings

Art Weiss shows off our fresh roasted chickens. Stew's sells over 2,000 a week!

Stew's TIP

There is no need to waste broccoli stems when a recipe calls for flowerets. Use the stems in a stir-fried meal. Cut the stems on the diagonal into 1/4-inch slices. Stir-fry them with a tablespoon of peanut oil in a wok or a large pan until nearly soft. Add slivers of chicken or seafood, minced ginger, and garlic. Moisten with a splash of soy sauce and dry sherry, and garnish with chopped scallions.

Bethy's Tortellini Salad

This vibrant salad from my sister Beth may be served as a luncheon main course or as a dinner side dish. Stew's sells a variety of tortellini stuffed with meat, cheese, and vegetables.

Preparation Time: 10 MINUTES
Cooking Time: ABOUT 10 MINUTES

LOW FAT SUPER FAST

13 ounces Stew Leonard's tortellini (fresh or frozen — when frozen they usually come in 9- or 13-ounce containers)
1 cup broccoli flowerets (about 2 stalks)
1 zucchini, quartered and cut into 1/4-inch-thick slices
1/3 cup prepared mayonnaise
1/3 cup grated Parmesan cheese
2 tablespoons milk
1 large red bell pepper, cored and cut into 1/4-inch-thick strips
1/4 cup pitted black olives
1/4 teaspoon salt
1/8 teaspoon freshly ground black pepper

1. Cook the tortellini in a large pot of boiling salted water for about 4 minutes — or until they rise to the surface. Remove them with a slotted spoon and set aside. Add the broccoli and zucchini to the same water and cook for 3 to 4 minutes. Drain and cool under cold running water. Set aside.
2. Blend the remaining ingredients in a salad bowl. Toss with the pasta and vegetables. Adjust seasonings to taste. Serve at room temperature or slightly chilled.

Yield: 4 servings

My dad and my sister, Beth, at our little farm.

"You'll love this one!"

Grilled Flank Steak Salad with Orange Vinaigrette

The popular Mexican dish of thinly sliced grilled flank steak is super for all sorts of summer entertaining. It's one of our most popular meats to marinate. This light salad combines the taste of the smoky grilled meat with refreshing sweetness of orange slices. Serve this salad at the next family picnic as a change from grilled hot dogs and hamburgers.

Preparation Time: 20 MINUTES
Cooking Time: ABOUT 20 MINUTES FOR THE STEAK
(see recipe page 112)

LOW FAT

12 cups mixed salad greens such as chicory, Romaine and Boston lettuce
1 small Bermuda onion, thinly sliced
2 seedless oranges, peeled and thinly sliced
1- to 2-pound Grilled Oriental Flank Steak (see recipe page 112)
¼ cup white wine vinegar
⅓ cup orange juice
⅔ cup vegetable oil
1 teaspoon fresh chives, chopped
Salt and freshly ground black pepper to taste

1. On a large serving platter, arrange the mixed salad greens. Layer rings of onion and slices of orange over the lettuce. Slice the cooked flank steak against the grain (thin slices taste best) and arrange the strips of meat over the salad.
2. Combine the vinegar, orange juice, vegetable oil, and chives in a small mixing bowl or blender. Blend, then season with salt and pepper to taste. Pour the dressing over the salad. Serve this salad with Stew's Country Hearth Bread.

Yield: 4 to 6 servings

Stew's TIP

While flank steak is the traditional ingredient in this Mexican salad, you could easily substitute barbecued pork tenderloin. Season tenderloin with salt, pepper, and a bit of cumin. Grill until medium rare and slice thinly. For a sweet edge, brush a little honey over the pork tenderloin in the last 15 minutes of cooking. The sweetness is complemented nicely by the sliced oranges in the salad.

"Low Fat and Fabulous!"

Diced Turkey-and-Clementines Salad

This sunny and sweet-tinged salad is an excellent way to use leftover turkey. You could also buy Stew Leonard's rotisserie-roasted turkey breast — or the hickory-smoked turkey breast — and simply cube the meat.

Preparation Time: 15 MINUTES
Cooking Time: NONE

LOW FAT

SUPER FAST

6 clementines (or 4 oranges)
Juice of 1 orange
Juice of ½ lemon
¾ cup prepared mayonnaise
1 tablespoon Dijon-style mustard
Salt and freshly ground black pepper to taste
½ tablespoon poppy seeds (optional)
1 pound roasted turkey breast, cubed
1 tablespoon chopped parsley
Lettuce leaves to cover plates

1. Peel the clementines (taking off all of the white pith) and cut them into sections. Set aside. In a blender combine the orange juice, lemon juice, mayonnaise, mustard, salt, pepper, and poppy seeds. Purée well.

2. In a bowl, combine the diced turkey and the clementine segments. Pour the sauce over them and toss well. Sprinkle the parsley over the salad. Chill for 1 hour before serving over the lettuce leaves. (Radicchio makes a nice color contrast.)

Yield: 4 servings

Note: See information on clementines, page 315.

Moroccan Couscous Salad

This is another of Chef George's creations. Sold in the take-out section of the store, it is a major seller!

Preparation Time: 10 MINUTES
Cooking Time: 5 MINUTES

2 tablespoons olive oil
Salt and freshly ground black pepper to taste
½ teaspoon cumin
1 pound box precooked couscous
½ cup cored, diced red pepper
½ cup cored, diced green pepper
¼ cup raisins
¾ cup chopped parsley
¼ cup fresh lemon juice

1. Bring a pot of salted water to a boil. Season with the olive oil, salt, and cumin.
2. Put the couscous in a large bowl. Pour the boiling water over the couscous and mix well with a wooden spoon.
3. Let the couscous rest until all of the water is absorbed. Let it cool and fluff it with a fork. Add the remaining ingredients and toss well. Taste for seasonings — it probably will need salt and pepper. Serve at room temperature or chilled.

Yield: 4 to 6 servings

Stew's TIP

Couscous is a delightful change of pace from rice or noodles. Technically, it is semolina pasta with a nice nutty flavor. It is mostly found in North African cuisines. The couscous sold at Stew's and most other markets is precooked, so all you have to do is add boiling water; the uncooked couscous is very time-consuming to prepare. Couscous can be seasoned and served like rice, or blended with vegetables and herbs of your choice. It is delicious hot, room temperature, or even cold.

Chef George tried this recipe in the store after talking to a customer. We are amazed at the popularity of couscous.

Barbecuing

Barbecuing is more popular than ever, so this chapter covers it in depth, showing you how to grill meat, fish, shellfish and vegetables. Check out Paul Newman's grilled asparagus! Also, look through our dozen or so marinades, which make any grilled food distinctive and delicious.

Better Barbecuing

The key to successful barbecuing is the same as that for stovetop cooking: a powerful, even source of heat; knowing how to judge your timing; and quality food. Probably the most common failing of amateur backyard chefs is trying to work with a fire that is weak or uneven.

Gas-powered grills have an advantage over charcoal in that they maintain even, high heat. Most use lava rocks to simulate charcoal. Many barbecue grills come with lids that can be used for an oven effect. Certain foods that take a relatively long time to cook — chicken legs, thick slices of steak, and so on — grill faster and better with the lid closed. Essentially, you are grilling and roasting at the same time. A lid traps much of the smoke, directing it into the food rather than allowing it to blow away. This is particularly important if you add apple, hickory, or mesquite chips to the fire.

If you are using charcoal, load the grill to capacity and let the coals turn 80% white before cooking. A weak fire fails to sear food and does not seal in juices. The result is a steak that is grayish-brown rather than nicely cross-hatched with black streaks. It also will lack a distinctive barbecue flavor. If you are cooking a large quantity of food and the fire begins to fade before you are through, add a small amount of charcoal to keep it alive.

Real charcoal, which looks like blackened shards of wood, is preferable to charcoal briquettes because it burns hotter. Charcoal can be found in many wood-stove shops as well as at some lumber yards.

Citrus-and-Hot-Pepper Marinade

This is particularly good with shellfish, fish and poultry.

Preparation Time: 10 MINUTES
Cooking Time: NONE

⅓ cup olive oil
⅓ cup orange juice
3 tablespoons fresh lime juice
1 tablespoon minced, seeded jalapeño pepper
1 tablespoon grated lime zest
1 tablespoon grated orange zest
Salt and freshly ground black pepper to taste

1. Combine all ingredients in a bowl. Mix well.

Yield: About 3 cups

Barbecue Tips:

- Trim most of the fat from meat before grilling. Too much flare-up can give the food a burned flavor.
- If you want to add wood chips to the fire, such as apple, cherry, hickory, or mesquite, soak them in water for 10 minutes before adding them. This prevents them from making flames that burn the food. Add them to the fire a few minutes before cooking.
- Clean the grill grate with a wire brush between uses. Just before cooking coat the grill with vegetable oil to prevent food from sticking, particularly fish.
- Steaks should be grilled fairly close to the coals — about three or four inches — to sear the outside of food, particularly steaks, and retain their juices. Chicken, on the other hand, should be grilled higher up, especially the legs, because they take longer to cook.
- Before grilling chicken legs or duck legs run a knife along both sides of the thigh bone and the leg bone (on the skinless side) to separate the meat a little from the bone. This allows the legs to sit flatter on the grate and cook more evenly. Also, slice three-quarters of the way through the joint that connects the thigh and the leg (from the skinless side).
- Most barbecue grills have hot spots. While cooking you should move food around periodically to assure even exposure to heat.
- Always let red meat rest for 5 to 10 minutes before carving. This allows the juices to redistribute in the meat.

Stew's TIP

Easy Marinades

Here is a variety of easy marinades that you can prepare in minutes. If you like, make them a day ahead to let the flavors intensify. The quantities here can be doubled or tripled depending on the size of the meat or fish to be marinated.

Stew's TIP

How to Ignite Charcoal

There is a simple and quick way to ignite charcoal without using fluid lighters. Buy a piece of stovepipe about 8 inches in diameter and about 15 inches long. Place it in the grill over a layer of charcoal and stuff a few sheets of crumpled newspaper in the bottom. On top of that place four or five handfuls of charcoal.

When you tilt the pipe and ignite the newspaper from the bottom, the flame will be concentrated and directed toward the charcoal, lighting it within a few minutes. When the coals begin to whiten, lift the pipe carefully, using thick kitchen mittens or potholders, allowing the white charcoal to scatter over the rest. Pour fresh charcoal over it and wait for it to turn white.

Garlic-Lemon Marinade

This is another marinade that is excellent with seafood and poultry.

Preparation Time: 10 MINUTES
Cooking Time: NONE

¼ cup Worcestershire sauce
¼ cup soy sauce
½ cup white vinegar
1 tablespoon minced garlic
1 tablespoon fresh lemon juice
2 teaspoons grated lemon rind
Salt and freshly ground black pepper to taste
1½ tablespoons ground cumin

1. Combine all ingredients in a mixing bowl and stir well.

Yield: About 1 cup

Citrus-Honey Marinade

This is particularly good with lamb and pork.

Preparation Time: 10 MINUTES
Cooking Time: NONE

SUPER FAST · LOW FAT · PREPARE IN ADVANCE

4 tablespoons freshly squeezed lemon juice
4 tablespoons olive oil
½ cup dry white wine
⅓ cup honey
1 tablespoon chopped fresh rosemary or ½ tablespoon dried
1 tablespoon minced garlic
2 teaspoons ground cumin
Salt and freshly ground black pepper to taste

1. Combine all ingredients in a mixing bowl and stir.

Yield: 1 cup

Ginger Teriyaki Marinade

This is wonderful with fatty fish like tuna and salmon. It also works with steaks. For a whole London Broil (see recipe page 113) you need to double this recipe.

Preparation Time: 10 MINUTES
Cooking Time: NONE

SUPER FAST · LOW FAT · PREPARE IN ADVANCE

5 tablespoons of soy sauce
(low-sodium soy sauce is okay)
4 tablespoon rice wine or rice vinegar
3 large garlic clove, minced
1 tablespoon minced fresh ginger or 1 teaspoon ground ginger

1. Stir all ingredients in a mixing bowl.

Yield: About ½ cup

What's better, charcoal or gas?

Grilling experts debate about which is better. About 80% of our customers at Stew's use gas, and 20% use charcoal. The "charcoal flavor" associated with outdoor grilling has little to do with charcoal. That smoky, woody taste is the result of fat or marinade dripping onto the fire, flaring up, and sending smoke into and around the food. It doesn't matter whether you cook over charcoal or a gas flame. You can, however, impart some flavors by adding aromatic wood chips like apple, pear, and mesquite.

Stew's TIP

When using yogurt in a recipe be sure to get the plain, unsweetened type. Also, do not get a yogurt that contains gelatin or stabilizers. They will ruin the texture of your dish.

Did you know that when yogurt is frozen to simulate ice cream it loses most of its beneficial bacteria?

Orange-Ginger Marinade

This sweet-tinged marinade is ideal for salmon and tuna, as well as shellfish.

Preparation Time: 10 MINUTES
Cooking Time: NONE

SUPER FAST · LOW FAT · PREPARE IN ADVANCE

½ cup orange juice
2 tablespoon rice vinegar or white wine vinegar
2 teaspoons of minced fresh ginger or ¾ teaspoon of ground ginger
2 teaspoons minced garlic
1 teaspoon of honey
1 teaspoon soy sauce
1 teaspoon grated orange rind
1 teaspoon of Dijon mustard

1. Blend all ingredients in a bowl. Refrigerate for about 30 minutes before using.

Yield: About ¾ cup

Herbed Yogurt Marinade

This marinade adds a nice herby flavor to chicken and turkey.

Preparation Time: 10 MINUTES
Cooking Time: NONE

SUPER FAST · LOW FAT · PREPARE IN ADVANCE

1 small yellow onion, coarsely chopped
2 tablespoons fresh dill or 2 teaspoons of dried dill
2 teaspoons lemon juice
1½ teaspoons Dijon mustard
¼ teaspoon ground turmeric
⅛ teaspoon freshly ground black pepper
1 cup plain lowfat yogurt

1. In a food processor or blender, combine all ingredients except the yogurt. Process for 45 seconds. Add the yogurt and process for about 10 to 15 seconds, or until all is well combined. Keep cool.

Yield: About 1 cup

ORDER MORE BOOKS at www.stew-leonards.com or Call... 1-800-SAY-STEW (729-7839)

Get a FREE COOKBOOK!

Mail Us Your Favorite Recipe or Idea!

We are collecting our customer's great family recipes and ideas for our next cookbook. You can be a part of it too! Just mail us your favorite recipe or great cooking tip. If we select your recipe, you'll get a free book and your name will appear with your recipe. You'll be a star!

Thanks for your help! — Stew

MAIL RECIPES TO:

Stew Leonard's
Cookbook Recipes
100 Westport Avenue
Norwalk, CT 06851

What do you like? What don't you like? I'D LOVE TO KNOW! -Stew

We get over 100 written suggestions each day
from our customers in our stores.
We love getting ideas and suggestions from YOU!
Please let us know what you thought of this book!

My overall rating of this book is: ❑ Very Good ❑ Good ❑ Okay ❑ Not so good

What I liked the most about Stew's Cookbook: ______________________

____

____

____

What needs improvement: ______________________

____

____

____

Green Chili-and-Cilantro Marinade

This is a zesty marinade for any kind of seafood.

Preparation Time: 10 MINUTES
Cooking Time: NONE

SUPER FAST · LOW FAT · PREPARE IN ADVANCE

4 tablespoons lemon juice
5 tablespoons plain lowfat yogurt
1 tablespoon minced fresh ginger or 1 teaspoon ground dry ginger
1 teaspoon seeded and finely chopped jalapeño
1 teaspoon ground cilantro
Salt to taste

1. Combine all ingredients in a bowl. Stir. Taste for seasonings.

Yield: About ½ cup

Lemon-and-Dijon-Mustard Marinade

This mild marinade could go either with seafood or meat.

Preparation Time: 10 MINUTES
Cooking Time: NONE

SUPER FAST · LOW FAT · PREPARE IN ADVANCE

6 tablespoons olive oil
3 tablespoons of fresh lemon juice
1 tablespoon Dijon mustard
¾ teaspoon grated lemon peel
Salt and freshly ground black pepper to taste

1. Whisk together all ingredients in a bowl. Taste for seasonings.

Yield: About ½ cup

Stew's TIP

Do marinades really tenderize meat?

Contrary to popular belief, marinades do not "tenderize" meat or poultry. A marinade, even one high in acid, penetrates meat only a quarter of an inch or so — it just flavors the surface. Fish, of course, take on the flavor of a marinade much more. That is why it is important not to over-marinate fish because the acid in the liquid will "cook" it.

As for marination times, meat can marinate for up to 12 hours or more (take it out of the refrigerator for the last 2 hours). Chicken needs only 2 to 3 hours, whereas fish should marinate for less than an hour.

A convenient way to marinate meat and seafood is to put it in plastic storage bags with the marinade and refrigerate. Every once in a while shake the bag.

Stew's TIP

When buying papayas look for those that are soft to the touch and brightly colored. Green papayas will ripen quickly at room temperature, especially if placed in a brown paper bag. If you buy a ripe papaya, store it in the refrigerator.

Papaya-Cilantro Marinade

This tropical marinade is great on fish or chicken.

SUPER FAST · LOW FAT · PREPARE IN ADVANCE

1 papaya, peeled, pit removed, and diced
1 medium ripe tomato, peeled, seeded, and diced
1 bunch of fresh cilantro (¾ to 1 cup)
½ red bell pepper, cored, seeded, and diced
½ green bell pepper, cored, seeded and diced
½ yellow bell pepper, cored, seeded and diced
2½ tablespoons of fresh lime juice
1 tablespoon olive oil
Hot pepper sauce to taste (such as Tabasco)

1. Whisk together all ingredients in a bowl. Taste for seasoning.

Yield: About ½ cup

Cuban-Style Marinade

This is particularly tasty with pork.

Preparation Time: 15 MINUTES
Cooking Time: NONE (it should be refrigerated for an hour)

SUPER FAST · LOW FAT · PREPARE IN ADVANCE

⅓ cup fresh orange juice
2½ tablespoons of fresh lemon juice
2 tablespoons fresh lime juice
10 garlic cloves, minced
2 teaspoons soy sauce
2 teaspoons freshly ground black pepper
2 teaspoons dried oregano, crumbled
1 teaspoon salt
4 bay leaves

1. In a bowl, stir together all ingredients. Refrigerate for about an hour to let the flavors meld.

Yield: About ½ cup

Jamaican Jerk Seasoning

This is a dry seasoning blend from the Caribbean that you rub onto pork, chicken or beef. Let the seasonings sit for 30 minutes or so before grilling.

Preparation Time: 5 MINUTES
Cooking Time: NONE

¼ teaspoon ground allspice
¼ teaspoon cinnamon
¼ teaspoon garlic powder
¼ teaspoon freshly ground black pepper
¼ teaspoon sugar
¼ teaspoon Worcestershire sauce
1 tablespoon minced scallion
Hot sauce (such as Tabasco) to taste.

1. Blend all ingredients in a bowl. Taste for seasonings.

Yield: ⅔ cup

Herbed Grilling Salt

All grill chefs seem to have their secrets for seasoning fish, meats, and vegetables before placing them on the fire. The Leonard family recipe is simple but flavorful. This spicy combination adds a subtle flavor but without dominating the seafood. Sugar contributes to the browning process but adds no sweetness to the cooked food. (If you use a combination of your own, always remember to apply it just before grilling.)

½ cup coarse kosher salt
½ teaspoon cayenne pepper
1 tablespoon ground fennel seeds
1 tablespoon sugar
1 teaspoon freshly ground black pepper

1. Combine all ingredients in a small bowl. Store in a sealed container.

Yield: 1 cup

Stew's TIP

Jerk seasoning comes from Jamaica, where a blend of spices is rubbed onto meat before grilling. There are many versions of jerk seasonings, but most include cinnamon, ginger, black pepper, allspice and sugar.

In Jamaica the seasonings are rubbed on chicken and pork.

Mango Salsa

This is not a marinade, but rather a sweet-tart salsa with a little kick of jalapeño pepper. It is great with any type of grilled meat, or even grilled seafood. We sell it fresh at the store and customers love it.

Preparation Time: 10 MINUTES
Cooking Time: NONE

SUPER FAST · LOW FAT · PREPARE IN ADVANCE

1 Granny Smith apple, cored, peeled, and cubed
2 ripe mangoes, peeled, pits removed and chopped
1 medium red onion, chopped
3 tablespoons fresh lime juice
4 garlic cloves, chopped
2 fresh jalapeño peppers, seeded and minced
¼ cup chopped fresh cilantro
Pinch of cumin

1. Place all ingredients except one mango in a mixing bowl. Place that mango in a blender and purèe well. Add this to the other ingredients and mix well. Cover with plastic wrap and refrigerate for at least one hour.

Yield: About 4 cups

We did a mango tasting at the store, and Wow! We sold more than 6,000 mangos that day!

Grilled Beef Tenderloin with Tarragon

Stew's customers love beef tenderloin for its buttery texture, subtle flavor, and ease of preparation. Our butchers will cut the tenderloin to order. We also sell tenderloins already seasoned with black pepper, so all you have to do is place them on a grill or in the oven. This recipe takes virtually no time to assemble — just remember to keep track of the cooking time!

3 tablespoons fresh tarragon, minced (or 1 tablespoon dried tarragon)
2 tablespoons olive oil
Salt and freshly ground pepper to taste
3 pounds beef tenderloin

1. In a bowl combine the tarragon, olive oil, salt and pepper. Stir well.
2. Rub the mixture all over the tenderloin. Roll the meat in aluminum foil. Place on the grill and close the cover. Cook for 20 to 25 minutes, turning the meat occasionally with tongs. Remove from the grill and let it sit for 10 minutes. Slice and serve with Mashed Potatoes with Roasted Garlic (see recipe page 244) and Green Beans with Arugula and Garlic (see recipe page 266).

Grilled Porterhouse Steak with Herb Butter

Preparation Time: 10 MINUTES (plus time for chilling flavored butter)
Cooking Time: ABOUT 15 MINUTES

4 tablespoons butter, at room temperature
1 tablespoon fresh minced tarragon, or ½ tablespoon dried
Salt and freshly ground black pepper to taste
2 medium porterhouse steaks, about 3½ pounds total and about 1-inch thick
1 tablespoon olive oil
Onion powder for steaks

1. In a mixing bowl, work together with your fingers the butter, tarragon, salt and pepper. Transfer the mixture to a sheet of wax paper and roll the butter into a cylinder. Refrigerate.
2. Preheat a charcoal grill or oven broiler to high.
3. Rub the steaks on both sides with olive oil. Salt and pepper generously. Sprinkle some onion powder evenly on both sides.
4. If the charcoal grill is used, put the grate on the highest position (if your grill has different levels). Place the steak on the grill (or on a broiler rack about 4 inches from the heat source).
5. Grill the steak for about 6 minutes. Turn it over and cook 5 minutes more for rare, 8 minutes for medium — always check with a sharp knife. Remove the steak from the grill or broiler to a sheet pan and let stand 10 minutes so the juices redistribute. Save any juices in the pan. Serve garnished with a slice or two of the herb butter and pour any pan juices over the steaks.

Yield: 6 servings

Note: If you have leftover herb butter you can use it with vegetables, on bread, or in sauces.

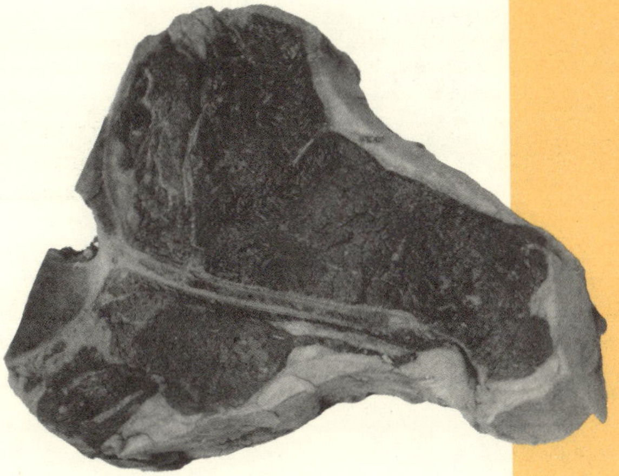

Stew's TIP

What is a porterhouse steak?

A porterhouse steak is actually two steaks in one. For that reason the porterhouse is considered by many the ultimate cut of beef. It consists of two steaks with different textures, connected by a single bone. The filet mignon, which is the most buttery and tender cut of beef, is on one side; on the other is the strip steak (also called shell steak), which is a bit less tender but extremely flavorful.

Porterhouse steaks are fantastic on the barbecue grill. Just don't overcook them. All they need is a little pat of herb butter.

Grilled Oriental Flank Steak

Flank steak, another big seller at Stew Leonard's, comes from the underside of the steer, just in front of the shank and the round. It is a particularly flavorful cut of meat — slightly sinewy but not tough — and ideally suited to broiling and barbecuing. My kids love this for dinner. Cut the flank steak very thin and on an angle.

Preparation Time: 10 MINUTES
Cooking Time: ABOUT 20 MINUTES

¼ cup soy sauce
1 tablespoon chopped fresh ginger
¼ cup white wine
1 teaspoon chopped garlic, about 2 cloves
1 2-pound flank steak

Tom Anrico, a 20-year veteran at Stew's, inspects meat at Arthur Stern's in the Bronx Terminal Market. "This meat is hand selected and ends up in the best steak houses in New York City," says Tom.

1. Combine the soy sauce, ginger, white wine, and garlic in a shallow pan large enough to hold the flank steak. Set aside.
2. Place the steak on a cutting board. Remove any excess fat on both sides.
3. Transfer the steak to the marinade, turning it to coat all over. Cover the meat with plastic wrap and refrigerate overnight, turning once to let the flavors of the marinade permeate all sides.
4. Preheat an outdoor grill or the broiler. Remove the flank steak from the refrigerator and let it warm up for about 30 minutes. Remove from the marinade and drain off excess liquid. Place the meat on the grill or under the broiler. Cook it for 2 minutes per side to sear, then another 6 to 8 minutes per side for medium rare (timing can vary significantly depending on the steak's thickness, so check by making a slice in the thickest part).
5. Place the steak on a sheet pan and let it sit for 10 minutes. Reserve the pan juices. Transfer the steak to a cutting board. Holding a long carving knife at a 75-degree angle, cut thin slices from one end of the meat — always cut against the grain. Serve several slices of flank steak with Mashed Potatoes with Chives (see recipe page 242) and a mixed green salad.

Yield: 4 to 6 servings

Grilled London Broil in Ginger-Teriyaki Marinade

This is one of the biggest-selling cuts of beef at Stew Leonard's. It is not the most tender cut, but it does have a full, beefy flavor. This marinade subtly infuses the meat with ginger.

1 London broil, 1-inch thick (about 3½ pounds)
Ginger-Teriyaki marinade (see recipe page 105), double the proportions
Freshly ground black pepper to taste

1. In a large shallow pan, coat the steak with the marinade. Let it sit for about 1 hour, flipping several times.
2. Heat a barbecue grill or broiler. Pepper the steak. Grill the steak for about 8 to 10 minutes and flip. Grill for another 8 to 10 minutes and check for doneness. When finished, let it rest in a sheet pan for 10 minutes before carving on a bias, against the grain. Pour pan juices over each serving.

Yield: Serves 8 to 10

Football Tailgate Party

Can't-Eat-Just-One Spiced Walnuts (see recipe page 33)
Spicy Roasted Chicken Wings (see recipe page 183)
Fresh Tomato and Balsamic Vinegar Relish (see recipe page 32)
Warm Red Potato Salad (see recipe page 92)
(This is equally good at room temperature.)
The Amazing Leonard Brownies (see recipe page 334)

Grilled Chicken Breasts with Spicy Peanut Sauce

Preparation Time: 10 MINUTES
Cooking Time: ABOUT 10 MINUTES

3 whole skinless, boneless chicken breasts (making 6 fillets), about 1½ pounds
2 tablespoons olive oil
3 tablespoons freshly squeezed lime juice
½ teaspoon chili powder
½ teaspoon ground turmeric
2 teaspoons chopped fresh or crushed dried rosemary leaves
1 teaspoon finely minced garlic
Salt and freshly ground black pepper to taste

1. Cut the breasts lengthwise down the center (so you have 6 fillets). Cut away and discard any fat and membrane.
2. Put the oil in a mixing bowl; whisk in the lime juice, chili powder, turmeric, rosemary, garlic, salt, and pepper. Stir to blend and add the chicken pieces. Turn them in the marinade to coat well. Cover and set aside until ready to cook — at least 30 minutes. If they are to be marinated for a long period, refrigerate them.
3. Place the chicken pieces on a preheated grill or on a broiler rack. Cover the grill or close the door to the broiler. Cook for about 3 to 5 minutes and flip the chicken. Continue cooking until done, about 3 to 5 minutes on the grill, possibly a little longer under the broiler. Check by slicing open a chicken fillet at its thickest point — it should be white all the way through.
4. Remove the chicken and serve with Spicy Peanut Sauce (see following recipe) served on top of the chicken breasts or on the side.

Yield: 4 to 6 servings

Spicy Peanut Sauce

It is best to make this before you cook the chicken.

Preparation Time: 10 MINUTES
Cooking Time: NONE

SUPER FAST · LOW FAT · PREPARE IN ADVANCE

½ cup soy sauce
6 tablespoons peanut butter
2 tablespoons sesame oil
3 tablespoons minced fresh ginger
1 garlic clove, chopped
2 tablespoons chopped scallions (green part only)
Cayenne pepper to taste

1. In a blender, combine all ingredients. Blend until it reaches a creamy consistency. Serve over chicken breasts, or on the side.

Yield: 4 to 6 servings

Here's a group at one of our cookbook testing parties. Every recipe in this book was tested in a home kitchen. We then tasted every dish at Stew's the next day.

Grilled Chicken Breasts with Rosemary and Lime

Preparation Time: 15 MINUTES
Cooking Time: ABOUT 10 MINUTES

3 whole skinless, boneless, chicken breasts, 6 fillets (about 1½ pounds)
2 tablespoons olive oil
3 tablespoons freshly squeezed lime juice
½ teaspoon chili powder
½ teaspoon ground turmeric
2 tablespoons chopped fresh rosemary or 1½ teaspoons dried rosemary
1 teaspoon minced garlic
Salt and freshly ground black pepper to taste

1. Preheat a charcoal grill or broiler.
2. Cut the breasts lengthwise down the center so you have 6 breast halves total (each one portion). Cut away and discard any excess fat and membrane.
3. Put the oil in a mixing bowl; add lime juice, chili powder, turmeric, rosemary, garlic, salt, and pepper. Stir to blend well and add the chicken pieces. Turn them in the marinade to coat well. Cover and set aside until ready to cook — at least 30 minutes. If they are to be marinated for a long period, refrigerate them.
4. Place chicken pieces on the grill or on the rack of a broiler. Cover the grill or close the door to the broiler. Cook about 3 to 5 minutes and turn the pieces. Continue cooking until done, about 3 to 5 minutes more on the grill (possibly a little longer under the broiler).
5. Remove the chicken and brush the tops with the melted butter.

Yield: 4 to 6 servings

Pork Kebobs with Soy Sauce and Honey

Preparation Time: 15 MINUTES
Cooking Time: 20 MINUTES

The marinade:
¼ cup soy sauce
½ cup water
¼ cup honey
2 tablespoons red wine vinegar
1 tablespoon finely chopped garlic
1 tablespoon freshly grated ginger
Salt and freshly ground black pepper to taste
1 teaspoon paprika

The pork:
2½ pounds boneless loin of pork, trimmed of fat
Oil for brushing pork
1 tablespoon lemon juice
4 tablespoons butter
1 tablespoon chopped fresh cilantro, optional

1. In mixing bowl combine soy sauce, water, honey, vinegar, garlic, ginger, salt, and paprika. If wooden skewers are to be used, soak them in water for 10 minutes.
2. Cut the pork into 1½-inch cubes and put into the soy sauce mixture. Cover. Let marinate for up to an hour.
3. Preheat a grill or broiler.
4. Drain the pork, but reserve the marinade. Arrange pork cubes on 8 skewers (about 5 pieces per skewer). Brush the meat with oil. Place the skewers on the grill or under the broiler. Cook, brushing with reserved marinade and turning often so the meat cooks evenly, about 15 minutes or until thoroughly cooked.
5. In a small saucepan combine ¼ cup of the marinade, lemon juice, butter, and cilantro. Reduce by about ⅓ over high setting. Spoon onto the meat and serve.

Yield: 8 servings

Stew's TIP

In summer I love to barbecue all kinds of kebobs. There are so many types to make, and so many ingredients to use: baby onions; sweet peppers; zucchini; cubes of chicken, beef or lamb; even scallops.

This soy-honey sauce is great with meat and poultry.

Remember to cut your vegetables and meats into equal sizes so they cook evenly.

Grilled Pork Chops with Mustard-Prune Sauce

Prunes go exceptionally well with the rich taste of pork. In fact, few cooks think of using prunes in sauces and casseroles. They can add a lovely mellow, sweet edge to all sorts of recipes. The sauce here would also be good with grilled German-style sausage. Pork chops also seem to go naturally with crisp and golden Chef George's Potato Pancakes (see recipe page 248).

Preparation Time: 15 MINUTES
Cooking Time: ABOUT 30 MINUTES

12 pitted prunes
1 cup red wine, beef stock or water
4 tablespoons vegetable oil
4 lean 6- to 7-ounce pork chops, trimmed of fat
Salt and freshly ground black pepper to taste
1 tablespoon olive oil
½ cup finely minced onion (about 1 small onion)
½ cup diced carrots (about 1 medium carrot)
½ cup diced celery (about 1 stalk celery)
2 tablespoons coarse-style French mustard

1. Preheat the oven to 250 degrees.
2. Place the prunes in a small bowl with the wine and oil. Set aside.
3. Heat a barbecue grill or a broiler to medium-high setting. Sprinkle the chops with salt and pepper and place them on the grill. Cook for about 5 to 8 minutes on each side, depending on thickness. Remove them to a baking tray and keep them warm in the oven.
4. Add the olive oil, onions, carrots, and celery to a pan. Cook for about 10 minutes or until vegetables are golden brown. Add the liquid from prunes. Stir. Blend in the mustard, then add prunes. Adjust the seasonings to taste and simmer for 5 minutes.
5. Serve each pork chop with 3 prunes and a few spoonfuls of sauce. Accompany with Mashed Potatoes with Chives (see recipe page 242) or Chef George's Unbelievable Potato Pancakes (see recipe page 248).

Yield: 4 servings

Grilled Butterflied Leg of Lamb with Herbs

The term "butterflied" refers to deboning a leg of lamb and cutting it down the center so it lays flat on the grill. Ask the butcher to do it for you.

Preparation Time: 10 MINUTES (plus up to 2 hours marination)
Cooking Time: 30 MINUTES

1 6-pound leg of lamb, boned, butterflied and well-trimmed of fat
Salt and freshly ground black pepper to taste
¼ cup olive oil
3 tablespoons mustard seed
1 teaspoon ground cumin
1 tablespoon finely chopped garlic
4 sprigs fresh thyme or 1 teaspoon dried
2 tablespoons chopped fresh rosemary or 1 tablespoon dried
4 tablespoons fresh lemon juice
2 tablespoons butter, melted
4 tablespoons finely chopped parsley

1. Lay the lamb flat and sprinkle with salt and pepper on all sides.
2. Pour the oil into a baking dish large enough to hold the lamb. Add the lamb and sprinkle on both sides with the mustard seed, cumin, garlic, thyme, rosemary, and lemon juice. Turn and rub the lamb so it is evenly coated. Marinate in a cool place for 1 or 2 hours, or up to 6 hours in a refrigerator. If refrigerated, let the lamb return to room temperature before cooking.
3. Preheat a charcoal grill or the oven broiler.
4. Remove the lamb from marinade and reserve the marinade. If a grill is used, put the lamb flat on the grill. If the broiler is used, place the lamb under the broiler 4 to 5 inches from the heat source. Cook the lamb, uncovered, on the grill or under the broiler about 15 minutes. Turn and cook 15 minutes on the second side. For medium or well-done meat, cook longer.
5. Meanwhile, bring the reserved marinade to a boil in a pan or casserole large enough to hold the lamb. Stir. Remove from the heat, and swirl in the butter and parsley. Transfer the lamb to the marinade pan, cover loosely with foil and keep warm. Let the meat rest 10 to 15 minutes before serving. Slice thinly and serve in the pan sauce.

Yield: 6 to 8 servings

Stew's TIP

How do I butterfly a leg of lamb?

First, buy a deboned leg of lamb. At home place it on a cutting board and, with a sharp knife, make a slice ¾ of the way through the middle of the lamb to lay it open flat. Then cover it with plastic wrap. With the bottom of a heavy pan or a mallet, pound the lamb so it is the same thickness all over.

Lou Trani, our Meat Manager, butterflies a leg of lamb for a customer. "The important thing is to follow the bone," says Lou.

Stew's TIP

What kind of fish is mahi-mahi?

Mahi-mahi is dolphin fish, a warm-water tropical species not to be confused with the mammal — like Flipper! The fish can be as small as 2 to 5 pounds each to as much as 50 pounds. These larger fish are filleted and crosscut into chunks. Its flesh is moderately fatty and very flavorful. It is usually sold as steaks.

Grilled Mahi-Mahi with Citrus Pepper Butter

The flesh of the mahi-mahi is meaty, firm and off-white. Its moderately fatty skin and somewhat dense texture make it excellent for grilling. This recipe also works well with tuna.

Preparation Time: 10 MINUTES
Cooking Time: ABOUT 20 MINUTES

SUPER FAST LOW FAT

$1\frac{1}{2}$ pounds fresh mahi-mahi steaks, divided into 4 portions
1 teaspoon vegetable oil
1 tablespoon minced garlic (2-3 cloves)
4 tablespoons unsalted butter or margarine, at room temperature
1 red bell pepper, seeded and chopped
1 tablespoon grated orange zest
$\frac{1}{4}$ teaspoon salt
3 tablespoons orange juice

1. Preheat a broiler or an outdoor grill. Lightly oil the fish fillets and refrigerate until ready to cook.
2. Place the garlic, butter or margarine, red pepper, orange zest, and salt in the bowl of a food processor or in a small mixing bowl. Process to combine the ingredients, or use a wooden spoon to blend them. Add the orange juice, and blend.
3. Place the mixture on a sheet of wax paper and form it into a cylinder. Refrigerate.
4. Place the fish on a preheated grill or in a pan under the broiler. Cook about 7 minutes for fillets $1\frac{1}{2}$-inches thick. Flip and cook for another 6 to 7 minutes.
5. Remove fillets from the grill or broiler. Cut the chilled butter mixture into slices $\frac{1}{4}$-inch thick. Place two slices on each portion of fish. (To melt the butter over the fish immediately, take a metal spatula and heat it over a gas flame or on an electric heating coil. Press the butter lightly so it melts over the fillets. Serve with Confetti Orzo (see recipe page 290).

Yield: 3 to 4 servings

Balsamic-Citrus Sauce

1 tablespoon butter
1 tablespoon brown sugar
1 cup freshly squeezed orange juice (or from concentrate)
1 cup freshly squeezed lemon juice
½ cup balsamic vinegar
1 tablespoon chopped chives

1. In pan, melt the butter and add the sugar, stirring. Cook until the sugar is caramelized — it will be a light brown color.
2. Add the orange and lemon juices. Reduce the sauce by half. Add the vinegar and cook for 1 minute, mixing well. Set aside to cool. Brush this over the lobster meat before cooking. Serve what is left as a dipping sauce.

Yield: 2 servings

Grilled Lobster Caribbean Style

In the French Caribbean lobsters are split and grilled over a wood fire. A spicy butter keeps the tender lobster meat moist while the smoke from the fire adds to the flavor. Serve this with Citrus-Balsamic Sauce (see preceding recipe page 121).

Preparation Time: 15 MINUTES
Cooking Time: ABOUT 25 MINUTES

5 tablespoons butter
1/4 teaspoon paprika
Pinch of curry powder
3 tablespoons lemon juice (about 1 medium lemon)
1/2 teaspoon hot pepper sauce, to taste
1 tablespoon fresh minced chives
1/2 teaspoon soy sauce
4 2-pound lobsters

1. Preheat an outdoor grill or a broiler. Melt the butter in a small saucepan with the paprika, curry powder, lemon juice, hot pepper sauce, chives, and soy sauce. Set aside and keep it warm.
2. Insert the top of a large knife into the top of the lobster shell a little behind the eyes. Don't worry, this is painless for the lobster! Turn the lobster over on its back and insert the knife between the rows of small claws. Bring the knife down and split the lobster tail in half lengthwise. Then cut through the body lengthwise (the lobster should be completely halved). Repeat with other lobsters. Pick out the intestinal tract that runs along the tail meat.
3. Brush the cut side of each lobster with some of the melted butter mixture. Place the lobsters, cut-side up, on the preheated grill (or cut-side up on a baking tray if broiling). Brush the meat with seasoned butter, and cook for 10 to 15 minutes — until the tail meat is to the touch. (The shell will also be bright red and the lobster meat white and flaky.)
4. Crack the claws of each lobster. If they look semi-raw, return them to the grill or broiler for another few minutes to finish. Place 2 lobster halves on each of four serving plates. Fill the cavity of each lobster with Mashed Potatoes and Chives (see recipe page 242). Serve with Balsamic-Citrus Sauce (see preceding recipe), additional melted butter, and lemon wedges.

Yield: 4 servings

Grilled Whole Red Snapper with Lemon-Herb Sauce

Small fish like red snapper, porgies and sea bass are good for grilling or broiling whole. The smokiness of the grill adds a delicious nuance. A fresh lemon-herb sauce is all it needs.

Preparation Time: 5 MINUTES
Cooking Time: ABOUT 15 MINUTES

1 cleaned red snapper or sea bass, 1½ to 2 pounds
1 teaspoon Herbed Grilling Salt (see recipe page 109)
Lemon-Herb Sauce (see recipe below) or 1 lemon cut into wedges

1. Preheat a broiler or prepare an outdoor grill.
2. Rinse the fish under cold running water and pat it dry with paper towels. Lightly coat it with the oil and season with the grilling salt.
3. Place the fish on a tray under the broiler or directly over the outdoor grill. If using the outdoor grill, be certain that the flames have died down. A fire that is too active will send flames onto the fish and char it.
4. Cook the fish for 5 to 7 minutes on each side (for a fish 1½-inches thick).
5. Serve the grilled fish on a platter with lemon wedges, or accompanied by the Lemon-Herb Sauce (see following recipe).

Yield: 2 to 3 servings

Lemon-Herb Sauce

Preparation Time: 5 MINUTES
Cooking Time: NONE

3 tablespoons freshly squeezed lemon juice
4 tablespoons olive oil
½ cup dry white wine
Salt and freshly ground black pepper to taste
1 tablespoon minced fresh rosemary, or ½ teaspoon dried

1. Place the lemon juice in a mixing bowl. Drizzle in the oil while whisking. Mix in the white wine, salt, pepper and rosemary. It is better if it sits for half an hour or more before using.

Yield: 1 cup

Grilled Whole Sea Bass with Lime Butter

This works with any white-fleshed fresh fish like snapper.

Preparation Time: ABOUT 15 MINUTES
Cooking Time: ABOUT 15 MINUTES

LOW FAT

4 whole, cleaned sea bass, about 1 pound each
¼ cup olive oil
½ cup freshly squeezed lime juice
8 tablespoons butter
1 tablespoon finely chopped shallots
1 cup dry white vermouth
¼ teaspoon finely grated or finely minced zest of lime
1 tablespoon finely chopped chives

1. Preheat an outdoor gas grill to high, or fire the coals of a charcoal grill until they are close to white hot.
2. With a sharp knife, score both sides of each snapper, slicing down to the bone at 3 equidistant spots.
3. Brush the grill lightly with oil. Brush the fish on both sides with oil and place them on the grill. Squeeze half of the lime juice on top of each fish. Grill the fish on one side for about 6 minutes. The cooking time will vary depending on the size of the fish. Turn and cook about 6 minutes longer.
4. Meanwhile, heat one tablespoon of the butter in a pan and add the shallots. Cook, stirring, about 1 minute. Add the vermouth, remaining lime juice, and lime zest. Cook over high heat until the liquid is almost evaporated.
5. Add the remaining butter, stirring rapidly with a wire whisk. Cook until the butter is melted and very hot. Remove from the heat.
6. Arrange the fish on a platter or serving dishes and pour the hot lime-butter sauce over them. Sprinkle with the chives and serve immediately.

Yield: Serves 4

Shrimp and Zucchini Kebobs

One of the best of all grilled foods is shrimp, which must be cooked quickly. If shrimp are overcooked, they become dry and chewy. The precise cooking time for them depends mainly on their size. Large shrimp, for example, cook for 2 to 3 minutes per side.

Preparation Time: 25 MINUTES (prepare skewers in advance)
Cooking Time: ABOUT 6 MINUTES

LOW FAT — PREPARE IN ADVANCE

20 large shrimp, shelled and deveined
2 small zucchini
Salt and freshly ground black pepper to taste
1 tablespoon coarsely chopped garlic (about 2 medium cloves of garlic)
1 tablespoon finely chopped fresh parsley, basil, rosemary, or dill
3 tablespoons olive oil
3 tablespoons fresh lime juice
1 teaspoon chopped fresh thyme or ½ teaspoon dried

1. Prepare a gas-fired or charcoal grill, or preheat a broiler.
2. Place the shrimp in a mixing bowl.
3. Trim off the ends of the zucchini and cut them into 20 rounds of approximately equal size.
4. Add the zucchini rounds to the shrimp. Add salt, pepper, garlic, parsley, olive oil, lime juice and thyme. Blend well. Let marinate for at least 15 minutes.
5. Arrange alternate pieces of shrimp and zucchini on each of 4 skewers. It is best when skewering the shrimp to skewer them through the thick upper part and again through the small tail section. That way they will lie flat on the grill. Brush the skewered ingredients with any oil remaining in the bowl.
6. If the skewers are to be broiled, arrange them on a baking sheet and place them 4 or 5 inches from the heat source. Broil about 3 minutes on one side and turn. Broil about 3 minutes on the second side.
7. If the skewered foods are to be grilled, place them over the hot coals and let cook about two or three minutes on one side. Turn and cook about 2 or 3 minutes on the second side. Serve alone or drizzled with melted butter with some lemon juice stirred into it.

Yield: 4 servings

Grilled Tuna with Ginger and Provençal Sauce

This calls for a dry rub of ginger rather than a liquid marinade. This can be done with any firm, meaty fresh fillet like tuna and swordfish.

Preparation Time: 10 MINUTES
Cooking Time: 10 MINUTES

SUPER FAST LOW FAT

4 tuna or salmon steaks, each about 1-inch thick (about 2 pounds)
Salt and freshly ground black pepper to taste
1 tablespoon freshly grated ginger
1 tablespoon lemon juice
1 tablespoon olive oil
Provençal Sauce (see following recipe)

1. Preheat an outdoor grill or a broiler.
2. Place the fish on a plate and sprinkle both sides with salt and pepper. Rub the ginger on both sides and sprinkle evenly with the lemon juice and oil. Cover closely with foil and let stand until ready to broil.
3. If broiling, arrange the steaks on a rack and place under broiler about 6 inches from the heat coils. Broil 5 minutes with the door partly open. Turn the steaks. Continue broiling, leaving the door open, about 5 minutes.
4. If grilling, put the steaks on a hot grill and close the lid. Cook 5 minutes. Turn the fish, cover the grill, and continue cooking about 5 more minutes.
   Serve with Provençal sauce on the side.

Yield: 4 servings

Provençal Sauce

Preparation Time: 10 MINUTES
Cooking Time: NONE

SUPER FAST

LOW FAT

PREPARE IN ADVANCE

1 large, ripe tomato
2 tablespoons red wine vinegar
¼ cup olive oil
¼ cup finely chopped shallots
1 teaspoon minced garlic
½ cup finely chopped fresh basil (parsley may be used)
1 teaspoon grated fresh lemon rind
Salt and freshly ground black pepper to taste

1. Put the tomato in boiling water for about 10 seconds. Remove, and when cool enough to handle, peel off the skin. Cut out the core and discard. Cut the tomato crosswise in half. Remove seeds by squeezing the halves, cut side down. Cut the tomato into ¼-inch cubes — there should be about ½ cup.
2. Put the vinegar in a mixing bowl and add the oil, shallots, garlic, basil, and tomato. Add the lemon rind, salt, and pepper. Blend well with a whisk.

Yield: About 1 cup

Stew's TIP

You may notice that this sauce features the holy trinity of Provençal cooking: garlic, tomatoes, and olive oil. In the south of France you also see olives, anchovies, eggplant, and mushrooms.

Our Danbury store. My great-grandfather, Patrick Leonard, settled in Danbury in 1888. He'd be shocked to see this store today!

Grilled Salmon with Fennel Butter

Preparation Time: 10 MINUTES
Cooking Time: 20 MINUTES

LOW FAT

2 pounds skinless, boneless salmon fillets
Salt and freshly ground black pepper to taste
2 tablespoons olive oil (optional if using a non-stick pan)
1 head fennel (about ¾ pound)
½ cup water
5 tablespoons butter, at room temperature
¼ teaspoon cayenne pepper
⅛ teaspoon freshly grated nutmeg

1. Carefully inspect the fish for any bones. Using a pair of pliers or tweezers, carefully pull away and discard the little bones in the center. Cut the fillets into 4 equal portions. Sprinkle with salt and pepper. Sprinkle with oil and rub to coat on all sides. Set aside.
2. Trim the fennel of stalks and hard bottom core, discard, and cut bulb into ¼-inch cubes. There should be about 1½ cups. Put the fennel in a saucepan and add the water and one tablespoon of the butter. Cook 7 to 8 minutes, or until the fennel is soft.
3. Pour the fennel and water into the container of a food processor or electric blender and add the remaining butter. Blend as finely as possible. There should be about 1¼ cups. Pour the mixture into a saucepan and bring to a boil. Add the salt, pepper, cayenne pepper, and nutmeg. Reduce the heat and let simmer about 3 minutes.
4. Meanwhile, heat a large non-stick pan over medium-high setting (or a grill) and add the salmon. Cook about 5 minutes on one side. Turn and cook about 5 more minutes. Transfer the fillets to a warm serving dish.
5. Serve with the hot fennel sauce spooned over or on the side.

Yield: 4 servings

Grilled Monkfish Kebobs with Orange-Butter Sauce

The firm, plump meat of monkfish is well suited to grilling. This orange-butter sauce is also delicious with lobster.

Preparation Time: 15 MINUTES
Cooking Time: 25 MINUTES

SUPER FAST · LOW FAT · PREPARE IN ADVANCE

2¼ pounds monkfish fillets, cut into 1 x by x 2-inch pieces
1 yellow bell pepper, cored, seeded, and cut into thick slices
1 red bell pepper, cored, seeded, and cut into thick slices
2 small ripe tomatoes, peeled and seeded (drop the tomatoes in boiling water for 10 seconds to loosen skin)
2 cups fresh orange juice
½ cup chopped scallions (including some of the green part), diced
Salt and freshly ground black pepper to taste
6 tablespoons butter
2 tablespoons vegetable oil
2 tablespoons chopped fresh cilantro (optional)

1. Place 6 pieces of monkfish on a skewer, alternating with slices of red and yellow bell peppers. Continue until all the fish and peppers are used. Set aside.
2. Dice the tomatoes. You should have about ¾ cup. In a saucepan, combine the orange juice, scallions, salt, and pepper. Reduce by half over the grill or stove — about 10 minutes. Add the butter, tomatoes, salt and pepper. Mix well. When the butter is melted, set aside in a warm spot while you cook the brochettes.
3. Coat the brochettes with oil and place them over the grill. Cook until done, about 15 minutes, turning occasionally. Place the brochettes on serving plates, pour the sauce over them, and garnish with fresh cilantro.

Yield: 6 servings

Grilled Eggplant with Mozzarella Cheese and Basil

Preparation Time: ABOUT 15 MINUTES
Cooking Time: 30 MINUTES

LOW FAT

3 large eggplants (about 1½ pounds each)
5 tablespoons olive oil
Salt and freshly ground black pepper to taste
1 bunch fresh basil leaves
3 medium ripe tomatoes, sliced thinly
1¼ pounds fresh mozzarella, cut into ¼-inch slices

1. Cut the stems off the eggplants. Slice each eggplant lengthwise into 4 even pieces. Rub some of the olive oil over the slices and season well with salt and pepper.
2. Lay the tomatoes over six of the eggplant slices. Place the basil leaves over the tomatoes. Drizzle with the olive oil and season with salt and pepper. Lay the mozzarella slices over the basil leaves. Coat them with the remaining olive oil and make sandwiches with the remaining eggplant slices. Wrap well in greased heavy-duty aluminum foil.
3. Place the eggplants over the grill and cook for about 30 minutes, turning occasionally, or until the eggplants are cooked thoroughly and the cheese is melted. To serve, use a spatula to gently transfer the eggplant sandwiches from the foil to a plate (they will be moist and slippery). Garnish with fresh basil leaves.

Yield: 6 servings

Paul Newman's Favorite Grilled Asparagus

Paul Newman, a longtime friend of our family, raves about these grilled asparagus, which are amazingly simple to make.

Preparation Time: ABOUT 10 MINUTES (plus 30 minutes marination)
Cooking Time: ABOUT 12 MINUTES

SUPER FAST LOW FAT

1 teaspoon minced garlic
½ cup olive oil
½ cup balsamic vinegar
Salt and freshly ground pepper to taste
24 to 30 asparagus, hard part of stalks snapped off

1. In a bowl combine the garlic, olive oil, vinegar, salt, and pepper.
2. Transfer the marinade to a wide shallow dish and add the asparagus. Marinate for 30 to 40 minutes, tossing occasionally.
3. Heat a barbecue grill. Place the asparagus on the hot center and cook for about 5 minutes, turning, or until they get slightly charred from the heat. Move the asparagus to the cooler rim of the grill and cook another 3 to 5 minutes, or until they are cooked but still a little crisp.

Yield: Serves 4

Stew's TIP

The best time for fresh asparagus is early spring, but with hot-house cultivation we get arparagus all year long. Asparagus plants live more than 10 years, and the size of the stem reflects the age of the plant from which it came. To store asparagus at home, place it in a few inches of water and cover with a plastic bag.

"Hey Paul, take off your sunglasses!" one customer cheered when Paul Newman visited our store to launch his new steak sauce. "I can't," Paul replied. "Every time I take off my sunglasses, my pants fall down!" Newman's Own has raised nearly $100 million and given every penny to charities!

Stew's TIP

What is a Portobello mushroom?

Portobello mushrooms are very large, brown, thick, and with fat stems. The meaty cap is ideal for grilling. The term portobello is just a fancy made-up name for a mushroom that growers could not sell prior to the 1980s.

Grilled Portobello Mushrooms

Meaty, earthy portobellos are delicious seasoned with this simple lemon-garlic vinaigrette, then grilled.

Preparation Time: 10 MINUTES (plus 15 minutes marination)
Cooking Time: ABOUT 10 MINUTES

4 tablespoons olive oil
3 tablespoons lemon juice
1 tablespoon minced garlic
2 tablespoon minced chives
½ teaspoon dried oregano
½ teaspoon dried basil
Salt and freshly ground black pepper to taste
4 large portobello mushrooms, 1 inch of stems trimmed, tops rinsed, and drained

1. Heat a charcoal or gas grill to high.
2. In a bowl, combine all of the seasonings and whisk well.
3. Place the mushrooms, stem-side up, on a flat surface. Drizzle the dressing over the inside of the caps. Rub the tops around in the bowl used for mixing the dressing (just to coat lightly). Season well with salt and pepper. Place the mushrooms on a plate, cover with plastic wrap, and refrigerate for about 15 minutes (to let the flavors sink in).
4. Place the mushrooms, stem side up, on the grill for 3 minutes. If using gas, turn down the grill; if charcoal, move the mushrooms to the perimeter of the grill. Cover loosely with aluminum foil and cook for another 7 to 10 minutes, or until the stems feel soft. Slice or serve whole, garnished with chopped chives.

Yield: 4 to 6 servings

Giovanni is putting out some freshly baked French baguettes. Stew's breads are all-natural and made from scratch with the finest ingredients. Bakery products not sold each day are given to charities in the area.

Grilled French Bread with Garlic and Parmesan

This is tasty accompaniment to any meal.

Preparation Time: 10 MINUTES (Cook before serving)
Cooking Time: 15 MINUTES

SUPER FAST · PREPARE IN ADVANCE

1 large French baguette or two small ones
3 tablespoons olive oil
2 cloves garlic, minced
¼ cup minced parsley
4 tablespoons grated Parmesan cheese

1. Slice the baguette lengthwise. Brush it with olive oil. In a bowl combine the garlic, parsley, and Parmesan cheese. Sprinkle the mixture over the bread. Recombine the loaf and wrap in aluminum foil.
2. Place the loaf over the grill and cook, turning occasionally, until well heated throughout, about 15 minutes.

Yield: 6 servings

Beef, Pork, Veal, and Lamb

Beef continues to be far and away the best seller at Stew's. In this chapter we give you a wide range of great, easy-to-prepare recipes — including tips on how to pick a perfect tenderloin. The same goes for lamb, veal and pork, which can be equally delicious when grilled, roasted or braised. For example, there is a wonderful recipe for Sautéed Veal Chops with Herb-Vinegar Glaze, and another of our favorites, Pierre Franey's Lamb Curry.

Stew's TIP

At Stew Leonard's we sell more than 50 tons of fresh beef each week. Indeed, beef is growing in popularity nationwide. We get most of our beef from Kansas, which is the heartland of the American meat industry. Our cattle ranchers and stockyards are in far southwestern Kansas, just 50 miles from the Colorado border. Kansas is a major corn producer, which makes it suitable for cattle ranching. Also, cattle are healthier in such low humidity environments.

"A Real Winner ..."

Pepper-Coated Whole Roasted Beef Tenderloin

This superb dish for the holidays or parties packs a double punch of white and black pepper. Use a heavy pan, like cast iron, to crush the peppercorns on a hard, flat surface — or use a spice grinder. If you don't want to go through the seasoning process, Stew's sells beef tenderloins already coated with black pepper.

Preparation Time: 5 MINUTES
Cooking Time: 20 MINUTES

1 beef tenderloin (about 6 pounds untrimmed)
⅓ cup Dijon mustard
5 tablespoons black peppercorns, crushed
5 tablespoons white peppercorns, crushed

1. Ask the butcher to trim the fat and sinew from the meat. The trimmed beef should weigh about 5-5½ pounds. (Stew Leonard's sells untrimmed 8-pound whole tenderloins that the butcher will cut to order.)
2. Preheat the oven to 450 degrees.
3. Coat the beef and rub it with mustard. Press the cracked peppercorns into all sides of the meat. Place the beef on a baking sheet.
4. Roast for about 20 minutes and check — the internal temperature should register 120 degrees on a meat thermometer (for rare). Cook longer for medium (130 degrees) or well done (140 degrees).
5. Remove the beef from the oven, cover with aluminum foil, and let stand for 15 minutes before carving.
6. Cut on the diagonal into ½-inch-thick slices. Overlap the slices around a serving platter.

Yield: 10 to 12 servings

Beef Filets in a Quick Red Wine Sauce

Filet mignon is one of the best meats for cooks who are in a hurry — it is so tender and rich that it cooks more quickly than other cuts. This recipe is ideal for entertaining.

Preparation Time: 5 MINUTES
Cooking Time: ABOUT 15 MINUTES

4 filet mignons, about 6 ounces each
Salt and freshly ground black pepper to taste
3 tablespoons butter
4 tablespoons minced shallots
1½ cups red wine
1 small bay leaf
2 sprigs fresh thyme
1 teaspoon tomato paste

1. Season the filets all over with salt and pepper. Place one tablespoon of the butter in a large pan over medium-high heat. When butter melts, add the filets and cook for 3 to 4 minutes per side, depending on desired doneness (always check by making a small incision on the top). Remove the filets and keep warm.
2. Remove half of the fat from the pan and add the shallots. Cook over low heat for about 2 minutes. Add the wine, bay leaf, thyme and tomato paste. Increase heat to medium high, and stir. Reduce the liquid to about ⅓ cup. Strain the sauce through a fine sieve into a small saucepan. Bring to a boil, remove from heat, and stir in remaining butter.
3. Place the filets on warm serving plates. Divide the sauce over four portions. Sprinkle with freshly ground black pepper.

Yield: 4 servings

Visiting one of our stockyards in Liberal, Kansas. This is also the town where Dorothy's house is located from the Wizard of Oz!

Stew's TIP

Is red meat good for you?

This is a common question from our customers. The answer is YES! In moderation, of course. Steaks sold in American markets today are significantly different from those of previous generations. To meet changing consumer habits, ranchers have bred beef cattle that are marketed younger and leaner. The leanest cuts of all are the sinewy ones: shoulder, rump and flank. They may need a little marination, but the flavor, in our opinion, is far superior to more expensive cuts like filet mignon. The American Beef Council recommends that we cook beef more quickly and at a higher heat for best results. Barbecuing, while controversial in some aspects, has at least one health advantage: excess fat drips down into the coals and flares up, adding flavor, but no fat, to the meat.

How do I pick a great whole tenderloin?

At Stew's you can buy the whole tenderloin. Our butchers will custom cut beef tenderloin to fit your needs. Here is how you pick a perfect filet. First, squeeze the meat. The softer it feels the better because you are buying more meat and less fat. A tenderloin that feels hard inside the vacuum pack has a lot of fat — and you don't want to pay for a lot of fat.

Our whole tenderloins weigh about 7 to 8 pounds, untrimmed. When trimmed, this will easily feed 8 to 10 people. A good rule of thumb when you are shopping is that one pound of untrimmed filet feeds one person.

Stew's Favorite Roasted Garlic Beef Tenderloin

When I visited Kansas my ranger friends were eager to tell me about their favorite steak recipes. Here is one that sounded great to me! The garlic browns on the outside of the beef and gives it a very special flavor.

Preparation Time: 10 MINUTES
Cooking Time: [NEED TIME FOR THIS]

4 cloves of chopped garlic
3 tablespoons olive oil
2 pounds beef tenderloin
Salt and freshly ground black pepper to taste

1. Trim any excess fat from the tenderloin — not all of it, just the thick pieces.
2. Chop the garlic and mix it with the olive oil.
3. Make small slits around the filet and generously rub the garlic oil all over.
4. Cover the tenderloin with plastic wrap and refrigerate for 2 hours or overnight.
5. Preheat the oven to 500 degrees.
6. Remove the plastic wrap and season the meat with salt and pepper. Place the filet in a roasting pan and cook for 15 minutes. Reduce the heat to 450 degrees. (This gives you a nice crust on the outside.) Continue cooking for another 15 to 20 minutes. Slice into the steak to check for desired doneness, or use a cooking thermometer (140 to 150 degrees is medium-rare).
7. Let the beef rest for 10 minutes before slicing.

Yield: 4 to 6 servings

Here's a picture of Roy Moore, owner of Maverick Ranch in Denver, Colorado. Maverick Beef is the official supplier to the United States Olympic Training Centers.

Poached Filet of Beef with Winter Vegetables

You may never have heard of poaching beef, but it is great! It is important to cook it in beef broth, which you can make at home (and freeze what you don't use) or buy commercially.

Preparation Time: 10 MINUTES
Cooking Time: 30 MINUTES

4 large carrots, peeled and trimmed
3 stalks celery
4 medium leeks, cleaned and trimmed (whites only)
8 cups fresh beef broth (see recipe page 143) or commercial broth
Salt and freshly ground pepper to taste
1 filet of beef (38 ounces), trimmed of fat, cut into 8 equal pieces
Dressing (see recipe)
Sprig of fresh parsley, thyme or coriander

1. Slice the carrots, celery, and leeks into sections about 2-inches long and $\frac{1}{4}$-inch wide. The slices should be the same size so they cook evenly. Place the carrots, celery and 1 to 5 leeks in a large pot and cover with lightly salted water. Bring to a boil, remove from the heat and drain immediately.
2. In another large pot bring the beef broth to a low simmer over medium-high heat. Add the salt, pepper, carrots, celery and leeks. Simmer for 15 to 20 minutes, or until tender. Do not let the broth boil.
3. Meanwhile, season the filets on both sides with salt and pepper. Add the filets to the simmering vegetables, and cook over low heat about 4 to 5 minutes. Do not let the liquid boil. The meat should be served medium rare.
4. Divide the vegetables in a decorative pattern over 4 warm serving plates. Place the beef pieces next to the vegetables. Spoon the dressing over the meat. Season if necessary. Garnish with fresh herbs. The broth can be served on the side in a consommé cup.

Yield: 4 to 6 servings

Roy Snider shows the technique of cutting a whole tenderloin for a customer at Stew's. Most customers request steaks that are $1\frac{1}{2}$- inches thick.

How do the pros pick the best meat?

When you are selecting meat in a store, look for the following:

- **Bright red color** – As soon as meat is cut, it begins to oxidize. The redder the color, the fresher the cut.
- **Cold and firm** – Make sure the refrigerated case is cold and that the meat doesn't feel "mushy." Some meat cases don't hold temperature well and the meat deteriorates quickly.
- **The bones** – Bones should be a "milky" white color. Dark bones indicate that the meat has been in the display case for at least 3 days.
- **Very little "purge" or juice** – This is the blood and water on the bottom of the package. Excessive purge is caused by beef sitting too long on the shelf or by fluctuating temperatures.
- **Expiration date** – If you go to a store and see expired meat or many different dates in the case, just walk away. These are indications that the store has a low turnover, or a poor product rotation program.

Pepper-Coated Filet Mignon with a Touch of Brandy

Preparation Time: 10 MINUTES
Cooking Time: 35 MINUTES

1½ tablespoons crushed black peppercorns (crush them with a mortar and pestle or the bottom of a heavy skillet)
4 beef filets, about 5 ounces each, trimmed of all fat
3 tablespoons butter
2 tablespoons vegetable oil
1 tablespoon brandy
¼ cup veal stock (see recipe page 164)
Salt to taste
¼ cup cream or half-and-half

1. Spread the crushed pepper on a flat surface. Lightly press the filets on top, then flip and repeat. Pat the pepper with your hands so it adheres well.
2. Heat a pan over high setting. Add 2 tablespoons of the butter and the vegetable oil. When it sizzles, add the filets. Cook for 4 minutes and flip. Cook another 4 minutes. Turn down the heat to medium. Cook another 8 minutes per side (time can vary with thickness) and check for doneness.
3. Remove the steaks from the pan and set aside in a warm place. Pour off the fat from the pan. Add the remaining tablespoon of butter and any peppercorns that remain on the counter. Add the brandy and tilt the pan so the flames ignite it (use a match if you have an electric range). Let the alcohol burn off. Add ¼ cup beef broth (preferably homemade) and turn up the heat to high. Reduce the sauce by one-third. Add a dash of salt and the cream. Stir and bring to a boil. Remove from heat and taste — it may need more salt.
4. Place the steaks on warm serving plates and surround with some of the sauce.

Yield: 4 servings

New York Strip Steaks with Burgundy Sauce

Preparation Time: 5 MINUTES
Cooking Time: 15 MINUTES

¼ cup finely chopped shallots
½ cup dry Burgundy wine
½ cup fresh or canned chicken broth
2 tablespoons red wine vinegar
3 tablespoons butter
4 boneless strip steaks, about ¾ pound each, most of the fat removed
Salt and freshly ground black pepper to taste

1. If you are grilling the steaks, ignite the charcoal. Or you may choose to cook the steaks in a skillet. The cooking time for either method will vary according to the intensity of heat of the charcoal grill or the skillet.
2. Sprinkle the steaks with salt and pepper. If a charcoal grill is used, cook the steaks about 3 minutes to a side and check them by slicing into the thickest part. If the steaks are to be cooked in a skillet, heat it (cast iron works best) about 5 minutes or until the surface is very hot. Do not add oil or fat. Cook the steaks about 4 minutes on one side or until well browned. Turn and continue cooking 4 minutes for medium-rare.
3. To prepare the sauce for the steaks, combine the shallots, red wine, chicken broth, and vinegar in a saucepan. Bring to a boil and cook over high heat until reduced to about ¾ cup.
4. Add the butter, a little at a time, shaking the pan to incorporate it.
5. Serve the steaks whole or sliced with the heated sauce spooned over.

Yield: 4 servings

Here is a special hammer used by the old-time meat men in New York. It puts your initials on each piece of meat for identification during the selection process.

Murray's Strip Steaks with Mustard-Peppercorn Crust

Murray's Steak House in Minneapolis is one of the oldest family-owned steak houses in the Midwest, open for more than 50 years. Its nickname is "Home of the Silver Butterknife Steak."

I was able to eat there one night and talk with the grandson, Tim Murray. He told me how the restaurant ages its beef for 30 days before his butchers cut it to order.

I asked him about his favorite steak recipe and he replied, "our Peppercorn Steak." This recipe is similar to our Mustard-Rubbed Beef Tenderloin, but with a few differences — like cooking the peppercorns in brandy! Murray's serves a 14-ounce New York strip steak that is broiled then slathered with a combination of mustard, garlic, and cracked black peppercorns. The steaks are put back under the broiler to crisp the top. My steak was sensational! Here is the recipe.

(In case you want to eat at Murray's Steak House in Minneapolis, here is the address: 26 South 6th Street, Minneapolis, MN 55402. Phone: 612-339-0909. Tell them Stew sent you!)

10 tablespoons cracked black peppercorns
½ cup brandy
½ cup water
6 boneless strip steaks, most of the fat removed (about ¾ pound each)
5 tablespoons Dijon or course-style mustard
1 tablespoon minced fresh garlic
5 tablespoons olive oil

1. Heat a broiler.
2. Combine in a saucepan the peppercorns, brandy and water. Bring to a boil, reduce heat to simmer, and cook until all of the liquid evaporates — it will resemble mud but don't worry.
3. Stir together in a bowl the mustard and the garlic.
4. Place the steaks 4 to 6 inches from the heating element and broil them for about 4 minutes per side (time varies with thickness of the steaks, so check by making an incision in the thickest part).
5. When the steaks are cooked, remove from the broiler and spread the mustard and garlic mixture on top. Pat the peppercorns over the mustard. (A thin coating will do.) Spoon the olive oil over the peppercorns and place the steaks back under the broiler — a little closer to the heating element if you can. Cook for about a minute, or until the mustard topping sizzles and darkens a little.

Yield: Serves 6

Homemade Beef Broth

This basic beef broth can be used for sauces, soups and other dishes. Freeze it in individual plastic containers or in ice cube trays.

Preparation Time: 10 MINUTES
Cooking Time: 3½ HOURS

PREPARE IN ADVANCE

2 pounds lean beef chuck
3 pounds beef bones (ask our butchers)
10 quarts water
2 large carrots, scraped and quartered
1 large onion, peeled and pierced with 4 cloves
Greens of 2 leeks, washed and cut into large chunks
4 ribs celery, trimmed and quartered
2 bay leaves
4 sprigs fresh thyme
10 peppercorns

1. Place the beef and the bones in a deep pot. Cover with 5 quarts of water and bring to a boil. Discard the water. Return the beef and bones to the heat, add 5 quarts water and the remaining ingredients. Bring to a boil.
2. Simmer 3½ to 4 hours. Skim the surface foam periodically. When cooked, strain and set aside.

Yield: About 3 quarts

What is aged beef?

Beef is aged to enhance tenderness and flavor. I asked our cattle ranchers how long they age their meat. They told me that if they are having guests over, they take the vacuum-packed pieces of fresh meat and leave them in the refrigerator for at least 2 weeks! Aging causes beef enzymes to break down the muscle fibers, and it also enhances the flavor. Aging acts as a natural tenderizer. As our rancher friends say, "I want my guests to be able to cut their steaks with a fork!"

There are two types of aging, dry and wet. In dry aging, beef hangs in a refrigerated room for days or weeks (only about 2% of all meat is dry-aged). At Stew Leonard's we wet-age our beef by keeping it in refrigerated rooms between 7 and 21 days, at 28 to 34 degrees. The meat ages in the vacuum packs and customers rave about it.

What's the best steak to buy?

1. Filet Mignon – This is called the "King of Tender Steaks!" You can't get more tender meat than this. Filet mignon ("cute filet" in French) comes from the small end of the tenderloin. In the colder months, our customers love to roast the entire tenderloin. In summer it's our #1 seller for barbecues. When we put whole tenderloins on sale for, say, $4.99 a pound, our Norwalk and Danbury stores sell more than 20 tons a week!

2. New York Strip Steak – This is a tender steak, rich in flavor, well-marbled, and great on the grill. When I first went to Kansas I discovered that out there they call it a "Kansas City Strip Steak."

3. Rib-Eye – This is a boneless cut from the rib section. It is also a well-marbled piece of meat that is very tender and full of beefy flavor. My cattle rancher buddies say it is their favorite cut of beef. You can grill it or roast it.

4. London Broil – This is essentially a very thick and large flank steak. It is quite lean so it needs marination before cooking. At $2 to $3 a pound, it is a real bargain — that's why we call it a "family steak."

5. Porterhouse/T-Bone – This is two steaks in one! It's part filet mignon and part strip steak. If you go to many of the famous steakhouses around the country, this is likely to be their signature steak. "Johnny O," the manager at Supreme Cattle Feeders in Liberal, Kansas, says he never orders a T-Bone unless it's at least 1½ inches thick! "It's juicier that way," he says.

6. Flank Steak – This lean but extremely flavorful cut is best when marinated. We have a grilled flank steak recipe on page 112 that my guests rave about. This steak normally sells in the $4 to $5 a pound range. It is also delicious stuffed with cheese or fresh herbs, then rolled and roasted.

7. Sirloin Steak – This is another premium steak with good marbling, full flavor and a tender texture. It normally sells in the $4 to $5 a pound range.

What's the best way to tell when meat is cooked?

There are three ways to tell if your steaks are cooked properly.

"Touch" method – Most chefs as well as cattlemen would never think of sticking anything into their beef, pork, veal, or even lamb. They told me that it allows the precious juices to escape. Instead, they use the "touch" method. When you are ready to check your meat, press it with your finger. If it is still very soft it is rare. If it is just slightly firm it is medium rare or medium. If it is tight and firm, it is well done. It takes a lot of experience, though, to perfect this method.

Cutting method – This is the easiest and probably most widely used. The minimal amount of juice that oozes out is more than offset by the assurance of having a precisely cooked steak. Slice into the thickest part of the steak and see if the center is done. It should be slightly red, or "rare," because the thinner parts of the steak will be medium rare.

Thermometer – In my opinion, this is the best and safest method. The USDA has published many articles recently warning that "visual cues" cannot determine whether dangerous bacteria like E. coli have been killed. The only way to be sure that ground meat has been cooked enough is with a thermometer. E. coli are killed at around 160 degrees.

Insert a thermometer into the meat's thickest part.

Rare	130-140°
Medium Rare	140-150°
Medium	150-160°
Medium Well	160-165°
Well Done	170-180°

Gorgonzola Stuffed Flank Steak

This is by far our most popular steak recipe at the store. And as you will see, it is so easy to make at home.

Preparation Time: 10 MINUTES
Cooking Time: 45 MINUTES

1 flank steak, about 1¼ pound, trimmed of excess fat and pounded with a mallet so it is the same thickness all over
1 pound of Gorgonzola cheese, crumbled
2 cloves garlic, peeled and crushed
3 tablespoons melted butter

1. Preheat the oven to 375 degrees.
2. Lay the pounded flank steak on a sheet tray. Drizzle with the melted butter and evenly disperse the garlic over it. Then sprinkle the crumbled Gorgonzola over it. Press the cheese firmly into the meat.
3. Roll the flank steak tightly and tie it in three places with kitchen twine.
4. Place the steak in the oven and roast for 40 to 45 minutes. Remove, let sit for 10 minutes, and carve portions crosswise. Serve with Mashed Potatoes with Chives (see recipe page 242).

Yield: Serves 4 to 6

How much meat should I buy for my family or guests?

Here's a good rule of thumb:

MEAT CUT	# LBS. PER PERSON
Trimmed and boneless, or ground beef	½ pound per person
Beef with the bone	1 pound per person
Wholesale cut (untrimmed)	1 pound per person

What kind of marinade do I use?

Here's an area where you can use your creativity. The only thing that I have found in common in my travels around the United States is the use of salt on steaks. All the best steak houses use salt to flavor their meat.

There are just a few basics to consider with marinades. You want to balance acidity, salt, and sweetness. Vinegar (regular and balsamic), wine, and citrus, all have acidity. They also have a little sweetness. The acidity penetrates the meat and flavors it — it doesn't really tenderize because it does not penetrate more than a fraction of an inch.

If you have a rich (well-marbled), flavorful piece of meat, you'll want to use a subtle marinade. If you have a leaner cut like a flank steak, you'll want a stronger marinade. Fresh herbs, oil, and citrus, are terrific when used sparingly. See pages 102 to 108 for 10 different types of quick marinades.

Stew's TIP

Pot roast can also be made with brisket, a flavorful cut that requires long braising.

Ask the butcher at Stew Leonard's for the first-cut brisket, sometimes referred to as the "flat cut." It has just the right amount of fat and is falling apart tender after it is braised for a long time.

Pot Roast Bolognese with Winter Vegetables

Bolognese sauce, usually served with pasta, is an Italian meat sauce full of vegetables and smokey Italian bacon. Here a pot roast gets the same treatment. The bacon adds a fabulous flavor to the roast and its chunky vegetable gravy.

Preparation Time: 15 MINUTES
Cooking Time: 2 HOURS AND 15 MINUTES

2½-pound beef round roast
Salt and freshly ground pepper to taste
3 medium carrots, peeled and finely chopped
½ pound lean slab bacon or thick-cut regular bacon (Stew Leonard's sells a thick-cut bacon), cut into little cubes
2 celery stalks, finely chopped
2 cups coarsely chopped onions (2 medium onions)
1 tablespoon olive oil
1 cup beef stock or water
2 cups white wine

1. Sprinkle the beef with salt and pepper. Heat a non-stick pan over medium-high. Brown the beef with bacon in the ungreased pan for about 3 to 4 minutes, until it is a deep mahogany color on all sides. Remove the pan from the heat.
2. Heat the oil in a pot large enough to hold the beef. Add the vegetable mixture and cook until soft and beginning to release moisture (about 6 minutes). Add the beef, the stock, and white wine. Bring to a boil. Cover, reduce heat, and simmer very gently for 2 hours.
3. Remove the beef from pan. Skim the fat from the cooking liquid and discard the fat. Bring the liquid to boil and simmer for 5 minutes. Adjust seasonings to taste.
4. Cut the beef into ¼-inch slices. Arrange on a tray or in a casserole dish. Spoon the sauce over the beef and serve.

Yield: 4 to 6 servings

Smoky Black-Pepper Burgers

One of the staples of French bistro cooking is steak au poivre, in which a steak is embedded with crushed black pepper before cooking. It seems like an awful lot of pepper, but somehow in cooking the spice is tamed.

This same technique works wonderfully with hamburgers, giving them a distinctive peppery edge.

Preparation Time: 10 MINUTES
Cooking Time: ABOUT 15 MINUTES

1 pound lean ground beef
2 tablespoons whole black peppercorns, crushed
2 tablespoon vegetable oil
3 tablespoon chopped shallots (or onion)
1 ounce Scotch whisky
1 teaspoon chopped fresh tarragon, or ½ teaspoon dried
Salt and freshly ground black pepper to taste
⅓ cup Worcestershire sauce.
1 tablespoon chopped fresh parsley

1. Divide the beef into 4 patties. Place the crushed peppercorns on a plate and dip each burger into them, making sure that some pepper adheres to each side of each burger.
2. Heat 1 tablespoon of the oil in a pan. Add the shallots and cook until they are translucent. Add the whiskey and tarragon and cook for a few minutes to loosen any particles stuck to the pan. Add the Worcestershire sauce and cook for 3 minutes over medium heat to combine flavors. Adjust seasonings to taste. (The sauce may be made ahead and reheated before serving.)
3. Place another pan over medium-high heat. Add the remaining oil, then the burgers. For rare burgers, cook for 3 to 4 minutes, turn, and cook for another 3 to 4 minutes. Slice into the center to test for desired degree of doneness. The meat should not be raw in the center!
4. To serve, place each burger on a crusty slice of bread or a roll, and drizzle with the sauce. Accompany with a fresh tomato salad or Warm Red Potato Salad (see recipe page 92).

Yield: 4 servings

These zesty burgers can also be grilled outdoors. Some of the black pepper inevitably falls off, so be extra careful to press the pepper into the meat firmly. The smokey flavor comes through. As a variation, add bourbon to the meat mixture instead of Scotch.

Stew's TIP

At Stew Leonard's we grind our hamburger meat hourly, whether it is chuck or sirloin, and you can choose your degree of leanness. The ground beef with 4% fat is good for blending with ground pork or veal to make meatloaf or burgers; 20% and 10% are best for grilling and barbecuing.

Whenever we make hamburgers at home or for a picnic we try different flavorings to jazz them up. If you like heat, try some Tabasco in the mix, or maybe cumin; soy sauce gives them a nice salty sweet sensation. Dijon-style mustard is a winner too. And of course there are all kinds of fresh and dried herbs — be imaginative, be daring!

Stew's TIP

There are endless variations of chili, both meat and vegetarian. Try combining beef and pork for a different flavor or, if you like, add some lamb. If you want to stoke it, add some red pepper flakes when you put the meat in the pot.

Here is a basic recipe for beef and pork chili:

Heat olive oil in a large deep pot. Add a cup of chopped onions, ½ cup chopped green pepper, 2 teaspoons chopped garlic, and cook for 3 minutes. Add ½ pound each of ground beef and ground pork and cook another 3 minutes, stirring. Add some chili powder, cumin and ground coriander seed to taste.

Stir in 1½ cups ripe, diced tomatoes (or one 14-ounce can diced tomatoes), ¾ cup beef broth, ½ cup red wine, 2 teaspoons tomato paste, and salt, black pepper, and red pepper to taste.

Bring to a boil, reduce to simmer, and cook for 25 minutes, stirring often. Add a 15-ounce can of drained kidney beans and cook 5 minutes more. Garnish with sour cream and chopped cilantro or parsley.

Super Bowl Chili

This all-vegetable chili makes a great winter supper or the perfect meal to enjoy while glued to sports on TV. For a more traditional dish, add 1 pound of cooked ground beef or turkey.

Preparation Time: 10 MINUTES
Cooking Time: ABOUT 50 MINUTES

LOW FAT · PREPARE IN ADVANCE

2 tablespoons vegetable oil
2 teaspoons minced garlic (2 large cloves)
½ cup chopped onion (1 medium onion)
2 tablespoons flour
1 28-ounce can crushed tomatoes
1 15-ounce can red kidney beans
1 12-ounce can chickpeas
1 cup cubed zucchini (1 medium zucchini)
½ cup chopped carrot (1 medium carrot)
2 tablespoons chili powder
1 teaspoon cumin powder
1 teaspoon salt and freshly ground black pepper to taste
Hot pepper sauce, like Tabasco
½ cup grated cheddar cheese
½ cup lowfat yogurt or sour cream

1. Heat the oil in heavy saucepan over medium setting. Add the garlic and onions and cook for 5 minutes until the onions are soft. Sprinkle with flour, and stir to blend.
2. Add ¾ of the tomatoes (use some of the rest if the chili seems dry as it cooks), kidney beans, chickpeas, zucchini, carrots, chili powder, cumin, salt, and a dash of pepper. Bring to a boil, reduce heat, simmer, and cook about 45 minutes, stirring occasionally. Adjust the seasonings to taste with salt, pepper, and a dash of hot pepper sauce.
3. Garnish each serving with grated cheese and a dollop of yogurt or sour cream.

Yield: 6 to 8 servings

Chef Bob Greene developed many of the prepared meals at Stew's. "I do the cooking for our customers. They just warm it up!"

Lean Meatloaf with Rosemary

Everyone seems to be nostalgic for meatloaf these days. It is showing up on restaurant menus in all different incarnations: loaded with garlic, à la Tex-Mex, laced with cheese, or infused with herbs.

The rich, homey taste of a good traditional meatloaf comes from the fat in the meat. Some of the fat here is replaced with fresh vegetables. Amazingly, this meatloaf is just as flavorful as Mom's best.

Preparation Time: 10 MINUTES
Cooking Time: 1 HOUR AND 10 MINUTES

LOW FAT

PREPARE IN ADVANCE

$1\frac{1}{2}$ pound lean ground beef
3 medium carrots, trimmed, sliced into thin rounds
2 cups finely minced onions (2 large onions)
$\frac{1}{2}$ cup wheat bran (or Wheat Germ)
$\frac{1}{2}$ cup breadcrumbs
1 tablespoon of soy sauce
$\frac{1}{2}$ teaspoon salt
Freshly ground black pepper to taste
$\frac{1}{4}$ teaspoon cayenne pepper
2 sprigs fresh rosemary, or 1 teaspoon dried rosemary
3 egg whites
3 tablespoons tomato paste dissolved in $\frac{2}{3}$ cup water

1. Preheat the oven to 350 degrees.
2. Bring a pot of salted water to a boil and add the carrots. Cook for 10 minutes (or until they are somewhat firm but tender), strain and set aside.
3. In a large mixing bowl, combine the beef, carrots, onions, wheat bran, breadcrumbs, soy sauce, salt, pepper, cayenne pepper, and rosemary. Blend well with your fingertips to distribute the seasonings evenly.
4. Add the egg whites and tomato paste-water mixture. Blend thoroughly. Add more breadcrumbs if the mixture seems too moist.
5. Press the mixture into a loaf pan and smooth over.
6. Bake for 1 hour. Remove the loaf from the oven and let it rest on the counter for 10 minutes before slicing.

Yield: Serves 6

How do I pick great ground beef?

The key to picking quality ground beef is looking for both freshness and fat content. Freshness is indicated by a bright red color. The longer ground beef sits, the darker brown it becomes.

Fat content adds juiciness and flavor to your ground beef. In supermarkets, ground beef is generally 75% to 94% lean. Watch out for the pricing! The fattier ground beef will often be the cheapest. And even though the leaner meat is less juicy and flavorful, it is often the most expensive.

At Stew's we have three different kinds of ground beef:

- **Ground Chuck** (80% lean) – Juicy, flavorful and good for burgers and meatloaf.
- **Stew's Choice** – Ground Sirloin (90% lean) – Customers who want a healthy but still moist and flavorful combination prefer this blend.
- **Ground Round** – (94% lean) – This is very lean, and popular among those on a low-fat diets.

"A Hearty Dish"

Shepherd's Pie

Shepherd's pie is one of the most popular items in the Stew Leonard takeout section. This shepherd's pie is a far cry from the one served in school lunchrooms. Red wine, abundant herbs, and fresh vegetables lighten and brighten this traditional dish. Most people think shepherd's pie is made with ground lamb; in fact, the original recipe calls for ground beef.

Preparation Time: ABOUT 20 MINUTES
Cooking Time: ABOUT 25 MINUTES

PREPARE IN ADVANCE

1 tablespoon vegetable oil
1 cup minced onions or shallots (about 1 large onion or 3 large shallots)
2 pounds ground lean raw beef (or minced cooked lamb if you prefer)
2 tablespoons all-purpose flour
2 cups chicken or beef stock
1 cup red wine
1 cup diced carrots, peeled (about 3 medium carrots)
1 cup diced celery (about 2 stalks)
¼ teaspoon dried rosemary
½ teaspoon dried thyme
Salt and freshly ground black pepper to taste

1. In advance, prepare a batch of Mashed Potatoes with Chives (see recipe page 242).
2. Heat the oil in a heavy pan over high setting. Add the onion or shallots and cook until soft, about 5 minutes. Add the ground beef and cook, stirring, for 6 to 8 minutes, or until the meat loses its red color. (If using cooked lamb, heat until lightly browned, 6 to 8 minutes.

3. Drain any excess fat from pan, sprinkle the meat with flour, and blend. Add remaining ingredients. Bring the mixture to a boil, reduce heat, and simmer, covered, for 10 minutes. Taste for seasonings.
4. When the meat is cooked, pour it into a 6-cup casserole. Cover the mixture with the mashed potatoes. Smooth the surface with a spatula and decorate with fork swirls.
5. Place the pie under the broiler until the top is golden, about 5 minutes. Serve with a mixed green salad.

Yield: 6 to 8 servings

Beer-Braised Beef Shortribs

This dish is inspired by a popular Belgian recipe called carbonnade, in which beef is cooked in beer. Here we choose flavorful beef ribs in place of the traditional stew meat, although either may be used. Because beef ribs are high in fat, prepare this dish the day before you plan to serve it. When the cooked beef is chilled, the excess fat will float to the surface and solidify, making removal easy.

Preparation Time: 5 MINUTES
Cooking Time: ABOUT 2 HOURS AND 20 MINUTES

2½ pounds beef shortribs (about 5 ribs)
Salt and freshly ground black pepper to taste
¼ cup flour
4 ounces diced bacon (about 3 strips)
2 cups chopped onions (about 2 medium onions)
1 sprig fresh thyme (or ½ teaspoon dried thyme)
1 tablespoon Dijon-style mustard
12 ounces dark beer
1 tablespoon brown sugar
1 tablespoon vinegar

1. Season the ribs with salt and pepper then dredge them in the flour. Shake off excess flour from each piece of meat. Set aside.
2. Place the bacon in a heavy casserole large enough to hold the ribs. Cook the bacon over medium-high heat for 4 to 5 minutes, or until some of the fat is rendered. Remove the cooked bacon and set aside. Brown the ribs in the bacon fat, turning until they are darkened on all sides.
3. Remove the ribs, set them aside, and brown the onions in the fat (about 8 minutes).
4. Return the ribs and bacon to the pan and add all of the remaining ingredients. Cover the pot and simmer for 2 hours until the meat is tender. Check seasonings.
5. Serve the ribs with boiled egg noodles, crusty rolls, and mustard.

Yield: 4 to 5 servings

Stew's TIP

Why would I want to marinate meat in beer?

Beer is an excellent marinade for seafood or meat. Its effervescence and active enzymes are particularly effective when it comes to infusing flavor and tenderizing sinewy cuts of meat. Belgian cuisine is replete with dishes that use beer as an ingredient, including fresh mussels cooked in dark beer.

One of our cattle ranchers, "Johnny O," loves to cook his meat with beer. "It really brings out the flavor," he told us.

What is Prime beef?

The USDA has eight grades of beef but only 3 really matter: Prime, Choice, and Select. Prime meat accounts for only 2% of all graded beef and is considered the best. Prime beef has the most marbling (fat) throughout and is very tender and flavorful. Personally, I don't care for prime meat — it's too rich for me. I prefer choice, which comprises about 44% of all graded beef in the U.S. It has sufficient marbling to be tender and has the same great flavor as prime.

The next grade, Select, represents 27% of all graded beef. This has the least amount of marbling and may not be as tender or juicy as prime or choice. It can have excellent flavor, though, when braised or stewed — long cooking breaks down the tough fibers.

Roast Prime Rib with Natural Juices

Prime rib is an enormous seller at Stew's, especially around the holidays. Here is the classic recipe.

1 prime rib of beef (ask the butcher for the first three ribs), about 4 pounds
Salt and freshly ground black pepper to taste
4 cloves garlic, chopped
2 tablespoons olive oil
½ teaspoon fresh thyme (or ¼ teaspoon dried thyme)
1 tablespoon black peppercorns, crushed
2 tablespoons red wine
1 tablespoon salt
1 cup dry white wine
1 cup beef stock (homemade or canned — see recipe page 164)

1. With a sharp knife, trim the layer of fat on the top of the prime rib, exposing the bones underneath (clean the bones well).
2. In a bowl, combine all of the remaining ingredients except wine and beef stock. Whisk well.
3. Rub the mixture over all of the prime ribs. Refrigerate for at least 2 hours, or overnight.
4. Preheat the oven to 400 degrees.
5. Place a roasting pan in the oven until it gets very hot. Carefully open the oven, pull out the tray, and place the prime ribs on the hot tray. (The hot tray makes the bottom of the prime rib crispy.)
6. Roast for 25 minutes, then turn down the oven to 375 degrees (it is a good idea to check your oven's accuracy with an oven thermometer). Cook for 1 hour and 15 minutes (for medium rare). For medium, roast another 15 minutes.
7. When finished, remove the prime rib from the oven and transfer it to a platter. Pour off all of the remaining fat — but not the juices if possible — in the roasting pan.
8. Place the tray on the stovetop over medium-high setting. Pour the white wine and beef stock into the tray. Reduce the liquid by half. Taste for seasonings and strain the juices into a bowl.
9. Carve the prime rib, place it on warm serving plates, and pour the juices around the meat. If desired, garnish the plate with watercress.

Yield: Serves 6 to 8

Beef Brisket Braised in Beaujolais

Brisket of beef is a sinewy cut, but when it is marinated and braised for several hours, the fibers break down and you have a superbly flavorful meal. It's also inexpensive. This recipe calls for braising the brisket with a little fruity Beaujolais wine. You could use any red wine, however.

Preparation Time: 10 MINUTES
Cooking Time: ABOUT 4 HOURS AND 15 MINUTES

LOW FAT

PREPARE IN ADVANCE

4 pounds beef brisket, well trimmed and cut into 1½-inch cubes
Salt and freshly ground black pepper to taste
2 tablespoon vegetable oil
2 cups chopped onions
1 tablespoon chopped garlic
1 pound fresh mushrooms, trimmed and cleaned
4 sprigs fresh thyme or 1 teaspoon dried thyme
¼ cup all-purpose flour
4 cups Beaujolais wine (or other fruity red wine)
1 cup beef stock (see recipe page 164) or chicken stock (see recipe page 63)
1 bay leaf
2 cloves
2 whole allspice

1. Sprinkle the brisket of beef with salt and pepper. Heat a non-stick pan that is large enough to hold the meat in one layer. Add 1 tablespoon of the vegetable oil and the cubed beef and cook over medium heat, stirring, until well-browned on all sides — about 10 minutes.
2. Transfer the meat to a heavy cast-iron kettle (or any large kettle). Add the remaining tablespoon of oil, the onions, garlic, mushrooms, and thyme. Stir for about 5 minutes. Add the flour and blend well for 1 minute.
3. Add the wine, beef or chicken stock, bay leaf, cloves, and allspice. Blend well and bring to a simmer. Cook, covered, over low heat for 3½ to 4 hours, or until the meat is tender. Remove the bay leaf. Taste for seasonings. Serve with noodles or rice.

Yield: 8 servings

Stew's TIP

What's the best way to store meat?

We wrap our meat in plastic atop Styrofoam trays, as do most stores. This is also the best way to store it in your refrigerator — use two or three paper plates if you do not have Styrofoam. We do not recommend refrigerating meat for more than 3 days. Keep it in the coldest part of your refrigerator — usually the bottom shelf.

Stew's TIP

Pork has an undeserved image problem. Many health-conscious eaters assume that because some pork-based products are high in fat, like sausages, bacon, hot dogs and spareribs, they should avoid pork altogether.

In fact, well-trimmed pork cut from the tenderloin is less fatty than tenderloin of beef, and nearly as lean as skinless chicken breast. A 4-ounce portion of trimmed pork has 4.8 grams of fat, compared with 9.6 grams for beef tenderloin and 3.6 for chicken breast. The same portion of pork contains 166 calories, compared with 207 for beef and 165 for chicken.

The pork industry has been well aware of the public's perceptions. Over the years it has modified breeding and feeding techniques to produce increasingly lean animals. Pork is also recognized as an excellent source of B vitamins, iron, zinc and protein.

Roasted Pork Loin with Rosemary

The Mediterranean flavor of rosemary complements the rich taste of pork. In this dish, crisp browned onions flavor the pork roast and add to the color and intensity of its simple pan gravy.

Preparation Time: 15 MINUTES
Cooking Time: 1 HOUR AND 20 MINUTES

2 pounds boneless pork loin or shoulder roast
2 cloves garlic, sliced thinly
2 sprigs of fresh rosemary, coarsely chopped (or 1½ teaspoons dried)
Salt and freshly ground black pepper to taste
2 teaspoons flour
3 medium onions, thinly sliced
¼ cup dry white wine
1¼ cups water

1. Preheat the oven to 375 degrees.
2. Pierce the roast all over with a knife and insert the slivers of fresh garlic. Pat the pieces of fresh rosemary around the meat, or sprinkle it with dried rosemary. Season it with salt and pepper, and rub with flour.
3. Transfer the meat to a roasting rack or a baking sheet. Roast for 30 minutes. Remove it from the oven and add the onions to the bottom of the pan. Return the pork to the oven for about 25 minutes. When the roast is cooked — use a meat thermometer (160 degrees is medium) — remove it from the pan and place it on a serving platter. Cover the meat with aluminum foil and keep it in a warm place while preparing the gravy.
4. To make gravy, skim any excess fat from roasting pan. Place the pan over medium-high heat. Add the wine and water and scrape loose the cooked onions sticking to the bottom of the pan. Cook the sauce for about 5 minutes, stirring and letting it reduce to develop intensity. Adjust seasonings to taste. The browned onions should flavor and color the sauce. Add a pinch of rosemary for more flavor if you like.

Yield: 4 servings

At what temperature is pork safely cooked?

Cooks used to roast pork until it reached an internal temperature of 185 degrees to avoid trichinosis — at which point the meat was overcooked and dry. Scientists have since discovered that trichinae are killed at 138 degrees. So cooking pork to 150 degrees — medium rare — is just fine. Always use a meat thermometer to be sure. Place the thermometer at the thickest part of meat to get the most accurate temperature.

"The Guthmans' favorite"

German-Style Marinated Pork Cutlets

Schnitzel is the German word for cutlet. My mothers' family, the Guthmans, are from Germany and love this meal. Many Germans and Austrians would use veal for this dish. Cold cooked schnitzel is delicious in a picnic basket or in a sandwich with hot mustard.

Preparation Time: 15 MINUTES
Cooking Time: 30 MINUTES

SUPER FAST

PREPARE IN ADVANCE

½ teaspoon ground cardamom (optional)
¼ teaspoon ground coriander seeds
½ teaspoon chili powder
Salt and freshly ground black pepper to taste
1 tablespoon vegetable oil
1 pork tenderloin (about 2 pounds)
2 eggs, beaten
1 cup flour
2 cups fine breadcrumbs
¼ cup vegetable oil
1 lemon cut into 6 wedges

1. In a large bowl, combine the cardamom, coriander, chili powder, black pepper, salt, and oil. Set aside.
2. Cut the pork into 12 slices about ½ inch thick. Place a slice of pork between two pieces of waxed paper. Pound with a meat mallet or the bottom of a small pan until the cutlet is about 4 inches in diameter. Repeat with other slices.
3. Place the cutlets in the spice mixture and toss to coat evenly. (This can be done a day in advance.)
4. Place in separate bowls the beaten eggs, the flour and the breadcrumbs. One by one, dip the cutlets into the flour, then the egg, and finally the breadcrumbs. Place them on a baking sheet.
5. Heat the oil in a large pan over high setting. When the oil sizzles (3 to 4 minutes), sauté 2 or 3 cutlets at a time for about 2 minutes on each side, or until golden brown. Remove to a tray lined with paper towels. Cook remaining cutlets.
6. Place two or three cutlets on each plate and garnish with a wedge of fresh lemon and some Pear Chutney (see following recipe).

Yield: 4 to 6 servings

Stew's TIP

A succulent loin of pork is a cinch to make short notice. At Stew Leonard's we sell regular pork tenderloins (roughly 2 pounds) as well as preseasoned tenderloins coated with black pepper. If you buy a plain loin of pork (2 to 3 pounds), rub it with olive oil and generously season with salt and pepper. Place it on a rack and roast in a 400-degree oven for 20 minutes. Gently turn it. Roast for 15 minutes more. Check with a meat thermometer.

Is it safe to eat a very rare hamburger?

Dr. Shams Alam, Stew's Quality Director, says emphatically "Don't do it!" E. coli and salmonella are killed at 160 degrees. The most common breeding ground for E. coli is ground beef. If there is E. coli present, the bacteria get mixed throughout the meat during the grinding process. If you cook a hamburger rare or even medium rare, you can't be assured that you have killed all the bacteria. I always cook my hamburgers medium or medium well just to be on the safe side.

Pear Chutney

This sweet chutney is also great with sandwiches, hamburgers, and grilled meats.

Preparation Time: 10 MINUTES
Cooking Time: 25 MINUTES

2 ripe pears
1 cup thinly sliced onion (about 1 large onion)
2 tablespoons minced fresh ginger
½ teaspoon red-pepper flakes
½ cup vinegar
½ cup brown sugar
¼ teaspoon ground cumin
½ teaspoon turmeric powder

1. Peel the pears, quarter them lengthwise, remove and discard cores. Cut the pear strips into 1-inch cubes.
2. Combine the remaining ingredients in a small pot and bring to a boil, stirring to dissolve the sugar. Add the pears, cover, and simmer for 20 minutes until pears begin to soften.
3. Serve warm with Marinated Pork Cutlets (see recipe page 155) or chilled with sandwiches. Homemade chutney will last for several months if covered tightly and refrigerated.

Yield: 2½ cups

The Basics of Food Safety

Dr. Shams Alam operates a USDA-certified food testing laboratory at Stew Leonard's. He also teaches more than 1,000 of Stew's employees the basics of food safety and hygiene. Here are some tips to keep you and your family healthy.

- **Never defrost meat, fish or poultry at room temperature!** Harmful bacteria grow between 40°F and 140°F. When meat is within that range for an extended period there is a risk of E. coli or salmonella growth. Therefore, if you defrost your meat in the refrigerator, you never enter the danger zone because your refrigerator is under 40 degrees F.
- **Before you cook, wash your hands with soap and hot water!** It is a little-known fact that most bacteria originate in your hair and fingernails. Wash your hands well and cover your hair to prevent hair from falling in your food.
- **Use clean equipment and utensils** — Wash your knives and cutting boards with soap and hot water after every use.
- **Don't cross contaminate** — If you have a raw product on a plate or pan, wash it before you reuse it again. Many people bring raw food to the grill, cook it, and use the same plate for the cooked product. You just exposed yourself, your family or guests to potential growth of E. coli or salmonella in your food and related sickness.
- **Get Your Food Cold Again!** When you're done eating, get your food back into the refrigerator or freezer quickly. Don't leave it in that danger zone (40-140)!

Ground-Pork-and-Garlic Stuffing

Preparation Time: 15 MINUTES
Cooking Time: 15 MINUTES

PREPARE IN ADVANCE

½ pound fresh spinach, tough stems removed
½ pound ground pork
1½ cups chopped onions (about 3 medium onions)
2 teaspoons finely chopped garlic
¼ pound fresh mushrooms of choice, finely chopped (about 1¾ cups)
2 sprigs fresh thyme, finely chopped, or 1 teaspoon dried thyme
1 cup fresh breadcrumbs
2 eggs, lightly beaten
Salt and freshly ground black pepper to taste

To assemble:

1. Clean and rinse the spinach well, but do not dry. Place in a saucepan. Cover and cook over high heat for 30 seconds, until wilted. Drain well. When the spinach is cool enough to handle, squeeze it to extract excess moisture. Chop and set aside.
2. Place the pork in a pan and add the onions and garlic. Cook, stirring, for about three minutes over medium heat. Add the mushrooms, thyme and bay leaf. Cook, stirring occasionally, for about 10 minutes. Add the chopped spinach and stir to blend well. Remove from the heat. Stir in the breadcrumbs and add the beaten eggs, salt and pepper. Stir and let cool. Stuff into the veal shoulder cavity.

Yield: 8 servings

Stew's TIP

Veal shoulder has a shape that is well-suited to stuffing. You might try this terrific stuffing of pork and spinach, which was given to us by the late Pierre Franey. It is plenty for a 5-pound roast.

Dr. Shams Alam, Stew's Quality Director, in his USDA certified lab.

Chilies Rellenos with Sausage

In Mexico, hot or sweet chilies are stuffed with a creamy cheese, battered, and deep-fried. Rellenos means stuffed. In this recipe a spicy stuffing of hot peppers and sausage makes the chilies a substantial main dish or the bracing first course of a Mexican dinner.

Preparation Time: 15 MINUTES
Cooking Time: ABOUT 1 HOUR

PREPARE IN ADVANCE

6 Anaheim chilies (a long, green, mild chili) or 6 sweet green peppers (see chili information page 267)
1 tablespoon vegetable oil
½ cup minced onion (about 1 small onion)
½ cup minced celery (about 1 stalk)
1 fresh or canned jalapeño pepper, seeded and minced
½ pound hot Italian sausage, its casing removed
¾ cup fresh prepared breadcrumbs soaked in ¼ cup milk (or 1 cup mashed potatoes)
1 cup grated Pepper Monterey Jack cheese, or regular Monterey Jack

1. Preheat oven to 375 degrees.
2. To prepare the chilies or peppers for stuffing, cut off the tops ½ inch from the stem. Set the tops aside. Remove the seeds. If using the green peppers, blanch them for 5 minutes in 3 quarts of salted boiling water. Drain the peppers and set aside.
3. Heat the oil in a pan. Add the onions, celery, jalapeño peppers, and cook over medium heat until soft — 8 to 10 minutes. Add the sausage, breaking it into small pieces with a fork, and cook thoroughly, about 6 minutes. Drain excess fat.
4. Blend the soaked breadcrumbs or mashed potato into the sausage mixture and stuff the peppers with it. Replace the pepper tops, securing each one with a toothpick.
5. Place the peppers on a greased baking tray and bake for 35 to 40 minutes, until lightly browned. If desired, sprinkle peppers with shredded Monterey Jack cheese and return to the oven for 5 minutes or until the cheese melts.
6. Serve one pepper per person as an appetizer or side dish, or two per person as a main course.

Yield: 4 to 6 stuffed peppers

Stew's TIP

One of the best sellers at our barbecue take-out counter is chilies stuffed with cream cheese, cheddar cheese, and herbs. In this recipe goat cheese melts beautifully and the herbs — fresh or dried — lend an aromatic edge. Experiment with all kinds of cheeses, along with minced vegetables and seasonings of your choice.

Fresh Baked Ham with Herb Gravy

This simple ham is a great dish for the holidays or parties. Serve it with potatoes and Braised Winter Vegetables (see recipe page 262). A great accompaniment is Gina's Blue-Ribbon Herbed Biscuits (see recipe page 160).

Preparation Time: 15 MINUTES (plus 4 hours marination)
Cooking Time: ABOUT 3 HOURS

PREPARE IN ADVANCE

The ham:
1 9-pound ham shoulder or a 6- to 8-pound boneless ham
1 cup carrots, coarsely chopped (about 3 medium carrots)
1 cup celery, coarsely chopped (about 2 stalks)
1 cup onion, coarsely chopped (about 1 medium onion)
12 cloves

The glaze:
½ cup sugar
1 teaspoon molasses
2 tablespoons vinegar
1 tablespoon grated orange zest (about 1 small orange)
1 teaspoon dry mustard
¼ cup Dijon-style mustard
½ cup water

1. In a large container, cover the ham with cold water and set in a cool place for at least 4 hours, or overnight.
2. Discard the water. Place the ham in a large kettle, cover with fresh cold water, and add carrots, celery, and onion. Bring to a boil over high heat, then reduce the heat and simmer gently for 3 hours.
3. Blend all glaze ingredients in a small bowl.
4. Preheat oven to 350 degrees.
5. Remove the ham from the pot (reserving liquid) and allow it to drain for a few minutes, then place it on a baking sheet. Spread the glaze over the ham. Using a sharp knife, score the surface fat, and stud it with the cloves. Bake for 30 minutes until top is bubbling and brown.
6. Serve the ham thinly sliced with Herb Gravy (see accompanying recipe) and coarse country mustard.

Yield: 12 servings

Herb Gravy

Preparation Time:
5 MINUTES
Cooking Time:
ABOUT 25 MINUTES

4 cups ham cooking liquid
2 cups beef broth
½ cup sweet red wine or sweet sherry
1 teaspoon dried tarragon
Salt and freshly ground black pepper to taste
1 tablespoon cornstarch dissolved in 2 tablespoons cold water

1. Place the cooking liquid, broth, and wine in a saucepan over high heat. Boil for 10 to 12 minutes or until reduced by one quarter. Add the tarragon, lower heat, and simmer for 10 minutes. Add the seasonings to taste.
2. Stir the cornstarch mixture into the gravy. Return to a boil and cook for about 2 minutes until slightly thickened.

Yield: 3½ to 4 cups

Gina's Blue-Ribbon Herbed Biscuits

Our friend Gina Fox of Rhinebeck, New York, won a blue ribbon at the Dutchess County Fair for these addictive country biscuits. Stew Leonard's carries all of the fresh herbs you need to season them.

Preparation Time: 15 MINUTES
Cooking Time: ABOUT 15 MINUTES

PREPARE IN ADVANCE

2 cups all-purpose flour
½ teaspoon salt
4 teaspoons baking powder
1 tablespoon sugar
½ cup chopped fresh herbs (mixture of rosemary, basil, sage, and mint), chopped
½ cup (1 stick) butter, cut in four pieces
⅔ cup half-and-half (or maybe a little more) for brushing the tops of the biscuits

1. Preheat the oven to 425 degrees.
2. In a bowl, blend the flour, salt, baking powder, and sugar. Mix in the chopped herbs.
3. In the bowl of a food processor with the metal blade (or by hand) mix the dry ingredients with the butter until the mixture resembles coarse corn meal. Gradually add the milk and mix until the dough forms a ball.
4. On a flat, lightly floured surface, knead the dough about a dozen times. Roll out the dough to a circle ½ inch thick.
5. Using a 2- or 3-inch cookie cutter (or drinking glass), cut out the biscuit shapes by pressing straight down on the dough (not in a rotation manner). You will have between 12 and 18 biscuits, depending on the size of your dough balls.
6. Place the biscuit rounds on a greased cookie sheet and bake for 12 to 15 minutes or until golden brown.

Yield: 12 to 18 biscuits

Smoked Ham with Pineapple Glaze

Stew Leonard's sells delicious smoked hams in various sizes. You could also make this recipe with a cooked ham. Count on 2 pounds feeding six.

Preparation Time: 5 MINUTES (plus 24 hours marination)
Cooking Time: 45 MINUTES

PREPARE IN ADVANCE

3/4 cup brown sugar
3/4 cup ketchup
3/4 cup Dijon-style mustard
3/4 cup diced fresh (or canned) pineapple
1/2 teaspoon ground cloves
3/4 cup honey
1 3-pound smoked ham (or cooked not smoked)

1. Combine all ingredients except the ham in a blender and purée well.
2. Trim all fat from the ham. Place the ham in a baking dish. Brush the marinade all over the ham. Reserve unused marinade. Cover the ham and refrigerate for 24 hours.
3. Preheat the oven to 345 degrees. Bake the ham for 45 minutes, brushing it with the marinade every 15 minutes. Serve with Mashed Potatoes and Parsnips (see recipe page 243) and Sautéed Beet Greens with Oyster Mushrooms (see recipe page 261).

Yield: Serves about 8

Here's a spiral-cut ham with pineapple glaze, a big seller in our catering department.

Easter Dinner

Asparagus Salad (see recipe page 90)

Baked Ham with Herb Gravy (see recipe page 159)
or **Poached Salmon with Dill** (see recipe page 218)

Mashed Potatoes and Parsnips (see recipe page 243)
Glazed Carrots with Sugar Snap Peas (see recipe page 269)

Strawberries with Balsamic Vinegar (see recipe page 320)
or **Crème Brûlée** (see recipe page 323)
or **Jill's Terrific Chocolate Cake** (see recipe page 312)
or **Aunt Helen Clark's Lemon Pie** (see recipe page 335)

Roasted Shoulder of Veal with Wild-Mushroom Sauce

Veal shoulder is a much-neglected cut of meat, which is too bad, for it is sublimely flavorful, moist and texturally pleasing. It is also less expensive than most other cuts of veal.

Ask the butcher at Stew's if you do not see it in the display case.

Preparation Time: 10 MINUTES
Cooking Time: ABOUT 1 AND ONE HALF HOURS

3-pound veal shoulder roast, or loin of veal
Salt and freshly ground black pepper to taste
1 tablespoon butter
½ teaspoon garlic
8 ounces sliced Portobello mushrooms, stems trimmed and sliced (3 to 4 mushrooms)
½ cup white wine
1 cup chicken stock or water
1 teaspoon cornstarch dissolved in 3 teaspoons water

1. Preheat the oven to 350 degrees.
2. Season the veal with salt and pepper.
3. Place veal in a large, lightly oiled pan over a high setting and brown until golden on all sides. Place the veal in a roasting pan. Roast it in the oven for 45 minutes to 1 hour, or until the internal temperature reaches 130 degrees. (Count on 25 minutes per pound.)
4. While the veal is roasting, melt the butter or margarine in a pan over medium heat, and cook the garlic and the mushrooms until tender, 6 to 8 minutes. Add salt and pepper to taste.
5. Remove the veal from oven to a platter and cover with aluminum foil to keep warm. Place the roasting pan over high heat on top of the stove. Add the white wine, chicken stock and scrape to loosen any particles stuck to bottom of the pan. Cook for 3 minutes, stirring occasionally, and add the mushrooms.
6. Simmer mixture over medium heat for a few minutes. Adjust seasonings to taste, then add the cornstarch mixture, stirring constantly. Boil for 2 minutes until slightly thickened.
7. Cut the veal into ½-inch-thick slices. Spoon some mushroom sauce over each portion. Accompany with Mashed Potatoes with Chives (see recipe page 242) or Chef George's Unbelievable Potato Pancakes (see recipe page 248).

Yield: 8 servings

Sautéed Veal Chops with Herb Vinegar Glaze

Veal chops are a delicate and tasty cut of meat. We like to cook them very simply, with just a light sauce so the subtle flavor of the meat comes through.

Preparation Time: 10 MINUTES
Cooking Time: 30 MINUTES

4 loin center cut veal chops, about 8 ounces each
Salt and freshly ground black pepper to taste
1/4 cup flour for dredging
4 tablespoons butter
4 bay leaves
4 whole cloves garlic, peeled
4 sprigs fresh thyme or 1 teaspoon dried thyme
2 tablespoons red wine vinegar
3/4 cup fresh or canned chicken broth

1. Sprinkle the chops with salt and pepper. Place the flour on a flat dish. Dredge each chop in the flour, shaking off the excess.
2. Heat 2 tablespoons of butter in a heavy pan over medium-high setting and add the chops. Brown them 5 minutes per side.
3. Add to the pan the bay leaves, garlic, and thyme. Cook about 3 minutes, shaking the pan. Pour the vinegar around the chops and cook until half reduced. Add the broth, cover tightly and simmer 15 to 20 minutes or until tender. Remove the chops to warm plates.
4. Increase the heat to high. Swirl in the remaining butter and remove the bay leaves. Serve with the sauce, garnish with garlic and thyme.

Yield: 4 servings

What about freezing meat?

There's nothing wrong with freezing meat. Don Stevenson, one of our suppliers who lives in Kansas and grew up around cattle, frequently freezes his meat for up to 6 months. I don't recommend this for most people. My home freezer is designed to maintain a very low temperature — it has to, because I have four kids opening it all the time to grab ice cream and popsicles. I don't like to freeze meat for more than 2 months. If it gets "freezer burn" (from slight thawing and refreezing) it will lose taste and tenderness.

If you freeze meat, wrap it in airtight ziplock freezer bags. Also, don't forget to date it!

What is the best way to defrost meat?

Always defrost meat in the refrigerator. If you defrost at room temperature the ice crystals on the meat penetrate the surface, making it mushy. In the refrigerator, slow thawing avoids this.

As I mentioned earlier, there is also a health element in defrosting. The bacteria danger zone for meat is 40 degrees to 140 degrees. When meat is within that range for an extended period there is a risk of E. coli or salmonella contamination. Therefore, if you defrost your meat in the refrigerator, you never enter the danger zone because your refrigerator is between 32 and 36 degrees.

Homemade Veal Stock

Veal stock (or beef stock) is one of the most important parts of the cooking repertory. Yes, it takes some time, but you can make a big batch and freeze it. A good stock is the foundation of so many fabulous sauces, soups, and stews. In a pinch you can use canned stock, but keep in mind that it is often salty.

Preparation Time: 10 MINUTES
Cooking Time: ABOUT 4½ HOURS

PREPARE IN ADVANCE

3 pounds veal bones, sawed in half (ask the supermarket butcher to do it)
2 unpeeled onions, quartered
2 carrots, chopped
2 ribs celery, chopped
4 unpeeled garlic cloves
½ cup flour
1 tablespoon tomato paste
6 parsley sprigs
1 teaspoon salt
½ teaspoon dried thyme
1 bay leaf
10 black peppercorns
14 cups water

1. Preheat the oven to 400 degrees.
2. Spread the veal bones on a baking sheet and roast them for 25 to 35 minutes, or until browned. Add to the baking sheet the onions, carrots, celery, and garlic. Roast for another 40 minutes.
3. Sprinkle the flour over everything and stir to distribute it. Add the tomato paste and stir. Scrape everything into a large pot (16 cups or more). Add the parsley, salt, thyme, black peppercorns, and bay leaf.
4. Add the water to the pot. Bring to a boil, skimming any froth that accumulates on top. Reduce the heat and simmer gently for 4 hours. Strain the stock well and let it cool. Refrigerate for several hours. Skim the fat that forms on the surface.

Note: This stock freezes well — in freezer bags, ice cube trays, or plastic containers.

Lamb Burgers with Feta Cheese

Lean ground lamb is an excellent alternative to ground beef and, to our taste, even better — of course you could use either. This recipe has a haunting Middle Eastern flavor from the cumin and rosemary. The crumbled feta cheese adds a tart, fresh touch. You could also use an aged goat cheese. This recipe was kindly provided by our dear friend, the late Pierre Franey of *The New York Times.*

Preparation Time: 10 MINUTES
Cooking Time: 15 MINUTES

SUPER FAST

1½ pounds ground lean lamb
Salt and freshly ground black pepper to taste
¼ teaspoon ground cumin
¼ teaspoon red pepper flakes
2 teaspoons finely chopped fresh rosemary leaves, or 1 teaspoon dried rosemary
¾ cup crumbled feta cheese
4 teaspoons finely chopped parsley

1. Divide the lamb into 8 portions of equal size. Shape each into a patty and season both sides with salt and pepper.
2. Sprinkle the top of each patty with an equal amount of cumin, pepper flakes, and rosemary. Pat to help the herb and spices adhere.
3. The patties may be broiled or cooked in a pan. If broiled, preheat the broiler. Place the patties on a baking sheet about 3 inches from the heat. Broil 2 to 4 minutes on one side for rare (depending on thickness), 5 minutes or more for well done. Turn the patties and cook 1 minute for rare, 2 minutes for well done.
4. If the patties are cooked in a pan, select one large enough to hold them in one layer. Brush the pan with a little oil and place over medium-high heat. Cook the patties for 3 minutes for rare, 5 minutes for well done. Turn the patties and continue cooking 1 minute for rare, 2 minutes for well done. Check for doneness.
5. Top each patty with a portion of crumbled feta cheese. Place under the broiler about 3 inches from the heat and cook until the cheese melts slightly.

Yield: 8 servings

Here are some master cheese makers we met during a trip to Wisconsin.

Pierre Franey's Lamb Curry

This vibrant recipe calls for diced apples and bananas cooked with onion, celery, garlic, and curry powder. The degree of hotness varies with the amount of curry powder added. A good curry powder is essential to achieve the complexity of flavors desired. Fortunately for us, Pierre Franey shared his recipe for homemade curry (see recipe page 231). The apples and bananas in the dish counterbalance the heat.

Preparation Time: 15 MINUTES
Cooking Time: ABOUT 20 MINUTES

PREPARE IN ADVANCE

1 loin of lamb, boned and trimmed of fat (about 3 pounds)
½ cup raisins
3 tablespoons butter
½ finely chopped onion
¼ cup diced chopped celery (½ stalk)
¾ cup diced apple (1 apple)
½ cup diced banana (1 banana)
1 teaspoon minced garlic
2 to 3 tablespoons curry powder, homemade or commercial (see recipe page 231)
½ cup crushed Italian tomatoes
1 cup fresh or canned chicken broth
Turmeric rice (see recipe page 167)

1. Place the loin of lamb on a flat surface and cut it diagonally into ¼-inch-thick slices. Cut the slices into large chunks.
2. Soak the raisins in warm water for about 30 minutes.
3. Heat 2 tablespoons of butter in a pan and add the onion. Cook, stirring, until wilted. Add the celery, apple, banana, garlic and curry powder. Cook briefly and add the tomatoes. Add the broth. Stir. Bring to a boil and simmer for 10 minutes. Pour and scrape the mixture into a food processor or blender. Blend until smooth. There should be about 2 cups.
4. Return the sauce to the pan and reheat. Drain the raisins and add them to the pan.
5. Heat the remaining tablespoon of butter in a pan and, when it is quite hot and starting to brown, add the meat. Cook over high heat, stirring constantly to separate the pieces and cook them evenly. Cook about 2 minutes per side, or just until the center is medium rare. Add the meat to the simmering sauce and remove from the heat. Do not let the meat cook in the sauce. Serve it immediately, with rice.

Yield: 4 servings

Turmeric Rice with the Lamb Curry

Turmeric is related to ginger, although its somewhat bitter and pungent flavor makes it different. In Indian cuisine it is used both to flavor foods and to color them — it turns rice yellow-orange. Used sparingly, it adds a compelling sharp edge to dishes.

Preparation Time: 5 MINUTES
Cooking Time: ABOUT 20 MINUTES

LOW FAT · SUPER FAST

2 tablespoons butter
2 tablespoons finely chopped onion
½ teaspoon minced garlic
1 cup converted rice
1 tablespoon turmeric
1½ cups fresh or canned chicken broth
1 bay leaf
2 sprigs fresh thyme or ½ teaspoon dried thyme
Salt and freshly ground black pepper to taste

1. Melt 1 tablespoon of butter in a saucepan and add the onion and garlic. Cook until the onion is wilted. Add the rice and turmeric. Stir to coat.
2. Add the broth, bay leaf, thyme, salt, and pepper. Cover and bring to a boil. Reduce to a simmer and cook for 17 minutes, covered. Uncover and stir in the remaining butter. Toss gently to blend well. Remove bay leaf and serve.

Yield: 4 servings

Stew's TIP

Like an aging prize-fighter, dried spices eventually lose their punch. Most last about one year in the cupboard. Keep them in a relatively cool place, tightly capped.

Christmas Dinner

Orange-Marinated Mushrooms (see recipe page 35)
or **Smoked-Salmon-and-Melted-Brie Wheel** (see recipe page 41)

Pepper-Coated Filet Mignon (see recipe page 140)
or **Roasted Shoulder of Veal with Wild Mushroom Sauce** (see recipe page 162)
or **Roast Prime Rib with Natural Juices** (see recipe page 152)

Mixed Green Salad with Lemon-Garlic Dressing (see recipe page 75)
Jean-Louis Gerin's Creamy Potatoes Gratin (see recipe page 247)
Simmered Red Cabbage with Apples (see recipe page 263)
Moroccan Carrots (see recipe page 254)

Jill's Terrific Chocolate Cake (see recipe page 312)
or **Pears in Spiced Red Wine** (see recipe page 316)
or **Chocolate Mousse** (see recipe page 322)

Broiled (or Grilled) Marinated Leg of Lamb

Leg of lamb is ideal for broiling or outdoor grilling. Ask the butcher to butterfly the leg, which means removing the center bone and joint, and then making an incision down the middle so it lays flat on the grill.

Preparation Time: 15 MINUTES
Cooking Time: 30 MINUTES

LOW FAT

1 4-pound boneless butterflied leg of lamb
1 tablespoon chopped garlic (about 3 cloves)
1 tablespoon chopped fresh ginger
½ teaspoon freshly ground black pepper to taste
1 teaspoon coarse mustard with seeds
¼ cup chopped parsley
2 tablespoons olive oil
Salt and freshly ground black pepper to taste

1. Trim any fat that remains on the surface of the lamb. Place the lamb on a large platter or in a 9 x 13-inch casserole. Combine in a bowl the garlic, ginger, pepper, mustard, parsley, and oil. Massage these ingredients into the surface of the lamb. Cover the lamb with plastic wrap and let it sit for 6 to 24 hours in the refrigerator.
2. Preheat a broiler or outdoor grill. Sprinkle the lamb with salt and pepper then place it on the heated grill or on a tray under the broiler. Cook the lamb for about 15 minutes on one side. Turn the lamb then continue cooking it for another 15 minutes. (Always check for doneness by making an incision in a thick part of the lamb — timing may vary due to the thickness of the lamb and intensity of the heat.)
3. Remove the lamb from the heat. Place it on a platter and cover it loosely with aluminum foil. Let the lamb rest in a warm place for 15 minutes before slicing.
4. Carve the lamb on an angle into ⅛-inch-thick slices. To reheat, if necessary, place the tray of sliced lamb, covered, in a warm oven for 5 minutes. Serve the lamb with some of its pan juices, fresh chopped parsley, and hot mustard. Mashed Potatoes and Parsnips (see recipe page 243) are a nice accompaniment.

Yield: 8 servings

Lamb Chops Provençal

Few other styles of cooking are more popular today than Provençal — and more misunderstood. For a dish to be Provençal, it should harmoniously combine some of the indigenous herbs of the south of France — particularly rosemary, basil, sage, thyme, fennel and oregano. Of course, garlic and tomato are essential. Olives are common as well.

On those counts, the lamb dish below is certainly authentic. The chops are cooked quickly in a hot skillet, preferably cast iron, and when they are done a quick sauce is made in the same pan. This is done simply by adding the garlic, onions, vinegar, tomatoes, black and green olives, and seasoning. Provençal cooking is more sensory than calculated, so you must taste for seasonings periodically — and always before serving.

Preparation Time: 10 MINUTES
Cooking Time: ABOUT 15 MINUTES

SUPER FAST

4 lamb chops, most of the fat removed (about ½ pound each)
Salt and freshly ground black pepper to taste
1 tablespoon olive oil
2 teaspoons chopped fresh rosemary or 1 teaspoon dried rosemary
4 sprigs fresh thyme or 1 teaspoon dried thyme
4 tablespoons chopped onion
2 teaspoons finely chopped garlic
1 tablespoon red wine vinegar
2 cups fresh tomatoes, cored, peeled, and cut into ½-inch cubes
1 bay leaf
½ cup pitted black olives
4 tablespoons chopped fresh basil or parsley

1. Sprinkle the chops with salt and pepper.
2. Heat the oil in a large heavy skillet, preferably cast iron. Add the lamb chops (in batches if you need to). Cook until brown on one side, about 5 minutes. Turn and sprinkle with rosemary and thyme. Cook 5 minutes more for rare, longer for medium-rare or well-done. Remove the chops to a warm platter.
3. Pour off most of the fat from the skillet and add the onion and garlic. Cook and stir until wilted. Add the vinegar, tomatoes, bay leaf, black olives, salt, and pepper. Cook, stir, and simmer for 5 minutes. Add any juices that have accumulated around the lamb chops.
4. Remove the bay leaf. Taste for seasonings. Pour the mixture over the lamb chops and garnish with basil.

Yield: 4 servings

Poultry

Every day in the store around 4 p.m. we see customers scrambling around trying to decide what to make for dinner. One of the most popular items is chicken breasts, which can be prepared quickly at home. In this chapter we help out those last-minute cooks by offering plenty of fast, tasty options for both chicken breasts and turkey breasts. Also, look for our fantastic recipes for Roasted Lemon-Garlic Chicken and the Holiday Roasted Turkey with Mushroom Gravy and Cranberry-Orange Relish.

Stew's TIP

To get the most juice out of a lemon, place it in your microwave for 30 seconds (on high) or in your oven at 350 degrees for 5 minutes. The lemon should be just warm to the touch. Cut it in half and squeeze it. Another technique is to place the lemon on a counter and press it while rolling it back and forth.

Bryan Rupp and his wife, Abbe, and daughter Charlotte.

"Malibu" Lemon-Apricot Chicken

This is a sensational dish that a friend of mine, Byron Rupp, loved to make when he lived in Malibu, California. This dish makes its own sauce during the long baking. It is just as tasty served cold the next day or in a picnic basket with many of the salads described in Chapter 4.

Preparation Time: 10 MINUTES (plus 12 hours marination)
Cooking Time: 50 MINUTES

LOW FAT · PREPARE IN ADVANCE

1 teaspoon grated lemon zest
½ cup lemon juice (about 2 lemons)
1 cup minced onion (about 1 medium onion)
1 teaspoon mustard seeds or Dijon-style mustard
1 tablespoon olive oil
2 teaspoons minced garlic (about 3 cloves)
½ cup dried apricots, sliced thinly
3 pounds of chicken breasts, legs and thighs
Salt and freshly ground black pepper to taste
2 tablespoons chopped fresh cilantro or parsley

1. In a large ceramic or glass bowl combine the lemon zest, lemon juice, onion, mustard seeds, olive oil, garlic, and apricot pieces. Toss the chicken pieces in the marinade and coat them well. Cover the bowl with plastic wrap and refrigerate for at least 1 hour (12 hours maximum).
2. Preheat the oven to 375 degrees.
3. Remove the chicken fillets from the marinade and place them in an ovenproof casserole. Spoon the onions and ½ cup of the marinade over the chicken. Tuck the apricot pieces between the chicken parts.
4. Place the casserole on the center rack of an oven and roast for 30 minutes. Baste with a few tablespoons of the remaining marinade and cook for another 15 to 20 minutes, until the chicken is golden brown and tender.
5. Sprinkle with the chopped cilantro or parsley. Serve with Orzo (see recipe page 290) or Curried Rice Pilaf with Almonds (see recipe page 305).

Yield: 4 servings

Roasted Lemon-Garlic Chicken

This is a tried and true recipe that yields a moist, evenly cooked bird every time.

Preparation Time: 15 MINUTES
Cooking Time: 1 HOUR AND 15 MINUTES

LOW FAT

1 chicken, 4 to $4\frac{1}{2}$ pounds, with giblets
1 lemon, halved
Salt and freshly ground black pepper to taste
2 sprigs fresh thyme (or $\frac{1}{2}$ teaspoon dried)
1 clove garlic
2 tablespoons olive oil
1 medium onion, peeled and quartered
2 tablespoons butter
$\frac{1}{2}$ cup chicken stock
$\frac{1}{2}$ cup water, or more as necessary

1. Preheat the oven to 425 degrees. Remove the giblets from the chicken's cavity; rinse them and reserve. Rinse the chicken under cold running water, inside and out, and pat dry with paper towels.
2. Sprinkle the chicken inside and out with salt and pepper. Insert the lemon, thyme, and garlic into the cavity of the chicken. Rub the outside of the chicken with the olive oil.
3. Place the chicken on its side in a shallow metal roasting pan. Scatter the neck, gizzard, liver, and onions on the bottom of the pan.
4. Place the chicken in the oven and roast for 25 minutes. Using large forks or tongs, gently turn the chicken onto its other side, being careful not to pierce the skin. Roast for another 25 minutes, basting once with the pan juices.
5. Carefully remove the roasting pan from the oven and close the oven door. Using a large spoon, skim any surface fat from the roasting pan juices. Turn the chicken on its back. Add the butter, chicken stock, and $\frac{1}{2}$ cup of water to the pan. Roast for another 25 minutes, basting with the pan juices. Take the chicken out of the oven and slice it at the point where the thigh meets the body — the juices should run clear. If the juices are pink, return the chicken to the oven. When cooked, lift up the chicken and let the cavity juices flow into the pan. Transfer the chicken to a carving board or serving platter and let it rest for 10 minutes.
6. Meanwhile, place the roasting pan on top of the stove. Remove and discard any burned pieces of giblets or onion. Add the water or broth if necessary to make about 1 cup liquid. Bring to a boil and reduce for 1 to 2 minutes. Stir and scrape the bottom of the pan. If desired, add fresh parsley, rosemary, tarragon, or other fresh herbs to taste. (If your roasting pan is too shallow to hold this liquid, scrape the bottom of the pan and transfer the contents to a saucepan.) Turn off the heat when the sauce is reduced to about $\frac{3}{4}$ cup. Taste the gravy for seasonings. Discard the lemon and thyme sprigs.
7. Carve the chicken into serving pieces (see instructions on carving a chicken page 189) and serve with the hot pan juices.

Yield: Serves 4

Stew's TIP

Instant Soup

If you have vegetable stock in the freezer you can make all kinds of great soups. For example, slice some carrots, chop some kale, chop a few stalks of celery and add all to the pot. Toss in egg noodles and simmer until the vegetables are tender.

Homemade Vegetable Stock

Vegetable stock can be used in many dishes instead of chicken stock or veal stock.

Preparation Time: 5 MINUTES
Cooking Time: 90 MINUTES

LOW FAT

PREPARE IN ADVANCE

1 small bunch parsley, rinsed
10 black peppercorns
5 sprigs of fresh thyme (or ½ teaspoon dried thyme)
1 bay leaf
Dash of cayenne
10 cups water
1 bottle dry white wine
5 carrots, scraped and cut into 2-inch pieces
2 medium onions, peeled, each pierced with a clove
2 leeks, split lengthwise down the middle, rinsed, and coarsely chopped (including green parts)

1. Tie the parsley, peppercorns, thyme, bay leaf, and cayenne in a sheet of cheesecloth or a patch of white cotton.
2. Combine with all of the remaining ingredients in a stockpot or other large pot and bring to a boil. Reduce the heat and simmer, uncovered, for 1½ hours, stirring occasionally and skimming the foam off the surface with a slotted spoon.
3. Strain the stock through a colander or sieve placed over a large bowl. Let cool. Discard the solids. Freeze the leftover stock in ice cube trays.

Yield: 9 to 10 cups

Southern Creole Chicken Breasts

Preparation Time: 20 MINUTES
Cooking Time: ABOUT 30 MINUTES

LOW FAT

PREPARE IN ADVANCE

2 skinless, boneless chicken breasts, halved (so you have 4 fillets)
1 tablespoon olive oil
¾ cup sliced onion
¾ cup cored, seeded, and julienned green peppers
¾ cup sliced celery
1 tablespoon finely chopped garlic
1 bay leaf
1 tablespoon paprika
1 cup peeled, diced tomatoes (or 1 cup canned, crushed tomatoes)
Salt and freshly ground black pepper to taste
1 teaspoon Worcestershire Sauce
1 teaspoon hot pepper sauce (like Tabasco)
1 tablespoon butter
1 tablespoon red wine vinegar
4 tablespoons water or chicken broth
4 tablespoons chopped parsley

1. Place half a chicken breast (one fillet) between sheets of plastic wrap. Using a mallet or the bottom of a heavy pan, pound it lightly to a thickness of ¼ inch. Repeat with the remaining fillets.
2. Heat the olive oil in a large pan over medium-high setting. Add the onions, green peppers, and celery. Cook until the onions are transparent and the celery is soft. Add the garlic. Stir for 2 minutes. Add the bay leaf, paprika, tomatoes, salt and pepper to taste. Stir well. Continue cooking for 4 to 5 minutes.
3. Add the Worcestershire Sauce and the hot pepper sauce. Simmer until the sauce reduces a little, about 5 minutes. Set aside.
4. Meanwhile, sprinkle the chicken with salt and pepper. Heat the butter in a large pan — or two smaller ones — over medium setting. Sauté the chicken breasts until golden on one side, about 4 minutes. Turn the chicken pieces and cook for 4 to 5 more minutes, or until the meat is just white in the center. Be careful not to overcook. Remove the chicken to a warm spot. Save any the butter left in the pan.
5. Add the vinegar to the sauce, along with the water or chicken broth, and cover. Bring to a boil and simmer for 4 minutes. Remove the bay leaf.
6. To serve, divide the Creole sauce among 4 serving plates. Place the chicken breasts over the sauce and pour any hot butter from the pan over them. Garnish with parsley.

Yield: 4 servings

Stew's TIP

One of the biggest sellers at Stew Leonard's is our prepared lemon-pepper chicken breast, which can be sautéed and served with a quick chicken broth sauce. After you have taken the cooked chicken breasts out of the pan and put them aside in a warm spot, add to the pan ¾ chicken broth (see chicken broth recipe page 63), a little chopped fresh thyme (or dried thyme), and a squeeze of lemon juice. Reduce to half volume; season with salt and pepper, and swirl in a tablespoon of butter — as soon as the butter melts serve the sauce over the chicken breasts.

"From the romantic La Panetière in Rye ..."

Chicken Breast Stuffed with Spinach and Wild Mushrooms

Jacques Loupiac (center) and Chef Bernard Bouissou (left) and Pastry Chef Didier Berlioz

If you are looking for an excellent restaurant with a romantic setting, La Panetière, in Rye, N.Y., is it. The dining rooms, done in the sand-and-soft-blue tones of the south of France, are as soothing as the superb cooking of Bernard Bouissou, the chef, and Didier Berlioz, the amazing pastry chef. In fact, the cooking is so special that we like to go even without romance in mind! Owner Jacques Loupiac is a welcoming and charming host. Here is one of the chef's easy-to-make specialties. (La Panetière is at 530 Milton Road, Rye, N.Y. (914) 967-8140.)

6 large boneless chicken breast fillets
3 cups chopped assorted mushrooms of choice (button, shiitake, dried porcini, etc.)
1 tablespoon olive oil
¼ cup cream
3 cups spinach, stems removed, and washed
1 tablespoon butter
2 shallots, chopped
2 cloves garlic, chopped
1 teaspoon chopped fresh thyme (or ½ teaspoon dried thyme)
Salt and freshly ground black pepper to taste

1. Preheat the oven to 375 degrees.
2. Peel off the tenderloin section of the breasts — it is a little strip of meat, about the size of your index finger, that runs along the bottom of the fillet and is partly detached already.
3. In a large pan, sauté the mushrooms in olive oil until they are golden and a little crisp. Add the garlic and the shallots. Season well with salt and pepper. Stir and cook for 2 minutes. Transfer the contents of the pan to a mixing bowl.
4. In the same pan sauté the spinach in the tablespoon of butter. Season very well with salt and pepper. Cook for 2 minutes, or until the spinach wilts. Transfer it to a plate and, when cool enough to handle, chop the spinach and transfer it to the mushroom bowl.
5. Place the little chicken tenderloin strips in the bowl of a food processor. Add some salt and pepper. Purée for 15 seconds. Drizzle in the cream while puréeing for another 15 seconds. The purée should be moist and malleable. If it is a little dry add a touch more cream. Add this to the mixing bowl. Mix well.
6. With a sharp knife, make a lengthwise slice in the chicken breast fillets, being careful not to go all the way through. With your hands

or a pastry bag with a plain tip, fill the slices with the mixture — let it come out of the slits and onto a little of the chicken. Salt and pepper well.

7. Grease a baking dish and place the stuffed chicken breasts on it. Cover with foil and bake for 30 minutes or more. Slice into one of the breasts to see if it is done. Remove and slice each breast on an angle into 5 pieces. Make fan patterns on the plates. You could place in the center of the plates Broiled Tomatoes with Parmesan (see recipe page 255) or Char-Grilled Sweet Peppers (see recipe page 255).

Yield: 6 servings

Chicken Breasts with Mushrooms and Baby Onions

Preparation Time: 10 MINUTES
Cooking Time: ABOUT 20 MINUTES

SUPER FAST LOW FAT

4 whole skinless, boneless chicken breast halves, 4 fillets, (about 1½ pounds total)
Salt and freshly ground black pepper to taste
26 small white onions, peeled (about ½ pound)
3 tablespoons olive oil
½ pound white button mushrooms, stems removed and left whole if small, otherwise sliced or quartered
8 fresh basil leaves
½ cup dry white wine
1 tablespoon butter

1. Cut each chicken fillet in half crosswise. Cut off and discard any bone or membrane.
2. Sprinkle the chicken with salt and pepper.
3. Peel the onions and put them in a pot. Add cold water to cover, and salt to taste. Bring to a boil and cook about 3 minutes. Drain.
4. Heat the oil in a large, heavy pan and add the chicken breasts. Cook about 30 seconds and add the onions.
5. Cook 10 minutes and flip the chicken pieces. Scatter the mushrooms over all and cook about 3 minutes.
6. Add the basil leaves, wine, and butter. Cover and cook about 3 minutes. Remove the chicken and place on 4 heated plates. Pour the sauce over them. Garnish with fresh basil leaves.

Yield: 4 servings

How can I tell if my chicken is fresh?

There are no bigger quality fanatics than Frank and Jimmy Perdue. Both are long-time friends, and we have walked around our store with them a number of times. It was quite an education. Here is what the Perdues look for in chicken:

• **Cold temperatures** – Chicken is one of the most perishable products and it is very temperature sensitive. The Perdues have exceptionally high quality-control standards and transport their chickens at very low temperatures. In the store, you should look for a chicken that is very well chilled.

Frank Perdue greets Costas Keramaris and Art Weiss in our Danbury store.

"Try this fabulous lowfat dish!"

Chicken Breasts Stuffed with Ricotta and Fresh Herbs

This turns a chicken breast into a special entree. Ricotta is also great under the skin of a small game hen.

Preparation Time: 15 MINUTES
(prepare in advance the seasoning and stuffing)
Cooking Time: 30 MINUTES

LOW FAT · PREPARE IN ADVANCE

2 whole chicken breasts, split in half (so you have 4 fillets on the breastbones), trimmed of excess fat
¾ cup skim-milk ricotta cheese
¼ cup chopped fresh chives
½ teaspoon fresh minced thyme (if fresh thyme is not available, use ¼ teaspoon dried thyme)
Salt and freshly ground black pepper to taste
Olive oil for drizzling over chicken
4 sprigs fresh thyme (optional)

1. Preheat the oven to 450 degrees.
2. In a small bowl, combine the ricotta, chives, thyme, and a generous amount of salt and pepper. Stir until well blended.
3. Slide a finger under each breast skin to loosen and form a pocket. Don't probe so far as to open the skin on the other side — leave the skin attached along the breastbone. Spoon ¼ of cheese mixture under the skin of each breast.
4. Place the breasts on a baking sheet. Drizzle some olive oil over each breast. Sprinkle with salt and pepper, and roast for 30 minutes or until done.
5. Garnish each breast with a sprig of thyme (optional). Serve with mixed salad greens tossed in Lemon-Garlic Dressing (see recipe page 75) and French Potato-and-Onion Casserole (see recipe page 246).

Yield: 4 servings

Chicken Breasts with Quick Dijon Mustard Sauce

This invigorating dish can be put together in about half an hour, making it ideal for weeknight cooking.

Preparation Time: 10 MINUTES
Cooking Time: ABOUT 25 MINUTES

SUPER FAST LOW FAT

4 skinless, boneless chicken breast halves, 4 fillets (about 1½ pounds total)
Salt and freshly ground black pepper to taste
1 tablespoon butter
4 tablespoons finely chopped onion
¼ teaspoon dried thyme
1 tablespoon red wine vinegar
¼ cup dry white wine
½ cup fresh or canned chicken broth
2 teaspoons tomato paste
¼ cup cream or half-and-half
1 tablespoon Dijon-style mustard
2 teaspoons finely chopped parsley (optional)

1. Sprinkle the chicken fillets generously with salt and pepper.
2. Heat the butter in a heavy pan over medium-high setting and add the breasts. Cook until browned on one side, about 8 minutes. Turn the chicken and cook another 8 to 10 minutes. (Test for doneness by slicing into the thickest part of the fillet — as soon as it turns from wet-looking and rosy to white, remove.)
3. Remove the chicken pieces to a warm platter and set aside. Add the onion and thyme to the pan and cook briefly, stirring, until the onion is wilted. Add the vinegar and wine and bring to a boil. Add the chicken broth and bring to a boil. Stir in the tomato paste. Cook until reduced by half and add the cream. Bring to a full rolling boil and stir in the mustard. There should be about ½ cup of sauce. Taste for seasonings. It may need salt and pepper.
4. Spoon the sauce over the chicken pieces and garnish, if desired, with chopped parsley.

Yield: 4 servings

How can I tell if my chicken is fresh?

- **A fresh looking product –** The Perdues love to see a nice yellow-skinned chicken. They feed their chickens all-natural marigold petals (along with corn and soy) to get that color. Whether the chicken has a yellow or white skin, it should be shiny and moist-looking. Also, check the dates stamped on the package.

- **Neat, tight packaging** – There should not be holes in the plastic wrap, or loose sections of wrap where air could get in. Moreover, there should not be a lot of juice in the package. That indicates that the chicken has been exposed to temperature fluctuations, or that it has been on the shelf too long.

Stew's TIP

Mascarpone is an Italian cheese that is exceptionally creamy and faintly tart. It can be used much like sour cream. It is also sweetened and used in desserts such as the ubiquitous tirami sù. It is also lovely served over fresh strawberries and dusted with sugar.

David Burke's Poached Chicken Breasts with Ratatouille and Orzo

This recipe comes from David Burke, chef of the famous Park Avenue Cafe in New York City. It's a fantastic tasting and great looking one-pot meal that is ideal for entertaining. (Park Avenue Cafe is at 100 East 63rd Street (at Park Avenue), Manhattan, (212) 644-1900).

Preparation Time: 20 MINUTES
Cooking Time: 25 MINUTES

LOW FAT

1½ cups chicken stock
1½ cups fresh or canned tomato sauce (see Fresh Tomato Sauce recipe page 181)
4 boneless, skinless chicken breast halves (about 6 ounces each)
Kosher salt to taste
Freshly ground black pepper to taste
1 red bell pepper, cored, seeded and diced
1 yellow bell pepper, cored seeded and diced
1 medium zucchini, diced (skin left on)
1 medium yellow squash, diced (skin left on)
1 small eggplant, outer 1½ inches cut off and diced (with skin)
½ small onion, diced
3 cloves garlic, minced
1 cup fresh basil, chopped (or 2 tablespoons dried basil)
2 cups orzo, cooked to al dente and set aside
½ cup mascarpone cheese or grated Parmesan
4 basil leaves or 4 twigs of parsley

1. In a large pot, combine the chicken stock and tomato sauce. Bring to a simmer.
2. Season the chicken with salt and pepper and add to the pot. Cover and simmer for about 8 minutes, or until the chicken is just about cooked.
3. Add all remaining ingredients except the cheese and basil. Stir and simmer for another 2 minutes.
4. Remove the chicken breasts and keep them warm. Add the orzo to the vegetable pot and cook until the vegetables are tender and the orzo is al dente. Taste for seasonings.
5. Spoon the vegetable-orzo mixture into 4 bowls. Cut each chicken breast in half widthwise and place on top of the mixture. Garnish with a dollop of mascarpone or grated Parmesan, and a basil leaf.

Yield: Serves 4

Chef David Burke at the Park Avenue Cafe in Manhattan.

Fresh Tomato Sauce

This is a good all-around tomato sauce that can be used in all kinds of dishes.

Preparation Time: 5 MINUTES
Cooking Time: 10 MINUTES

SUPER FAST · LOW FAT · PREPARE IN ADVANCE

2 tablespoons olive oil
1 medium onion, peeled and chopped
4 medium ripe tomatoes, cored and chopped
½ teaspoon dried oregano
½ teaspoon dried rosemary (crushed)
1½ teaspoon salt
Freshly ground black pepper to taste

1. In a large pan over medium-high heat, add the olive oil, let it get hot, and then add the onions. Cook, stirring, until the onions wilt. Add the chopped tomatoes, the oregano, the rosemary, and the salt and pepper. Reduce heat to medium low and cook for about 8 minutes. Pass the sauce through a fine sieve. (If you wish, add some shredded fresh basil to the sauce after passing it through the sieve.)

Yield: About 2 cups

Stew's "Genovese-Style" Pesto

This is a sauce made with fresh basil, garlic, pine nuts, olive oil and Parmesan or Pecorino cheese. We like to use both cheeses here at Stew's because we feel it gives an exceptional flavor. This is a classic sauce that originated in Genoa, Italy. It is great for not only pasta but also seafood, chicken, veal and pork. When you're warming your pesto, be careful not to overheat. Otherwise you will lose the nice green color and delicate flavor.

SUPER FAST · LOW FAT · PREPARE IN ADVANCE

1 bunch fresh basil (about 20 large leaves)
4 cloves garlic
⅓ cup pine nuts
½ teaspoon salt
2 tablespoons olive oil
¼ cup grated Parmesan and Pecorino Romano cheese (in equal amounts)

1. Place the basil and garlic in the bowl of a food processor or blender. Process until the mixture becomes a smooth paste (about 2 minutes). Add the pine nuts and salt. Drizzle in the oil while processing, then add the cheese. Process again until smooth. Taste for seasonings.

Stew's TIP

While chicken parts are certainly convenient for the busy cook, buying whole chickens gives you a lot of creative options. For example, you could remove the wings from a chicken and save them in the freezer until you have enough for Spicy Roasted Chicken Wings (page 183). With two whole chickens you have enough chicken breasts for Chicken Breasts Stuffed with Ricotta and Herbs (page 178). Save the legs for Roasted Chicken Legs with Herb Gravy (page 187). Each time you remove the legs and breasts from a chicken, put the carcass in a plastic bag and freeze it. When you have two or more chicken carcasses, use them to make Homemade Chicken Stock (page 63).

Chef George's Chicken and Penne with Pesto

This aromatic dish, sweetened with peppers and onions, comes from Spain's Basque country, which is known for its earthy maritime cuisine. If you are in a rush, Stew Leonard's sells delicious freshly made pesto. You would use between ½ and ¾ cup of the premade pesto for this dish.

Preparation Time: 10 MINUTES
Cooking Time: 30 MINUTES

LOW FAT

Chicken:
4 tablespoons olive oil
1 cup coarsely chopped onion (1 medium onion)
1 red bell pepper, cored, seeded, and sliced
1 yellow bell pepper, cored, seeded, and sliced
Salt and freshly ground black pepper to taste
10 to 12 ounces boneless, skinless chicken breasts, cut into 1-inch cubes (2 small breasts)
10 ounces hot Italian sausage, cut into 1-inch pieces (you also could use Stew's spicy Turkey or Chicken sausages)
1 pound penne
Grated Parmesan cheese
Chopped fresh basil

1. Heat half of the oil in a large non-stick pan over medium-high heat. Cook the onions for 3 minutes to soften. Add the peppers, season to taste, and cook for 6 minutes. Remove from the pan and set aside.
2. Heat the remainder of the oil in the same pan over medium-high setting. Add the chicken and sausage and cook for 8 to 10 minutes, or until the sausage has lost its pink color and the chicken is firm. Drain the pan of fat, then add the meats to the reserved vegetables. Set aside and keep warm.
3. While the meat is cooking, cook the pasta in 4 quarts of rapidly boiling salted water for about 7-8 minutes.
4. Place the drained pasta in a large bowl with the vegetable-meat mixture and the pesto sauce. Toss well. Taste for seasonings and serve. Sprinkle each serving of pasta with grated Parmesan cheese and chopped basil.

Yield: 4 servings

Spicy Roasted Chicken Wings

Save those wings from whole chickens and freeze them. They make great appetizers or nibbles while watching a football game. The simple recipe here makes wings that are slightly spicy.

Preparation Time: 10 MINUTES
Cooking Time: 35 MINUTES

PREPARE IN ADVANCE

3 pounds chicken wings (about 24 whole wings)
Salt to taste
1 tablespoon chili powder
1 tablespoon dry mustard
3 tablespoon vinegar
1 tablespoon honey
1 tablespoon minced garlic (about 3 large cloves)

1. Preheat the oven to 400 degrees.
2. Remove the tips from the chicken wings. (Save them for chicken stock. See recipe page 63.) Cut each wing through the center joint. Place the wings on a baking tray, sprinkle them with salt, and bake them for 15 minutes.
3. While the wings are baking, combine the remaining ingredients in a small bowl.
4. Remove the wings from the oven, coat with the sauce, and bake for another 10 minutes. Turn the wings over, coat again, and bake for another 10 minutes.

Yield: 48 pieces

Stew's TIP

Buffalo, New York, holds the lofty distinction of being "Chicken Wing Capital of America." In 1964, at a working-class bar called The Anchor, the celebrated Buffalo chicken wing was born. As the story goes, Teressa Bellissimo, whose family still operates the bar, received a giant order of chicken wings from a customer. She decided to deep fry them and set them out with some hot pepper sauce and a bleu cheese dip. They were an immediate hit. If you go to The Anchor today you will get your wings with a mug of dressing that combines mayonnaise, onion, garlic, sour cream, vinegar and blue cheese. To make them lighter, we roast the wings instead of deep frying them.

Stew's TIP

The pot pie, or "potpie," as it was called when it first appeared in an American recipe collection in 1792, was a common method of cooking meats and vegetables. The pies were much larger than the single-portion frozen entrees found in supermarkets today. The first commercial frozen pot pie (chicken) was introduced in 1951 by the C.A. Swanson company, according to *The Dictionary of Food and Drink*, by John Mariani (1983 Ticknor & Fields). If you make your own, prepare 6 or more and freeze those you don't use right away.

Mrs. Leonard's Traditional Chicken Pot Pie

Here's one of our bestsellers in the stores. It's a recipe that my Mom always made around the house. Kids love it too! The secret is leaving some of the vegetables in big chunks!

1 quart chicken stock or water (see stock recipe page 63)
2 chicken breast fillets, boneless and skinless, cubed
½ cup chopped onions
½ cup diced carrots
½ cup diced celery
½ cup fresh or frozen peas
1 teaspoon fresh tarragon (or ½ teaspoon dried tarragon)
1 teaspoon fresh chopped parsley (or ½ teaspoon dried parsley)
3 tablespoons butter
4 tablespoons flour
Salt and freshly ground black pepper to taste

1. In a large pot, bring the chicken stock to a boil. Put in the chicken breasts and cook for 15 minutes. Remove the chicken breasts and set aside.
2. Add the onions, carrots, celery, and peas to the pot. Add the tarragon and the parsley. When the vegetables are cooked, remove them with a slotted spoon and set aside. Reserve cooking water.
3. In another pot over medium heat melt the butter. Whisk in the flour. Cook, stirring, until it turns golden — this is called a roux.
4. Bring the stock to a boil. Pour the roux into the stock and stir well. Continue boiling over medium heat for 6 minutes. There should be no lumps. If there are pass the liquid through a sieve.
5. Return the vegetables and the chicken to the pot. Let it boil for 1 minute. Transfer equal portions of the mixture to 6 small, ovenproof pie dishes. Or you could make one large pie. Cover with the Parmesan Crust page 185.

My mother, Marianne Leonard, shares some of her family recipes with our chefs. In my book, she's the best cook of them all!

Parmesan Crust for Pot Pies

Preparation Time: 10 MINUTES
Cooking Time: NONE

PREPARE IN ADVANCE

¾ cup all-purpose flour
2 ounces unsalted butter (½ stick cut into small pieces)
1 tablespoon grated Parmesan
½ teaspoon dried thyme
1 tablespoon minced chives
2 to 3 tablespoons water

1. Place the flour, butter, cheese, thyme and chives in the bowl of a food processor fitted with the plastic dough attachment, or in a large mixing bowl. If using a food processor, blend the mixture for 10 seconds until it resembles a coarse meal. Add 2 tablespoons of ice water and blend another 10 to 15 seconds until the dough begins to form a ball — it may need a little more water.
2. To blend the mixture by hand, crumble the pieces of butter and the remaining ingredients between your fingers for a few minutes until the mixture resembles coarse corn meal. Add the cold water and stir with fingertips until the dough begins to form a ball.
3. Gather the dough into a ball. Press any small pieces of dough that cling to the bowl into the ball. Wrap it with plastic wrap and chill until ready to use.
4. To roll out the dough, place it on a lightly floured piece of wax paper. Flatten the dough with a rolling pin. Sprinkle it with more flour then cover it with a second sheet of waxed paper. Roll the dough out to about ¼-inch thickness, and large enough to overlap the pot pie's casserole dish.
5. Use this crust for pot pies (see recipe pages 184 and 198) or any other type of savory pies.

Yield: Covers an 8-x-12 casserole, or up to 6 smaller pie plates

Summer Weekend Menu

Spinach-and-Scallion Salad with Mustard Vinaigrette
(see recipe page 87)

Baba's California "Quick Blender" Gazpacho
(see recipe page 70)

Malibu Lemon-Apricot Chicken
(see recipe page 172)

Gingered Strawberry Salad
(see recipe page 319)

What is the difference between a broiler chicken, a roaster, and a fryer?

At Stew Leonard's and most other supermarkets you will find chicken identified in all three ways. Technically, a broiler is the smallest (under $2\frac{1}{2}$ pounds); a fryer is slightly larger, and a roaster is the biggest of all (about 4-5 pounds). Actually, any of these can be roasted, braised, or cut up and fried. In cooler weather our largest seller by far is the roaster.

"You'll Be a Hero at the Grill!"

Grilled Chicken-and-Sausage Kebabs

The popularity of kebabs has exploded here at Stew's. Our customers love to put these on the grill or under a broiler. If you want different variations, experiment with the different marinades in Chapter 5 (Barbecue).

Preparation Time: ABOUT 25 MINUTES
(put meat and sausage on skewers and make onion mixture)
Cooking Time: ABOUT 30 MINUTES

LOW FAT

PREPARE IN ADVANCE

4 chicken legs and thighs, and 2 chicken breasts (or any combination weighing about 2 pounds)
1 pound Stew's All-Natural Turkey Sausage, or Chicken Sausage, cut into 2-inch pieces
Juice of 1 lemon
Salt and freshly ground black pepper to taste
2 large white onions, peeled and sliced
1 green pepper, cored, seeded, and sliced
1 hot cherry pepper, diced
$\frac{1}{4}$ cup white wine
$\frac{1}{4}$ cup chopped fresh cilantro or Italian parsley
8 lemon wedges

1. Preheat a barbecue grill or a broiler.
2. Using a sharp knife, cut the chicken meat into 2-inch chunks.
3. Place a piece of chicken on a bamboo or metal skewer and add a piece of sausage. Add another piece of chicken and another piece of sausage. Finish with a third piece of chicken. Arrange 7 additional skewers the same way.
4. Place the finished kebabs in a shallow dish and cover with the lemon juice. Salt and pepper generously and set aside.
5. Heat the olive oil in a heavy pan. Sauté the onion, green pepper and cherry pepper over medium-high heat for about 10 minutes or until the onions are soft and translucent. Add the white wine and season the mixture with salt and pepper to taste. Simmer, covered, for another 5 minutes. Remove from the heat and keep warm.
6. Once the onion mixture is cooked, place the chicken skewers in a shallow baking tray. Broil on a rack about 6 inches from the heat source for 8 to 10 minutes (use the same timing for an outdoor grill). Turn the kebabs and broil for another 6 to 8 minutes or until the chicken is well cooked.
7. Serve the brochettes, 1 per person, over some of the onion mixture, garnished with cilantro or parsley and accompanied by Curried Rice Pilaf with Almonds (see recipe page 305) or Confetti Orzo (see recipe page 290).

Yield: 6 to 8 servings

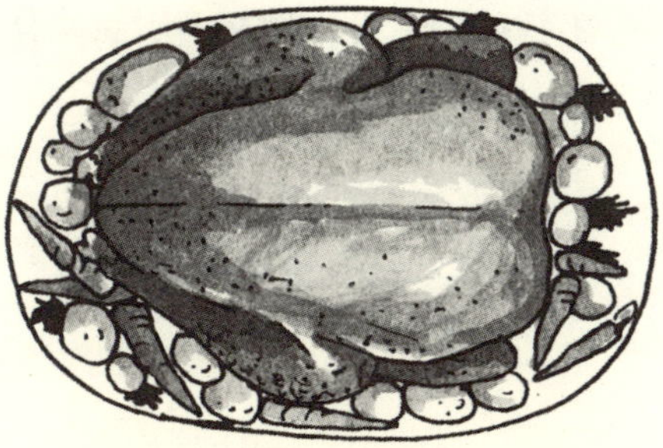

Family-Style Roasted Chicken Legs and Herb Gravy

Here is a quick and inexpensive family dinner, made with chicken legs, the most succulent part of the chicken.

Preparation Time: 10 MINUTES: 5 MINUTES
Cooking Time: 30 MINUTES:40 MINUTES

PREPARE IN ADVANCE

4 chicken legs (about 1 pound)
Salt and freshly grated black pepper to taste
Cayenne pepper to taste
1 cup chicken stock (see recipe page 63)
1 tablespoon chopped fresh thyme (or ½ teaspoon dried thyme)
1 tablespoon chopped fresh chives or scallion greens
1 tablespoon chopped fresh tarragon (or ½ teaspoon dried tarragon)

1. Preheat the oven to 375 degrees
2. Place the chicken legs in a roasting pan. Season with salt, black pepper, and cayenne pepper. Place the pan in the oven and roast for about 30 to 45 minutes (time varies with size of legs) or until the chicken legs are well browned and tender.
3. Remove the chicken legs from the roasting pan. Place them on a plate near the stove to keep warm while the gravy is prepared. To make the gravy, place the roasting pan on a burner over high heat. Add the chicken stock and stir to scrape the bottom of the pan. Add the herbs and cook the sauce for 2 or 3 minutes, or until one-third of the liquid has boiled away. Taste for seasonings.
4. Place a chicken leg on each of 4 dinner plates. Top each with a few spoons of the herb gravy. This is delicious served with Mashed Potatoes and Parsnips (see recipe page 243) and Simmered Red Cabbage with Apples (see recipe page 263).

Yield: 4 servings

Do I have to worry about salmonella in my chicken?

"The answer is no, if you cook the chicken thoroughly and avoid cross contamination," says Stew's Quality Director Dr. Shams Alam. According to the FDA, salmonella bacteria in poultry are killed at 165 degrees. The most common cause of cross contamination is the cooked chicken coming into contact with the raw juices. Just to be safe, before you cook chicken, remove the wrapping and rinse it thoroughly under cold tap water. Wash your hands, cutting board and utensils thoroughly.

Mike Derivan, who's been at Stew's for more than 20 years, inspects some fresh chicken.

Stew's TIP

Almost every Thanksgiving at the Leonard house we experiment with a new roasted turkey recipe. The terrific recipe here originated with the famous Boston chef, Jasper White.

Jasper explained in an interview with Craig Claiborne, the former *New York Times* food editor, that he got the basic recipe from the *Fannie Farmer Cookbook*, first published in 1896, and then gave it his own spin. It involves an unusual technique of blending butter and flour, then massaging the skin of the turkey for several minutes. The turkey then stands for half an hour or so outside the oven and then is cooked at a high temperature for about 40 minutes. You then turn down the oven and continue roasting, basting occasionally with melted butter, for about an hour and a half. The turkey emerges perfectly cooked, moist and tender. It just shows that we could all use a good massage once in a while!

How to Cook a Perfect Thanksgiving Turkey

Stew's Roasted Holiday Turkey with Fresh Herbs and Garlic

Wednesday before Thanksgiving:

LOW FAT

½ tablespoon olive oil
1 medium onion, chopped
4 cloves of garlic, peeled and sliced
1 medium apple, peeled, cored, and cubed
2 stalks celery, trimmed, washed and chopped
4 bay leaves, broken into fingernail-size pieces
1 tablespoon fresh thyme, chopped (or ½ tablespoon dried thyme)
1 tablespoon fresh sage, chopped (or 2 teaspoons dried sage)
Salt and freshly ground black pepper to taste
½ orange, skin and white pith removed, cut into wedges
2 tablespoons white wine vinegar
18- to 20-pound fresh turkey

1. In a large pan over medium-high heat, combine the olive oil, onions, and garlic, and cook, stirring, until the garlic is golden — 4 to 5 minutes. Add the other ingredients (except the turkey) and sauté, stirring, until everything is moist and blended. Remove from the heat, place in a covered container, and refrigerate.
2. Remove everything from the inside of the turkey, including the neck, gizzards, heart, and liver. Put aside. Fill your sink with cold water and add a handful of salt and 2 tablespoons of white wine vinegar. Place turkey in the water and, using your hands, rinse the turkey well inside and out. Remove the turkey and rinse under the faucet with fresh cold water inside and out.
3. Dry the turkey with paper towels. When the marinade is cool, remove from the refrigerator and fill the cavity of your turkey. (This orange mixture is a marinade not a stuffing, because it flavors and moistens the turkey during cooking.) Put the turkey in a roasting pan and cover tightly with plastic wrap. Place in the refrigerator.

On Thanksgiving Day:

Salt and freshly ground black pepper to taste
2 tablespoons olive oil

1. Place an empty roasting pan in the oven and preheat to 400 degrees. You want to heat the pan in order to give the bottom of the turkey a crisp texture — we do not recommend a roasting rack.

2. Season the turkey well with salt and pepper. Rub it all over with two tablespoons of olive oil. Carefully remove the hot roasting pan and place the turkey in it. If the turkey has a pop-up timer (all Stew Leonard's turkeys have them), make sure it faces the front so you can see it.
3. Place the turkey in the oven. After 30 minutes turn down the heat to 350 degrees. Place a sheet of aluminum foil over the turkey. Every 30 minutes baste the turkey with the pan juices. (Remember, every time you open the oven it increases your cooking time by approximately 5 minutes, so be quick.) The turkey takes about 3 hours and 15 minutes to cook.
4. About 30 minutes before the turkey is done, remove the aluminum foil. When the pop-up timer is activated, remove the turkey from the oven and let it sit for 15 to 20 minutes to redistribute the juices. (See instructions on carving a turkey.)

Yield: About 20 or more

Is there any flavor difference between a fresh turkey and a frozen one?

Yes. When a turkey is frozen its natural juices turn into ice crystals. When thawed, these crystals disrupt the protein cell membranes in the flesh and cause some of the natural juices to leak out. Thus, a frozen turkey will not be as moist or juicy as a fresh turkey.

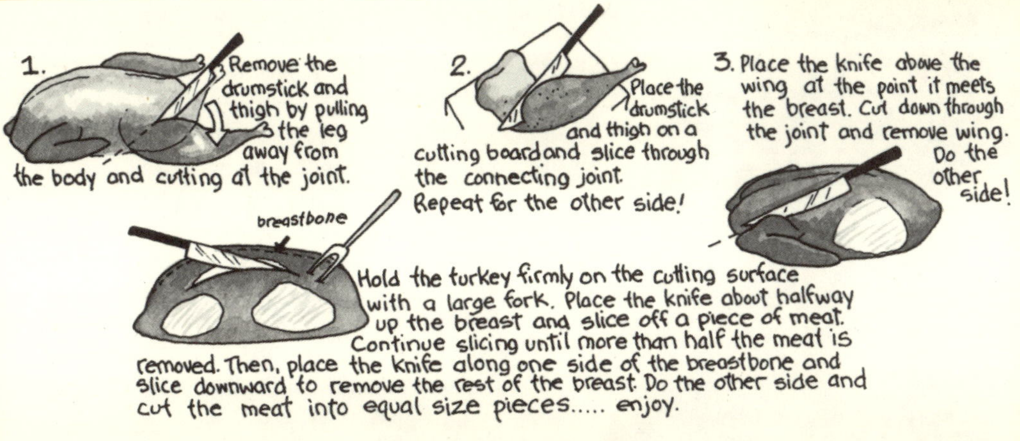

Carving a turkey

1. Remove the drumstick and thigh by pulling the leg away from the body and cutting at the joint where the thigh meets the body.
2. Place the drumstick and thigh on a cutting board and slice through the connecting joint, which is right in the middle. Repeat on the other side.
3. Place the knife above the wing at the point where it meets the breast. Cut down through the joint and remove the wing. Repeat on the other side.
4. Hold the turkey firmly on the cutting surface with a large fork. Place the knife about halfway up the breast and slice off a piece of meat. Continue slicing until more than half the meat is removed. Then place the knife along one side of the breastbone and slice downward to remove the rest of the breast. Repeat on the other side. Slice the breast meat into equal size pieces.

What is so special about Stew Leonard's turkeys?

We visit our turkey farmers and inspect their operations. Our turkeys are fed a special blend of corn, soy and other natural feed. Their diet is closely monitored by a nutritionist to ensure that Stew's turkeys are tender and juicy.

We visited the Shenandoah Valley and met our turkey farmers.

New England Chestnut Stuffing

This is the most popular among our customers. Chestnuts are harvested in the fall and they add a wonderful sweet taste to your stuffing. This is great with turkey, chicken or pork.

Preparation Time: 10 MINUTES
Cooking Time: 20 MINUTES

SUPER FAST · LOW FAT · PREPARE IN ADVANCE

1 cup shelled chestnuts
2 cups milk
1 stalk celery, chopped
2 tablespoons olive oil
2 cups chopped onions
1 tablespoon fresh thyme, chopped (or 2 teaspoons dried thyme)
1 tablespoon fresh sage, chopped (or 2 teaspoons dried sage)
2 bay leaves
¼ teaspoon ground cloves
2 quarts chicken stock, homemade or canned
½ baguette or equivalent amount of other stale bread
2 cups croutons, fresh or boxed (if fresh see instructions page 84)
Salt and freshly ground black pepper to taste

1. In a pot, combine the chestnuts, milk, and celery. Bring the milk to a boil, cook for 1 minute, and drain well.
2. Pour the olive oil into a large pan. Cook the onions over high heat until they begin to turn golden. Add the thyme, sage, bay leaves, and clove. Stir well.
3. Add the chicken stock and bring to a boil. Break up the bread and add to the stock. Simmer for 15 minutes. Add the chestnuts and bring to a boil. Cook for 5 minutes.
4. Put all of the croutons into a large bowl. Add the hot mixture to it and stir to mix.

Yield: 4 servings
(Note: You may double or triple this recipe.)

Turkey Roasting Chart

Weight	Unstuffed Cooking Time	Stuffed Cooking Time
8 to 12 pounds	2¾ to 3 hours	3 to 3½ hours
12 to 14 pounds	3 to 3¾ hours	3¼ to 4 hours
14 to 18 pounds	3¾ to 4¼ hours	4 to 4¼ hours
18 to 20 pounds	4¼ to 4½ hours	4¼ to 4¾ hours
20 to 24 pounds	4½ to 5 hours	4¾ to 5¼ hours

Holiday Roasted Turkey with Mushroom Gravy and Cranberry-Orange Relish

Here is another roasted turkey recipe. Some other stuffing recipes are on pages 157 and 190.

Preparation Time: 10 MINUTES: 10 MINUTES
Cooking Time: 30 MINUTES: 3 HOURS

LOW FAT

1 10- to 12-pound turkey
2 12-inch squares of cheesecloth, optional
4 tablespoons butter, melted
4 tablespoons vegetable oil, optional
Salt and freshly ground black pepper to taste

1. Preheat oven to 375 degrees.
2. Remove the neck, giblets and liver from the turkey. Reserve them for the stuffing and gravy. Rinse the turkey under cold running water. Pat it dry with paper towels. Season the turkey inside and out with salt and pepper.
3. Place the turkey in a shallow roasting pan or on a baking sheet with sides. For the most golden skin, drape the breast of the turkey with the two layers of cheesecloth dipped in the melted butter and oil. Or, lightly oil the skin of the turkey before placing it in the oven.
4. Place the turkey in the preheated oven and roast it for 2½ to 3 hours. The internal temperature of the turkey, measured by a meat thermometer inserted in the thickest part of the leg, should be 180 degrees. Transfer the cooked turkey to a serving platter and cover it with aluminum foil. Save the contents of the pan in which the turkey was cooked for the Mushroom Gravy (recipe follows). Let stand in a warm place for 20 minutes before carving.

Yield: 9-10 generous servings, with leftovers

Should I baste my turkey, and if so, how frequently?

Basting is not essential, but it does give the skin a more golden color. If desired, baste roughly every 30 minutes during the last 2 hours of cooking.

Should I stuff the turkey before cooking?

No. The reason this has become such a major question among our customers has to do with food safety. By the time the inside of your stuffed turkey reaches a safe temperature of 165 degrees, the outside of your turkey will be over-cooked. To be on the safe side for you, your family and guests, always cook and serve your stuffing separately.

Are Stew Leonard's turkeys "all natural?"

Yes. They receive no artificial additives, hormones, or preservatives.

After I buy a turkey how long can I store it before cooking?

A fresh turkey will last for two to three days in your refrigerator. Remember that turkeys last longer in the cold. The coldest spot in your refrigerator is on the bottom shelf.

Holiday Turkey Mushroom Gravy

Preparation Time: 10 MINUTES
Cooking Time: ABOUT 2 HOURS

6 cups water
Giblets and neck from one turkey
1 small carrot, chopped
1 small onion, peeled and halved
1 clove garlic
1 sprig parsley
1 small stalk celery, chopped
¼ teaspoon dried thyme
1 tablespoon vegetable oil (for mushrooms)
1 cup sliced portobello mushrooms (about 2 medium portobellos)
Salt and freshly ground black pepper to taste
1 tablespoon cornstarch dissolved in 2 tablespoons cold water

1. While the turkey is roasting, place the water, giblets, neck, carrot, onion, garlic, and parsley in a pot over high heat. Bring to a boil, then reduce heat and simmer for 1½ hours. Strain and discard the turkey neck, giblets, and vegetables. Set the stock aside.
2. Pour the drippings from the roasting into a 2-cup measuring cup. Let sit for 10 minutes before removing as much grease as possible from the surface. In a saucepan, combine the drippings with the turkey stock and thyme. Bring to a boil, reduce heat, and simmer for 15 minutes.
3. While the gravy is simmering, heat the oil in a non-stick pan over high heat. Add the sliced mushrooms and cook for 5 minutes or until they are lightly browned. Add the cooked mushrooms to the gravy. Adjust seasonings to taste and remove from heat.
4. Ten minutes before serving, return the gravy to a simmer and stir in the cornstarch. Increase heat to high and boil for 3 to 4 minutes, stirring constantly until the gravy is smooth and slightly thickened. Taste for seasoning before serving.

Yield: 2 to 3 cups gravy

Stew's turkey mushroom gravy is a huge hit at the holidays. It's proof that customers don't want to spend extra time in the kitchen.

Cranberry-Orange Relish

This is a delectable side dish for your Thanksgiving meal — or any meal for that matter.

Preparation Time: 15 MINUTES
Cooking Time: NONE

SUPER FAST · LOW FAT · PREPARE IN ADVANCE

1 bag fresh cranberries, washed and picked through for crushed or bad ones
3 tablespoons honey, or more to taste
2 tablespoons grated orange zest (about 2 medium oranges)
½ cup fresh orange juice (about 2 medium oranges) or from concentrate

1. Place all of the ingredients in a food processor or blender. Process until the cranberries are evenly chopped but not a purée. Add more honey as needed to taste. This relish keeps for several weeks in the refrigerator.

Yield: About 6 servings (You may double or triple this recipe.)

Stew's TIP

Cranberries are harvested between Labor Day and Halloween. Central New Jersey's "Pine Barrens" are a major source. Discard any shriveled or discolored berries.

A Thanksgiving Menu

Smoked Salmon with Horseradish Cream Sauce (see recipe page 41)

Stew's Roasted Holiday Turkey with Chestnut Stuffing (see recipe pages 188-190)

Cranberry-Orange Relish (see recipe page 193)

Mashed Potatoes and Parsnips (see recipe page 243)

Sautéed Beet Greens with Oyster Mushrooms (see recipe page 261)

Green Beans with Arugula and Garlic (see recipe page 266)

Aunt Helen's Fresh Apple Cake (see recipe page 310)

What can I do with turkey parts sold at Stew's?

Turkey parts are a great bargain! Anything you can do with chicken breasts or veal you can do with turkey cutlets. Here's a quickie: Place them between two pieces of plastic wrap and — using a mallet or the bottom of a heavy pan — pound them gently so they are of uniform thickness. Sauté them in a mixture of butter and olive oil and make a quick pan sauce — pour off most of the fat from the pan and then add to the pan, over high heat, some chicken stock, salt, pepper and a touch of lemon juice. Bring to a boil and swirl in some butter, then serve over the Stew's Turkey Cutlets. Turkey legs can be braised or roasted.

"The clock is ticking!"

Turkey Cutlets à la Minute

This recipe is so quick and simple, not to mention delicious, that you will find yourself making it on weeknights when you're pressed for time.

Preparation Time: 5 MINUTES
Cooking Time: 5 MINUTES

SUPER FAST · LOW FAT

4 turkey cutlets (about $1\frac{1}{4}$ pound total)
Salt and freshly ground black pepper to taste
2 tablespoons olive oil
2 tablespoons butter
Juice of $\frac{1}{2}$ lemon
$\frac{1}{2}$ cup canned chicken stock (or fresh if you have it)

1. Place the turkey cutlets between sheets of plastic wrap and pound them with the bottom of a pan so they all are the same thickness. Season generously with salt and pepper.
2. In a pan over medium-high setting, heat 1 tablespoon of olive oil with 1 tablespoon of butter and the lemon juice. Cook the turkey cutlets about 2 minutes per side and check for doneness — they should be nicely browned. Remove the turkey to a warm plate. Add the chicken stock and scrape the bottom of the pan with a plastic spatula.
3. Turn heat to high and reduce the chicken stock by a third. Swirl in the remaining butter. Taste for seasonings. Pour a little sauce over each turkey cutlet.

Yield: Serves 4

How do I tell what size turkey is needed to serve 10, 15 or 20 people?

Around Thanksgiving time many of Stew Leonard's customers ask us what size turkey to buy for a certain number of people. A quick rule of thumb is *one pound of uncooked turkey per person*. It never hurts to overestimate because turkey sandwiches on the weekend after Thanksgiving are a tradition!

Uncooked Turkey	Number of Servings
6 to 8 pounds	6 to 8 people
8 to 12 pounds	8 to 12 people
12 to 16 pounds	12 to 20 people
16 to 20 pounds	20 to 28 pounds
20 to 24 pounds	28 to 32 people

Turkey Cutlets with Prosciutto and Gruyère

Preparation Time: 25 MINUTES
Cooking Time: ABOUT 7 MINUTES

4 turkey breast steaks, sometimes sold as turkey tenderloins (about 1¼ pound total)
Salt and freshly ground black pepper to taste
2 tablespoons flour
2 tablespoons olive oil
2 tablespoons butter
1 tablespoon finely chopped shallots
¼ cup Marsala or sherry wine
4 very thin slices prosciutto, or any thinly sliced ham (about 2 ounces)
4 very thin slices Gruyère or Swiss cheese (about 2 ounces)

1. Put the turkey slices on a flat surface between 2 pieces of plastic wrap and pound lightly with a mallet or the bottom of a pan to make them all the same thickness. Each should be about ¼ inch thick.
2. Sprinkle the turkey pieces on both sides with salt and pepper.
3. Dip the turkey cutlets in flour to coat well on both sides. Shake off the excess.
4. Preheat the broiler to high.
5. Heat the oil and butter in a pan over medium-high setting and add the turkey pieces. Cook about 2 minutes, or until lightly browned on one side. Turn and cook about 2 minutes longer, turning the pieces occasionally. Scatter the shallots around the turkey pieces. Cook briefly and add the Marsala. Cook about 1 minute.
6. Transfer the turkey pieces to a heatproof dish and pour the wine sauce over them. Cover each piece with a slice of prosciutto. Cover the prosciutto neatly with a slice of cheese.
7. Place the covered turkey pieces under the broiler, about 3 inches from the heat source. Cook until cheese melts, 45 seconds to 1 minute. Serve immediately.

Yield: Serves 4

We visited Roth Kase in Wisconsin, a premier Gruyère maker.

What does it mean when I see chickens in the store identified as "Free Range," "Free Roaming," "Antibiotic free," "Hormone free," "Organic," and "Amish?"

We don't feel that "free range" chickens taste any better than any other chickens. *Consumer Reports* did a taste test last year and agreed. In most cases you are paying a lot more for nothing other than a fancy title. The key thing to remember is that chickens and turkeys reflect what they eat and where they are raised. If growers feed chickens high-quality grain, and raise them in a clean, disease-free environment, you will get a great tasting chicken!

In the early 1980s, we started to hear the term "free range," which implied that the chickens were raised on small, local farms, and allowed to run free. Some indeed were, but they were the exception. The free-range chicken prices were higher, presumably because of small-scale production. There were no USDA regulations defining the term "free range," so breeders used it very loosely.

Today, the USDA requires that chicken growers sign an affidavit saying they will provide free-range chickens "access" to the outdoors. This is an improvement, but one thing I learned while interviewing poultry experts was that chickens stick around their food supply. Since the food is in the barn, the chickens stay in the barn, whether the door is open or not! I've have seen this phenomenon first hand many times.

"Free Roaming" was another term used to describe chickens until the government strictly defined the term. Now, free roaming must meet the same criteria as "free range."

"Hormone free" is not an issue because virtually no chickens or turkeys are given hormones. They don't need them.

"Antibiotic free" means that no drugs can be used to cure sick chickens. Just like yourself, when you get a cold or flu, you might go to the doctor and get a prescription for antibiotics The chickens can't be cured that way if they are to be called antibiotic free (even though the USDA approves these antibiotics).

"Organic" means that no hormones or antibiotics are administered, and that the chickens and turkeys are fed certified organic feed. Always look for the term "certified organic." This also means that the farmland where the feed is grown cannot be treated with any pesticides or chemical fertilizers.

"Amish" is a regional description for the Amish country in Pennsylvania, and not a government definition. Many people feel that this area, with its deep German roots and anti-technology lifestyle, produces healthy, meaty chickens.

Lowfat Turkey-and-Corn Meatloaf

Preparation Time: 15 MINUTES
Cooking Time: 50 MINUTES

LOW FAT

PREPARE IN ADVANCE

14 ounces ground turkey (thigh meat is the best)
½ cups diced yellow bell peppers (about 1 medium pepper)
½ cup diced red bell peppers (about 1 medium red pepper)
1 cup diced onions (about 1 medium onion)
1 cup corn kernels, fresh or frozen (reserve the husks if using fresh)
1 tablespoon cornmeal
¼ teaspoon salt
Generous grating of fresh black pepper
½ teaspoon chili powder
½ teaspoon paprika
½ cup diced scallions (about 4 scallions)
2 tablespoons tomato paste dissolved in 2 tablespoons water
2 eggs
1 cup breadcrumbs

1. Preheat the oven to 350 degrees. Lightly oil a 5 x 9 x 3-inch loaf pan with the vegetable oil. Set aside.
2. Place the ground turkey in a large mixing bowl. Add the yellow and red peppers, onion, corn kernels, cornmeal, salt, pepper, chili powder, paprika, and scallions. With a wooden spoon or your hands, knead the ground turkey to blend all the ingredients.
3. Stir in the tomato mixture, eggs, and breadcrumbs. Thoroughly mix all ingredients.
4. Pat the turkey mixture into the prepared loaf pan. Cover the loaf with reserved cornhusks if you have them — otherwise leave it uncovered. Place the turkey loaf in the oven and bake for 45 to 55 minutes. The internal temperature should measure 160 degrees to be thoroughly cooked.
5. Cut the turkey loaf into 1½-inch-thick slices. Serve it with Fresh Tomato Sauce (see recipe page 181).

Yield: Six 1½-inch-thick slices

Stew's TIP

Crumble leftover slices of cooked Turkey-and-Corn Meatloaf and use them as a filling for taco shells, perhaps with melted cheese. Serve with Lima-Beans-and-Fresh-Fennel Salad (see recipe page 80) and sangria or beer.

Is a small turkey more tender than a large one?

No. Most turkeys today are raised with similar feed and under similar conditions. Their flavor and texture are more or less the same if cooked properly.

Turkey-and-Mushroom Pot Pie

This irresistible pie is a family favorite, especially in the fall. You can make this pie with Thanksgiving leftovers then freeze it.

Preparation Time: 15 MINUTES
Cooking Time: ABOUT 45 MINUTES

PREPARE IN ADVANCE

1 pound skinless, boneless turkey cutlets, cut into 1-inch chunks
1 tablespoon olive oil
1 cup sliced mushrooms, portobello or shiitake if available
1 teaspoon minced garlic
¾ cup carrots, peeled and cut into ½-inch cubes (about 2 medium carrots)
1 cup chopped fennel, about ½ bulb
4 cups chicken stock (see recipe page 63)
4 tablespoons cornstarch dissolved in ¼ cup white wine
1 teaspoon chopped fresh thyme or ½ teaspoon dried thyme
1 cup fresh or frozen peas
Salt and freshly ground black pepper to taste

1. Preheat oven to 350 degrees.
2. Pour the olive oil into a medium-size pan over high heat. Add the turkey and cook, stirring, for 2 minutes. Add the mushrooms and cook for 3 minutes. Add the garlic and cook just until the mushrooms release their juices, about 3 minutes more. Add the carrots and fennel, reduce heat, and cook for 5 minutes to soften the vegetables.
3. Add the stock. Bring the mixture to a boil then stir in the dissolved cornstarch. Bring the stock to a boil and cook for 2 minutes, stirring occasionally, until it thickens. Add the cubed turkey, thyme and peas. Adjust seasonings to taste with salt and pepper. Bring the mixture to a boil, reduce the heat, and simmer for 5 minutes, covered.
4. While the pot pie filling is simmering, roll out the Parmesan Pastry Crust (see recipe page 185) into one rectangle large enough to cover a 3-quart casserole. Lightly flour the crust then fold it in half. Fold it in half again and set it aside.
5. Pour the filling into a shallow 3-quart casserole. Unfold the Parmesan Crust (see recipe page 185) and evenly cover the top of the casserole. Pinch the edges of the crust over the lip of the casserole to form a decorative border. Cut three slits in the top of the crust to allow steam to escape as the pie bakes.
6. Bake the pot pie for 30 to 35 minutes, or until the top is golden brown.

Yield: 6 servings

"You'd Never Know It's Lowfat!"

Tangy Turkey Chili

This is a good lowfat party dish. Better yet, you can make it in advance and the flavors will intensify.

Preparation Time: 10 MINUTES
Cooking Time: ABOUT 1 HOUR AND 40 MINUTES

LOW FAT
PREPARE IN ADVANCE

2 tablespoons olive oil
1 medium onion, peeled and chopped
6 cloves garlic, peeled and minced
2 to 3 Anaheim (or comparable) chilies, diced (see chili chart page 267)
1 teaspoon diced jalapeño pepper, minced
1 pound ground turkey, from thigh
1 tablespoon dried oregano
¼ teaspoon ground clove
¼ teaspoon cayenne
Salt and freshly ground black pepper to taste
2 16-ounce cans Great Northern white beans (can weight may vary slightly)
1 cup chicken broth

1. Pour the olive oil into a large pot over medium heat. Add the onion and garlic. Cook, stirring, until the garlic is just golden (not brown!). Add the Anaheim peppers, jalapeño pepper, ground turkey, oregano, clove, cayenne, salt, and pepper. Stir for 2 minutes. Add the beans and chicken stock.
2. Simmer the chili, stirring occasionally, for 1½ hours. Taste for seasonings. Serve.

Yield: Serves 8 to 10

Seafood

This chapter is filled with tempting international recipes for all kinds of fish and shellfish. We also feature exclusive recipes from some of the most famous chefs in New York and Connecticut. Among the great dishes you will find are Charley Palmer's Steamed Halibut in Clam Broth (from Aureole restaurant in Manhattan) and Jean-Louis Gerin's Seared Monkfish with Tomato and Tarragon (from Jean-Louis restaurant in Greenwich).

Crispy Flounder Fillets with Lemon

The battering technique here — first in flour, then eggs, then breadcrumbs — can be used for all kinds of fish, as well as for scallopini of veal, chicken, or beef. It gives the main ingredient a slightly crispy texture.

Preparation Time: 10 MINUTES
Cooking Time: ABOUT 8 MINUTES

LOW FAT

PREPARE IN ADVANCE

8 small flounder fillets (about 1¼ pounds total)
Salt and freshly ground black pepper to taste
1 cup flour
2 eggs
2 tablespoons cold water
2 cups breadcrumbs
3 tablespoons corn or vegetable oil
4 tablespoons butter
Juice of 1 lemon

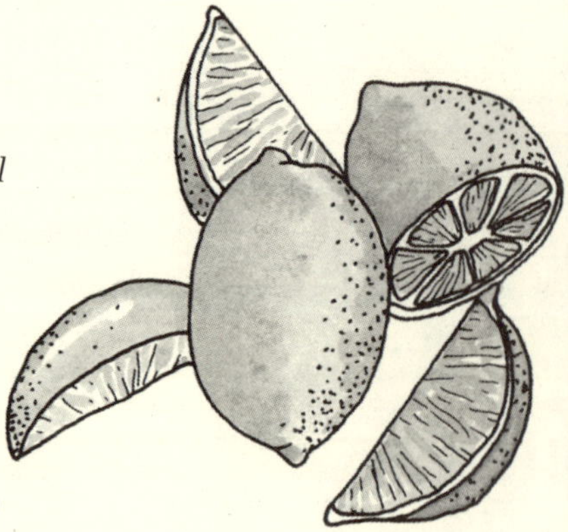

1. Sprinkle the flounder fillets on both sides with salt and pepper.
2. Dip the fillets in flour to coat both sides. Shake off the excess.
3. In a bowl, beat the eggs with the water. Dip the flour-coated fish in the egg mixture to coat all over, and then coat with the breadcrumbs. Pat the fillets on both sides so the breadcrumbs adhere.
4. Heat the oil in a pan over medium setting and add a few fillets in one layer. Cook about 2 minutes per side, or until golden brown. When the fillets are cooked, transfer them to warm serving dishes. Continue cooking, adding a little more oil to the pan if needed.
5. When all the fish are cooked, pour off any oil in the skillet and add the butter. Cook until it is lightly browned. Add the lemon juice and pour the sauce over the fish.

Yield: 4 servings

Whether we're walking the docks in Boston, visiting the Fulton Fish market, or accepting seafood deliveries at Stew Leonard's, we look for certain things in order assure we get the freshest fish. You should do the same. Here are some tips:

Buy from quality sellers — Whether you are eating fish at a restaurant or buying it at a store, a reputation for quality and freshness is a key. Fish is highly perishable and a few hours at the wrong temperature can destroy it. Buy from the best people you can find. That's what Stew's does!

Make sure that the fish you buy is icy cold — The seafood counter of a store should have mounds of crushed ice — fish usually are set out on trays over the ice. Fish kept at 32 degrees have twice the shelf life of fish kept at 40 degrees (the temperature of a home refrigerator). As soon as seafood gets warm it begins to dry out and lose flavor.

Every year Boston hosts the International Seafood Show. Every supplier in the industry attends, and it's a terrific place to look for new products and ideas.

Great fish doesn't smell! If you go to a fish counter and detect a "fishy" smell, keep walking. Something is fishy!

Great fish have clean, shiny skin and feel firm! Fresh fish "springs back" when pressed. When fish begins to age, the meat gets mushy. When judging fillets, look for vibrant colors: rosy red tuna, pearly white sole, and so on. If a fish has a browning rim, that is a sure sign of age.

Look it in the eye! The eyes should be sparkling and clear, not cloudy.

Don't buy on price alone! There are many ways that stores cut corners and sell inexpensive fish — but it is no bargain. Previously frozen fish that is thawed is less expensive than fresh — and the customer may not be aware of what is happening. Buy from a store where you can trust them to sell the best quality fresh fish.

Look for a big turnover. A busy seafood counter is more likely to have very fresh fish than an empty one. This is also good indication that deliveries are made daily. If you buy packaged fish, make sure it's dated.

Stew's Best Selling Fish

Mild Flavor

Fish Name	Where It's From	Characteristics	Best Way to Cook
Cod or Scrod	The cod that we catch weigh between 8 and 25 pounds. We get them off Cape Cod and along the southern Massachusetts coastline.	White, mild, and flaky. A real New England beauty! A scrod is a young cod.	Cook this any way except grilling. The fish is too delicate and breaks apart on the grill. It's great to bake, sauté or fry.
Fillet of Sole (also called Flounder or Fluke)	It comes from the deep cold waters off the U.S. and Canada.	Very delicate. Milky white meat. It has a very low fat content.	Fillet of sole is best sautéed or baked because it is so fragile. It is also good rolled and stuffed.
Monkfish (referred to as "poor man's lobster!")	Caught off Cape Cod and Maine. We buy it at the Boston seafood market.	Firm, thick meat, somewhat like lobster in texture, but not in flavor. An increasingly popular fish at the store.	Great on the grill. It's a versatile fish that can be cooked just about any way.
Orange Roughy	Caught in the South Pacific and flash frozen aboard fishing vessels.	Very light texture, flaky and with a mild flavor. It is a red-skinned fish with white, tender meat (dark meat indicates inferior quality).	Ideal for pan-frying or baking. Too flaky for the grill.
Tilapia	Farm raised in Costa Rica.	Lean, light meat, somewhat flaky, and sweet.	Versatile all-around fish. It has become one of our customers' favorites.
Halibut	Caught in the North Atlantic and North Pacific.	White, lean, firm, and with a flaky texture.	Best grilled, broiled, or roasted. Firm texture. Ideal for kebabs.

Moderate Flavor

Red Snapper	Caught in the Florida Keys and Southern warm waters.	Mild flavor with a white-to-off-white color when cooked.	Excellent when grilled. Soft to firm texture.
Mahi-Mahi	Caught in the tropics and sub-tropics.	Sweet, strong flavor, fairly oily and has an off-white-to-pink-color.	Versatile cooking fish. Can be cooked any way.

Fish Name	Where It's From	Characteristics	Best Way to Cook
Striped Bass	Found off Atlantic and Pacific coasts.	Mild flavor and a white-to-off-white color when cooked.	Can be sautéed, pan-fried, grilled or roasted. Firm-textured meat.
Grouper	Caught in Southern waters and the Gulf of Mexico.	Distinct, mild flavor, flaky and with a white color when cooked.	Baking, pan-frying and roasting are the most popular methods of cooking. Firm texture.
Mako Shark	Caught off the East Coast.	Sweet and mild flavor.	Great on the grill, or sautéed with lemon and butter. Meaty texture.
Chilean Sea Bass	Caught in the deep waters off southern Chile.	Loved by professional chefs because it is the only white fish with a high oil content. It always stays moist!	Usually cut thick, it is best grilled, baked or broiled. Easy to cook, it is difficult to overcook.

Rich Flavor

Fish Name	Where It's From	Characteristics	Best Way to Cook
Salmon	Mostly farm-raised in Maine and Canada.	Mild to full flavor, has a pinkish-red color when cooked. It is also rich in Omega-3 fatty acids.	Poach, broil or grill. Medium texture.
Swordfish	Caught off the East Coast.	Firm, rich, juicy flavor. Cut into steaks.	Chef's choice for grilling. Can also be baked or broiled. Meaty texture.
Yellowfin Tuna ("Ahi" is its Hawaiian name)	Found all over the world. We catch ours off the East Coast and the Gulf Coast.	Popular because of its rich, firm, flavorful meat. Stew's buys only #1 grade, which is called sushi quality.	Excellent on the grill, baked, or sautéed. Meaty texture.
Trout	Farm-raised all over the US.	Rich flavor and pink-to-off-white meat.	Great for grilling, pan-frying and roasting. Soft texture.
Catfish	Farm-raised in Mississippi, South Carolina, and growing in popularity all over the U.S.	Mild to rich flavor. White in color. Firm texture.	Pan-frying and sautéing are popular cooking methods.
Bluefish	Found along the East Coast.	Rich full flavor. Oily flesh. Many customers say it is too oily.	Excellent when broiled. Great smoked. This is a highly perishable fish and needs to be kept very cold before cooking.

Stew's TIP

The recipe for Monkfish with White Pepper calls for crushing the white peppercorns. To do this, place the peppercorns on a flat surface and, using the bottom of a heavy pan, lean down and crush them. An easier way is to put the peppercorns in an electric spice grinder

Monkfish "Poor Man's Lobster" with White Pepper

Monkfish, called lobster fish because its firm texture resembles that of lobster, has a pleasing sweet flavor. This recipe plays off that with its subtle spiciness from white peppercorns. You could use black peppercorns.

Preparation Time: 5 MINUTES
Cooking Time: 10 MINUTES

4 fillets of monkfish, about $1\frac{1}{4}$ pounds
$1\frac{1}{2}$ teaspoons crushed white peppercorns (or black)
Salt to taste
2 tablespoons olive oil
2 tablespoons finely chopped shallots
4 tablespoons dry white wine
4 tablespoons soft butter
Chervil or dill sprigs for garnish

1. Coat the fish on both sides with the crushed peppercorns. Sprinkle with salt to taste.
2. Heat the oil in a pan (black cast-iron is best) over medium setting. Add the fish and cook for about 2 minutes, or until lightly browned. Turn the fillets, lower the heat a little, and cook for 3 minutes. Transfer the fillets to warm plates and keep in a warm place.
3. Add the shallots to the skillet, stir, and cook over medium heat until they are wilted. Add the wine and bring to a boil, stirring. Reduce by half over high heat. Add the butter and blend well. As soon as the butter melts, spoon the sauce over each fillet. Garnish with sprigs of chervil or dill.

Yield: 4 servings

"From the superb restaurant Jean-Louis in Greenwich, Connecticut ..."

Jean-Louis Gerin's Seared Monkfish with Tomatoes and Tarragon

This is another recipe from Jean-Louis Gerin, chef-owner of the acclaimed Jean-Louis restaurant in Greenwich. My wife Kim enjoyed this meal when we ate at Jean-Louis's restaurant for our last anniversary!

Preparation Time: 15 MINUTES
Cooking Time: ABOUT 10 MINUTES

SUPER FAST

4 ounces butter (4 tablespoons)
1 tablespoon olive oil
2 pounds monkfish, cleaned, trimmed, and cut roughly into 2-inch rounds (½-inch thick)
2 cups white wine
1 cup clam broth
1 tablespoon minced shallots
½ tablespoon minced garlic
1 teaspoon fresh tarragon, chopped (or ½ teaspoon dried)
2 tablespoons chopped scallions (white and green section)
½ medium ripe tomato, chopped
Salt and white pepper to taste

1. In a large non-stick pan over medium-high heat, combine 2 tablespoons of the butter with the olive oil. Place the monkfish in the pan and season well with salt and pepper. Sauté until browned — about 3 minutes on one side, 2 minutes on the other. Remove the monkfish to warm serving dishes.
2. Add the garlic to the same pan and cook for 1 minute, stirring — do not let it turn brown. Add the shallots and the wine. Bring to a boil and add the clam juice. Cook over high heat to reduce the liquid by about ⅓. Return the monkfish to the pan and cook about 4 minutes, or until the fish is tender. Add the scallion, tarragon, and chopped tomatoes. Bring to a boil again, taste for seasonings, and whisk in the remaining 2 tablespoons of butter. As soon as the butter dissolves, pour the sauce over the fillets and serve.

Yield: 4 to 6 servings

What's the best way to store fish at home?

Two important things to remember are (1) maintaining fish's moisture and (2) keeping it ice cold. The best way to store fish is in airtight plastic wrap. Place it in the coldest part of your refrigerator, which is the bottom shelf because hot air rises. Shrimp and scallops need to breathe and should be kept either in plastic wrap with little "breathing holes," or in a bag that is partially open. In general, don't keep seafood for more than 2 or 3 days.

Jean-Louis Gerin is right at home in his restaurant in Greenwich, Connecticut.

Where is "cod" from?

Cod has played a vital role in New England for centuries. Bartholomew Gosnold, the English explorer who sailed south from Nova Scotia along the northeastern coast of America in 1602, was so in awed by the abundance of cod that he named a curved peninsula there "Cape Cod." Many New England fortunes were built on the cod industry. In recognition of the fish's importance to the economy, the Massachusetts House of Representatives voted in 1784 to hang a cod over its grand assembly room. It remains there today.

New England Roasted Cod with Tomato-and-Balsamic-Vinegar Relish

I think that the combination of sweet tomatoes and slightly sharp balsamic vinegar is fantastic! You could also use monkfish or catfish in this recipe.

Preparation Time: 10 MINUTES
Cooking Time: ABOUT 15 MINUTES

SUPER FAST LOW FAT

½ cup yellow cornmeal
2 tablespoons all-purpose flour
½ teaspoon salt
¼ teaspoon freshly ground black pepper
¼ teaspoon paprika
3 tablespoons minced chives
2 egg whites
¼ cup milk
6 cod or scrod fillets, 6 to 7 ounces each, about 1-inch thick
2 tablespoons vegetable oil

1. Preheat the oven to 350 degrees.
2. Combine the cornmeal, flour, salt, pepper, paprika, and herbs in a shallow bowl. In another bowl, beat the egg whites and milk.
3. Dip one cod fillet in the egg white-milk mixture, then in the cornmeal mixture. Set aside and repeat with other fillets.
4. Heat 1 tablespoon of oil in a non-stick skillet over medium heat. Brown 2 or 3 fillets for a minute. Turn and cook until golden brown. Place them on a baking tray. Sauté the remaining fillets, adding more oil to the pan if necessary, and place on the tray.
5. Bake the fillets for 6 to 8 minutes, or just until the fish becomes firm to the touch. Fillets 1-inch thick should be done in about 8 to 10 minutes.
6. Serve with Fresh Tomato-and-Balsamic-Vinegar Relish (see following recipe).

Yield: 6 servings

Tomato-and-Balsamic-Vinegar Relish

This would be a fine accompaniment to grilled meats or poultry.

Preparation Time: 5 MINUTES
Cooking Time: ABOUT 15 MINUTES

SUPER FAST · LOW FAT · PREPARE IN ADVANCE

2 large onions, peeled
6 plum tomatoes
3 tablespoons olive oil
Salt and freshly ground black pepper to taste
3 tablespoons balsamic vinegar

1. Cut the onions in half through the root. Slice into thin strips. Dice the plum tomatoes.
2. In a lightly oiled non-stick pan, sauté the onions over medium-high heat for about 5 minutes, or until soft. Add the tomatoes, salt, and pepper. Lower the heat and cook for 6 to 8 minutes. Add the vinegar, stir well, and serve with the roasted cod (previous recipe).

Yield: 4 to 5 servings

How much fish should I buy for my family?

To calculate how many portions you get from a whole fish, use a 3-to-1 ratio. For example, a cleaned fish that weighs 3 pounds will yield about 1 pound of boneless meat, enough to serve 2 people. If you buy lobster, figure on 1 pound of meat for every 4 pounds of whole lobster. The rule of thumb is: for whole fish, buy 1 pound per person; for cleaned fish on the bone, ¾ pound per person; and for fillets, ⅓ to ½ pound per person.

Debbie Emond, of our Seafood Department, sells so much fresh fish that we have to replenish the supply every few hours!

"From the elegant Homestead Inn in Greenwich, Connecticut ..."

Thomas Henkelmann's Provençal-Style Codfish with Potatoes

In the fall of 1997, Thomas Henkelmann took over the stately Homestead Inn, on Field Point Road in Greenwich, and he has been earning effusive praise for his cooking ever since. He was generous enough to give us one of his favorite recipes, called "brandade" in French. It is essentially a garlic-flavored purée of codfish, potatoes, olive oil and fresh herbs. Brandade is traditionally made with salt cod. In this recipe fresh cod is used. Chef Thomas says he prefers the fresh version because it is lighter and more delicate.

Preparation Time: 10 MINUTES
Cooking Time: 20 MINUTES

LOW FAT

PREPARE IN ADVANCE

1 pound small white potatoes or red potatoes, peeled
1½ pounds fresh cod (no bones)
6 tablespoons olive oil
Salt and freshly ground black pepper to taste
Cayenne pepper to taste
1 branch fresh thyme, chopped, (or ½ teaspoon dried)
1 branch fresh tarragon, leaves removed and diced (or ½ teaspoon dried)
2 cloves garlic, minced
2 shallots, minced
1 French baguette, cut crosswise into ½-inch-thick slices
2 medium tomatoes, seeded and cut into cubes (for garnish)
2 cloves garlic, minced (for the croutons)

Theresa Carroll and Thomas Henkelmann at The Homestead Inn, Greenwich, Connecticut.

1. Boil the potatoes in lightly salted water until tender.
2. Place the codfish in a dish. Drizzle with 1 tablespoon of the olive oil. Season well with salt, black pepper, and cayenne. Sprinkle over the fish the chopped thyme and tarragon leaves. Cover with plastic wrap and refrigerate for an hour.
3. After the cod has marinated, remove it from the refrigerator and wipe off the herbs. In a pan (preferably non-stick) over medium-high setting, add 1 tablespoon of olive oil. Add the codfish and shallots and cook, turning once, about 4 to 5 minutes per side (timing varies with the cod's thickness, so check by slicing into the center).

4. When the fish is cooked, cut it into large cubes and place it, along with the garlic and shallots, in the bowl of a food processor. Use the pulse lever to chop it just enough to break it up — do not make a purée. Add the cooked potatoes and blend lightly. Add the remaining olive oil and garlic and blend lightly — you want a slightly chunky purée. If the mixture seems dry, add ¼ to ⅓ cup of cream or half-and-half, and purée for 15 seconds. Taste and adjust seasonings with salt, black pepper, and cayenne.
5. Preheat the oven to 400 degrees. Place the bread slices on a baking sheet. Rub the bread with the garlic cloves. Brush the bread with the olive oil. Bake until golden.
6. To serve: Spoon a generous amount of brandade over the toasted bread. Sprinkle some tomato cubes around as garnish.

Yield: 4 servings

What is a fish stock?

A freshly made fish stock is the most important building block for many fabulous soups and sauces. And it is easy to make. At Stew Leonard's we package the heads and bones of filleted fish every day. Just put them in a stockpot with vegetables and seasonings. Here is a recipe for a good basic fish stock.

Homemade Fish Stock

Preparation Time: 5 MINUTES
Cooking Time: 20 MINUTES

LOW FAT

PREPARE IN ADVANCE

4 pounds fish bones from a non-oily fish, including heads (gills removed)
1½ cups coarsely chopped onion
1 stalk celery, chopped
6 parsley sprigs
1 bay leaf
1 teaspoon dried thyme, or 2 sprigs fresh thyme
10 whole black peppercorns
6 cups cold water
2 cups dry white wine

1. Chop the fish bones so they fit in a deep pot.
2. Add the remaining ingredients to the pot and bring to a boil. Reduce the heat and simmer for 20 minutes. Strain the liquid into a bowl or jar. This broth can be stored in a refrigerator, covered tightly, for several days. You can also freeze it for a month or longer.

What is the best way to freeze fish?

If you freeze fresh fish, do so as soon as you get home. Place it in an airtight bag — it should last for up to 3 months. If you buy packaged fish at a store, freeze it in the package without opening it. Many stores sell fish that have been frozen and then thawed. If you refreeze this kind of fish it will become mushy and virtually inedible. This is because seafood is mostly water, and each time you freeze and thaw it, you lose moisture. Fish should be frozen only once.

"Guests will rave about this!"

Sesame-Coated Snapper Fillets

We love to surprise dinner guests with unusual flavor and texture combinations. This crunchy fish invariably gets applause. There is really nothing to it — just make sure you coat the fish completely with the sesame seeds.

Preparation Time: 5 MINUTES
Cooking Time: ABOUT 20 MINUTES

SUPER FAST LOW FAT

4 skinless, boneless snapper fillets (or another white-fleshed fish like weakfish, sole, flounder, or blackfish)
1/4 cup freshly squeezed lemon juice or lime juice
2 tablespoons Worcestershire Sauce
1 egg, lightly beaten
1 tablespoon milk
Salt and freshly ground black pepper to taste
3/4 cup sesame seeds
3/4 cup grated Parmesan cheese
1/2 cup flour
1/4 cup olive oil
2 tablespoons butter
4 lemon wedges

1. Put the fish fillets in a shallow dish and pour over them the lemon juice and Worcestershire Sauce. Turn the fillets in the mixture and let stand.
2. Put the beaten egg, milk, salt, and pepper in a bowl and whisk to blend. Combine the sesame seeds and grated cheese on a flat dish — stir so they are evenly distributed.
3. Lift the fillets one at a time and, using your fingers, wipe off some of the marinating liquid. Dip the fillets one at a time in the flour, then the egg mixture, and finally the sesame seed mixture to coat well. Set aside.
4. Heat the oil and butter in a skillet over medium setting and add the fish fillets (it may be necessary to cook the fish in batches). Cook for 2 to 3 minutes and turn carefully with a spatula. Cook about 2 minutes more on the second side. Transfer the fish to warm serving plates. Squeeze some lemon or lime juice over them and serve with lemon or lime wedges.

Yield: Serves 4

"From the stellar Aureole restaurant in Manhattan ..."

Charlie Palmer's Steamed Halibut in Clam Broth

This healthful and spectacular-looking dish was given to us by Charles Palmer, chef-owner of the elegant Aureole on East 61st Street in Manhattan (212-319-1660). He is the author of *Great American Food*, (Random House). The cooking technique for the fish is unconventional, but it works great.

Preparation Time: ABOUT 20 MINUTES
Cooking Time: ABOUT 20 MINUTES

LOW FAT

6 5-ounce squares of halibut, skinless and boneless
Salt and freshly ground white pepper to taste
Leaves from 3 branches of tarragon (about 36 leaves)
3 tablespoons olive oil (preferably extra-virgin olive oil)
4 cups fish stock (see recipe page 211), or clam juice
2 cups dry white wine
2 pounds manila clams, scrubbed and rinsed
½ cup minced carrots (minced very fine, like confetti)
½ cup sugar snap peas, cut on a bias
½ cup pearl onions, dropped in boiling water for 30 seconds
¼ cup diced ripe tomatoes

1. Lightly season each piece of halibut with salt and freshly ground white pepper. Place 3 tarragon leaves on each side of the halibut, pressing them to adhere.
2. Cut six 10-x-10-inch squares of plastic wrap and spread them on a flat surface. Using a pastry brush, coat the top sides with 1 tablespoon of the olive oil. Securely enclose each piece of fish in the plastic wrap.
3. Bring a pot of water to a boil. Place a steamer rack on top. Arrange the fish in the steamer and cover (you may have to do it in batches). Steam for about 8 minutes per inch of thickness, or until the fish is just firm but still slightly underdone in the center. Remove the fish from the steamer and keep warm.
4. In a large pan, combine the fish stock and white wine. Add the clams, cover, and cook for about 8 minutes or until all of the clams have opened (discard any that do not). Using a slotted spoon, lift the clams from the broth, place them in a bowl, and keep warm. Lower the heat and add to the pan the carrots, peas, onions, and tomato. Simmer for 1 to 2 minutes, or until the carrots are tender. Taste for seasonings.
5. To serve: Spoon equal portions of the broth and vegetables into six shallow bowls. Unwrap the fish and place one piece in the center of each bowl. Garnish with some of the rosemary. Place equal portions of the clams around the fish. Drizzle remaining olive oil over the top of the fish and serve immediately.

Yield: 6 servings

How do I know how long to cook fish?

According to the "Canadian Fish Rule," your fish should be cooked 10 minutes per inch of thickness, no matter what the cooking method. If the fish is stuffed or rolled, consider that as part of the total fish's thickness. A ½-inch-thick swordfish steak, therefore, should be cooked for a total of 5 minutes, or 2½ minutes per side. This is a good general rule but just to be safe check your fish sooner, especially if you like tuna and salmon a little rare. If you use a thermometer, look for an internal temperature of 140 to 145 degrees.

Charlie Palmer at his Manhattan restaurant, Aureole.

"It's too simple to believe ..."

Pan-Fried Whole Red Snapper

An exquisitely fresh fish needs no elaborate preparation. The recipe below sounds too simple to believe, but if the fish is absolutely fresh, this is a wonderful way to savor it.

Preparation Time: 5 MINUTES
Cooking Time: ABOUT 20 MINUTES

SUPER FAST LOW FAT

1 whole red snapper or sea bass, cleaned (about 2 pounds)
Salt and freshly ground black pepper to taste
2 tablespoons olive oil
6 lemon wedges

1. At home, rinse the fish under cold running water and pat dry with paper towels. Season the fish well with salt and pepper.
2. Heat the oil in a large, heavy pan. (If you have fresh herbs like tarragon, thyme, or rosemary, stuff some inside the fish's cavity.) Place the fish in the pan, sprinkle with juice from 2 lemon wedges, and cook over medium-high heat for 8 to 9 minutes (for a fish 1½- to 2-inches thick). The fish will sizzle and crackle as it cooks.
3. Carefully turn the fish and cook for another 8 minutes. The skin should be crisp and golden on each side, and the flesh should be flaky.
4. Serve the whole fish on a platter with lemon wedges. Sprinkle over it some Lemon-Garlic Dressing (see recipe page 75) and serve with Confetti Orzo (see recipe page 290).

Yield: 2 servings

"From the tantalizing Spanish restaurant, Meson Galicia, in Norwalk, Connecticut ..."

Grilled Striped Bass with Little Neck Clams

Ignacio Blanco has been a friend of ours for years, and we're lucky to have his charming and authentic Spanish restaurant just minutes from the store. Ignacio gave us this fantastic recipe for an authentic Galician seafood dinner. (The province of Galicia is in the far northwest corner of Spain, which is a major fishing region.) Not only does it taste great, it is beautiful looking on the plate. (Meson Galicia is at 10 Wall Street, Norwalk, Connecticut (203) 866-8800.)

8 fillets of striped bass, about 8 ounces each (or almost any other mild-flavored fish)
6 tablespoons olive oil
Salt and freshly ground black pepper to taste
2 cloves garlic, sliced
1 pasilla chili (or any mild-hot chili, or cayenne to taste)
1 bunch parsley, stems removed, and leaves chopped
4 ounces sherry vinegar (or balsamic vinegar)
32 littleneck clams

1. Preheat a grill or the oven to 375 degrees. Place the fish fillets on a baking sheet and drizzle them with 4 tablespoons of the olive oil. Season generously with salt and pepper.
2. Grill or sauté the fillets for about 3½ minutes per side (it varies with the fillet's thickness). Set aside in a warm place on a heated dish.
3. In a large pan add 2 tablespoons of olive oil. Cook the garlic and the chili until the garlic is golden. Remove the chili and discard. Add the parsley and vinegar. Cook for one minute, stirring, and remove the pan from the heat and set aside.
4. In a large pot holding 1 cup of boiling water, cook the clams, covered, until they open. Add the clams and the cooking liquid to the pan holding the parsley sauce. Return the pan to the heat on high setting and stir for about 2 minutes. Taste for seasonings.
5. Place the fillets on warm serving plates, and spoon some of the sauce and clams over each portion.

Yield: Serves 6 to 8

Ignacio Blanco at Meson Galicia in Norwalk, Connecticut.

Is it better to buy the salmon steak or the fillet?

Stew's buys whole 10- to 12-pound salmons and cuts them fresh at the store.

Customers prefer the filleted salmon because they don't have to worry about bones.

Seared Salmon Fillets with Tomato-Basil Sauce

Customers at Stew Leonard's are buying more salmon than ever, and they often ask me or our staff how to cook it. The tender pink flesh of salmon is delicious when cooked just long enough to firm up the fillet — sort of medium rare. One good method is to sear the salmon in a very hot pan then finish it in the oven just before serving — this keeps the fillet wonderfully moist. The recipe here can be adapted for just one or two portions if you like.

Preparation Time: 10 MINUTES
Cooking Time: 20 MINUTES

SUPER FAST · LOW FAT

1½ to 2-pound side of fresh salmon, with skin on one side
Salt and freshly ground black pepper to taste
1 teaspoon vegetable oil

Salmon steaks are great on a hot grill. The fillets are best seared, baked, poached, or sautéed.

1. Preheat the oven to 400 degrees.

2. Place the salmon, skin side down, on a cutting board. With a sharp knife trim any little pieces of fat along the edges of fish. Remove the 1-inch-wide piece of belly fat from the bottom of the fillet — or ask one of our fish sellers to do it for you. Locate the row of "pin bones" that run along the thickest part of the salmon fillet. Remove them with needle-nose pliers or a strawberry huller. Grasp each bone and pull to remove as many as possible before cooking the fish.

3. Cut the fillet crosswise into 6 pieces, each about 2- to 3-inches wide. With the skin side up, make two parallel slices in each portion of fish.

4. Heat the oil in a large non-stick pan over high heat. Add the salmon fillets, skin side down, and cook for about 2 minutes, or until the skin is crisp. With a spatula, pick up the fish fillets and place them,

flesh side down, on a baking tray. Roast for 2 minutes. The salmon may be prepared up to this point and held for an hour, refrigerated, before finishing it. (This might be helpful if you have dinner guests.)

5. When ready to serve, place the tray of partially cooked fish fillets in the preheated oven and bake for 6 to 7 minutes or until fish is just firm to the touch and the center is pinkish. Carefully transfer each portion of salmon onto a serving plate and dress with some of the Fresh Tomato-Basil Sauce (see following recipe).

Yield: 6 servings

What are those white lines running through salmon fillets?

These "lines" are the natural fat in the fish that contain the healthful Omega 3 oils. It is the same fat that gives the fish flavor and moisture.

Tomato-Basil Sauce

This quick and easy all-purpose sauce could be used with other dishes like pasta and pizza.

Preparation Time: 5 MINUTES
Cooking Time: NONE

SUPER FAST
LOW FAT
PREPARE IN ADVANCE

2 bunches fresh basil
¾ cup olive oil
2 cups coarsely chopped plum tomatoes (about 4 tomatoes)
Salt and freshly ground black pepper to taste

1. Pick the leaves from the stems of the basil. Place the basil leaves and all remaining ingredients in the bowl of a food processor or blender. Process or blend for 30 seconds. There should still be chunks of tomato visible in the sauce. Adjust the seasonings to taste.

   Warm in a pot before serving. You can also serve this at room temperature.

Yield: 2½ to 3 cups

What is farm-raised salmon?

There are "wild" and "farm-raised" salmon. In the last 10 years farm-raised salmon production has exploded. Wild salmon is just what the name says, "from the wild." The salmon spawn in rivers then live in the sea. Farm-raised salmon are kept in floating corrals under controlled conditions, and fed a special high-nutrient diet. They are pampered until they reach a certain weight to be sold. The whole process takes about 2½ years. As our fish director, Dave Zavarelli, says, "A farm-raised salmon is a salmon that doesn't have to work for a living!" Stew's buys its salmon from the Fundy Bay where our supplier, Heritage Salmon Company, has a large farm.

This whole poached salmon is one of our best sellers for catering. Our customers rave about the presentation.

Poached Salmon with Dill

Preparation Time: 10 MINUTES
Cooking Time: 10 MINUTES

SUPER FAST · LOW FAT

4 tablespoons soft butter
1 tablespoon chopped fresh dill (or tarragon, rosemary, or chervil)
4 boneless salmon steaks (about ½ pound each)
4 tablespoons white wine vinegar
1 cup sliced onions
⅛ teaspoon cayenne pepper
Salt to taste
6 whole black peppercorns

1. In a bowl, blend the butter and dill with your fingers. Roll the mixture into a cylinder on wax paper. Refrigerate until needed.
2. Arrange the salmon over a shallow pan, like a sheet pan with high sides. Cover with cold water and all of the other ingredients.
3. Bring to a boil, lower heat to simmer, and poach for about 5 minutes, or until the center is pink. Drain. Rub a pat of herb butter over the top of the fillets, and serve.

Yield: 4 servings

Pietro's Herb-Perfumed Salmon Roasted in Parchment

Our friend in nearby Westport, Connecticut, Pietro Scotti runs an award-winning and charming restaurant called Da Pietro's. Pietro contributed this unique and tasty dish, in which you enclose salmon fillets in parchment paper before roasting — this preserves the fish's moisture.

Preparation Time: 10 MINUTES
Cooking Time: 17 MINUTES

2 7-ounce pieces of fillets of salmon
4 plum tomatoes, sliced
3 medium potatoes, peeled and thinly sliced
¾ cup olive oil
1 leek, cleaned (split the white bulb and some of the green and run tap water over it to remove sand), thinly chopped
½ cup fresh basil
4 cloves garlic, peeled and thinly sliced
2 tablespoon fresh parsley, chopped
5 branches fresh tarragon (or 1 teaspoon dried tarragon)
Salt and freshly ground black pepper to taste

1. Preheat a 400-degree oven.
2. Cut 4 sheets of aluminum foil into 14-x-14-inch squares. Place them on a sheet pan. Cut parchment paper to the same dimensions and lay over the aluminum foil.
3. Take half of the ingredients and divide them over each piece of parchment, starting with the potatoes, then the salmon, tomatoes, leeks, garlic, basil, parsley, lemon zest, tarragon, salt and pepper. Drizzle the olive oil over them.
4. Carefully fold up the edges of parchment paper and aluminum foil and seal very well. Place in the oven and cook for 17 minutes. Remove from the oven and serve. (Diners should open the packets very carefully.) Using a spatula, transfer the contents to the plate.

Yield: 4 servings

Pietro Scotti is one of our favorite Italian chefs. My father would love to get his Bolognese recipe!

Is farm-raised salmon as good as wild salmon?

The great thing about food is that there are so many debates about it. Is a female lobster more tender than a male? Does coffee taste as good if it's put in the freezer? Can you taste a big difference between dry-aged and wet-aged beef? Does farm-raised Atlantic salmon taste as good as wild salmon? The professional fishermen and packers we talk with disagree with each other! Some say wild salmon has a more firm texture and a pronounced briny flavor. Others say that farm-raised salmon, which are fed a special diet, have a more fatty and flavorful flesh. We have done taste tests here at Stew's and we cannot tell the difference. Why don't you try and let us know what you think!

What accounts for salmon's wide price variations in different stores?

There is one species of Atlantic salmon and 6 species of Pacific salmon. There is an abundance of Pacific salmon in the fall, especially off Alaska. Prices drop when that happens. Many of these varieties don't have the flavor of the Atlantic Salmon. We have tried selling Pacific salmon at the store but too many customers complained that it didn't taste right. It's only Atlantic salmon now for Stew's!

"From the famous Oceana in New York City ..."

Rick Moonen's Grilled Salmon over Arugula with Salsa Cruda

This recipe comes from our friend Rick Moonen, one of the great seafood chefs in America. He cooks at the restaurant Oceana, on East 54th Street in Manhattan (212-759-5941). The peppery flavor of arugula is fantastic with the buttery salmon.

Preparation Time: 5 MINUTES
Cooking Time: ABOUT 5 MINUTES

SUPER FAST LOW FAT

4 6-ounce salmon fillets, skinless and boneless
Kosher salt and freshly ground black pepper to taste
2 tablespoons fresh cilantro, stems removed, and chopped
⅓ cup olive oil
4 cups arugula, cleaned and loosely packed (do not bruise the leaves)
Salsa Cruda (see following recipe)

1. Season both sides of the salmon generously with salt and pepper.
2. In a bowl, blend together the cilantro and olive oil.
3. Brush the cilantro oil on both sides of the salmon. Let the salmon stand at room temperature for about 30-45 minutes.
4. Place the salmon on a hot grill or in a hot pan and cook for 2 to 3 minutes per side, depending on the fish's thickness (if it is ¾-inch thick, the time is closer to 2 minutes; for 1-inch thick, it is closer to 3 minutes).
5. Place a mound of arugula over the center of 4 plates. Place a salmon fillet on top of each and surround the arugula with salsa cruda (see recipe following).

Yield: 4 servings

Rick Moonan at Oceana restaurant in New York City.

What is Omega 3 oil and is it good for you?

Omega 3 fatty acid is the healthy part of fish oil. Without getting too scientific here, suffice to say that it helps prevent clogged arteries. Omega 3 fatty acids are primarily found in deep, cold-water fish, especially salmon.

Salsa Cruda

Preparation Time: 15 MINUTES
Cooking Time: NONE

SUPER FAST LOW FAT

3 ripe tomatoes
1 red bell pepper, cored, seeded, and cut into ¼-inch-wide strips
1 yellow bell pepper, cored, seeded and cut into ¼-inch-wide-strips
1 poblano pepper, seeded and diced
3 tablespoons chopped fresh cilantro
4 tablespoons fresh basil, rinsed and chopped
¼ cup fresh lime juice
¼ cup fresh lemon juice
6 tablespoons capers
¾ cup olive oil
2 tablespoons chopped garlic
Salt and freshly ground pepper to taste

1. In a bowl, combine all of the ingredients and let the mixture stand, refrigerated, for at least 1 hour before serving (overnight is preferable).

Yield: 6 to 8 as a garnish

What does "sushi-grade" tuna mean?

Stew Leonard's buys only sushi-grade tuna, which is determined by the tuna's freshness, bright red color and fat content. "High fat content in tuna gives the fish a sweet, buttery texture," says Anthony Valenti, who began as a commercial fisherman over 20 years ago and is now the owner of Valencambo Seafood in New York. Anthony also has fishing vessels in the Caribbean and Venezuela. "The most prized sushi in Japan is the bluefin and the big-eye tuna," Anthony says.

Grilled (or Broiled) Salmon with Orange Glaze

Preparation Time: 5 MINUTES
Cooking Time: ABOUT 10 MINUTES (plus 30 minutes marination)

SUPER FAST · LOW FAT

4 salmon (or tuna) steaks, each 7 to 8 ounces
Salt and freshly ground black pepper to taste
3 tablespoons olive oil
2 tablespoons Dijon mustard
1 tablespoon lemon juice
1½ tablespoons grated orange rind

1. Preheat a charcoal grill or an oven broiler.
2. Sprinkle the salmon with salt and pepper.
3. Put the oil in a shallow platter and stir together the mustard, lemon juice and orange rind. Place the salmon in the marinade and coat well on both sides. Cover with plastic wrap and let stand in a cool place (not the refrigerator) for 30 minutes.
4. Remove the salmon from the marinade.
5. If broiling, place the fish about 5 inches from the heat source. Cook 3 minutes on one side, and about 4 to 5 minutes on the other. Check for doneness by slicing open a fillet at its thickest part. If it is still raw-looking in the middle, cook a little more — do not overcook. If grilling, the timing is roughly the same.
6. When done, transfer the salmon back to the marinade. Turn the salmon to coat it on both sides. Cut diagonally into thin slices. Serve over mixed greens if you like.

Yield: Serves 4

Mr. Masatoshi Ito, Founder, Ito-Yokado Japan, holds up a Stew Leonard bag during a visit to Japan. Mr. Ito is a master retailer and entrepreneur. In Tokyo, we also visited the market where all the local fish arrives called "Tsukiji" (pronounced "Skiggi"). The Japanese pride themselves in fresh fish!

Seared Tuna with Peppery Ginger Marinade

Preparation Time: 10 MINUTES
Cooking Time: ABOUT 15 MINUTES (plus 1 to 2 hours marination)

LOW FAT

½ cup red wine vinegar
¼ cup soy sauce
Juice of 1 lemon
Juice of 1 lime
1 tablespoon cayenne
1 tablespoon chopped garlic
3 tablespoons minced fresh ginger
1 teaspoon minced red pepper flakes
2 tablespoons chopped cilantro
¼ cup sesame oil
½ cup vegetable or peanut oil
1 tablespoon butter
2 pounds tuna steaks, skinless, boneless, and cut into 4 steaks (about 1-inch thick)

1. Combine all the ingredients except the butter and tuna in a flat pan. Stir. Add the tuna, turning it a few times, and marinate in the refrigerator for 1 to 2 hours.
2. When the tuna is marinated, heat a non-stick pan over high setting. Add the butter and the oil. Place the tuna in the pan and sear it on each side for 2 minutes (reserve the marinade). Reduce the heat to medium-low. Cook for 4 to 5 minutes per side (checking to make sure it does not overcook; it should be pink in the center). Remove the tuna steaks and set aside in a warm place.
3. Pour off the fat from the pan. Add ½ cup of the reserved marinade to the pan over high heat. Bring to a boil. Place the tuna steaks on warm serving plates and pour a little hot marinade over each fillet.

Yield: Serves 4

Where does your tuna come from?

In the summertime, we get our tuna from the waters off Montauk, Long Island, as well as the New Jersey coast. We sell about 3,000 pounds each week. Tuna is a great grilling or sautéing fish, and continues to grow in popularity among our customers. Our customers prefer yellowfin tuna for its milder flavor.

Tuna is one of the most requested items at our fish bar. This seared tuna recipe is one of my family's favorites.

Where does swordfish come from?

Stew's swordfish is bought right from fishing boats off Montauk, Long Island, and Cape May, New Jersey. In winter we get our swordfish from our own chartered boats off the coast of Australia. It is iced there and flown directly to JFK International in New York. Our trucks pick it up early in the morning and bring it to the store. Our fresh swordfish weigh between 100 and 200 pounds, and we cut them every day into 1½-pound steaks. Stew's sells more than 3,000 pounds of fresh swordfish per week!

Broiled Swordfish Steaks with Tomato-Grapefruit Salsa

At Stew Leonard's we carry beautiful fresh fillets of swordfish. This unusual but sprightly garnish adds a delightful touch of citrus from the grapefruit and sweetness from the tomatoes.

Preparation Time: 5 MINUTES
Cooking Time: ABOUT 12 MINUTES

SUPER FAST · LOW FAT

1¾ pounds of fresh swordfish, divided into 4 steaks
2 tablespoons olive oil
Juice of 1 lemon
1 teaspoon fresh thyme, chopped (or ½ teaspoon dried)
1 teaspoon fresh rosemary, chopped (or ½ teaspoon dried)
¼ teaspoon freshly ground black pepper
4 lemon wedges
Tomato-Grapefruit Salsa (see following recipe)

1. Place the swordfish pieces in a shallow pan and drizzle the oil and lemon over them. Sprinkle them with thyme, rosemary, and pepper. Turn the fish and repeat. Refrigerate for at least one hour, or overnight.
2. If broiling, place the fish on a baking tray. Slide the tray under the broiler, about 4 inches from the heating element, and cook for 5 to 7 minutes. Turn the fish and cook for another 3 to 4 minutes.
3. Transfer the fish to a serving platter and garnish with lemon wedges. Serve with Tomato-Grapefruit Salsa and White Beans and Onion Salad (see recipe page 81).

Yield: 4 to 5 servings

Tomato-Grapefruit Salsa

This zesty salsa goes wonderfully with grilled swordfish, tuna, halibut or cod.

Preparation Time: 10 MINUTES
Cooking Time: NONE

SUPER FAST
LOW FAT
PREPARE IN ADVANCE

1 grapefruit
2 medium tomatoes, seeded and diced
1 teaspoon cayenne pepper, or to taste (you might stir in ½ teaspoon and taste it)
½ cup minced onion (about 1 medium onion)
¼ teaspoon salt
2 tablespoons fresh cilantro

1. Using a sharp knife, peel the grapefruit, removing all the white membrane. Separate sections of the peeled fruit, working over the bowl to save the juice. Cut the sections into small pieces.
2. Combine the grapefruit sections with the remaining ingredients in a glass or stainless steel bowl. Refrigerate for at least 1 hour to allow the flavors to meld.

Yield: 2 cups

Note: The salsa keeps for 1 week in the refrigerator. Hotness increases as it ages.

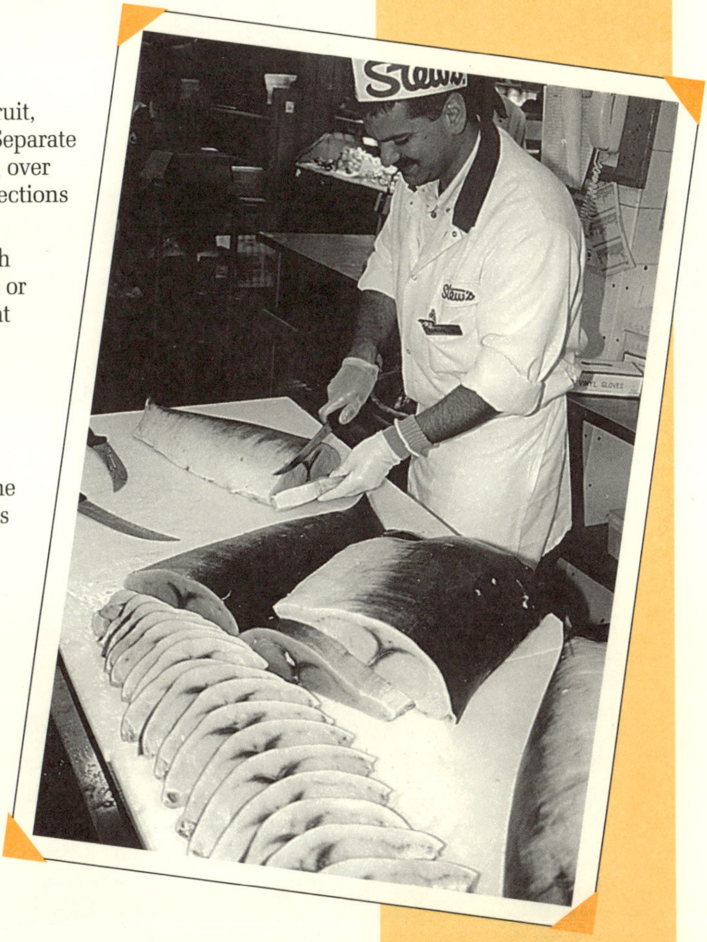

Dave Zavarelli, our Fish Director in Danbury, cuts up some fresh fish that just arrived at our store.

Stewed Bayou Catfish with Leeks and Carrots

Just a decade ago catfish was considered a southern oddity, something no self-respecting Yankee would go near. At Stew's, when we sold it as "Southern Scrod," customers bought it like crazy. When we sold it as "Catfish," sales dried up. But with the recent popularity of regional American cuisine, and the willingness of customers to experiment, catfish has become a star. It is now one of the top five fish consumed in America, and it is one of our best sellers at Stew's! Catfish is meaty and firm, with mild-tasting white flesh.

Preparation Time: 15 MINUTES
Cooking Time: 20 MINUTES

LOW FAT

2 small leeks, washed (and split from the root lengthwise, about 3 inches, then rinsed under cold tap water to eliminate any sand), and trimmed (all but 2 inches of green cut off — save the green part for stocks)
3 medium carrots, peeled and trimmed
¼ cup celery, finely minced
1 tablespoon butter
½ cup white wine
1½ cups water
1 sprig fresh thyme (or ¼ teaspoon dried)
Salt and freshly ground black pepper to taste
2 pounds catfish fillets, cut into strips about 1-inch thick and 3-inches long
Minced fresh parsley for garnish

1. Cut each leek all the way through lengthwise then cut crosswise into 3-inch-long pieces. Cut each of those sections lengthwise into ¼-inch-wide strips. Do the same with the carrots.
2. Place the leeks, carrots, celery, and butter in a shallow pan. Cook over medium heat for 5 minutes, stirring occasionally. Add the wine, water, and thyme. Bring the mixture to a boil, reduce the heat, and simmer for 5 more minutes. Adjust the seasonings to taste.
3. Place the catfish strips in the vegetable liquid. Bring to a boil, reduce heat, and cover. Simmer for 7 to 8 minutes, or until the fish is firm to the touch. Taste the liquid for seasonings.
4. To serve, use a slotted spoon to place the cooked vegetables in shallow soup bowls. Place on top a few strips of catfish for each portion, then add some of the broth. Garnish with minced fresh parsley.

Yield: 4 to 6 servings

Variation: Sea scallops may be used in place of the catfish.

"From the Historic Roger Sherman Inn in New Canaan, Connecticut ..."

Raymond Peron's Sautéed Mountain Trout with Mushrooms

Stew Leonard's carries fresh mountain trout, and many customers ask us how to cook it. We went to an expert for a recipe, our friend Raymond Peron, who is the chef at the Roger Sherman Inn in New Canaan, Connecticut.

6 trout, about 8 ounces each, cleaned
Salt and freshly ground white pepper to taste
½ cup flour
8 white button mushrooms (or any other type), minced and with stems removed
1½ sticks butter
1 cup breadcrumbs
2 hard-cooked eggs, forced through a sieve
1 tablespoon chopped fresh parsley

1. Season the trout with salt and pepper. Place the flour on a dish and dredge each fish in it, coating thoroughly. Shake off the excess.
2. In a large pan over medium-high setting, melt half of the butter. Sauté the trout, turning and basting frequently, for 12 to 15 minutes. (If you do not have a large enough pan cook the trout in batches.) Remove the trout from the pan and keep warm, while reserving the butter in the pan.
3. Brown the mushrooms in the same butter over medium-high setting. Salt and pepper to taste. Remove the mushrooms from the pan and keep warm. Discard the butter.
4. Melt the remaining butter in the pan and add the breadcrumbs. Stir for about 30 seconds. Add the eggs and the parsley. Stir. Cook until the breadcrumbs are browned.
5. To serve, spread the mushrooms over a warm serving platter. Lay the trout on top, and cover them with the breadcrumb mixture. Garnish with parsley. (Or serve on individual warm plates the same way.)

Yield: Serves 6

Raymond Peron at his historic Roger Sherman Inn, in New Canaan, Connecticut.

What is the difference between sea scallops and bay scallops?

Sea scallops, harvested in the deep waters of the North Atlantic, can grow to about the circumference of a silver dollar. They are exceptionally sweet and tender. Bay scallops are smaller, about the size of nickel. They come from the tidal waters along the East Coast, and are prized for their sweetness and succulence. Sea scallops are wonderfully tender, too, and have a mild, oceanic flavor when absolutely fresh. At Stew's, we sell about 500 pounds of scallops each week.

Sautéed Sea Scallops with Snow Peas and Fresh Thyme

At Stew Leonard's we carry big, sweet sea scallops as well as tiny bay scallops (in season, beginning in April). This recipe works with either. The crunchy snow peas are a nice addition to the buttery scallops. This recipe is equally good with bay scallops — just cook them for a shorter time.

Preparation Time: 10 MINUTES
Cooking Time: ABOUT 7 MINUTES

SUPER FAST

LOW FAT

$\frac{1}{2}$ pound snow peas, trimmed and rinsed
2 tablespoons olive oil
2 teaspoons finely chopped garlic
2 plum tomatoes, about $\frac{1}{4}$ pound, peeled and cut into $\frac{1}{4}$-inch cubes
1 teaspoon chopped fresh thyme, or $\frac{1}{2}$ teaspoon dried
Salt and freshly ground black pepper to taste
1 tablespoon butter
1$\frac{1}{4}$ pounds sea scallops — cool, but not icy from the refrigerator (cut in half if very large)
4 tablespoons chopped fresh cilantro
Juice of 1 lemon.

1. In a small pot, bring 4 or 5 cups of salted water to a boil (the water should cover the peas). Add the peas, bring to a boil, and cook for 1 minute. Drain.
2. Heat the oil in a non-stick skillet. Over medium-high setting, add the garlic and tomatoes, and toss for 1 minute. Add the snow peas, thyme, salt, and pepper. Cook and stir for 1 more minute.
3. Using a non-stick skillet large enough to hold the scallops in one layer, heat the butter over high setting. Add the scallops, season with salt and pepper, and cook, shaking the pan so that the scallops cook evenly and quickly — for about 2 minutes. Be careful not to overcook them.
4. Add the tomato-snow pea mixture, cilantro, and lemon juice. Cook, stirring, for 1 minute. Serve immediately.

Yield: 4 servings

Broiled Sea Scallops with Garlic and Lemon

This recipe is equally good with bay scallops — just cook them for a shorter time.

Preparation Time: 15 MINUTES
Cooking Time: ABOUT 20 MINUTES

LOW FAT

4 tablespoons butter
2 tablespoons olive oil
2 teaspoons minced garlic
1¼ pound sea scallops — cool, but not frigid from the refrigerator (halved if very large)
Salt and freshly ground black pepper to taste
2 tablespoons grated Parmesan cheese
½ pound snow peas, trimmed and washed
2 plum tomatoes, peeled and cut into ¼-inch cubes (about ¼ pound)
1 teaspoon chopped fresh thyme, or ½ teaspoon dried
4 tablespoons chopped fresh cilantro or parsley
Juice of 1 lemon
4 lemon wedges

1. In a small saucepan over medium heat, melt 1 tablespoon of the butter with 1 tablespoon of the olive oil. Sauté two teaspoons of garlic until golden. Set aside.
2. In a small saucepan, bring salted water to a boil. Add the snow peas and cook for one minute. Drain. Set aside.
3. Heat 1 tablespoon of oil plus 1 tablespoon of butter in a non-stick skillet over medium-high setting. Add the tomatoes and stir for a minute. Add the snow peas, thyme, salt and pepper, then stir for another minute.
4. Using a non-stick skillet large enough to hold the scallops in one layer, heat the remaining tablespoon of butter over high setting. Add the scallops, season with salt and pepper, and cook, shaking the pan, for about 2 minutes. Be careful not to overcook the scallops.
5. Add the tomato mixture to the pan along with the cilantro and lemon juice. Cook, stirring, for a minute. Serve immediately with lemon wedges.

Yield: Serves 4

What's the best way to cook shrimp or scallops?

Shrimp and scallops turn firm and opaque when cooked. It takes from 3 to 5 minutes to boil or steam one pound of medium shrimp, and 3 to 4 minutes to cook scallops. It is important to cook scallops precisely — if they are undercooked or overcooked they get rubbery.

Fresh sea scallops are put on display by Jack Driscoll. We sell about 500 pounds of scallops each week.

How many calories do I save by cooking with yogurt instead of sour cream?

A lot. Eight ounces of unsweetened yogurt has about 150 calories and 7 grams of fat, as opposed to 493 calories and 9.8 grams of fat for sour cream. A little sour cream is often necessary in sauces, however, because yogurt alone tends to break down in cooking.

"A creamy taste without the calories!"

Zita's Favorite Shrimp in Light Curry Sauce

Zita Sebastian is our Director of Operations at Stew's. She is from India and loves to cook. Here is one of her favorite dishes, made with shrimp. Shrimp is one of the best sellers at our seafood department. One reason is that they cook so quickly. With a quick sauce like the one here, dinner can be on the table in less than 30 minutes. This recipe includes an aromatic homemade curry powder (see Pierre Franey's Homemade Curry Powder, page 231). As in all curry dishes, this one includes a sweet counterbalancing ingredient. Here Zita uses apple. She also lightens the sauce by replacing sour cream with Stew Leonard's lowfat yogurt.

Preparation Time: 20 MINUTES
Cooking Time: 10 MINUTES

LOW FAT

PREPARE IN ADVANCE

1½ pounds medium shrimp
1 tablespoon olive oil
½ cup finely chopped onions
¼ pound finely chopped celery
½ cup peeled and diced apple, cut into ¼-inch cubes
1 teaspoon minced garlic
Salt and freshly ground black pepper to taste
1 bay leaf
1 tablespoon curry powder (see recipe for making homemade curry powder page 231), or commercial powder
1 tablespoon lemon juice
½ cup sour cream
1 cup plain yogurt
2 teaspoons chopped cilantro

1. Peel and devein the shrimp and rinse them.
2. Heat a large non-stick pan over medium-high setting. Add the onions, celery, apples, and garlic. Season with salt and pepper. Cook over medium heat until the ingredients have wilted. Do not brown.
3. Add the shrimp, bay leaf, and curry powder. Cook, stirring often, for about 3 minutes over high heat. Add the lemon juice, sour cream, and yogurt. Stir. Gently bring the mixture to a boil while stirring. Check seasonings. Sprinkle with the cilantro and serve immediately.

Yield: 4 servings

Zita Sebastian and her three boys — Michael, Joshua, and John Paul — visit her homeland of India. Zita gave us her family's recipe for Shrimp in Light Curry Sauce, which is popular in the southern part of India.

Pierre Franey's Homemade Curry Powder

Store this curry powder in an airtight container.

4 tablespoons ground turmeric
3 tablespoons ground coriander
2 tablespoons ground cumin
1 tablespoon white peppercorns
1 tablespoon whole cloves
2 tablespoons ground ginger
1 tablespoon ground cardamom
1 tablespoon fenugreek seeds
2 teaspoons cayenne
1 tablespoons ground mace

1. Combine all ingredients in a spice grinder. (You can also add a tablespoon of dried fine herbs; commercial packages usually contain thyme, oregano, sage, rosemary and basil.

Yield: About 1 cup

What does "deveining" shrimp mean?

Shrimp have a thin black vein that runs below the surface on the top side. It can be bitter and is best removed (although many cooks don't bother). Run a sharp paring knife down the center of the top of the shrimp, making a shallow incision. You will see the black vein. Use the knife and your fingers to remove it. It is more important to remove the vein if you are grilling the shrimp or serving them without a sauce. Otherwise, you could leave it in.

Is fresh shrimp better than frozen?

Donald Julich, the owner of Crown Seafoods at the Fulton Fish Market in New York City, told me that "Ninety-nine per cent of the people wouldn't be able to tell the difference between fresh and frozen shrimp."

Shrimp and Snow Peas with Tomato-Vodka Sauce

We developed a pasta sauce made with tomatoes, herbs and a shot of vodka, which adds a smooth, warm nuance. Customers went wild for it, and we now make it every day and sell more than 2,000 quarts each week! Here is a version that you can make at home; don't worry, the vodka cooks off.

1¼ pounds medium shrimp, peeled and deveined (see instructions page 231)
3 tablespoons fresh lemon juice
1 tablespoon grated fresh ginger
2 tablespoons lemon-flavored vodka (or add a squeeze of fresh lemon juice to regular vodka)
½ teaspoon red-hot pepper flakes
Salt and freshly ground black pepper to taste
½ pound snow peas
4 ripe plum tomatoes
2 tablespoons butter
2 tablespoons olive oil
1 tablespoon minced garlic
2 tablespoons chopped cilantro or parsley.

1. In a bowl, combine the shrimp, lemon juice, ginger, vodka, pepper flakes, and salt and pepper to taste. Blend well. Cover with plastic wrap and let stand for at least 15 minutes.
2. Pluck off and discard the tips of each snow pea.
3. Drop the tomatoes into a pot of boiling water for about 10 seconds. (This loosens the skins.) Remove, and when cool enough to handle, peel off the skins with a sharp paring knife. Cut away the cores, then cut the tomatoes into ½-inch cubes.
4. Melt the butter and olive oil in a large non-stick pan over high heat. Add the snow peas. Cook, stirring occasionally, for 30 seconds. Add the tomatoes and cook for 1 minute, continuing to stir. Add the garlic, shrimp, and the marinade. Cook for about 3 minutes. Taste for seasonings. Add cilantro, blend well, and serve immediately.

Yield: 4 servings

Spanish-Style Steamed Mussels

If you get the chance to go to Spain, definitely visit a few of the "tapas bars," where an array of colorful appetizers lines the bar. Customers nibble their way through the tidbits while sipping local red wine. One of the most popular items in tapas bars is mussels cooked in white wine with garlic, herbs and tomato sauce. With a chunk of country bread and a glass of stout red wine, it's heaven! Here is a recipe from Stew's executive chef, George Llorens, who was born in the fishing village of Sitges, just south of Barcelona.

Preparation Time: 15 MINUTES
Cooking Time: ABOUT 12 MINUTES

SUPER FAST

LOW FAT

3 pounds mussels
¼ cup olive oil
1½ cups chopped white onion (about 1 large onion)
2 tablespoons minced garlic (about 4 large cloves)
½ cup dry white wine
½ teaspoon ground cumin
1 cup fresh tomato sauce (see recipe page 181), or canned
2 tablespoons minced fresh cilantro, or parsley

1. Wash and scrub the mussels and pull off any beards that protrude from the shells. (See instructions on cleaning mussels, page 60.)
2. Place the oil, onions, and garlic in large pot over medium-high heat. Cook until the onions soften (about 4 minutes).
3. Add the wine, cumin, tomato sauce, and mussels. Cover the pan and shake gently to toss the mussels. Cook for 5 to 8 minutes, or until all the mussels open (discard any that do not open). Taste the sauce for seasonings.
4. Divide the mussels into four bowls, pour some of the sauce over them, and top each serving with a pinch of cilantro or parsley.

Yield: 4 servings

Why does "large" shrimp in some stores look like medium size?

Unfortunately, there are no government regulations regarding shrimp size. One store may sell "jumbo shrimp" that are equal to "large" or "colossal" shrimp in another store. The best method for determining size is the count — that is, the average number of shrimp per pound: 36 to 40, 16 to 20, or U-15 (which means under 15 per pound). This is the industry standard for selling shrimp, however it has not yet caught on at the retail level. Always ask the number per pound when you buy shrimp.

Where does the shrimp come from?

Wow! We sell 50 tons of shrimp during the Christmas holidays alone! It is definitely not only the season for giving but also for eating shrimp! Stew's shrimp is farm-raised in Ecuador. There are many types of shrimp available on the market today. We feel that Ecuador has the most flavorful shrimp and the most consistent quality. Seventy per cent of our shrimp are cooked, cleaned, and then flash frozen for transport.

"Exquisite" Mussels with Garlic and Basil

This fabulous, and easy, recipe makes a great appetizer. It is similar to the Spanish-Style Steamed Mussels recipe preceding this, except this one has basil and garlic. I could eat a bushel of these! It's great with fresh garlic bread.

Preparation Time: 15 MINUTES
Cooking Time: 10 MINUTES

SUPER FAST LOW FAT

4 tablespoons olive oil
¼ cup chopped scallions
¼ cup chopped fresh Italian parsley leaves
2 tablespoons chopped fresh basil leaves, or 1 tablespoon dried basil
1 tablespoon minced garlic
¼ cup minced green pepper
1 tablespoon dried oregano
½ cup dry white wine
1 tablespoon chopped fresh mint leaves (or 1 teaspoon dried mint)
Salt to taste
Hot red pepper flakes to taste
4 pounds mussels, well scrubbed with beards removed

1. Heat the oil in a deep pot. Add all the ingredients except the mussels and cook over high heat for 3 minutes. Add the mussels, cover, and continue cooking over high heat until the mussels have opened, about 5 to 6 minutes. Shake the pan from time to time.
2. Drain the cooking liquid equally into individual serving bowls. Serve the mussels in separate bowls. As you extract the mussel meat, dip it into the hot broth. Serve with French or Italian bread.

Yield: 4 servings

"You'll love 'em ..."

Chef George's Fantastic Lemon-and-Herb Crab Cakes

During one of our cookbook taste tests at Stew's, people went crazy for Chef George's fantastic crab cakes. They are golden, plump with crab, and beautifully seasoned with lemon and scallions. You'll love them!

Preparation Time: 15 MINUTES
Cooking Time: 10 MINUTES (per batch)

1 pound lump crab meat
Juice of 1 medium lemon
1 cup cracker crumbs
1 egg
$\frac{1}{3}$ cup prepared mayonnaise
Hot pepper sauce (like Tabasco) to taste
$\frac{1}{4}$ cup minced fresh chives or parsley
2 tablespoons minced fresh tarragon (or $\frac{1}{2}$ teaspoon dry)
$\frac{1}{2}$ teaspoon mustard
$\frac{1}{2}$ teaspoon salt
$\frac{1}{4}$ teaspoon freshly ground black pepper
$\frac{1}{2}$ cup all-purpose flour
2 tablespoons butter or vegetable oil

1. Remove any crab shell or cartilage from the meat, and combine the crab meat and lemon juice in a bowl. Stir in the crumbs, then set aside.
2. In a separate bowl, combine the egg, mayonnaise, hot pepper sauce, chives or parsley, tarragon, and mustard. Add salt and pepper to taste, and beat thoroughly. Combine with the crab.
3. Form the mixture into 8 cakes (about $\frac{1}{3}$-cup mixture for each) about 1-inch thick. Lightly flour each cake, then refrigerate, covered, until ready to cook (up to 6 hours).
4. To cook the cakes, heat butter (or vegetable oil) in a non-stick pan set over medium-high heat. Reduce heat to medium and cook the cakes a few at a time for 5 minutes; do not crowd the pan. Turn the cakes and cook for another 5 minutes, until golden brown and lightly puffed.
5. Keep the cooked cakes warm in a low oven while cooking the others. Serve with wedges of fresh lemon and some Tartar sauce.

Yield: 8 appetizer servings or 4 main course servings

How do I keep my crab cakes from falling apart in the pan?

Some of our customers have told us that they have a hard times keeping crab cakes together when they cook them. Here is a tip: Take a biscuit or cookie mold that is about $\frac{3}{4}$ of an inch deep. Place the mold on a flat surface and stuff it compactly with the crab mixture. Let the molds sit on a rack for about 20 minutes to let some moisture seep out. At that point you can take them out of the mold (tap them into one hand). Then coat them with breadcrumbs. Voila!

Chef George has cooked for many of the local celebrities, including Martha Stewart, Paul Newman, Phil Donahue, and others.

What is the biggest lobster you've ever seen?

Stew Leonard's sells lobsters sells lobsters in the 1-to-5 pound range. One day, Larry Lariviere at Westbrook Lobsters in Connecticut, called and said that he had just caught a 23-pounder! We brought it into the store and put it in a display tank. It was estimated to be more than 100 years old! After about two weeks of showing off this attraction, we returned our friend to the ocean. The #1 customer question asked was "Is a big lobster tougher than a small lobster?" Our lobstermen in Canada say, "Absolutely not — that is, if you cook it right!"

Classic New England-Style Steamed Lobster

If you are near the ocean use sea water for steaming the lobsters. Otherwise, just add table salt to tap water.

Preparation Time: 5 MINUTES
Cooking Time: ABOUT 20 MINUTES

Water for the steamer
½ cup sea salt or regular salt
2 pounds seaweed (optional)
6 live lobsters (about 2 pounds each)

1. Pour 2 inches of water into the bottom of a large steamer. Bring it to a boil. Add seaweed.
2. Place the lobsters in the pot. Cook, covered, for about 15-18 minutes, or until the shells are bright red. Remove the lobsters from the heat, place them on a baking sheet, and let them sit on their backs for 5 minutes. (This keeps the meat more moist.)
3. With a large knife, split the lobsters in half lengthwise. Crack the claws. Remove the small sac near the eyes and the intestine that runs through the middle of the tail. Serve with lemon wedges and hot melted butter.

Yield: Serves 6

Here I am, a little nervous, the first time I held Larry. Customers loved having him in the store. He's alive and happy today on the bottom of the ocean!

What are the different ways to cook lobster?

When we mention to customers that there is more than one way to cook a lobster, they are invariably surprised. By far, boiling is the most popular. Fred Papp, who works at our fish bar, talks to hundreds of customers a day. "Ninety per cent of our customers boil their lobsters," says Fred. No matter what method you use there is one common element to delicious lobster: adding salt to the water, which enhances the lobster's natural sweetness and also maintains the natural sea flavor. We use a 1-to-6 ratio: 1 cup of sea salt for every 6 lobsters.

Here are the four best ways to cook lobsters:

1. Boiling
Every time my in-laws come from California, we have the traditional New England lobster dinner. Boiling is the fastest and most widely used method. Use a large enough pot to immerse the lobsters. Fill the pot with salted water, cover, and bring to a boil. Add the lobsters. Start timing as soon as you drop the lobster in the pot. After I remove the lobsters from the water, I remove all the claws and tail section and do all the cracking on the kitchen counter. This makes everyone happy. Just don't do too much tasting as you're cracking (like I do!).

Chef George of Stew Leonard's likes to cook lobster in court bouillon (a broth made from various vegetables and herbs).

Lobster Cooking Rule of Thumb
1-pound lobster = 8 minutes
2-pound lobster = 15 minutes
3-pound lobster = 22 minutes

2. Steaming
This easy method yields tender and juicy meat (see Classic New England Style Steamed Lobster, page 236). Put 2 inches of salted water in a large pot, place a rack in the bottom of the pot, cover, and bring water to a boil. When water is boiling place lobsters on the rack and cover immediately.

1-pound lobster = 10 minutes
2-pound lobster = 18 minutes
3-pound lobster = 25 minutes

3. Stuffing and Baking
This is a delicious way to enjoy lobster. Split the lobster down middle of the underside (not all the way through) and remove the head sac and intestine. Discard. Crack the claws. Loosely add a stuffing of your choice — herbs and breadcrumbs, or maybe a vegetable purée — into the split

How do you judge the quality of a lobster?

Look for lobsters that are lively in the tank. Lobsters do not eat in captivity, so if they sit too long in a tank they slowly die. If a lobster is moving around in the tank, that is a good sign. At Stew's, we have installed special lobster tanks just like those used by our lobstermen in Canada. The tanks are specially designed to keep lobsters healthy.

How long can I keep lobster after I cook it?

Cooked lobster can be kept in the refrigerator for up to three days. It can also be frozen for up to a month. However, it is recommended that if you freeze it you should pick out the meat.

How do you store lobsters at home?

First of all, lobsters are like corn and bread: it's best to eat them the same day you buy them. Our good friend, Wolford MacCormack, is Stew's "eyes and ears" on the lobster docks of Prince Edward Island, in Canada. He has been in the lobster business for more than 40 years. If you have to store a lobster, Wolford says the best way is to wrap it in a wet towel then place it in a plastic bag (but don't tie it closed). He also advises that you set the bag over crushed ice in the refrigerator. This way you give the lobster what it loves, moisture and an ice cold environment (35 degrees is ideal).

tail. Lightly brush the stuffing and the exposed tail meat with butter and bake at 425 degrees.

1-pound stuffed lobster = 15 minutes
2-pound stuffed lobster = 24 minutes
3-pound stuffed lobster = 28 to 30 minutes

4. Grilling

Scilly Cay's Famous Grilled Lobster

Anguilla is a beautiful little island in the Caribbean that is noted for wonderful beaches, crystalline water and, not least, its luscious lobsters and sweet tender crayfish.

When our family goes on vacation together, one of the highlights of the trip is when our mom and dad take us to one of their favorite restaurants: Scilly Cay (pronounced "Skilly Key" by the locals). Owners Eudoxie and Sandra Wallace have graciously agreed to share their famous grilled lobster recipe. (Scilly Cay is on Anguilla, British West Indies, Tel: (809) 497-5123.)

4 $1\frac{1}{2}$- to 2-pound lobsters
Juice of 4 limes
Herb-seasoned salt (see description in recipe)
Lemon-Garlic Dressing (see recipe page 75)

1. Insert a knife into the top shell of the lobster just behind the eyes. Split the lobster down the middle of the underside (not all the way in half) and remove the head sac and intestines.
2. Crack the claws on the side that will not be directly exposed to the grill. You may need to use a mallet or hammer for this.
3. Brush the entire lobster with fresh lime juice and season with Abodo seasoning salt (a combination of hot chilies, herbs, and salt — you can improvise with salt, some cayenne pepper, and a little dried thyme and basil).
4. Place the lobster on a hot grill, cut side up.
5. Place the cover on the grill and cook for about 10 to 15 minutes.

Here's a photo of gorgeous Scilly Cay in Anguilla, British West Indies. Ask for the owners, "Doxie" or "Sandra," if you visit.

6. When the lobster meat starts to pull away from the shell, remove it from the grill. Just before you take the lobster off the grill, brush it with some Lemon-Garlic Dressing (see recipe page 75), or simply eat it with lemon butter.

Yield: 4 servings

Scilly Cay's famous marinade

Scilly Cay's has an equally famous marinade. We tried to get Sandra's secret marinade recipe but all we could do is get the ingredients (no quantities!). Sandra said "Stew, *Time Magazine* did an article on us and I wouldn't even give them the recipe!" You can experiment for yourself. Here's what Sandra uses:

Honey, tarragon, roasted peanuts, Dijon mustard, curry powder, olive oil, orange juice, orange marmalade, and seasoning. (Although Sandra has divulged the ingredients to us, the quantity of each remains a secret.)

Is there really any difference between a male and female lobster?

This has always been a debate. At Stew's, we have cooked "female" and "male" lobsters and eaten them side-by-side and can't taste the difference. We feel that buying a fresh lobster and cooking it right have more to do with tenderness than its gender. Our friend Wolford from Canada disagrees. He says, "The female is more tender!" If you want to do your own testing, here's how to determine gender. Flip the lobster on its back. Where the body meets the tail there are two prongs. If the prongs are soft, it is a female lobster; if they are very hard, it is male.

Vegetables

Vegetable dishes in this section range from the luxurious — Creamy Vegetables Gratin — to the fresh and lean — Green Beans with Arugula and Garlic — and a lot in between. Don't miss our simple recipe for grilled summer corn!

Stew's TIP

When it comes to mashing potatoes it is best done by hand with a masher or a ricer. Food processors whip potatoes too fast and make them gummy. When mashing by hand, just do it long enough to remove the lumps.

Potatoes are a staple at Stew's, and we sell more than 40,000 pounds each week! Here are a few basics you should know about potatoes.

• **Idaho potatoes**, of course, are grown primarily in Idaho. They are actually russets, the traditional baking potato. If you go into a restaurant and order a steak and potato, chances are you are going to get an Idaho. They are big, with thick brown skin, and have a low moisture content. Idahos store well, too. Aside from baking, use them for French fries and mashing.

Mashed Potatoes with Chives

The biggest seller at Stew Leonard's take-out counter is mashed potatoes, which reveals the enduring popularity of whipped spuds. In most mashed potato recipes, the potato skins are discarded. In this dish, they are left on to add color, texture, and nutrition. Serve these country-style mashed potatoes with any kind of roasted meat.

Preparation Time: 10 MINUTES
Cooking Time: 20 MINUTES

SUPER FAST · PREPARE IN ADVANCE

2 pounds red potatoes, peeled and halved (about 8 potatoes)
1 tablespoon unsalted butter
$\frac{3}{4}$ cup finely minced fresh chives
$\frac{1}{2}$ cup lowfat sour cream
$\frac{3}{4}$ cup milk
Salt and freshly ground pepper to taste

1. Place the potatoes in a pot, cover with salted cold water, and bring to a boil. Simmer until the potatoes are tender, about 20 minutes.
2. Drain the water from the pot. Add the butter to the potatoes and mash coarsely. Add the chives, sour cream, and milk and continue to mash until the potatoes are smooth. Adjust seasonings to taste. If necessary, reheat on low setting, stirring.

Yield: 3 to 4 servings

Mashed Potatoes and Parsnips

If you have never cooked parsnips you should give this easy recipe a try. Parsnips have a sweet flavor that makes ordinary mashed potatoes irresistible.

Preparation Time: 10 MINUTES
Cooking Time: ABOUT 25 MINUTES

SUPER FAST · PREPARE IN ADVANCE

1 large sweet potato
2 medium size Idaho or Yukon Gold potatoes
Salt and freshly ground pepper to taste
2 medium parsnips
3 tablespoons butter
⅓ cup milk
Pinch of nutmeg

1. Peel the potatoes. Cut them into 3-inch cubes and place then in a pot. Cover with cold water and add some salt. Cover the pot and bring to a boil. Reduce the heat and simmer the potatoes for 15 minutes.
2. While the potatoes are cooking, peel and cube the parsnips. Add them to the pot and continue cooking for 8 minutes, or until they are soft enough to mash with a fork.
3. Drain the pot and mash the potatoes and parsnips. Add the butter. Beat the mixture with a spoon or stiff whisk until smooth. Add the nutmeg, salt, and freshly ground black pepper to taste.

Yield: 4 servings

One of our best-selling prepared foods is mashed potatoes. We prepare more than 1,000 pounds every day!

Stew's TIP

- **Maine or Easterns** are all-purpose potatoes. This is a smaller, moist variety with a medium moisture content. Since they are grown in the Northeast, transportation costs are lower and they are generally a bargain. Maine potatoes are normally sold in 10- to 20-pound bags.
- **New potatoes** are just about any potatoes that are harvested when still very small. They can be red or white. New potatoes also go by the name "creamers." Their skins are thin and the flesh is tender and white. These potatoes are excellent for pan roasting, boiling or steaming.
- **Red potatoes** – called new potatoes when small — are very popular because of their thin skin and flaky flesh. We buy these from Florida, but the spring harvest season is quite short.
- For a distinctive tasting potato try **Yukon Golds.** This newer hybrid — available for the last 5 to 8 years — is pale yellow both inside and out. It is sweeter than most potatoes and ideal for mashing. In my opinion its light, buttery flavor and smooth texture are worth the slightly higher price.

Stew's TIP

"How to Make 15-Minute Mashed Potatoes"

If you have a microwave oven you can cut way down on the preparation time of mashed potatoes. Cut the peeled potatoes into 1-inch cubes and arrange on a plate. Cook in the microwave for 7 to 10 minutes or until tender. If you're adding other vegetables to the potatoes, put them in the microwave too.

Mashed Potatoes with Roasted Garlic

Roasting the entire head of garlic makes the pulp mildly sweet, perfect for adding to mashed potatoes.

Preparation Time: 10 MINUTES
Cooking Time: 90 MINUTES (includes roasting the garlic)

PREPARE IN ADVANCE

1 large head of garlic
1 tablespoon olive oil
7 peeled red or white potatoes, halved (a little over 2 pounds)
1 cup milk, or enough to make the potatoes creamy (you may use a lowfat milk)
Salt and freshly ground black pepper to taste

1. Preheat the oven to 375 degrees.
2. Remove the white papery skin from the garlic. Rub the garlic all over with olive oil. Wrap it in aluminum foil. Bake for 45 minutes to 1 hour, and let cool. Separate the cloves and squeeze out the pulp onto a plate. Reserve.
3. While the garlic is baking, place the potatoes in a pot and cover with water. Bring to a boil and cook for 15 to 20 minutes, or until tender. Drain.
4. Heat the milk in a pan over medium setting — it should be hot but not boiling. In a bowl combine the potatoes, salt, and pepper. Mash slightly with a potato masher, then add the milk, salt and freshly ground black pepper to taste. Use an electric mixer to whip the potatoes to a smooth consistency. Add the garlic pulp and stir. Taste for seasonings. Serve.

Yield: 6 servings

Baked Potatoes Stuffed with Creamy Goat Cheese

The tangy flavor of goat cheese makes this the perfect potato to serve with lamb (see Grilled Marinated Leg of Lamb page 168). Stew's carries several brands of French goat cheese, mostly the young, creamy type. Remember that the fresher and softer the cheese (squeeze the package slightly), the milder the flavor and creamier the texture. Goat cheese gets harder and sharper as it ages, which many people prefer. These excellent potatoes can be prepared ahead of time and reheated before serving.

Preparation Time: 20 MINUTES
Cooking Time: 50 MINUTES

PREPARE IN ADVANCE

4 medium baking potatoes, washed
3 tablespoons goat cheese
2 teaspoons butter or margarine, soft
2 tablespoons chopped fresh chives
¼ cup lowfat milk (or more if needed)
Salt and freshly ground black pepper to taste

1. Preheat the oven to 350 degrees. Place the washed potatoes on a baking tray and bake for 35 minutes or until a fork can be easily inserted into the center.
2. When the potatoes are cool enough to handle, make a lengthwise slice about 1½-inches deep in each potato. Carefully empty the skins with a spoon, placing the contents in a mixing bowl (reserve the skins). Use a fork to mash the potatoes with the cheese and butter. Add the chives, milk, salt, and freshly ground black pepper to taste. Mix well. Refill the skins.
3. Place the stuffed potatoes on baking tray and reheat at 350 degrees for 15 minutes before serving. If the potatoes were refrigerated after being stuffed, leave in the oven for about 30 minutes to reheat thoroughly.

Yield: 4 servings

STEW'S TIP

Mashed potatoes can be combined with an endless variety of ingredients: cooked carrot purée, chives, scallions, almost any sautéed and minced vegetable (spinach, kale, cabbage), parsnip purée, onions, puréed sweet potatoes, fresh herbs, Parmesan cheese, bacon and much more. Cook the ingredients well and mince, then stir into the mashed potatoes. Always check for seasonings.

Stew's TIP

The variety of stuffings for baked potatoes is limited only by your imagination. Try adding braised chopped cabbage or melted cheese and butter. Another good combination is chopped parsley, garlic and onions. A French recipe called "chasseur," or "of the hunt," calls for stuffing potatoes with sliced chicken livers and mushrooms that have been sautéed in butter. Or season with fresh herbs of your choice and sprinkle some Parmesan over them before popping them under the broiler for a few minutes.

What is the difference between scallions and onions?

Scallions, or green onions, are onions that are harvested very young, while the tops are still green. They are a popular item for salads and are used extensively in Chinese cooking. The flavor is slightly milder that of onions.

French Potato-and-Onion Casserole

In the days before home ovens in rural France, it was common for women to prepare casseroles or roasts and take them to the local baker, who had the biggest and hottest oven in town. Sometimes the baker's services were in such demand that residents had to make appointments. This wonderful and simple potato-and-onion casserole is typical of those dishes.

Preparation Time: 10 MINUTES
Cooking Time: 55 MINUTES

SUPER FAST

LOW FAT

PREPARE IN ADVANCE

3 pounds Idaho (russet) potatoes (about 6 medium potatoes)
4 cups white onions, thinly sliced (about 2 large onions)
3 cloves garlic, sliced
3 tablespoons butter
3 tablespoons olive oil
Salt and freshly ground black pepper to taste
½ cup chicken broth
½ teaspoon dried thyme
3 tablespoons Parmesan cheese
1 cup crushed tomatoes

1. Preheat the oven to 375 degrees.
2. Peel the potatoes and slice into ¼-inch-thick rounds. Place the sliced onions, garlic, some butter, and oil in a large pan (or two smaller ones) over medium-high heat. Sprinkle with salt and freshly ground black pepper to taste. Cook, shaking the pan for about 10 minutes. Set aside in a bowl.
3. Cook batches of potatoes, flipping once, for 10 minutes.
4. Place the onions and potatoes in a 9 x 13 x 3-inch casserole (approximately). Add the chicken broth, thyme and tomatoes. Cover loosely with aluminum foil and bake for 20 minutes. Remove the foil, sprinkle with cheese and bake another 25 minutes.

Yield: 8 to 10 servings

"From the superb restaurant Jean-Louis in Greenwich ..."

Jean-Louis Gerin's Creamy Potatoes Gratin

This is the real thing, a sumptuous, creamy casserole that is a delight with roasted meats or poultry. The recipe comes from Jean-Louis Gerin, chef/owner of the exquisite Jean-Louis restaurant in Greenwich, Connecticut. It was voted the state's most popular dining spot in the 1998 Zagat Survey. Jean-Louis told me that this is "the classic preparation" of this homey dish. It can be cooked a day or two in advance and refrigerated. Then reheat it gently in a 275-degree oven.

Preparation Time: 15 MINUTES
Cooking Time: 1 HOUR

2 tablespoons minced garlic
2 pounds Yukon Gold potatoes, peeled
2 cups cream
1 cup milk
Salt and freshly grounded white pepper to taste

1. Preheat the oven to 350 degrees.
2. Sprinkle the minced garlic over the bottom of casserole measuring roughly 9 x 5 x 3 inches.
3. Cut the potatoes into ½-inch-thick slices and layer them over the bottom of the casserole.
4. In a saucepan, combine the milk and cream and bring to a boil. Season the cream liberally with salt and white pepper. Pour this over the potatoes. Bake for about an hour, or until the potatoes are tender and the surface is golden.

Yield: Serves 4 to 6

Stew's TIP

Grilled onions are a special treat with any meal. Slice the onion into rings about ½-inch thick. Spray or brush the onion with olive oil, or marinate it (see 10 suggested marinades on pages 102-108). Grill for about 5 minutes on each side — this also works with a broiler. Garnish with grated Romano or Parmesan cheese.

Stew's TIP

We sell a lot of Vidalia onions in the store. These are exceptionally sweet, large onions from Vidalia County, Georgia. They say these onions are so sweet "you can eat them like an apple!" I've tried this, and I suppose you can, but you really have to love onions! Their peak season is May to August, although Stew's carries them until November.

Chef George's Unbelievable Potato Pancakes

George Llorens, the executive chef of Stew Leonard's, makes a potato pancake that our customers love. They are sublimely tasty and have a beautiful golden crust.

Here is the recipe. The pancakes are terrific with any type of roast meat or stew. They are particularly good with roast pork (see recipe page 154).

Preparation Time: 15 MINUTES (reheat in the oven)
Cooking Time: 20 MINUTES

2 large russet potatoes, Idaho or Washington, peeled (or 3 medium potatoes)
1 medium Vidalia onion (or other onion)
4 tablespoons chopped parsley
½ cup chopped scallions, including green part (about 2 scallions)
2 eggs
½ cup flour
Salt and freshly ground black pepper to taste (season generously!)
3 tablespoons vegetable oil

1. Grate the potatoes (using the large holes of a grater, or do it with a food processor) into a large mixing bowl. Add all of the remaining ingredients except the vegetable oil. Stir well to combine.
2. In a large pan (preferably non-stick) heat the oil over medium-high setting. When it is hot, spoon some of the mixture into the pan. (You can make the pancakes as large or small as you wish.) Cook for 5 to 6 minutes on one side, flip carefully, and cook another 5 to 6 minutes (the pancakes should be golden brown on both sides). Drain on paper towels for 1 minute per side and serve hot.

Yield: 4 very large pancakes or 12 small ones

How do you keep fresh herbs at home?

Fresh herbs, with the exception of basil and oregano, can be refrigerated or kept in a cool place. Treat fresh herbs as you would fresh flowers. Cut them at the stem and place them in room-temperature water, then refrigerate.

Aunt Margot's Swiss "Rösti" Potatoes

Another spectacular potato pancake is called rösti, from Switzerland. When I brought my family to Switzerland to visit our Aunt Margot, she made these potato pancakes and everyone loved them.

5 medium russet potatoes, peeled
Salt and freshly ground black pepper to taste
4 tablespoons butter

1. Shred the potatoes on a grater and into a bowl. Drain out any liquid that accumulates in the bowl.
2. Season the potatoes very well with salt and freshly grated black pepper — toss the spices all around so the potatoes are seasoned evenly.
3. Melt 2 tablespoons of the butter over medium-low heat. Add enough potatoes to make a fairly thick pancake. Let the potatoes cook for about 20 minutes, or until golden brown on the bottom. Flip carefully with a spatula and cook for another 15 to 20 minutes. Remember to keep the heat low — check once in a while to make sure the potatoes are not burning. Repeat with a second batch of potatoes. These potatoes can be reheated in a 300-degree oven for about 15 minutes.
4. Cut the potato pancakes into wedges and serve.

Kim and Stew with three of their daughters, visit Aunt Margot in Switzerland.

Stew's TIP

Shallots are part of the onion family. We use them in dishes where we want a sweeter, more delicate flavor than regular onions.

Stew's TIP

Did you know that sugar snap peas have only been around for only about 25 years? They are a hybrid vegetable, a cross between the snow pea and the bigger garden pea. Scientists developed these sweet little peas so you could eat them pod and all — although the hard stems should be broken off as well as the strings that sometimes run down the side.

The best way to cook them is by boiling the peas in salted water until cooked but still a bit crisp. Drain immediately and plunge the peas into a bowl of ice water to preserve their color. You can also cook them in a microwave. Place them in a plastic container and add a few tablespoons of water. Cook on high setting for about 3 minutes. This method retains the vitamins better than boiling!

Herbed Sugar Snap Peas

Preparation Time: 5 MINUTES
Cooking Time: 10 MINUTES

SUPER FAST · LOW FAT

3 cups sugar snap peas (or snow peas)
3 tablespoons chopped shallots
½ teaspoon vegetable oil
¼ cup water
½ teaspoon salt
1 tablespoon butter

1. In a pan over high heat, combine the peas, shallots, oil, water, and salt. Toss well and cook for 5 minutes.
2. Reduce the heat to medium. Add the herb butter and continue cooking, covered, until the peas are tender (about 5 minutes). Serve.

Yield: 4 servings

Sugar Snap Peas with Lemon and Mint

Preparation Time: 10 MINUTES
Cooking Time: NONE

SUPER FAST · LOW FAT

1 pound sugar snap peas (green beans or snow peas could be used), stems cut off and strings removed
2 tablespoons olive oil
1 tablespoon fresh mint, chopped
Grated zest of 1 lemon
2 teaspoons fresh lemon juice
6 large fresh basil leaves, cut into thin strips
Salt and freshly ground black pepper to taste.

1. Bring a pot of salted water to a boil. Drop the snow peas in and cook for 4 minutes. Drain and plunge the peas into a bowl of ice water.
2. In another pan over medium heat, combine the olive oil, mint and the lemon zest. Stir for 1 minute. Add the peas and lemon juice. Stir for 30 seconds. Add the basil. Season with salt and freshly ground black pepper to taste. Taste for seasonings.

Yield: 6 servings

Roasted Garlic

Many people would be aghast at the notion of eating a whole clove of garlic. However, when garlic is roasted it becomes extremely mild, almost sweet. You can squeeze out the pulp and spread it on toasted bread, or mix it in with mashed potatoes (see Mashed Potatoes with Roasted Garlic page 244).

Preparation Time: 5 MINUTES
Cooking Time: ABOUT 30 MINUTES

SUPER FAST

LOW FAT

PREPARE IN ADVANCE

1 large bulb of fresh garlic, papery outer skin removed
1 tablespoon olive or vegetable oil

1. Preheat the oven to 350 degrees.
2. In a small bowl, toss the garlic bulb in oil to coat thoroughly.
3. Wrap the garlic in aluminum foil and bake for 20 to 30 minutes, until a fork can be easily inserted.
4. To serve, slice the bulb in half horizontally. Serve the roasted bulb as an accompaniment to roasted meat. Diners can squeeze out the pulp themselves and spread it on toasted bread or use it as a condiment.

Yield: 4 servings

Stew's TIP

Just as roasting causes garlic to lose its harsh flavor, so too does cooking cloves with their skins on. Many chefs cook with unpeeled garlic when they want the sweetness and aroma of garlic, but without its acidity. When buying garlic look for bulbs that are hard to the touch (and sometimes with a bluish tint). Soft cloves are over the hill. Also avoid garlic that has begun to sprout.

What is lemon, lime and orange zest?

The "zest" is the shavings from the skin of any citrus fruit, such as grapefruit, lemons or oranges (just the outside, not the bitter white pith underneath). Citrus zest is commonly used in baking, marinades and sauces.

When is the best time to buy apples?

Apples are available year-round, but the best time is October through January. In the Northeast the official apple season begins in August with the Tydemans and Paula Reds. These early varieties aren't the sweetest available but they are good eating apples. The best New England eating apples early in the season are the Jona Macs and the McIntosh.

When we visit our apple farmers, they predict that the Gala variety (relatively new) is going to be the most popular eating apple in the next five years. They can hardly grow enough of them today!

Alan Simon, Dave Peden, and Scott Varanko check out this year's apple crop. We buy directly from the best growers.

Scotch-Baked Apples

These heady apples go well with Roasted Pork Loin with Rosemary (see recipe page 154). The alcohol in the Scotch evaporates in the oven, leaving a hint of the wood-aging flavor.

Preparation Time: 5 MINUTES
Cooking Time: ABOUT 30 MINUTES

SUPER FAST LOW FAT

4 large McIntosh apples
4 teaspoons of Scotch whisky

1. Preheat the oven to 375 degrees.
2. Make a well in the top of each apple by cutting out the core to a depth of about 1 inch. Place the apples in a shallow baking dish and carefully pour a teaspoon of Scotch whiskey into each apple.
3. Bake the apples for 25 to 30 minutes.
4. Serve as a side dish with Roasted Pork Loin with Rosemary (see recipe page 154). Spoon some juice from the baking dish over each of the apples before serving.

Yield: 4 servings

Harvest time is a fun time at Stew's. Kids love our free hayrides through our pumpkin patch.

Variety	Flavor/Texture	Eating Fresh	Baking	Sauce	Pies	Season
Red Delicious	sweet/crisp	Very Good	Good	Good	Good	Year Round
Granny Smith	slightly tart/firm	Good	Excellent	Very Good	Excellent	Year Round
McIntosh	slightly tart/juicy	Very Good	Good	Excellent	Good	Aug.-Nov.
Golden Delicious	sweet/tender	Good	Excellent	Good	Excellent	Year Round
Gala	sweet/crisp	Excellent	Good	Good	Good	Year Round
Fuji	spicy sweet/crisp	Excellent	Good	Good	Good	Year Round
Cortland	sweet/juicy	Very Good	Excellent	Good	Very Good	Sept.-Nov.
Macoun	very sweet/crisp	Excellent	Good	Good	Good	Oct.-Nov.
Empire	juicy/crisp	Very Good	Very Good	Excellent	Good	Sept.-Oct.
Rome	slightly tart/firm	Good	Excellent	Good	Excellent	Sept.-Oct.
Mutsu/Crispin	slightly tart/crisp	Very Good	Excellent	Excellent	Good	Oct.-Nov.
Paula Red	sweet/firm	Good	Very Good	Good	Good	Aug.-Sept.
Jonagold	sweet-tart/crisp	Excellent	Very Good	Excellent	Very Good	Sept.-Dec.
Ida Red	sweet/juicy	Good	Excellent	Very Good	Very Good	Sept.-Oct.

(whole apple) = Excellent (bitten apple) = Very Good (apple core) = Good

Stew's TIP

Fennel is a refreshing, tasty vegetable that is a bright addition to salads. It can be eaten fresh or cooked. Fennel has a large bulb and a stalk with light green leaves. The bulb has a lovely hint of licorice. Cut off the stalk and slice the bulb. The recipe here for roasted fennel goes particularly well with seafood. Stew Leonard's carries fennel from November until mid-April.

"An Explosion of Flavor!"

Moroccan Carrots

This is another recipe from our friend and avid gardener, Brenda Sachs, who is also the restaurant critic for the *Poughkeepsie Journal.*

Preparation Time: 15 MINUTES
(You can save time by washing but not peeling the carrots.)
Cooking Time: 10 MINUTES

2½ pounds carrots, peeled and cut into ½-inch slices on the diagonal
¾ cup olive oil
¾ cup red wine vinegar
1 bunch parsley
8 cloves garlic, peeled, smashed with the side of a large knife
⅛ cup ground cumin
¼ cup paprika
Salt and freshly ground pepper to taste

1. Steam the carrots until tender but not mushy. Place in a salad bowl.
2. In a bowl, whisk together all remaining ingredients and pour over the carrots. Toss and refrigerate until cool.

Yield: 6 to 8 servings

Roasted Fennel

Preparation Time: 5 MINUTES
Cooking Time: 45 MINUTES

2 large fennel bulbs, stalks removed
1 tablespoon olive oil
Salt and freshly ground pepper to taste

1. Preheat the oven to 400 degrees. Cut each fennel bulb into 6 equal slices. Place the fennel in a roasting pan and drizzle with the olive oil. Generously season with salt and freshly ground black pepper.
2. Roast for 45 minutes to an hour, or until tender.

Yield: 4 servings

Broiled Tomatoes with Parmesan

Preparation Time: 5 MINUTES
Cooking Time: 3 TO 5 MINUTES

SUPER FAST · LOW FAT

3 ripe tomatoes
2 cloves garlic, thinly sliced
3 tablespoons olive oil
Salt and freshly ground black pepper to taste
⅓ cup grated Parmesan cheese

1. Preheat a broiler.
2. Halve the tomatoes. Stick the slivers of garlic into the cut side of the tomatoes. Drizzle with olive oil. Season with salt and freshly ground black pepper to taste. Sprinkle evenly with Parmesan cheese. Place about 3 inches from the broiler's heating element and cook until golden.

Yield: 4 to 6 servings

Char-Grilled Sweet Peppers

At Stew Leonard's these peppers come already trimmed, seeded, and cut into strips suitable for grilling or making kebabs. We also sell pre-seasoned and marinated kebobs, so all you have to do is crank up the grill and cook them.

Preparation Time: 10 MINUTES
Cooking Time: 15 MINUTES

LOW FAT · PREPARE IN ADVANCE

4 sweet red peppers, cored and seeds removed
(or 2 red and 2 yellow peppers)
4 tablespoons olive oil
Salt and freshly ground pepper to taste

1. Coat the peppers with olive oil and season generously.
2. Place the peppers on the charcoal grill and char the skins all over — about 15 minutes. Remove the peppers from the grill and place them in a brown paper bag for 10 minutes. (The steam created by the bag makes the skins much easier to peel off.)
3. Peel off the charred skin. Slice the peppers and toss them in some Lemon-Herb Vinaigrette (page 88). You may also toss these with mixed greens.

Yield: 4 servings

Stew's TIP

A little tomato history ...

If you like tomatoes you must thank Colonel Robert G. Johnson. On September 26th, 1820, he stood on the steps of the courthouse in Salem, New Jersey, and ate a basketful of tomatoes. This sounds relatively uneventful, but prior to his demonstration it was thought that tomatoes were poisonous. People believed that certain death would come to anyone who ate these bright red "berries." Yes, a tomato is in fact a berry. But in the late 19th century the Supreme Court ruled that this controversial food was indeed a vegetable, thus imports could be taxed. Prior to Colonel Johnson' public consumption the tomato was grown only as an ornamental flower.

Stew's TIP

What about greenhouse tomatoes?

Growing tomatoes in greenhouses is much more efficient than growing in the field because the crop is not exposed to harmful elements. Growers can control virtually all aspects of the cultivation process, with the exception of sunlight. For this reason some of the most productive greenhouses are found in Canada because of the extended periods of daylight in summer. The western province of British Columbia grows beefsteak and many other varieties of tomatoes. They are all grown hydroponically and are harvested from February to November. All of the growing conditions are monitored by computers, even the feeding.

Sweet Onion Tart

This luscious, sweet tart makes a fine first course, or even a main course for lunch. If you do not want to make the dough you can buy a 9- to 12-inch frozen pastry shell.

Preparation Time: 25 MINUTES
(make in advance the tart shell)
Cooking Time: ABOUT 35 MINUTES

The dough:

2 cups all-purpose flour
6 tablespoons unsalted butter, diced
1 teaspoon salt
3 egg yolks
3 to 4 tablespoons cold water

1. In a food processor using the plastic dough attachment, combine the flour, butter and salt. Use the pulse lever to beat the mixture until it resembles fine breadcrumbs. Add the egg yolks and pulse some more. Add the water and pulse until the mixture forms a ball. Roll the dough into a ball and cover with plastic wrap. Chill for 2 hours. (If doing by hand, place the flour, butter and salt in a bowl and work it until it resembles breadcrumbs. Add the eggs and water and mix. Form into a ball.)

The tart filling:

6 tablespoons butter
1 pound finely sliced onions
½ cup flour
2 cups milk
Salt and freshly ground pepper to taste
Grating of fresh nutmeg
2 egg yolks, beaten

1. Preheat the oven to 425 degrees.
2. In a pan over medium heat, melt 2 tablespoons of the butter. Add the onions and cook, stirring, until they are soft and golden. Set aside.
3. In another pan over low heat, melt 4 tablespoons of the butter and add the flour. Stir for one minute. Then slowly whisk in the milk until it thickens.
4. Remove from the heat and season with salt, pepper, and nutmeg. Stir in the egg yolks. Stir in the onion mixture.
5. On a lightly floured surface, roll out the dough into a 12-inch diameter circle. Lay the dough into an 11-inch tart pan. Fill with the egg-onion mixture. Bake for 30 to 35 minutes, or until firm. Cool for about 30 minutes before serving.

Yield: 6 servings

Grilled Corn on the Cob with Lemon Butter

Preparation Time: 10 MINUTES
Cooking Time: 5 MINUTES

8 tablespoons butter (not too chilled)
Juice of ½ lemon
Salt and freshly ground pepper to taste
8 ears fresh corn, shucked

1. In a bowl, combine the butter and lemon juice. Place it on wax paper and, using your hands, roll the butter into a cylinder. Refrigerate until used.
2. Place the corn, with husk, over the barbecue grate. Cook, turning often, for about 10 minutes, or until it is lightly charred all over. Serve with slices of the herb butter.

Yield: 4 servings

Stew's TIP

All kinds of vegetables can be cooked on a barbecue grill or broiled, including carrots, potatoes, onions, sweet peppers, corn, and fennel. The microwave can be used to save time. I always spray my vegetables with olive oil, then cook them in the microwave. I finish them on the grill to get that smoky flavor.

We recommend microwaves for three reasons. First, the grill may be too hot to cook the vegetables (I often get a burned outside and an undercooked inside). Second, you don't lose any vitamins or minerals in the microwave, versus boiling. And third, it's much quicker! As a rule of thumb, each pound of vegetables like asparagus, eggplant, zucchini, squash, and green beans cooks for 6 to 8 minutes. (Adjust timing according to the power of your microwave oven.)

How to Pick Sweet Corn Every Time

Fresh corn is a huge customer favorite at Stew's. We'll sell more than 2,000,000 ears of corn in summer! We contract with a local farmer to assure that we get the very best available. Here's how you can pick sweet corn every time!

Know the Source.

Genetic engineering over the past decade has produced exceptionally sweet corn. Look for these new hybrids. How do you know which is which? Ask when you buy corn if they know the farm it came from. If they don't know, it probably means they are buying from a "middle man," in which case the quality and provenance are questionable.

At Stew's, we buy two types of new corn, with the unappetizing names "8101" and "8102." But believe me, these are the best on the market.

Why don't all farmer's grow this genetically enhanced corn?

Farmers are great people and some of the nicest folks you'll ever meet, but they sometimes do things the way their dads' did it, and shun certain new technology. Even though you can get fresh corn at farmers' markets, it may not be the new variety. Ask the farmer.

Honey, is the water boiling?

The adage about cooking corn says that you should get the water boiling before buying it, then sprint home. No matter what kind of corn you buy, as soon as it's picked the sugar starts turning to starch. You can retard this process by refrigerating corn, but you're better off eating it the same day. When our trucks leave our Connecticut farms in the morning, there is usually steam rising from the corn!

Look for moist silk.

Sometimes the silk at the narrow tip of the corn is brownish. That is okay. It probably means that the corn has been on a refrigerated truck, and that is good. Look for moist silk. Silk begins drying out as soon as the corn is picked. Moisture means freshness!

My brother, Tom, and I inspect some corn with our farmer, John Chapman. John grows the best varieties of corn available.

Please don't shuck the corn!

I cringe when I stand at our corn bin each summer day. Customers love to strip the corn and take it home shucked. Why? It's less of a mess, they say. True, but you are taking away nature's natural casing and moisturizer. John Chapman, who runs our 1,000-acre farm in Connecticut, says "As soon as the husk comes off, the kernels are exposed to the air. The sugars begin to break down and turn to starch."

What's the best way to store corn?

Our farmer John says, "Only store corn in an emergency!" If you have to store it, put it in a plastic bag and refrigerate.

Can I freeze corn?

Yes. Here's the best way. Husk the ears and put them in boiling water for about 30 seconds (this seals in the juices). Cool them by plunging them into ice water. Then towel dry the corn and put it in airtight plastics bags and freeze. When ready to eat the corn, just boil it until done — don't let it thaw first.

What's the best way to cook corn?

Some people add sugar or honey to the boiling water. Others add some milk. This is unnecessary, especially with the new breed of super sweet corn. Just boil it for 5 to 8 minutes.

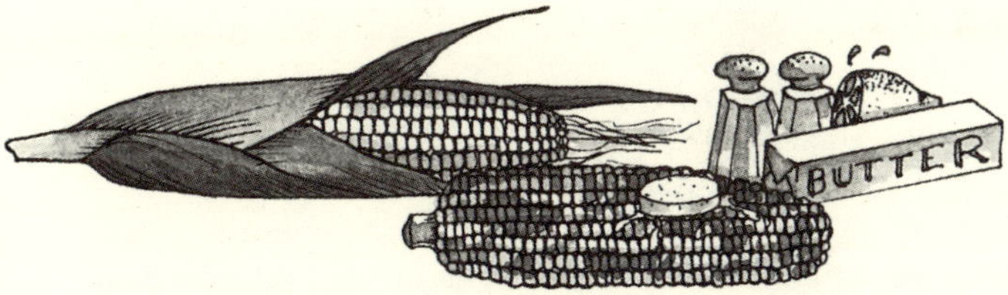

Our Favorite Grilling Methods

We're lucky to have a real corn expert at Stew's. Robert Cherubin, a native of the Haiti, manages our Hoe-Down Grill, where he serves thousands of grilled ears of corn each summer. When we were testing different ways to get the best taste from grilled corn, Robert told me about how his family used to have barbecues on the beach in Haiti. When the grill was hot, the kids would run into a nearby cornfield, grab some fresh corn, and grill it right away — that's what I call fresh!

A customer once came up to him and said that he had been grilling corn for 30 years, and that he always soaked it in water first. Robert asked him to taste his corn. "Wow!" the customer said. "I'll never soak corn again! This has such a nice roasted flavor and a great crunch!"

Robert's grilled corn recipe couldn't be easier. You simply place the ear of corn, in the husk, directly on a hot grill. Turn it occasionally until the outer husk become charred, about 10 to 15 minutes (possibly a little longer for larger ears). Take it off the grill and carefully husk it (this is the messy part). Then slather over it some butter, salt and pepper.

Another technique is to peel back the husks, remove the silk, brush the kernels with butter, sprinkle with salt, and replace the husk. I prefer the first method, which leaves the corn more crunchy.

You can also completely remove the husk and place the ear of corn directly on the grill.

Robert Cherubin is a great cook and a gentleman with our customers. Everyone loves meeting Robert.

Quick Microwaved Corn

This is actually better than boiling because you don't lose any flavor in the water. Peel the husks from the corn. Wrap each ear in a wet paper towel (this prevents the microwave from dehydrating the corn). Cook on high for about 4 minutes per ear.

Stew's TIP

Buying Winter Vegetables

When buying cabbage look for one that is firm and has no discolored or limp leaves on the outside. Carrots should also be firm with no big cracks in them or discoloration. The same goes for parsnips. Kale should be deep green and with firm leaves. Potatoes (not technically a winter vegetable) must be hard and not sprouting. Cauliflower should be white and firm all over with no brown spots.

Vegetable Custard

This delicious and light custard is a wonderful way to use vegetable odds and ends. You may substitute almost any vegetable you like.

Preparation Time: 20 MINUTES
Cooking Time: 50 MINUTES

PREPARE IN ADVANCE

2 cups light cream, or 2 cups half-and-half
¼ teaspoon paprika
½ teaspoon salt
½ teaspoon freshly grated black pepper
2 tablespoons butter, margarine, or olive oil
1½ cups minced onion (about 1 large onion)
1½ cups very small diced carrots (about 2 carrots)
1 cup sliced leeks, sliced into 1-inch-wide rings (1 medium leek)
6 cups chopped fresh spinach (about a pound if frozen)
1 bunch broccoli rabe, stems removed, and cut into 1-inch pieces (1 pound)
1 cup water
2 tablespoons flour
4 eggs, lightly beaten in a large bowl

1. Preheat the oven to 350 degrees. Grease a shallow 6-cup casserole and set aside.
2. Combine the cream, paprika, salt, and freshly ground black pepper in a pan over low heat.
3. Heat the butter evenly in 2 large fry pans or a wide pot over medium-high heat. Add half of the onion, carrots, leek and spinach to each. Cook for 5 minutes until the vegetables are wilted. Add the broccoli rabe and ½ cup water to each pan. Cover the pans and simmer the vegetables for 5 minutes. Adjust the seasonings.
4. Drain the cooked vegetables well and transfer to a large bowl. Sprinkle with the flour and stir. Whisk the warm cream into the eggs. Mix into the vegetables. Add more salt and freshly ground black pepper, and pour everything into the prepared casserole.
5. Set the casserole in a pan of warm water (the water should come about 1 inch up the side of the casserole). Place in the oven and bake for 35 to 40 minutes or until the custard is set in the center (verify by sticking a knife into the center — if it comes out clean it is done).

Serve the vegetable custard as a side dish with any fish, poultry or roasted meats, or as a main course accompanied by a Spinach and Scallion Salad (see page 87).

Yield: 8 to 10 side dish servings, or 6 main course servings

Sautéed Beet Greens with Oyster Mushrooms

Oyster mushrooms are medium sized and fan shaped. They also go by the name "tree mushrooms." The stems are grayish white and the flavor is quite mild when they are cooked. For this recipe you could substitute any other mushrooms you like.

Preparation Time: 10 MINUTES
Cooking Time: ABOUT 10 MINUTES

1 tablespoon olive oil
1 teaspoon minced garlic (about 2 cloves)
1 cup sliced oyster mushrooms (about 3 ounces)
12 ounces beet greens (about 1 bunch)
Salt and freshly ground black pepper to taste

1. Heat the oil in a large pan over high settings. Add the garlic and mushrooms and cook for 2 to 3 minutes. Reduce the heat to medium-high and add the beet greens. Cover, and cook for 8 minutes until the greens are tender. Add salt and freshly ground black pepper to taste.

Yield: 3 to 4 servings

Stew's TIP

How do you keep mushrooms from turning brown?

Keep mushrooms in a brown paper bag in the refrigerator. Mushrooms are sensitive to light and moisture. The bag protects them from light when the refrigerator door is opened.

What is a "crimini" mushroom?

A crimini mushroom is a young Portabello mushroom.

Looking at mushrooms on a visit to Franklin Mushroom Company in Connecticut. There's nothing like visiting a mushroom farm on a hot summer day!

Stew's TIP

This restorative and healthful combination of winter vegetables can be converted into an instant soup should the need arise. Just cook all the contents and add to a food processor or blender and purée to a fine texture. Place the purée in a deep saucepan and add ½ cup cream. Stir, adjust seasonings, heat the soup (do not boil) and serve with Pita-Bread Croutons (see recipe page 86).

Braised Winter Vegetables

Preparation Time: 15 MINUTES
Cooking Time: 25 MINUTES

SUPER FAST · LOW FAT

1 tablespoon olive oil
1 whole onion, peeled and diced
1 bulb of celery root, peeled and sliced into ½-inch strips (or 1 turnip)
½ head of cabbage, diced
1 head radicchio, shredded
2 cups of chicken stock or water
Salt and freshly ground black pepper to taste

1. Pour the oil into a heavy skillet over high heat. Add the onions, celery root, and cabbage. Brown for 5 minutes, stirring.
2. Add the radicchio and stock or water. Add salt and freshly ground black pepper to taste. Cover the pan and simmer over low heat for 20 minutes or until all of the vegetables are tender. Adjust seasonings to taste — very important!

Yield: 4 servings

"A Delicious Powerhouse of Vitamins and Minerals!"

Sautéed Escarole

This is the basic formula for sautéing any type of greens (kale, spinach, chard and the like). This whole family of vegetables is a dynamo of vitamins, minerals, and fiber. This recipe also is terrific with broccoli rabe.

Preparation Time: 5 MINUTES
Cooking Time: ABOUT 12 MINUTES

SUPER FAST · LOW FAT

2 tablespoons olive oil
1 tablespoon minced garlic (2 large clove)
1 pound escarole, washed and coarsely chopped
¼ teaspoon hot red pepper flakes
Salt and freshly ground black pepper to taste

1. Heat the oil in a large heavy skillet. Add the garlic and sauté until just golden (about 4 minutes).
2. Add the escarole. Season to taste with the red pepper flakes, salt, and pepper. Cook, stirring occasionally, until the greens are tender (about 6 to 8 minutes). Taste for seasonings.

Yield: 4 servings

Simmered Red Cabbage with Apples

This sweet-tangy side dish is particularly good with Roasted Pork Loin with Rosemary (see recipe page 154) or Roasted Chicken Legs and Herb Gravy (see recipe page 187).

Preparation Time: 15 MINUTES
Cooking Time: ABOUT 35 MINUTES

LOW FAT

3 tablespoons vegetable oil
1 cup chopped onions (1 medium onion)
3 apples, peeled, cored, quartered and sliced
4 tablespoons red wine or cider vinegar
1 tablespoon brown sugar
2 teaspoons Dijon-style mustard
1 teaspoon caraway seeds
½ cup white wine or water
1 cup grated carrots (about 6 medium carrots)
4 to 5 cups shredded red cabbage (1 small head)
Salt and freshly ground black pepper to taste

1. Heat the oil in a heavy pan over medium setting. Add the onions and apples, and sauté until the apples soften (about 8 minutes).
2. Add the vinegar, sugar, mustard, and caraway seeds. Heat for a few minutes to melt the sugar. Add the wine or water, carrots, and cabbage. Add seasonings to taste. Simmer, covered, for 25 to 35 minutes.

Yield: 6 servings

Stew's TIP

Red cabbage, which has a mild, faintly sweet flavor, is just one of the many members of the cabbage family. They include green cabbage (Savoy), bok choy, kale, and mustard greens.

For a quick side dish try boiling some sliced red or white cabbage, draining it extremely well, chopping it and sautéing it in olive oil with chunks of bacon. Season with salt and freshly ground black pepper to taste before serving.

Stew's TIP

Any other kind of dried beans can be added to this chili for a different texture or flavor. White beans have a subtle, semisoft texture, while pinto beans and black-eyed peas add more bulk and a toothy consistency. (See more information on dried beans, pages 80-81.)

"They'll never know it's vegetarian!"

All-Star Vegetable Chili

This chili makes a great winter supper or the perfect meal to enjoy while the family is sitting in front of the TV watching football. For a more traditional dish, add 1 pound of cooked ground beef or ground turkey.

Preparation Time: 10 MINUTES
Cooking Time: 50 MINUTES

2 tablespoons olive oil
¾ cup chopped onion (1 small onion)
2 teaspoons minced garlic (3 large cloves)
2 tablespoons flour
1 16-ounce can crushed tomatoes
1 12-ounce can red kidney beans
1 cup diced zucchini (1 small zucchini)
½ cup chopped carrot (1 small carrot)
2 tablespoons chili powder
1 teaspoon cumin powder
1 teaspoon salt and freshly ground black pepper to taste
Hot pepper sauce (like Tabasco) to taste
½ cup grated cheddar or Monterey Jack cheese
½ cup lowfat yogurt or sour cream

1. Heat the oil in a heavy pan over medium heat. Add the onions, cook a few minutes, stirring, then the garlic — you want the onions to wilt without burning the garlic. Sprinkle with flour and stir to blend.
2. Add the tomato, kidney beans, zucchini, carrot, chili powder, cumin, salt, and black pepper. Bring to a boil, reduce heat, and simmer for about 45 minutes, stirring occasionally. Adjust seasonings to taste with salt, pepper, and a dash of hot pepper sauce.
3. Garnish each serving with grated cheese and a dollop of plain yogurt or sour cream.

Yield: 6 to 8 servings

Lentils with Sweet Red Peppers

Preparation Time: 5 MINUTES
Cooking Time: 30 MINUTES

LOW FAT · PREPARE IN ADVANCE

1 cup brown or green lentils
1 sweet red pepper, cored, seeds removed
1 tablespoon chopped fresh mint (or 1 teaspoon dried)
2 tablespoons fresh lemon juice
2 tablespoons olive oil
¾ teaspoon salt
¼ teaspoon freshly ground black pepper

1. Preheat the oven to 375 degrees. Rinse the lentils well.
2. In a pot, add the lentils and enough water to cover by 2 inches. Bring to a boil. Reduce heat to medium-low, cover, and cook for 20 to 30 minutes, until the lentils are tender.
3. While the lentils are cooking, roast the red pepper in the oven for about 15 to 20 minutes, or until soft. When cool, cut into ¼-inch-wide slices.
4. Drain the lentils well. In a bowl, combine the sweet pepper, lentils, mint, lemon juice, olive oil, salt, and freshly ground black pepper to taste. Taste for seasonings. Serve.

Yield: 4 servings

Bob Greene demonstrates the art of roasting peppers. "It's really easy, and becoming more and more popular among our customers," says Bob.

Stew's TIP

I love garlic, but when my wife Kim and I are in a hurry to put together dinner, it's so convenient to have on hand Stew's Fresh Peeled Garlic, which is sold in plastic containers. The garlic lasts about 2 weeks in the refrigerator. If you cover the cloves with olive oil, they will last more than 3 months in your refrigerator!

Green Beans with Arugula and Garlic

Arugula has become quite popular at the store in recent years. This room-temperature summer dish is a perfect accompaniment to grilled foods.

Preparation Time: 10 MINUTES
Cooking Time: NONE

SUPER FAST · LOW FAT · PREPARE IN ADVANCE

1 pound of green beans, trimmed and cut into $1\frac{1}{2}$-inch pieces
3 cups arugula, rinsed and well dried with paper towels
2 tablespoons extra virgin olive oil
$1\frac{1}{2}$ tablespoons red wine vinegar
2 to 3 cloves garlic, minced
Salt and freshly ground black pepper to taste

1. Steam the green beans in a pot for about 8 minutes, or until tender. Rinse under cold water and pat dry with paper towels.
2. In a salad bowl, combine the green beans and all of the other ingredients. Toss. Taste for seasonings (you may like more vinegar).

Yield: 4 servings

Summer is my favorite time of the year. We bring all the local farmers' produce directly into the store. Our customers love it!

Summer Vegetable Medley

Stew Leonard's has private contracts with farmers all over the Northeast who deliver the finest and freshest produce. In summertime our bins are overflowing with colorful vegetables. This vegetarian stew makes a great cold salad or warm side dish with your favorite grilled foods.

Preparation Time: 20 MINUTES
Cooking Time: 20 MINUTES

LOW FAT

PREPARE IN ADVANCE

2 small zucchini (about ½ pound)
2 sweet red bell peppers, cored and seeded
1 yellow pepper, cored and seeded
2 Anaheim green chilies
1 pint cherry tomatoes
3 ears corn (or 2 cups frozen corn)
¼ cup olive oil
1 cup minced white onions
1 teaspoon minced fresh thyme, dill or basil
1 teaspoon salt
Salt and freshly ground black pepper to taste

1. Cut the zucchini in half lengthwise. Place the zucchini, cut side down, on a flat surface and slice each strip in half again. Then slice these strips widthwise into ½-inch pieces. There should be about 4 cups. Cut the red and yellow peppers into ½-inch cubes. Cut the Anaheim peppers in half and remove the veins and seeds. Cut into small cubes. Quarter the cherry tomatoes. There should be about 2 cups. Remove the kernels from the ears of corn. There should be about 2 cups.
2. Heat the oil in a large casserole. Add the onions and cook them until they soften, about 4 minutes. Add the remaining vegetables and herbs. Cook them for about 10 minutes, covered, over medium heat. Add the salt and freshly ground black pepper to taste and cook the stew for another 5 minutes or so or until soft. Taste for seasonings.

Yield: 6 to 8 servings

Stew's TIP

We carry a variety of chilies at Stew Leonard's, each one packing its own amount of heat. As they become more popular among our customers we are carrying more varieties than ever. Here is a rundown of the most common ones.

Ancho: Mild, often found in chili con carne. It is roughly heart shaped and has a wrinkled skin.
Anaheim: These are long, green, generally mild chilies that can be stuffed or added to all sorts of casseroles.
Pasilla: A dried chili, almost black on the outside, that has a mild kick.
Jalapeño: A small, green, medium-hot chili that is used in sauces, casseroles, soups and the like.
Serrano: A thin, greenish-red chili, about an inch long, and very hot, especially the seeds (which you discard). This is found in Southwestern and Mexican cooking.

Stew's TIP

What is celery root?

If you have never tried celery root you have been missing one of the more interesting vegetables on the market. Celery root is an uncomely, knobby-looking thing with orange-tinted flesh. The flesh is as firm as a turnip's, and it has an intense celery flavor. When buying celery root (also called celeriac) look for ones that are hard and with no dark blotches.

A sprightly salad can be made by peeling and thinly slicing celery root, tossing it in boiling water, draining, and then mixing with Stew's Balsamic Vinaigrette. Celery root is particularly popular among our customers around the holiday.

Vegetables au Gratin

This crunchy gratin combines fresh vegetables and crisp breadcrumbs. Serve it with broiled fish or roasted chicken.

Preparation Time: 20 MINUTES
Cooking Time: 20 MINUTES

1 large stalk broccoli
½ head fennel or celery root
2 large carrots
6 asparagus spears, hard stems snapped off
2 tablespoons lemon juice
Chopped fresh chives or chopped herbs of choice
Salt and freshly ground black pepper to taste
½ cup seasoned breadcrumbs
2 tablespoons butter

1. Preheat oven to 350 degrees. Butter a 10-inch ovenproof casserole. Set aside.
2. Trim the florets from the broccoli. Slice the fennel or celery root into ½-inch-thick rounds, then cut each round into ½-inch-wide strips. Do the same with the carrots.
3. Bring 3 quarts of salted water to a boil. Add the broccoli and cook 2 minutes, then add the asparagus and cook until both are tender, about 5 minutes. Remove the broccoli from the water and cool under cold running water. In the same water cook the carrots and celery root strips for at least 8 minutes or until tender. Cool under tap water.
4. Place the broccoli, asparagus, celery root and carrots in the casserole. Sprinkle the vegetables with the lemon juice and fresh herbs. Season well with salt and freshly ground black pepper to taste. Cover vegetables with breadcrumbs and dot the top with pieces of butter.
5. Bake for 15 to 20 minutes or until the breadcrumbs are browned and the vegetables heated.

Yield: 4 servings

A traditional gratin has cheese or some sort of white sauce on top. When it is broiled the topping bubbles and gets golden. We have made a leaner version of a vegetable gratin, using seasoned breadcrumbs instead. It works splendidly, yielding a crusty yet lowfat crust.

Carrots with Sugar Snap Peas

Preparation Time: 5 MINUTES
Cooking Time: ABOUT 8 MINUTES

SUPER FAST

½ pound sugar snap peas, trimmed and strings removed
4 medium carrots, scraped and trimmed (about ½ pound)
2 tablespoons butter
Salt and freshly ground pepper to taste

1. Scrape and trim the carrots. Cut the carrots crosswise into 1½-inch-thick lengths. Cut the pieces lengthwise into ¼-inch strips about ¼-inch wide.
2. Bring salted water to a boil and add the carrots and cook about 5 minutes; add the sugar snap peas and cook about 3 minutes more. Drain immediately.
3. Place the peas and carrots in a pan over medium heat. Add the butter, salt, and freshly ground black pepper to taste. Stir well to coat. Taste for seasonings.

Yield: 4 servings

Summer Vegetarian Menu

The first three dishes in this menu can be made a day in advance. The custard and the turnover could be made ahead of time as well, although they are better if served the same day.

Orange-Marinated Mushrooms (see recipe page 35)
Baba's California "Quick Blender" Gazpacho (see recipe page 70)
Grilled Eggplant with Mozzarella Cheese and Basil (see recipe page 130)
Vegetable Custard (see recipe page 260)
Blueberry Granité (see recipe page 317)

How do you keep asparagus fresh at home?

Asparagus should be treated like cut flowers. Trim ½ inch from the base of each stem and place upright in water, then refrigerate. If you don't have space for this, wrap all but the tips in damp paper towels.

Stew's TIP

Can you grill a tomato?

To grill a tomato, cut it in half. Sprinkle salt, pepper, and grated Parmesan or Romano cheese on the cut part. Place the tomato, skin side down, on the grill. Grill approximately 5 minutes or until heated through. Serve with balsamic vinaigrette dressing.

Better yet, broil tomatoes so they do not drip juices into the fire.

"Clean out the garden!"

Zucchini with Tomatoes and Onions

Preparation Time: 10 MINUTES
Cooking Time: 15 MINUTES

2 tablespoons olive oil
1 large or two small zucchini, trimmed and cut into ⅛-inch slices (skin left on)
½ cup minced onion
3 ripe plum tomatoes, peeled and cut into ½-inch cubes
¼ teaspoon dried thyme
Salt and freshly ground black pepper to taste
8 fresh basil leaves, chopped (or parsley, chervil or tarragon)

1. Heat the oil in a non-stick skillet. Add the zucchini. Cook over high heat, shaking the skillet and tossing the zucchini pieces gently with a spatula. Cook about 5 minutes.
2. Add the shallots and cook 1 minute. Add the tomatoes, thyme, salt, pepper, and basil. Cook and toss 2 minutes more. Taste for seasonings. Serve immediately.

Yield: Serves 4

Broccoli Rabe with Sausage

Italians are crazy for broccoli rabe, and this is the way they usually prepare it. If you like you could add some sun-dried tomatoes, ripe regular tomatoes, roasted sweet peppers, or onions. You could cut down on fat here by using Stew's lean Turkey Sausage.

Preparation Time: 10 MINUTES
Cooking Time: ABOUT 15 MINUTES

SUPER FAST · LOW FAT · PREPARE IN ADVANCE

1 bunch broccoli rabe, rinsed (about 1 pound)
1½ pounds Italian sausage (hot or sweet), cut into ½-inch pieces
8 cloves garlic, peeled and chopped
½ cup olive oil
Salt and freshly ground black pepper to taste

1. Trim the hard stalks from the broccoli rabe. Bring a pot of salted water to a boil. Blanch the broccoli rabe for 1 minute. Drain very well and pat with paper towels.
2. In a large pan over medium-high setting, heat the olive oil and sauté the garlic until light golden (not brown). Add the sausage and cook for about 3 minutes, stirring. Drain the excess fat from the pan. Add the broccoli rabe and cook, stirring, for 5 to 8 minutes, or until the greens are wilted. Check for seasonings and serve.

Yield: 4 servings

Stew's TIP

What is the best way to keep tomatoes at home?

Unless a tomato is at its peak of ripeness, do not put it in the refrigerator. A tomato should be left out at room temperature. It's also good to cover them to avoid fruit flies.

Here's an all-star produce team in our Danbury store. They arrive in the store at 3:00 a.m. to put out the fresh produce for that day. Dave Lindsay (second from left) just graduated from college and has been promoted to Produce Manager.

Pasta and Grains

If you love pasta — and who doesn't? — but always find yourself making the same two or three recipes, this chapter is for you. To name just a few: Marie's Penne with Roasted Red Peppers and Basil; Linguine with Fresh Asparagus; Lemon-Chive Fettuccine with Spicy Shrimp; and Penne with Grilled Chicken, Sun-Dried Tomatoes, and Spinach.

Fusilli with Tomatoes, Mozzarella, and Basil

One evening my neighbors, Marie and John Garofalo, invited us for dinner. We sat outside and Marie made this pasta, which was perfect for a warm summer night. It's one of those dishes you can pull together in minutes.

Preparation Time: 10 MINUTES
Cooking Time: 10 MINUTES

SUPER FAST LOW FAT

4 cloves garlic, sliced thinly
$\frac{1}{2}$ cup olive oil
6 medium tomatoes, diced (or 1 28-ounce can of crushed tomatoes)
Salt and freshly ground black pepper to taste
$\frac{3}{4}$ cup fresh basil, coarsely chopped (or $1\frac{1}{2}$ teaspoons dried)
8 ounces fresh mozzarella, cubed
1 pound fusilli (corkscrew pasta)

1. Bring a large pot of salted water to a boil. Meanwhile, in a pan, sauté the garlic with $\frac{1}{4}$ cup of olive oil until the garlic turns golden — do not let it brown.
2. In a large bowl, combine the tomatoes, salt, pepper, remaining olive oil, basil, and mozzarella. Add the garlic. When the pasta is al dente, drain it well and add to the bowl. Toss well, check for seasonings, and serve.

Yield: 4 servings

We attended the wedding of one of our team members, Imma Discala, in Ischia, Italy. While there we visited a business that makes beautiful hand-painted dishware. My daughter, Blake, models some plates we bought.

Mrs. Leonard's Marinara Sauce

Preparation Time: 10 MINUTES
Cooking Time: 40 MINUTES

PREPARE IN ADVANCE

3 tablespoons olive oil
1 medium onion, chopped
2 tablespoons minced garlic
1 cup water
1 28-ounce of crushed tomatoes
1 28-ounce can of peeled tomatoes, chopped
½ bunch Italian flat-leaf parsley, stems removed and chopped
1½ cup grated Pecorino-Romano cheese
1 teaspoon sugar
⅛ teaspoon dried oregano
Salt and freshly ground black pepper to taste

1. In a pot over high setting, heat the olive oil and sauté the onions and garlic until the onions are translucent. Add the crushed tomatoes. Add ½ cup of water. Stir until all lumps are dissolved. Add the remaining water. Stir until smooth.
2. Add the peeled tomatoes and stir well. Add all of the other ingredients. Stir. Bring to a boil, reduce heat to medium-high, and simmer for half an hour.

Yield: Serves 4 to 6

Why do you call for canned tomatoes in many recipes?

This is because, for most of the year, tomatoes are not very ripe or flavorful. Good canned tomatoes — imported are the best — are packed at their peak of ripeness and invariably are tastier than out-of-season tomatoes. Of course, in mid-summer Stew's is overflowing with wonderful Connecticut-grown, vine-ripened tomatoes. You could can them to use them the rest of the year.

My mother, Marianne, is so good that we bottled her!

Marie's Penne with Roasted Sweet Peppers and Basil

Some people are excited about food, and others are passionate about food. Marie Garofalo, whose family roots are in Sicily, definitely has the passion! She also happens to be my neighbor, so I have been lucky enough to sample a lot of her fantastic cooking. I asked Marie to contribute some of her favorite easy-to-make family dishes to the book.

This dish evokes all of the freshness and color of summer. The reason we call for canned tomatoes is that, for most of the year, they are more flavorful and sweet than fresh tomatoes. If you find nice ripe tomatoes in summer by all means use them.

Preparation Time: 10 MINUTES
Cooking Time: ABOUT 35 MINUTES

LOW FAT

3 medium red bell peppers
4 cloves of garlic, peeled and minced
6 tablespoons olive oil
1 28-ounce can of crushed tomatoes (or about 6 medium ripe tomatoes, seeded, peeled, and chopped)
1 cup of fresh basil leaves, chopped
3 teaspoons salt
Freshly ground black pepper to taste
1 pound penne
Freshly grated Parmesan cheese

1. Place the bell peppers about 4 inches from a broiler's heating element. Char the peppers on all sides — use tongs to turn them. When they are blackened, place them in a brown paper bag to cool (this loosens the skin). When they are cool enough to handle, remove the skins and the seeds and slice them into ¼-inch strips.
2. In a large pan over medium-high setting, sauté the garlic in olive oil until it begins to turn golden — about 2 minutes. Add the tomatoes and simmer for 10 minutes.
3. Add the sliced peppers, ½ of the basil, salt, and pepper, and simmer an additional 5 to 6 minutes.
4. Meanwhile, bring a large pot of salted water to a boil. Add the penne and cook until it is tender but still slightly firm. Drain the pasta and return it to the pot. Add ½ of the sauce and toss gently. Taste for seasonings — very important! Transfer the pasta to a serving bowl and spoon the remaining sauce on top. Garnish with fresh basil leaves. Serve with freshly grated Parmesan cheese.

Yield: 4 servings

Marie Garofalo is a regular customer (and neighbor), and has fantastic recipes. Wait until you try them. We love getting invited over for dinner!

Bucatini with Broccoli Pesto

This is a twist on conventional basil pesto. It requires a food processor to blend everything. This is a kid-tested healthy dish — don't even tell them it's broccoli. The report from George Bush will be in shortly.

Preparation Time: 5 MINUTES
Cooking Time: 25 MINUTES

SUPER FAST LOW FAT

¼ cup pine nuts
⅓ cup olive oil plus 1 teaspoon for the pine nuts
2 bunches broccoli buds, stalks removed and discarded
4 cloves garlic, peeled and crushed
¼ cup grated Romano cheese
Salt and freshly ground black pepper to taste
1½ pounds bucatini

1. Toast the pine nuts by placing them in a pan with 1 teaspoon of olive oil over medium-high heat. Cook, shaking the pan for 4 to 5 minutes, or until they turn golden. Set aside.
2. Place the broccoli buds in a large pot and cover with salted water. Bring to a boil. When they are tender (about 5 minutes), remove with a slotted spoon and reserve the water.
3. While the broccoli is cooking, sauté the garlic with ⅓ cup olive oil until it begins to turn golden. Remove the cooked broccoli and drain well. Place the broccoli in the bowl of a food processor. Add the garlic, pine nuts, grated Romano cheese, salt, and pepper. Drizzle in the olive oil while puréeing. (You may have to do this in two batches.) Purée until rough-textured — you do not want a paste. If necessary, add some of the reserved broccoli cooking water to give it a sauce-like consistency. Taste for seasonings.
4. Meanwhile, add more water to the broccoli pot and bring to a boil. Cook the pasta until al dente. Drain, saving about ½ cup of water in a container. Return the pasta to the pot. Add ½ of the sauce to the pasta. Toss gently. Transfer the pasta to a large serving bowl and spoon over it the remaining sauce (or toss everything in the big pot and serve from that). Sprinkle with more Romano cheese and freshly ground black pepper.

Yield: 6 servings
(For 4 servings, cut the pasta to 1 pound. Freeze extra sauce.)

Stew's TIP

Many people pour a little oil into pasta cooking water so the pasta does not stick together. Many chefs say that if you boil the pasta in a very big pot, oil is not necessary.

Secondly, always save a little of the pasta water after cooking. You can use this to moisten a sauce that is too thick — the starch in the water acts as a binder for the sauce.

Wisconsin Farmers' Macaroni and Cheese

You can't get much more all-American than a golden, bubbling casserole of macaroni and cheese. This soothing dish has been a staple around the Leonard home for years.

Little additions to the standard recipe can make a diverting difference. In this recipe, we add some powdered mustard and cayenne for extra spice. We also experimented with two kinds of cheeses. The variations are endless.

Preparation Time: 15 MINUTES
Cooking Time: ABOUT 40 MINUTES

PREPARE IN ADVANCE

1 clove garlic, peeled and halved
5 tablespoons unsalted butter
1 cup fresh breadcrumbs
1 pound penne
4 tablespoons flour
4 cups milk
½ cup minced red onion (about 1 medium onion)
1½ teaspoons powdered mustard
½ pound grated sharp cheddar cheese
½ pound grated Jarlsberg or Swiss cheese
½ teaspoon salt and freshly ground black pepper to taste
¼ teaspoon cayenne pepper

1. Preheat the oven to 375 degrees.
2. Rub the interior of an 8-by-12-inch casserole with the garlic, then grease with 1 tablespoon of butter. Coat evenly with ¼ cup of the breadcrumbs. Set aside.
3. Boil the pasta in 4 quarts of salted water for 4 to 6 minutes, until barely cooked. Pour into a colander, rinse under cold running water, and drain well.
4. Melt the remaining butter in a large pan over medium heat. Add the flour and stir. Add the milk, onions, and mustard. Cook, stirring continuously, until the sauce begins to thicken (about 5 minutes). Add the cheeses and cayenne and stir until the cheeses melt.
5. Add the drained pasta to the sauce and toss until it is evenly coated. Adjust seasonings to taste. Pour into the prepared casserole. Top with the remaining breadcrumbs. Bake for 25 to 35 minutes, or until the surface is golden brown and bubbling.

Yield: 6 to 8 servings

For a variation, add 1 cup of diced cooked turkey or ham to the pasta-cheese mixture before placing it in the oven.

To make Mexican-style macaroni and cheese, substitute ½ cup of grated Jack cheese for one of the other cheeses. Stir into the cheese mixture 1 can jalapeño peppers, chopped, and ½ cup of diced red peppers.

Spaghetti Puttanesca

The story has been told many times, how this dish translates as "whore's pasta." Evidently the spicy, haphazard nature of its creation earned it such a dubious label. It is one of our favorites, salty with anchovies, bursting with garlic, and faintly hot from the pepper flakes.

Preparation Time: 15 MINUTES
Cooking Time: ABOUT 25 MINUTES

PREPARE IN ADVANCE

¼ cup olive oil
2 ounces mashed anchovy fillets (about 8 fillets)
4 medium cloves garlic, chopped
3 tablespoons capers
½ teaspoon red pepper flakes
½ cup black olives, pitted and chopped
1 28-ounce-can chopped Italian plum tomatoes (or 8 ripe fresh plum tomatoes)
1 teaspoon fresh minced oregano (or ½ teaspoon dried oregano)
1 pound spaghetti
1 tablespoon unsalted butter or margarine
¼ cup grated Parmesan
2 tablespoons fresh parsley, chopped

1. In the bottom of a heavy pan (not aluminum) over medium heat, combine the oil, anchovies and garlic for 2 minutes to soften the garlic (do not brown the garlic). Add the capers, red pepper flakes, olives, tomatoes, and oregano. Simmer, stirring occasionally, about 10 minutes to meld the flavors.
2. Boil 4 quarts of water. Add salt and the spaghetti. Cook until al dente (about 10 to 12 minutes).
3. Drain the spaghetti. Toss with butter and 2 tablespoons of the cheese. Divide into 4 servings. Top each with sauce, grated Parmesan cheese, and chopped parsley.

Yield: 4 servings

Stew's TIP

Stew's Tips for Perfect Pasta

- Start out with plenty of water, roughly 4 quarts per pound. This prevents the pasta from sticking together — and you don't have to add oil to the pot.
- Stir frequently to keep the pasta moving around in the boiling water.
- Keep the water boiling. If it stops when you put the pasta in, place a lid on the pot to hasten bringing it back to a boil.
- Drain the pasta well before saucing it. Wet pasta dilutes the sauce.
- Count on about 4 ounces of pasta per person — about ¼ of a 1-pound box.
- To test pasta for doneness, taste a strand. It should be slightly firm to the bite — just short of al dente. The pasta will continue to cook in the colander and under the hot sauce.

Foolproof Tomato-and-Garlic Sauce

Here is a tasty, all-purpose tomato sauce that can be used with pasta, vegetables, pizza, or even chicken. At Stew Leonard's we make various fresh tortellini that go well with this sauce, including three stuffed with different cheeses, another filled with mushrooms, and a spinach-and-cheese combination.

Preparation Time: 5 MINUTES
Cooking Time: 10 MINUTES

SUPER FAST · LOW FAT · PREPARE IN ADVANCE

4 teaspoons extra virgin olive oil
1 tablespoon minced garlic (about 3 cloves)
1 28-ounce can Italian crushed tomatoes
½ teaspoon dried oregano
½ teaspoon dried basil
½ teaspoon salt
¼ teaspoon freshly ground black pepper to taste

1. Heat the olive oil and garlic in a heavy pan over low heat for 4 to 5 minutes. Do not let the garlic brown.
2. Add the tomatoes, oregano, and basil. Season with salt and pepper to taste.
3. Raise the heat and bring the sauce to a boil. Cook for 1 minute.
4. Remove the pan from the heat. If not using right away, let it cool completely, then refrigerate in a covered container, or freeze. Use for pizza (see Baked Ciabatta with Melted Cheddar and Tomatoes recipe page 14), or pasta.

Yield: 1 quart

Tomatoes on the vine (which are greenhouse grown) surpass all other tomato sales in our stores. Customers love them because of the aroma and taste. They're like home grown!

Fettuccine with Fresh Tomatoes and Basil

As we said, in midsummer, when the local tomatoes at Stew Leonard's are deep red and bursting with flavor, this dish is wonderful. Fresh basil is perfect with ripe tomatoes.

Preparation Time: 15 MINUTES
(make in advance the sauce)
Cooking Time: 20 MINUTES

LOW FAT

PREPARE IN ADVANCE

4 ripe plum tomatoes (or three ripe regular tomatoes), about 1 pound
Salt to taste
¾ pound fettuccine or any pasta of your choice
2 tablespoons olive oil
1 tablespoon butter
1 tablespoon minced garlic
Freshly ground black pepper to taste
2 tablespoons grated Parmesan cheese
10 fresh basil leaves, coarsely chopped

1. Core the tomatoes. Peel them by dropping them in boiling water for about 10 seconds, draining, and removing the loose skin with a sharp knife. Cut the tomatoes into ½-inch cubes, about 1 cup total.
2. Bring about 10 cups of water to a boil and add the salt. Add the fettuccine and cook for 10 to 12 minutes or to the desired degree of doneness. Drain the pasta, reserving ¼ cup of the water.
3. While the fettuccine is cooking, heat the oil and butter in a pan over medium-high setting. Add the garlic. Cook and stir briefly. Do not brown. Add the tomatoes, salt, and pepper. Cook and stir for about 3 minutes. Add the cooked spaghetti and the reserved ¼ cup liquid. Cook and stir for about 1 minute. Add the cheese and basil. Toss well and taste for seasonings.

Yield: Serves 4

Scott Varanko fills our display of local tomatoes from Belta Farms in Westport, Connecticut.

Fettuccine with Tomatoes and Zucchini

Preparation Time: 15 MINUTES
Cooking Time: 10 MINUTES

SUPER FAST LOW FAT

Salt to taste if desired
2 medium zucchini
3 tomatoes, about ½ pound, cored and seeded
9 ounces fresh or dried fettuccine
2 tablespoons olive oil
½ teaspoon minced garlic
¼ teaspoon dried hot red-pepper flakes
Freshly ground black pepper to taste
2 tablespoons butter
2 tablespoons chopped basil.

1. Bring a large pot of salted water to a boil.
2. Cut the zucchini into strips about 1½-inches long and ¼-inch thick.
3. Cut the tomatoes into ½-inch cubes. There should be about 2 cups.
4. Drop the fettuccine into the boiling water, and when the water returns to a boil, cook 2 to 2½ minutes if fresh pasta is used; cook 7 to 9 minutes or longer if dried pasta is used.
5. Meanwhile, heat the oil in a saucepan and add the garlic, tomatoes, pepper flakes, salt, and pepper to taste. Cook about 2 minutes, stirring, then add the zucchini strips and cook about 3 minutes.
6. Just before the fettuccine is cooked, scoop out ¼ cup of the cooking liquid. Set aside.
7. When the fettuccine is cooked to the desired doneness, drain it. Return it to cooking pot and add the tomato and zucchini mixture, the reserved cooking liquid, salt and pepper. Swirl in the butter and basil. Taste for seasonings.

Yield: 4 servings

Spaghetti with Olive Oil and Parsley

Preparation Time: 5 MINUTES
Cooking Time: ABOUT 15 MINUTES

SUPER FAST · LOW FAT

1 pound spaghetti
2 tablespoons olive oil
2 tablespoons chopped Italian parsley
Salt and freshly ground pepper to taste
Grated Parmesan cheese to taste
½ cup sliced fresh basil

1. Cook the spaghetti in boiling salted water until al dente. Drain and reserve ¼ cup of the cooking liquid. Return the spaghetti to the pot and add oil, parsley, reserved cooking liquid, salt, pepper, Parmesan cheese, basil.
2. Bring to a simmer, toss well, and serve immediately.

Yield: 4 servings

Variation: You can substitute any seasonal fresh herb for parsley in this sauce. If you like it hot, add a little hot pepper flakes.

I'm in a super rush to get dinner on the table. Do you have a super quick recipe?

If you are really in a rush, you can make a meal by placing drained pasta of choice in a large bowl and drizzling over it good olive oil. Salt and pepper generously, squeeze over it the juice of ½ lemon, and add your favorite fresh herbs (chopped). Sprinkle some Parmesan or Romano cheese over everything and toss. Serve immediately.

Every summer is exciting at Stew's, with all our locally grown fruits and vegetables in front of the store.

Farfalle with Basil and Parmesan

It doesn't get easier than this. Farfalle are the bow tie noodles. The combination of basil and Parmesan is a surefire winner.

Preparation Time: 5 MINUTES
Cooking Time: 10 MINUTES

¾ pound thin farfalle
Salt to taste if desired
2 tablespoons butter
2 tablespoons olive oil
½ cup finely shredded basil leaves or 1 teaspoon dried basil
Freshly ground pepper to taste
½ cup freshly grated Parmesan cheese, plus additional cheese to be served on the side

1. Bring a large pot of salted water to a boil and add the farfalle, stirring down so the pasta is completely immersed in the water. Cook until tender, stirring the strands often. Drain.
2. Return the pasta to the pot over medium-high setting and add the butter, olive oil, basil, pepper, and ½ cup cheese. Toss to blend. Serve with additional Parmesan cheese on the side.

Yield: 4 servings

Creamy Vegetable Fettuccine

This rich, satisfying assembly is a great dish for entertaining.

Preparation Time: 15 MINUTES
Cooking Time: ABOUT 30 MINUTES

2 teaspoons olive oil
1½ teaspoons minced garlic (about 2 medium cloves)
½ cup white mushrooms (about 4 mushrooms, stems removed and quartered)
¼ pound prosciutto, finely chopped (optional)
1 cup minced onion (about 1 medium onion)
3 cups cream or half-and-half
1 cup chicken stock
1 tablespoon minced sun-dried tomatoes, or tomato paste
½ cup finely chopped carrot (about 1 large carrot)
½ cup fresh or frozen peas
1 pound fettuccine
4 quarts water
½ cup grated Parmesan cheese
Freshly ground black pepper
½ cup minced fresh basil or parsley

1. Heat the oil in a saucepan over high setting. Add the garlic, mushrooms, prosciutto, and onions. Reduce the heat to medium, cover the pan, and cook until the onions are soft (about 5 minutes).
2. Add the cream, chicken stock, sun-dried tomatoes or tomato paste, carrots, and peas. Cook over low heat for 5 to 8 minutes.
3. While heating the sauce, cook the fettuccine in 4 quarts of rapidly boiling salted water for about 10 minutes.
4. Place the drained pasta in a large bowl and toss with the sauce and grated cheese. Add pepper to taste. Sprinkle each serving with the basil or parsley.

Yield: 4 servings

Children love to be entertained by our costumed characters. Cynthia-the-Chick, "Wow"-the-Cow, and Daphine-the-Duck.

Linguine with Fresh Asparagus

In spring at Stew Leonard's we carry the most beautiful asparagus, so sweet and tender you could almost eat them raw. This pasta dish is a real winner for asparagus lovers.

Preparation Time: 10 MINUTES
Cooking Time: 20 MINUTES

SUPER FAST LOW FAT

2 pounds fresh asparagus (about 2 bunches)
4 quarts of salted water
1 pound linguine
4 ounces unsalted butter
2 tablespoons chopped fresh parsley
1 cup grated Parmesan
Salt and freshly ground black pepper to taste

1. Trim each stalk of asparagus by bending each spear 2 or 3 inches from the bottom. The tough end of the asparagus will snap off at the point where the stem begins to get tender. Cut each spear into 2-inch-long pieces.
2. Cook the asparagus in 4 quarts of rapidly boiling salted water for about 5 minutes, or until they are cooked but still slightly firm. Remove the asparagus from the water, reserving the liquid for the linguine. Immediately plunge the asparagus into ice water to prevent overcooking. Set aside.
3. Cook the linguine for 8 to 9 minutes in the rapidly boiling water. While it is cooking, heat the butter in a large pan. Add the cooled asparagus and parsley.
4. Drain the linguine and toss it in the pan with the asparagus. Add ⅔ cup of the Parmesan cheese and adjust the seasonings with salt and pepper.
5. Divide the pasta among 4 serving plates. Offer the remaining Parmesan cheese at the table.

Yield: 4 servings

Penne with Zucchini

If your summer garden has a tidal wave of zucchini threatening to take over the neighborhood, here is a great recipe to use some of it.

Preparation Time: 10 MINUTES
Cooking Time: 15 MINUTES

SUPER FAST LOW FAT

3 small zucchini, washed and trimmed
1 tablespoon olive oil
Salt and freshly ground black pepper to taste
½ teaspoon finely chopped garlic
Pinch hot red-pepper flakes
1 pound penne
1 tablespoon butter
4 tablespoons grated Parmesan cheese

1. Cut the zucchini crosswise into very thin slices. Heat the oil in a large non-stick pan and add the zucchini slices (you may have to do this in batches). Salt and pepper them liberally. Sauté them over high heat until all are lightly browned. Remove to a plate. Add the garlic and pepper flakes. Cook for about 2 minutes. Set aside.
2. Bring a pot of salted water to a boil. Add the penne. Bring to a boil again, stirring, and cook about 10 to 12 minutes or until the pasta is al dente. Reserve 1 cup of the cooking liquid. Drain the pasta.
3. Add the pasta to the drained pot and add the zucchini, garlic, reserved cooking liquid and butter. Cook, stirring, until the mixture is hot. Sprinkle with cheese, salt and pepper to taste, and serve.

Yield: Serves 4

Variation: Combine zucchini, yellow squash, and fresh asparagus in the sauce.

What is broccoli rabe?

Broccoli rabe is a wonderfully tasty — somewhat tart and peppery — vegetable. It's great in pastas and as a side dish with roasted meats. To cook it as a side dish, trim the thick stems and rinse the buds under cold tap water. Do not drain — place directly in a pot. Add ½ cup water or chicken stock, cover, and cook for about 10 minutes, or until the broccoli rabe is wilted. Drain well and serve with butter, salt and pepper.

Rigatoni with Broccoli Rabe

Preparation Time: 15 MINUTES
Cooking Time: 35 MINUTES

LOW FAT

1 pound broccoli rabe, all but 1 inch of stems cut off
¾ pound rigatoni or other thin pasta
4 tablespoons olive oil
1 tablespoon finely chopped garlic
½ teaspoon red pepper flakes, or to taste
2 large red sweet peppers, cored, seeded and cut into 1½-inch-long strips
1 teaspoon chopped fresh rosemary or ½ teaspoon dried
1 teaspoon chopped fresh oregano or ½ teaspoon dried
2½ cups crushed tomatoes
Salt and freshly ground back pepper to taste
4 tablespoons grated Parmesan cheese

1. Cut the broccoli rabe into bite-sized pieces. Wash in cold water, and drain.
2. Bring a large pot of salted water to a boil. Cook the broccoli rabe until tender. Do not overcook. Remove the broccoli rabe with a slotted spoon and set aside. Reserve the cooking liquid in the pot.
3. Bring the cooking water to a boil. Add the pasta and cook according to the package instructions. Drain, reserving ½ cup of the cooking liquid.
4. Meanwhile, heat 2 tablespoons of olive oil in a deep pan, and add the garlic. Cook briefly — do not brown. Add the pepper flakes, the sweet pepper, rosemary, and oregano, and cook, stirring briefly. Add the crushed tomatoes and salt and pepper to taste. Bring to a boil, reduce heat, and simmer for 8 minutes, stirring often.
5. Add to the pan the drained pasta, the cooked broccoli rabe, the reserved cooking liquid, the remaining olive oil, and the Parmesan cheese. Cook, stirring and tossing, for 1 minute. Check seasonings. Serve immediately on hot serving plates.

Yield: 4 servings

Fettuccine with Goat Cheese and Asparagus

Preparation Time: 15 MINUTES
Cooking Time: 15 MINUTES

SUPER FAST LOW FAT

1¼ pounds fresh asparagus
2 quarts water
Salt to taste
1 pound fettuccine
4 ripe plum tomatoes
2 tablespoons olive oil
2 tablespoons butter
2 teaspoons finely chopped garlic
¼ pound soft goat cheese
4 tablespoons coarsely chopped fresh basil leaves
Freshly ground black pepper to taste
Freshly grated Parmesan cheese

1. Scrape and trim (bend until stalk snaps off) the asparagus. Slice the spears on the bias, creating ½-inch lengths.
2. In a large pot boil the water and add salt. Add the fettuccine and cook for about 9 minutes, or until al dente. Do not overcook. Reserve ¼ cup of the cooking liquid. Drain the pasta.
3. Drop the tomatoes into boiling water for 10 seconds. Remove them from the water and, when cool enough to handle, remove the skins with a paring knife. Core, seed, and dice them.
4. Heat the oil and butter in a large pan and add the asparagus, tomatoes and garlic. Cook over medium heat for about 3 minutes, stirring. Add the fettuccine, goat cheese, basil, reserved cooking liquid, salt and pepper. Toss well. Check seasonings. Serve immediately with Parmesan cheese on the side.

Yield: 4 servings

What is orzo and what can I do with it?

Orzo, the Greek rice-shaped pasta, has become exceedingly popular in recent years, both in restaurants and among home cooks. It has a wonderful texture that is both slippery and firm, and it blends nicely with all kinds of sauces. Orzo actually resembles some forms of baby food, which adds to its appeal as a comfort dish!

Confetti Orzo

We call this "confetti" because of the colorful minced vegetables mixed with the white orzo.

Preparation Time: 15 MINUTES
Cooking Time: 20 MINUTES

SUPER FAST · LOW FAT

2 tablespoons olive oil
1 tablespoon minced garlic (3 large cloves)
1 cup finely chopped onion (about 1 large onion)
1 cup finely minced celery (about 1 stalk)
1 cup finely minced carrot (about 2 medium carrots)
1 cup minced sweet red pepper
1 teaspoon chopped fresh rosemary (or ½ teaspoon dried)
1½ cups orzo
¼ cup water

1. In a pan, add olive oil and sauté the garlic, onion, celery, carrots, red pepper, and rosemary for 5 minutes, stirring. Add the water, and simmer for 7 minutes or until vegetables are tender.
2. Boil the orzo in three quarts of salted water for 7 minutes.
3. Drain the cooked orzo in a colander. Briefly rinse under cold water. Stir into the vegetable mixture. Adjust seasonings to taste. Serve as a side dish.

Yield: 6 cups

Chef George Llorens creates all of our prepared foods.

Linguine with Clam Sauce

Preparation Time: 10 MINUTES
Cooking Time: 20 MINUTES

SUPER FAST LOW FAT

2 tablespoons olive oil
⅓ cup chopped shallots (or onions)
1 tablespoon finely chopped garlic
4 6½-ounce cans of clams (in natural juices), or Stew Leonard's fresh, shucked clams in their juices (sold in 16-ounce containers, so you would need two)
Salt and freshly ground black pepper to taste
1 pound linguine
⅛ teaspoon hot red pepper flakes
½ cup Italian parsley, stems removed and chopped

1. Bring a large pot of lightly salted water to a boil.
2. Meanwhile, pour 2 tablespoons of olive oil in a pan. Cook the shallots or onions, stirring, until they wilt. Add the garlic and stir — do not brown. Add the clams and their juices. Add salt and pepper, then the red pepper flakes. Heat just to warm — do not boil.
3. Cook the pasta according to the instructions on the box. Drain well (reserving 1 cup of cooking liquid). Return the pasta to the cooking pot and add the sauce. If the pasta seems a little dry, add some of the reserved cooking liquid. Taste for seasonings. Serve, garnished with chopped parsley.

Yield: 4 servings

Spaghetti with Grilled Tuna, Tomato and Olives

Preparation Time: 10 MINUTES
Cooking Time: ABOUT 35 MINUTES

LOW FAT

4 cloves garlic, peeled and minced
⅓ cup olive oil
Salt and freshly ground black pepper to taste
1 28-ounce can crushed tomatoes (or 6 medium tomatoes, cored, seeded and chopped)
1½-pounds tuna steaks
½ cup kalamata olives, without pits, chopped
⅓ cup small capers, drained
½ cup fresh basil, chopped
¼ cup chopped Italian parsley
1 pound spaghetti

1. Heat a barbecue grill or broiler. Place a large pot of salted water over a burner on high.
2. In a large pan, sauté the garlic in the olive oil until it turns golden, about 3 to 4 minutes. Add the tomatoes, season with salt and pepper, and simmer for about 15 minutes.
3. Brush the tuna with some olive oil, salt and pepper, and grill about 3 minutes per side for rare (check by slicing in the middle). Undercook it slightly because it will continue cooking when added to the sauce. Remove the tuna from the grill or broiler and slice into ½-inch-thick strips about 1-inch long.
4. When the water is boiling, add the spaghetti. Cook until al dente. While the spaghetti is cooking, add to the tomato sauce the capers, olives and tuna. Bring to a simmer and cook for 5 minutes. Stir in the fresh basil and parsley.
5. Drain the spaghetti and return to the large cooking pot. Add ½ of the sauce and toss gently — try not to break up the tuna. Transfer to a serving platter and top with remaining sauce. (Or, if you prefer, add all of the sauce to the pot and serve from that.) Check seasonings (this is very important — it may need more salt and pepper).

Yield: Serves 4

Linguine and Fresh Shrimp in Quick Marinara Sauce

Preparation Time: 15 MINUTES
Cooking Time: 1 HOUR

LOW FAT

1 small onion, minced
¼ cup olive oil
4 cloves garlic, minced
2 28-ounce cans of peeled, crushed tomatoes (or 6 ripe tomatoes, cored, peeled and chopped)
Salt and freshly ground black pepper to taste
¼ cup coarsely chopped fresh basil leaves (about 12)
1½ pounds large shrimp, peeled and deveined (see instructions page 231)
1 pound linguine

1. Start a large pot of boiling water. In a large pan, sauté the onions in olive oil over medium setting until slightly golden, about 8 minutes. Add the garlic and cook until it just starts to turn golden. Add the tomatoes and bring to a boil. Reduce the heat and simmer.
2. Add salt (about 1 teaspoon) and pepper, stirring occasionally. Keep the saucepan covered and simmer for about 30 minutes. Stir in the fresh basil. Stir in the shrimp and cook for 2 minutes. Taste for seasonings.
3. Cook the pasta until al dente. Drain. Add to the sauce and toss well. Taste for seasonings and serve.

Yield: Serves 6 to 8

Is fresh pasta really better than dried pasta?

Americans went through a fresh pasta craze in the 1970s, and pasta-making machines were all the rage. Hand-cranked devices were followed by fancy electric machines, and you couldn't go to a dinner party without having fresh pasta on the menu.

Today, the fad is over and Americans are learning that, while freshly made pasta is excellent for certain dishes, so, too, is dried. Fresh pasta is more delicate and eggy than dried. It is particularly good with light, subtle sauces, especially those made with seafood. Dried pasta has more of a toothy texture and often more of a nutty flavor. It stands up better to assertive sauces like puttanesca and Bolognese.

Lemon-Chive Fettuccine with Spicy Shrimp

This tangy lemon pasta is an ideal accompaniment to any sautéed or grilled fish. It is also delicious cold. If you serve it cold, omit the butter from the sauce and replace it with an equal amount of olive oil.

Preparation Time: 20 MINUTES
Cooking Time: ABOUT 20 MINUTES

For the shrimp:
½ teaspoon paprika
½ teaspoon cayenne
1 teaspoon minced fresh garlic, about 2 cloves
3 tablespoon olive oil
2 tablespoons butter
1½ pounds large shrimp, peeled and deveined (about 24 shrimp)
2 tablespoons fresh lemon juice
Salt and freshly ground black pepper to taste

For the pasta:
Salt and freshly ground pepper to taste
1 pound fettuccine
3 tablespoons olive oil
2 tablespoons unsalted butter
Freshly ground black pepper to taste
¼ cup fresh lemon juice (about 1 lemon)
⅓ cup chopped chives or scallions

1. In a small bowl, combine the paprika, cayenne, garlic, and 2 tablespoons of the oil. Add the shrimp and toss to coat them. Cover and set aside in a cool place. (The mixture may be refrigerated overnight.)
2. In a small saucepan over medium heat, melt the butter with the remaining tablespoon of oil. Add the lemon juice, salt and pepper. Pour this into a bowl that is large enough to hold the cooked fettuccine. Set aside in a warm place.
3. Boil a large pot of lightly salted water. Add 1 teaspoon of salt and the fettuccine. Cook for about 8 minutes, or until tender.
4. While the pasta is cooking, heat 3 tablespoons of oil and 2 tablespoons of butter over high flame. Add the shrimp and cook for 1 minute on each side, or until golden brown and crisp. Season with salt and pepper. Remove and keep warm. (The shrimp may be broiled or grilled instead.)
5. Drain the cooked pasta. Put it in lemon-butter sauce. Add chives or scallions and toss well. Adjust seasonings to taste.
6. Top each serving of pasta with shrimp, and drizzle with pan juices.

Yield: 4 servings

"Angel Hair from Heaven!"

Rick Moonen's Angel Hair Pasta with Roasted Tomatoes and Shrimp

Rick Moonen, the chef at our favorite seafood restaurant, Oceana, in New York City, gave us this smashing angel hair pasta recipe. (Oceana, 55 East 54th Street, in Manhattan, 212-759-5941)

LOW FAT

3 tablespoons chopped garlic
1 cup diced onions
½ cup black kalamata olives, pitted
1 teaspoon fresh thyme or ½ teaspoon dried thyme
4 large ripe tomatoes, cored and sliced in half horizontally (or 1 28-ounce cans of whole tomatoes)
4 tablespoons olive oil
2 tablespoons capers
Salt and freshly ground black pepper to taste
1 pound fresh shrimp, peeled and deveined (see instructions page 231)
1 pound angel hair pasta
2 scallions, chopped on the diagonal

1. Preheat the oven to 450 degrees. In a large roasting pan, sprinkle the garlic, onions, olives, capers, and thyme as if you were topping a pizza. Add the tomatoes, cut side down, and drizzle 2 tablespoons of olive oil over everything. Place the pan on top of a burner until the vegetables just begin to cook (1 to 2 minutes).
2. Place the pan in the oven and roast until the tomato skins start to blister — about 15 minutes. Remove the pan from the oven. When the tomatoes are cool enough to handle, peel them. Season everything well with salt and pepper.
3. Place the contents of the pan in a food processor. Pulse a few times to make the sauce chunky (not smooth). Return the mixture to the pan and keep warm.
4. Season the shrimp well with salt and pepper. Place 2 tablespoons of olive oil in a large pan over high heat and add the shrimp. Sauté the shrimp for 1 to 2 minutes or until they turn pinkish and curl up a little. Set them aside in the sauté pan with the cooking oil in it.
5. In a large pot of rapidly boiling salted water, cook the angel hair pasta to the al dente stage (about 2 minutes — do not overcook!). Strain into a fine colander, reserving a few tablespoons of the cooking water. When the pasta is drained, add it to the shrimp pan and mix with the shrimp's cooking oil and 3 tablespoons of reserved pasta water (or more if necessary).
6. Divide the shrimp pasta among four plates. Surround with the vegetable sauce. Garnish with fresh scallions.

Yield: Serves 4

How do I reheat leftover pasta?

The best way to reheat pasta is to place it in a glass bowl and pop it in a microwave oven for a minute or two. Another method is to place the pasta in a colander, boil some water, and pour the water over the pasta. Drain well and sauce it immediately.

Margie's Shrimp Primavera

An entertaining staple in the Leonard family for years, this easy and quick recipe is nearly foolproof. Just remember not to overcook any of the ingredients. They all get a second heating just before serving.

Preparation Time: 30 MINUTES
Cooking Time: 25 MINUTES

1 head of broccoli florets, trimmed
2 cups fresh or frozen peas
1 pound spaghetti
3 tablespoons olive oil
2 tablespoons butter
2 tablespoons minced garlic (about 5 large cloves)
1 cup sliced white mushrooms, stems trimmed (about 5 medium-sized mushrooms)
30 large shrimp, peeled and deveined, about 1½ pounds
2 cups chopped tomato (1 medium tomato)
Salt and freshly ground black pepper to taste
⅓ cup grated Parmesan
½ cup chopped fresh basil

Here is a picture of my Aunt Margie. Her Shrimp Primavera is awesome!

1. Bring a large pot of lightly salted water to a boil. Cook the broccoli florets for about 5 minutes, or until tender. Remove the broccoli with a slotted spoon and set aside. Cook the peas just until al dente — do not let them get mushy. Remove them with a slotted spoon and set aside. Save the cooking water. Return the water to a boil and add the spaghetti. Cook until slightly firm to the bite, about 8 minutes.
2. While the pasta is cooking, combine the olive oil and butter in a very large pan or ovenproof casserole over high heat. Add the garlic and cook for about 1 minute, or until golden. Add the mushrooms and cook for another minute, stirring. Add the broccoli, tomatoes, and shrimp. Cook for 4 to 5 minutes, stirring constantly, until the shrimp are cooked through. Season with salt and pepper to taste. Reduce the heat to medium.
3. Drain the cooked pasta (save a cup of cooking liquid) and return it to its cooking pot. Add the vegetables and shrimp. Toss the spaghetti with the vegetables and shrimp then add the cheese and basil. If the sauce seems a little dry, add some of the reserved cooking water. Cook for another minute to heat thoroughly. Adjust the seasonings to taste.
4. Divide the spaghetti and shrimp among 4 heated bowls.

Yield: 4 servings

Linguine with Shrimp and Sweet Peppers

This dish couldn't be easier. For the shrimp sauce, you first cook the garlic, peppers, tomato and seasonings — that is the base. Then the linguine is cooked. While the pasta is cooking, the shrimp are sautéed. When the shrimp are cooked, they are combined with the tomato sauce and basil. As soon as the pasta is cooked, everything is mixed together.

Preparation Time: 15 MINUTES
Cooking Time: 25 MINUTES

LOW FAT

1¼ pounds medium shrimp
Salt to taste
4 tablespoons olive oil
1 tablespoon finely chopped garlic
1 medium-size red sweet pepper, cored, seeded and cut into 1-inch cubes
1 medium-size green pepper, cored, seeded and cut into 1-inch cubes
3 cups canned crushed tomatoes
Freshly ground black pepper to taste
1 teaspoon dried oregano
¾ pound linguine
¼ teaspoon red-pepper flakes
4 tablespoons chopped fresh basil, or chopped Italian parsley.

1. Peel and devein the shrimp (see instructions page 231).
2. Bring a large pot of salted water to a boil.
3. Heat 2 tablespoons of the oil in a large saucepan over medium-high heat and add the red and green peppers. Cook for 3 minutes. Add the garlic and cook for 2 minutes more. Add the tomatoes, salt, pepper, and oregano. Bring to a simmer and cook, stirring, for 10 minutes.
4. Meanwhile, cook the linguine in boiling water until it is al dente. Drain quickly and reserve about ½ cup of the cooking liquid.
5. While the linguine cooks, heat the remaining oil in another pan over medium-high setting. Add the shrimp, pepper flakes, salt, and pepper. Cook, stirring, about a minute or two. Add to tomato sauce.
6. Return the linguine to its cooking pot over medium heat. Add the sauce and reserved cooking liquid (if necessary). Add the basil to the mixture. Heat thoroughly. Toss well, check for seasonings, and serve immediately.

Yield: 4 servings

Linguine with Fresh Mussels

Preparation Time: 20 MINUTES
Cooking Time: ABOUT 20 MINUTES

LOW FAT

4 pounds small mussels
1 tablespoon plus ¼ cup olive oil
2 teaspoons finely chopped garlic
3 tablespoons plus 10 cups water
2 cups fresh new peas or a 10-ounce frozen package
1 cup ricotta cheese
9 ounces fresh or packaged dried linguine
⅛ teaspoon dried hot red-pepper flakes
¼ cup finely chopped basil or 2 tablespoons dried
Salt and freshly ground black pepper to taste.

1. Pull off the stringy "beards" that protrude from the mussel shells. Cut off any barnacles clinging to the shell (see instructions on cleaning mussels page 60). Rinse the mussels thoroughly under cold running water and drain. There should be about 12 cups.
2. Heat 1 tablespoon oil in a large pan. Add the garlic and cook, stirring, without browning — about 1 minute. Add the mussels and 3 tablespoons water. Cover closely and cook about 4 minutes or until the shells open (discard any that do not open). As the mussels cook, shake the pan to redistribute them so they steam evenly.
3. Place a large colander over a bowl and drain the mussels. There should be about 1½ cups of broth. Reserve the broth.
4. If fresh peas are used, drop them in a pot of boiling water, cook 3 minutes and drain. If frozen peas are used, put them in a sieve and run very hot tap water over them until defrosted. Set aside.
5. When the mussels are cool enough to handle, remove the meat from the shells. There should be about 1½ cups. Set aside. Discard the shells.
6. Pour the reserved mussel liquid through a fine strainer into a large pan over medium-high setting. Add ricotta cheese. Stir until blended and simmering.
7. Meanwhile, bring a large pot of salted water to a boil and add the linguine. If fresh pasta is used, cook 1½ to 2 minutes, or to desired degree of doneness. If dried linguine is used, cook 7 to 9 minutes, or until al dente. Drain the linguine and add it to the ricotta sauce. Add the remaining ¼ cup oil and stir. Add the peas, hot red-pepper flakes, basil, salt, pepper, and mussels. Cook until the mussels are heated through. Taste for seasonings and serve.

Yield: 4 servings

Linguine with Fresh Salmon and Pesto Sauce

The combination of richly flavored salmon and aromatic pesto is sublime. Since salmon tends to fall apart when cut up and tossed with pasta, it is preferable to sauté it and lay it atop the pasta. The salmon fillets in this recipe are seared in a non-stick pan coated with a tablespoon of olive oil. They should cook only for about two minutes.

If you are short on time, Stew Leonard's sells excellent freshly made pesto.

Preparation Time: 15 MINUTES
Cooking Time: 15 MINUTES

LOW FAT

2½ cups loosely packed basil leaves
½ cup plus 1 tablespoon extra-virgin olive oil
3 tablespoons pine nuts
1 tablespoon coarsely chopped garlic
Salt and freshly ground black pepper to taste
½ cup grated Parmesan or Pecorino cheese
1¼ pounds boneless, skinless salmon fillets
¾ pound linguine, fresh or dried
4 quarts water
1 teaspoon hot red pepper flakes
3 tablespoons finely chopped shallots.

1. Remove and discard all the tough stems from the basil. Put 2 cups of the basil leaves in the container of a food processor. Add ½ cup of olive oil, pine nuts, garlic, salt and pepper. Blend well to a fine texture. Add the cheese, and blend some more.
2. Cut the salmon on the diagonal into 1-inch-wide slices.
3. Cook the linguine in a large pot of salted water until al dente. Drain, but reserve ¼ cup of the cooking liquid. Return the pasta to the pot in which it was cooked. Add half of the pesto sauce, the reserved cooking liquid, salt and pepper. Toss well, and keep warm.
4. Add the remaining 1 tablespoon of olive oil to a non-stick pan large enough to hold the salmon in one layer. Add the salmon slices, and season with salt, pepper, and pepper flakes. Cook for about 1 minute. Add the shallots, flip the salmon pieces, and cook 1 to 2 minutes more. Keep warm.
5. Divide the linguine equally on each of 4 serving plates. Spoon equal portions of the sauce over each. Lay several strips of salmon over each portion. Garnish with the remaining ½ cup basil leaves. Serve immediately.

Yield: 4 servings

Spaghettini with Scallops and Sugar Snap Peas

The lemon vodka in this sauce, blended with a little bit of cream, gives a warm, smooth sensation on the palate. Most of the alcohol evaporates during cooking.

Preparation Time: 10 MINUTES
Cooking Time: 15 MINUTES

SUPER FAST

1 pound sea scallops (cut in half any exceptionally large ones)
1 pound sugar snap peas or snow peas
12 cups water
Salt to taste
1 pound spaghettini
2 tablespoons olive oil
1 tablespoon finely chopped garlic
5 ripe plum tomatoes, cut into ½-inch cubes (about 1 pound)
1 jalapeño pepper, seeded and minced
Freshly ground black pepper to taste
½ cup cream or half-and-half
½ cup coarsely chopped fresh basil
½ cup lemon-flavored vodka, or regular vodka flavored with 1 tablespoon of fresh lemon juice
Freshly grated Parmesan or Pecorino cheese

1. Trim off the ends of the snap peas and remove their strings.
2. Bring water to a boil in a large pot, add salt, and cook the snap peas for 3 minutes or until al dente. Drain, and reserve the cooking liquid.
3. Bring the reserved cooking liquid to a boil. Add the spaghettini, stir, and cook for about 6 minutes. Drain, but reserve ½ cup of the cooking liquid in a bowl or a mug.
4. Meanwhile, heat the oil in a large pan. Add the garlic and cook briefly, stirring, without browning. Add the tomatoes, jalapeño pepper, salt and pepper.
5. Add the scallops and cook for 1 minute, stirring. Return everything to the large pot, including the drained pasta and reserved cooking. Turn on the heat to medium-high. Stir, bring to a simmer, and add the snap peas, cream, basil and vodka. Toss and cook for about 2 minutes. Taste for seasoning. Serve immediately with cheese, if desired.

Yield: 4 to 6 servings

Penne Bolognese

This is one of my father's favorite dishes. Every time we go to an Italian restaurant, he orders a side dish of pasta with Bolognese sauce. This soul-satisfying sauce also freezes well. Keep it on hand for the evenings when you have no time to cook.

Preparation Time: 10 MINUTES
Cooking Time: ABOUT 1 HOUR AND 25 MINUTES

LOW FAT

PREPARE IN ADVANCE

1 medium onion, minced
1/3 cup olive oil
3 cloves garlic, peeled and minced
2 28-ounce cans crushed tomatoes
1 1/4 pounds ground sirloin, crumbled with your fingers
1 1/2 pounds ziti, bucatini or penne
1/4 cup chopped Italian parsley
Freshly grated Pecorino or Romano cheese

1. In a pan, sauté the onions in the olive oil until translucent. Add the garlic and cook until golden. Add the tomatoes, season with salt and pepper, and simmer for about 20 minutes.
2. Place the ground sirloin in a large pan. Cook over medium heat, stirring and breaking it up with a wooden spoon — about 7 minutes.
3. Add the tomato sauce to the ground meat. Stir and check seasonings. Simmer for 30 minutes.
4. When the sauce has cooked for 15 minutes, bring a large pot of salted water to a boil. Add the pasta and cook until al dente. Drain the pasta and return it to the pot. Add enough of the sauce to coat the pasta. Transfer the pasta to a large serving bowl and spoon the rest of the sauce over it. Sprinkle with parsley. Serve with the grated cheese.

Yield: Serves 6

What is the difference between flat-leaf parsley and regular parsley?

You may notice that many of these recipes call for Italian flat-leaf parsley. There are more than 30 varieties of parsley, although the two most common are curly leaf and flat leaf. The Italian parsley has a stronger flavor. If you can't find flat-leaf parsley use the other kind.

Here's a great shot of my Uncle Leo Leonard and my dad in the Danbury store. My father has always counted on Leo's advice over the years!

Penne with Grilled Chicken, Sun-Dried Tomatoes, and Spinach

You can save time by using Stew Leonard's savory rotisserie-cooked chicken. Just cut off the meat and add it to the pasta.

Preparation Time: 15 MINUTES
Cooking Time: ABOUT 35 MINUTES

LOW FAT

¼ cup toasted pine nuts
½ cup olive oil
4 cloves garlic, peeled
2 10-ounce bags of spinach, stems removed, and coarsely chopped (or 2 8-ounce containers of Stew Leonard's Petite Spinach)
½ cup sun-dried tomatoes (packed in olive oil), chopped
1⅓-pounds boneless chicken breasts (4 fillets), split and pounded to even thickness
1 pound penne
Salt and freshly ground black pepper to taste
Freshly grated Parmesan cheese

Pierre Philitas proudly shows off a Stew's Rotisserie-Cooked Chicken.

1. Toast the pine nuts by placing them in a pan with 1 teaspoon of olive oil over medium-high heat. Cook, shaking the pan, for about 5 minutes, or until they turn golden. Set aside.
2. In a large pan, sauté the garlic in all but 2 tablespoons of the olive oil until just golden. Add the spinach and cook, gently stirring, until it wilts. Remove the pan from the heat. Add the toasted pine nuts and sun-dried tomatoes, and stir to combine. Season well. Cover the pan to keep the ingredients warm.
3. Bring a large pot of salted water to a boil. Heat the grill or broiler.
4. Brush the chicken breasts with olive oil, and season well with salt and pepper. Cook until just white in the center, about 4 minutes per side. Slice the chicken into ½-inch-thick strips and keep warm.
5. Add penne to the boiling water and cook until al dente. Drain well and return penne to the pot. Add to the pot the spinach mixture, ½ of the chicken slices, and toss well. Check for seasonings. Transfer to a large serving platter and arrange the remaining chicken strips on top. Sprinkle with Parmesan cheese.

Yield: Serves 4

Spaghetti with Sizzling Southwestern Meatballs

Preparation Time: 30 MINUTES
(make in advance meatballs and sauce)
Cooking Time: 45 MINUTES

LOW FAT · PREPARE IN ADVANCE

The meatballs:
2 tablespoons olive oil
¾ cup finely chopped onions
2 teaspoons finely chopped garlic
1½ pounds ground chuck
¼ cup fresh breadcrumbs
¼ cup chopped cilantro (optional)
1 egg, lightly beaten
1 teaspoon cumin powder
1 to 1½ teaspoon chili powder
½ teaspoon Tabasco sauce
Salt and freshly ground black pepper to taste

The sauce:
2 tablespoons olive oil
1 cup finely chopped onions
1 tablespoon finely chopped garlic
1 cup sweet red peppers, cored, cleaned, and cut into ½-inch pieces
1 cup green pepper, cored, cleaned, and cut into ½-inch pieces
1 teaspoon chopped jalapeño pepper (optional)
1 28-ounce can crushed tomatoes
¼ teaspoon red pepper flakes
1 cup water
Salt and freshly ground black pepper to taste

The spaghetti:
8 cups water
Salt to taste
2 tablespoons olive oil
1 pound spaghetti

1. To make the meatballs, heat 1 tablespoon of the oil in a skillet and add the onions and garlic. Cook, stirring, until the onions are wilted. Let cool.
2. Combine all other ingredients except the remaining tablespoon of oil, and blend well.
3. Shape the mixture into 20 or more 1½-inch meatballs.
4. Heat the remaining tablespoon olive oil in a large non-stick skillet and add the meatballs. Cook over medium heat, turning so they brown evenly, about 10 minutes. Set aside and keep them warm.
5. To make the sauce, heat all the ingredients except the 2 tablespoons of the oil in a pan. Blend well and bring to a boil. Reduce heat and simmer for 10 minutes. Add the meatballs and simmer for 10 more minutes.
6. Meanwhile cook the spaghetti in a large pot of salted water until al dente. Drain. Return the spaghetti to the pot. Add the sauce, the meatballs, the olive oil, and butter. Toss. Serve immediately with the meatballs and the sauce.

Yield: Serves 4 to 6

Baked Pasta with Mushrooms and Capicola

This is a variation of northern Italian pasta dishes that are finished off in an oven so the crust is golden-brown. It's a great entree for parties.

Preparation Time: 15 MINUTES
Cooking Time: 25 MINUTES

PREPARE IN ADVANCE

1 tablespoon olive oil
8 ounces Portobello or domestic mushrooms, washed and stems trimmed
4 ounces hot Capicola ham, diced
2 tablespoons minced garlic
1 pound plum tomatoes (about 6 tomatoes), seeded and diced
2 cups zucchini (about 1 large zucchini), cut into ½-inch dice
½ cup water
1 pound shell pasta
1 cup half-and-half
1 cup grated Parmesan cheese

1. Preheat the oven to 400 degrees.
2. Heat the oil in a large pan over high setting. Add the mushrooms and ham, and cook for about 3 minutes. Add the garlic and cook, stirring, for another 2 minutes. Add the tomatoes, zucchini, ½ cup water (or enough to give it a sauce consistency), and cook, covered, for 5 minutes or until zucchini are tender. Adjust seasonings to taste.
3. While the sauce is cooking, boil the pasta shells in 4 quarts of salted water for 6 minutes, or until just short of al dente. Drain the shells in a colander, pass under cold water, and transfer to a greased casserole.
4. Pour the sauce over the shells and add half-and-half and grated cheese. Stir briefly.
5. Bake the casserole for 15 to 20 minutes, until the pasta is golden brown and crispy on top. (You could broil the crust for a minute or two for an extra crispy crust.) Serve with mixed greens or Caesar Salad (see recipe page 83).

Yield: 6 servings

Curried Rice Pilaf with Almonds

Serve this deliciously crunchy rice dish as an accompaniment to Malibu Lemon-Apricot Chicken (see recipe page 172) or any dish that has gravy. It may also be served as a cold salad with the addition of chopped tomatoes and cucumbers, or perhaps with cooked shrimp or scallops.

Preparation Time: 10 MINUTES
Cooking Time: 30 MINUTES

LOW FAT

2 tablespoons vegetable oil
2 cups minced onions (about 2 medium onions)
3 tablespoons Indian-style curry powder (see Pierre Franey's Homemade Curry Powder page 231)
½ cup sliced almonds
1½ cups rice
4 cups chicken stock or water
2 peeled and cored apples, cut into ¼-inch dice
1 teaspoon salt and ¼ teaspoon freshly ground black pepper

1. Heat the oil in a pot over medium-high flame. Add the onions and cook until translucent (about 4 minutes).
2. Add the curry powder, almonds, and rice. Cook for 2 minutes, stirring to mix well. Add the stock and salt and bring to a boil.
3. Reduce the heat to medium and cover pan. Simmer for 15 minutes. Stir in the apples and cook, covered, for another 5 to 8 minutes — if it gets a little dry, add more stock. Adjust seasonings to taste.

Yield: 4 servings

What is the best type of rice for all-around home cooking?

There are as many types of rice as there are pastas. Unless you are making risotto or some other specialized dish, a good all-around choice is long-grain Carolina-style rice. It absorbs flavors well, has a nice semifirm texture, and is fluffy if you cook it according to instructions.

Annually we attend the National Restaurant Association Convention. We come back with many new ideas for our kitchens.

What is risotto?

Risotto is an Italian dish usually made with Arborio rice, a variety that makes a creamy sauce when it is slowly cooked with stock, butter, and cheese.

Mara Mori Prologo's Authentic Risotto

Our friend Mara is from Montecatini, in northern Italy, and she now lives up in the Hudson Valley, in Tivoli, New York. Mara is a fantastic Italian cook who works for Pierre Moulin, the co-founder of Pierre Deux, the elegant French store specializing in products from Provence. One evening Mara invited Bryan Miller over to her kitchen for a lesson on risotto making. A lot of people shy away from risotto because they think that it requires endless stirring. As you will see in Mara's classic recipe, that is not true.

"You don't have to stare into the pot for half an hour," says Mara. Once you learn this simple risotto technique you can add all kinds of ingredients to it, like peas, zucchini, spinach, scallops, shrimp, mushrooms, and much more.

4 tablespoons butter, cut into 4 pieces
6 tablespoons olive oil
½ cup minced onions
2 cups Arborio rice, usually available in gourmet shops (Carolina converted rice also works)
½ cup vermouth or dry white wine
4 cups chicken stock (see recipe page 63)
Salt and freshly ground black pepper to taste
⅓ cup grated Parmesan cheese

1. In a large pot over medium-high setting, combine the butter and the olive oil. Add the onions. Reduce the heat to medium-low and cook, stirring occasionally, for about 10 minutes.
2. Add the rice and stir for about 2 minutes. Add the vermouth and the chicken stock. Stir. Simmer, stirring every 4 or 5 minutes, for about 20 minutes, adding more broth if the mixture gets too thick — it should have a creamy consistency.
3. Season with salt and pepper. Taste the rice — it should be al dente but not hard. Stir in the grated Parmesan cheese. Serve immediately.

Yield: 4 to 6 servings

Bryan Miller getting a lesson in the art of making risotto. "Maria is a master," Bryan says.

Barley Risotto with Fresh Tomato

Pearl barley, which is super-healthful and high in soluble fiber, is a delicious variation on risotto. (Butter has been omitted from the recipe to remove excess fat.)

Preparation Time: 10 MINUTES
Cooking Time: 45 MINUTES

LOW FAT

1 tablespoon olive oil
1 teaspoon minced garlic (2 small cloves)
¾ cup chopped onion (1 medium onion)
1½-cups pearl barley
¼ cup dry white wine
4 cups vegetable stock (see recipe page 174) or water
1 cup diced fresh tomato
1 cup fresh or frozen peas
Salt and freshly ground pepper to taste

1. In a large pan coated with the olive oil, cook the garlic and onions for 5 minutes over medium high heat, stirring.
2. Add the pearl barley and cook for 5 minutes to slightly toast the grains. Add the white wine and cook for a minute, then add 3 cups of the stock or water, the tomato, and some salt. Bring to a boil, cover, and reduce the heat to low. Simmer for 25 minutes, stirring frequently.
3. Add the peas and, if the risotto gets too thick, some of the remaining stock or water. Stir. Cook for 10 minutes. Taste the barley — it should be slightly firm, but not hard. Stir in the cheese and add salt and pepper to taste.

Yield: 4 servings

Desserts

There are sweets for everyone in this chapter. If you are intimidated by baking, try one of the foolproof recipes like Heavenly Angel Hair Pudding, or The Amazing Leonard Brownies. And if you want to really impress dinner guests, try our luxurious Crème Brûlée or the Mocha Walnut Tart.

Aunt Helen's Fresh Apple Cake

This moist, firm-textured cake is so simple to make. It requires no icing and is delicious when eaten as a tea time snack or after a sumptuous meal.

Preparation Time: 10 MINUTES
Cooking Time: 40 MINUTES

PREPARE IN ADVANCE

2 cups all-purpose flour
1 teaspoon salt
1 teaspoon baking soda
1 teaspoon ground cinnamon
2 cups sugar
1 cup vegetable oil
3 eggs, beaten
4 cups Granny Smith apples (or other apple), peeled and sliced thinly (about 3 large apples)
½ cup raisins
1 cup chopped walnuts

1. Preheat the oven to 350 degrees. Grease a 9 x 13-inch baking pan. Set aside.
2. In a large bowl, sift together the flour, salt, baking soda, cinnamon, and 1¾ cups of the sugar. Make a well in the center of the flour and pour in the oil and eggs. With a wooden spoon or a large whisk, stir the mixture until it begins to come together. Add the apples, raisins and walnuts. Stir until all ingredients are well distributed in the batter. The batter will be relatively dry and there will be more apples than batter.
3. Spread the batter into the prepared pan. Smooth the batter with a rubber spatula then sprinkle it with ¼ cup sugar before baking. Place the cake in the preheated oven and bake for 35 to 45 minutes. The cake is done when a toothpick inserted into the center comes out clean.
4. Serve warm or room temperature, directly from the pan in which it was baked.

Yield: 12 servings

Here's a great photo of my dad and his brothers and sisters. (Left to right: Helen (her apple cake recipe is on this page), Leo, Dorothy, Stew, Jim, Anna Lane, and Marion.

Crazy Chocolate Spice Cake

Preparation Time: 15 to 20 MINUTES
Cooking Time: 35 MINUTES

PREPARE IN ADVANCE

2½ cups all-purpose flour
2 cups sugar
7 tablespoons cocoa powder
½ teaspoon salt
1 teaspoon baking soda
¼ teaspoon cinnamon
¼ teaspoon ground ginger
½ cup chopped walnuts
1¼ sticks butter or margarine, softened
1 teaspoon vanilla
1 teaspoon white or cider vinegar
2 cups cold water

1. Preheat the oven to 350 degrees.
2. Sift the flour, sugar, cocoa powder, salt, baking soda, cinnamon, and ginger into a 9 x 12 x 2-inch ungreased cake pan. Stir in the walnuts.
3. Place the softened margarine in one corner of the mixture, pour vanilla in another corner, and the vinegar in a third. Pour water over entire mixture and blend thoroughly with a hand-held electric mixer or a rubber spatula.
4. Smooth the surface of the batter with a spatula and bake for 35 minutes. The cake is done when a toothpick inserted into the center comes out clean.

Yield: 12 servings

Stew's TIP

A cross between gingerbread and devil's food cake, this dessert is baked in the pan in which it is mixed. Take it on a picnic or to a football tailgate party.

Chef George did a tailgate party at Giants Stadium for FOX TV.

Football Tailgate Picnic

Can't-Eat-Just-One Spiced Walnuts
(see recipe page 33)

Fresh Tomato-and-Balsamic-Vinegar Relish
(see recipe page 32)

Spicy Roasted Chicken Wings
(see recipe page 183)

Bethy's Tortellini Salad (see recipe page 96)
or **Warm Red Potato Salad**
(served room temperature, see recipe page 92)

Crazy Chocolate Spice Cake
or **The Amazing Leonard Brownies** (see recipe page 334)

Stew's TIP

It is important to remember a few things when you are working with chocolate. For one, when you melt it always use gentle heat, preferably a double boiler. Also, chocolate is very sensitive to water so do not splash any in the pot.

A quick way to melt a large block of chocolate is in a microwave. Set the microwave on 50% power to prevent overheating.

Jill's Terrific Chocolate Cake

My sister Jill always loved chocolate! She makes this chocolate cake that is "to die for." This all-time family favorite is essentially a flourless chocolate cake. It is easy to make, almost foolproof, and intensely chocolatey. The cake gets its lift from beaten egg whites.

Preparation Time: 45 MINUTES
Cooking Time: 20 MINUTES

PREPARE IN ADVANCE

¼ cup light cream
10 ounces bittersweet chocolate, broken into pieces the size of a quarter
8 tablespoons sweet butter, softened and cut into finger-thick pieces
1 teaspoon rum (optional)
4 eggs, separated
2 tablespoons sugar
1 tablespoon flour
Pinch of salt

1. Preheat oven to 300 degrees. Butter and flour a 9-inch-round cake pan. Set aside.
2. Heat the cream in a saucepan over medium setting to almost boiling. Add the chocolate, cover, lower to simmer, and let sit for 5 minutes. Remove the pan from the heat and remove the cover. Whisk the chocolate until it is smooth. Stir in the butter until it is melted, then the rum.
3. While the chocolate is melting, in another bowl beat the egg yolks and sugar with an electric mixer or a whisk until light and foamy, about 5 minutes. Whisk the egg mixture into the melted chocolate-butter mixture. Gradually fold in the flour (folding means stirring the flour in with a circular motion of the spatula).
4. Beat the egg whites and the salt in an electric mixer until they form stiff peaks. Gently fold the egg whites into chocolate mixture. Pour the mixture into the greased and floured pan. Smooth the surface of the batter with a spatula.
5. Bake on the middle rack of the oven for 30 minutes, then check by inserting a toothpick into the center — if it comes out clean it is done. The cake will be slightly firm but somewhat moist in the center.
6. Cool the cake on a wire rack for 10 minutes. Unmold the cake onto a serving dish. Sprinkle with powdered sugar. The cake tastes best when served fresh, perhaps with a topping of unsweetened whipped cream.

Yield: 8 to 10 servings

My sister Jill just opened our Photo Cake Department at Stew's. A computer will put any photo onto your cake. It's done in edible food coloring and looks just like the photo!

Gina Fox's Hudson Valley Carrot Cake

Gina Fox, our friend from Rhinebeck, New York, is an award-winning baker. She gave us this easy and delicious carrot cake recipe.

Preparation Time: 15 MINUTES
Cooking Time: ABOUT 55 MINUTES

SUPER FAST PREPARE IN ADVANCE

The cake:
3 large eggs
¾ cup oil
1 cup sugar
1 teaspoon cinnamon
1 teaspoon vanilla extract
1 teaspoon baking soda
½ teaspoon salt
1½ cups all-purpose flour
1 cup sweetened coconut
1 cup shredded carrots (about 3 medium carrots)
½ cup chopped walnuts
1 8-ounce can crushed pineapple (drained)

1. Preheat the oven to 350 degrees.
2. Lightly grease and flour a 9-inch-square baking pan (metal or glass is okay). In a large mixing bowl, beat together the eggs, oil and sugar. Add the cinnamon, vanilla extract, baking soda, salt, and flour. Stir in the remaining items.
3. Pour everything into the baking pan and cook for 50 to 60 minutes. Remove, let cool.

Gina Fox, an award-winning baker, from Rhinebeck, New York.

The icing:
8 ounces softened cream cheese
3 ounces (1 stick) softened butter
Pinch of salt
3 cups powdered sugar
2-3 tablespoons milk
½ cup chopped walnuts

1. In a bowl, combine the cream cheese, butter, salt, powdered sugar, and milk. Blend well.
2. Apply the cream cheese frosting with a spatula (the long, thin, rounded metal type; or a butter knife). Sprinkle with chopped walnuts.

Yield: Serves 8 to 10

What is yogurt cheese?

Yogurt cheese is something you should know how to make. It is delicious, healthful, and versatile. All you do is take a colander and line it with cheesecloth or paper towels. Scoop the unflavored yogurt into the colander (the regular type, not the no-fat, which is too gelatinous). Let the yogurt sit in the lined strainer for at least 6 hours, or up to 24 hours. (If you drain for more than 6 hours refrigerate it.) The excess liquid drains out of the yogurt and it becomes more dense and creamy. It will loose about half its volume in the process — so, in the cheesecake recipe, which calls for 3 cups of yogurt cheese, you would start with 6 cups of yogurt.

Use yogurt cheese as you would use creamy mascarpone cheese or sour cream.

Stew's Silky Cheesecake

For the crust:

$\frac{1}{4}$ cup butter, soft, cut into four pieces (2 tablespoons, or $\frac{1}{4}$ stick butter)
$\frac{1}{4}$ cup sugar
$1\frac{2}{3}$ cup Graham cracker crumbs

For the cheesecake:

3 8-ounce packages of cream cheese, softened
2 eggs
$\frac{3}{4}$ cup granulated sugar
1 teaspoon lemon juice
1 teaspoon vanilla extract
Pinch of salt
1 teaspoon almond extract
1 tablespoon lemon zest

1. Preheat the oven to 325 degrees.
2. Mix all of the ingredients in a large bowl. Transfer to the springform pan, and bake for 45 to 55 minutes, or until the cheesecake is slightly firm.

   Set aside to cool.

Topping:

2 cups sour cream
$\frac{1}{2}$ cup granulated sugar
1 teaspoon vanilla extract

1. Mix in a bowl, with a wooden spoon, the sour cream, sugar, and vanilla. Spread the mixture neatly on top of the cooked cheesecake and return to the oven and cook for 10 more minutes.

Yield: Serves 8

When you walk through Bethy's Bakery at Stew's, the smell of fresh baked bread is everywhere. We bake for more than 16 hours every day.

Winter Fruit Compote

In New England, the best season for citrus is the dead of winter. That is when the Florida crop is at its peak and, barring frost or other setbacks, Stew Leonard's bins are piled high. The dried fruit in this recipe adds a nice textural contrast to the compote as well as a burst of intense flavor. This healthful and refreshing dessert always reminds us that warmer days are around the corner.

Preparation Time: 15 MINUTES
Cooking Time: COOKING TIME

3 whole pink grapefruit
4 temple oranges
6 tangerines or clementines, peeled and sectioned
1 vanilla bean, split in half (or 1 tablespoon vanilla extract)
2 tablespoons honey
2 tablespoons grated orange zest
1 cup chopped dates, dried bananas or dried cranberries (or a mixture of the three)
Citrus sherbet or fresh mint

1. Peel the grapefruits and oranges in the following manner: Using a sharp knife, cut a slice from the bottom and top. Place one of the cut sides down on a counter, and carefully slice off half of the peel, removing all of the white membrane. Repeat with the other half. Once the grapefruit and oranges are peeled, section them.
2. In a salad bowl, combine the grapefruit and orange sections with peeled and sectioned tangerines. Drain off and save any juice that has accumulated in the bowl.
3. Heat the juice (add some water if necessary) with the vanilla, honey and orange zest. Bring to a boil, then simmer for 2 minutes. Allow to cool, and add to sectioned fruit.
4. Stir the dates or dried-fruit combination into the fruit mixture. Serve the salad by itself or with lemon, lime, or orange sherbet, garnished with sprigs of fresh mint.

Yield: 6 to 8 servings

What is a clementine?

This super sweet, small fruit has exploded in popularity in the last 10 years. The season begins in November and ends in February. They are imported from southwestern Spain and are renowned for their juiciness and flavor. Their size and ease of peeling makes them ideal for snacking without getting juice all over your shirt.

Stew's TIP

This quick, delicious pear recipe was given to us by the late Pierre Franey, the author, television personality, and 60-Minute Gourmet columnist for *The New York Times* (with his partner, Bryan Miller). We have been great admirers of Pierre for many years. We finally got a chance to meet him when he came to Stew Leonard's for a book signing and cooking demonstration several years ago.

When it comes to easy, unpretentious cooking, nobody compared with Pierre, who started cooking in Paris when he was 13 years old and came to America to cook at the 1939 World's Fair in New York City. He eventually became chef of Le Pavillon, in Manhattan, the most influential restaurant in this country after World War II. Later, he became a culinary journalist at *The New York Times*.

Pears in Spiced Red Wine

Stew Leonard's carries various types of seasonal pears. This is one of our favorite light and healthful desserts that can be made with any pear variety, as long as the pears are ripe. The black peppercorns add a nice spicy undercurrent.

Preparation Time: 10 MINUTES
Cooking Time: 15 MINUTES

SUPER FAST · LOW FAT · PREPARE IN ADVANCE

4 pears, such as Bartlett, about 1¾ pounds total
2 cups dry red wine
1 cup water
½ cup sugar
1 bay leaf
¼ teaspoon black peppercorns
6 whole allspice
6 whole cloves
1 2-inch-long cinnamon stick

1. Peel the pears but leave the stems on. Use a melon ball cutter or an apple corer to cut out a little bit of the bottom center of each pear.
2. Combine the remaining ingredients in a deep pot and add the pears. Bring to a boil and let simmer, covered, for 10 to 15 minutes, turning the pears in the syrup periodically so that they cook evenly. Remove the pears and cook down the syrup by half over high setting. Return the pears to the sauce. Turn off the heat and let stand until ready to serve. Serve on a plate surrounded by the sauce. Vanilla ice cream is great with them. These pears are also delicious cold.

Yield: Serves 4

"My kids go crazy for this!"

Blueberry Granité

Granités are terrific summer coolers, and they couldn't be easier to make. This "Ice" is called "Granité" in France and "Granita" in Italy. They are literally flavored water that is frozen and scraped with a fork to form ice crystals. Kids love these — let them help scrape. You can experiment with all kinds of flavors. Here is a basic recipe for a blueberry granité.

Preparation Time: 10 MINUTES
Cooking Time: 1 HOUR AND 10 MINUTES (includes freezing)

2 cups (16 ounces) fresh blueberries, rinsed and stems removed
8 tablespoons sugar
Juice of 1 lemon
½ cup water

1. In a blender, purée the blueberries. Transfer them to a medium-sized pot.
2. Add to the pot the sugar, lemon juice, and water. Bring to a boil and remove from the heat.
3. Strain into a shallow metal pan (or ice cube trays without the dividers). Place in the freezer.
4. Every 30 minutes, scrape the ice with a fork. Continue working back and forth until you reach all the way to the bottom. Break up any big ice chunks with the fork. After the third time — that is, after 90 minutes — the ice should be ready to be broken up into many little shards, without any big chunks left. Serve in a wine glass or any conical container, perhaps with a little whipped cream.

Yield: 6 servings

What is the difference between an ice and a sorbet?

There is a major difference between frozen ices (called granités) and sorbets. Both are easy to make at home, as opposed to ice cream, which calls for a custard base. Ices can be made with the juice of fresh fruit or berries plus a simple sugar syrup (water and sugar boiled for about 3 minutes). A sorbet, on the other hand, requires a "stabilizer" in the form of egg whites, cooked meringue, or gelatin. Thus, sorbets have a slightly thicker, smoother consistency. Sherbet also contains milk or egg whites as a stabilizer.

Frozen Citrus-and-Berry Bombe

Preparation Time: 25 MINUTES
Cooking Time: NONE

LOW FAT

PREPARE IN ADVANCE

This impressive-looking dessert, made of rainbow-colored layers of fresh fruit and sorbet, is low in fat and easy to prepare. Serve it after a rich holiday meal.

2 cups strawberries, stemmed and sliced
8 ounces all-fruit strawberry preserves
2 cups peeled, sliced pineapple rounds (about 1 peeled and cored pineapple)
1 quart good commercial lemon sorbet
1 quart good commercial strawberry sorbet
½ cup vanilla-wafer or graham-cracker crumbs

1. Line a deep 2-quart bowl or decorative mold with plastic wrap, letting about 10 inches of plastic overlap all around.
2. Stir the strawberry slices into the preserves. Set aside.
3. Place a 1½-inch-thick slice of pineapple in bottom of the bowl. Spread 1 cup strawberry mixture over pineapple. Spoon half the lemon ice over the fruit and a little higher along the sides of the bowl. Cover this layer with more pineapple slices topped by 1 cup of strawberry sorbet. Add another cup of strawberry mixture and top with remaining lemon ice. Layer remaining strawberries and top with remaining strawberry sorbet. Sprinkle surface with the crumbs.
4. Gather the plastic wrap over the top of the bombe. Wrap in another layer of plastic and place in freezer overnight. It will keep for up to three days in the freezer.
5. To unmold the bombe, move from freezer to refrigerator one hour before serving. Unwrap, peel back the original plastic wrap, and reverse onto a large serving platter. Garnish with slices of cut fruit, whipped cream, and sprigs of mint.

Yield: 8 to 10 servings

Gingered Strawberry Salad

Something as simple as a dish of strawberries is transformed with the addition of just two ingredients, orange juice and ginger. Though there is no sugar in this dessert, it has a natural sweetness that satisfies your end-of-meal cravings.

Preparation Time: 5 MINUTES
Cooking Time: 5 MINUTES

SUPER FAST · LOW FAT

1 pint strawberries
¾ cup orange juice
1 tablespoon grated fresh ginger

1. Hull the strawberries and slice them vertically. Set aside.
2. Combine the orange juice and ginger in a small saucepan. Heat the juice over medium setting for 2 to 3 minutes to extract the flavor of the ginger. Let cool.
3. Pour the gingered orange juice over the strawberries, with a little sugar if needed, and serve well chilled with a garnish of whipped cream.

Yield: 4 servings

Can you freeze strawberries?

This is a question we get often at the store. Strawberries can be frozen; however, once thawed they are suitable only for recipes that call for chopping or purée-ing. Partially thawed strawberries can be blended to make milkshakes, smoothies and daiquiris. Fresh strawberries are great on Stew Leonard's Angel Food Cake, too.

How do you pick a great cantaloupe or honeydew?

We've seen it all in the store! Customers holding melons to their ears as if listening to a radio; shaking the melons, smelling them, and squeezing them. During the season we sell more than 60,000 melons a week. Here's how we tell our customers to pick a perfect melon.

Go for size – There are many different sizes and sometimes you may be lured into a store by low prices for small melons. At Stew's we sell only extra large, which are almost always more flavorful because they have ripened longer in the field.

Appearance – Cantaloupes should have a golden-yellow tint, and Honeydews have a white, creamy skin. If one side of a honeydew has a pale whitish color, that is where the melon was resting on the ground, that's fine.

Give it a squeeze – If a melon gives a little, chances are the flesh will be sweet. If it is very soft, it could be overripe.

Smell the stem end – The stem of cantaloupes should have a faintly sweet aroma. Honeydews, on the other hand, have very little aroma.

Shake it up baby! If the seeds rattle, chances are the cantaloupe has been grown in excessive heat, which means it is too ripe.

How do you pick a ripe melon? Smell, squeeze, or shake? Read this.

What's the best way to ripen fruit at home?

Just about all the fruits you buy continue to ripen after they are picked (with the exception of figs and pineapples). There are two ways to speed up or, slow down, the ripening process. To slow it down, place the fruit in the refrigerator — it makes the fruit "go to sleep." To speed up the ripening process, keep your fruit at room temperature. In your refrigerator, always protect your fruit from blowing and circulating air.

Another trick to ripen fruit is using natural ethylene gas. This is a natural gas emitted by apples, tomatoes, melons and bananas — so if you store them in paper bags they will ripen. Our Produce Director, Alan Simon, ripens hard, green bananas in our Danbury store by placing them in specially designed ripening rooms where ethylene gas is pumped in. After 24 hours they emerge beautifully yellow and ripe.

Aside from adding gas, he keeps the room at 58 degrees. Virtually all bananas you buy today are ripened in this fashion.

"Instant fat-free dessert!"

Strawberries with Balsamic Vinegar

This may sound like a strange combination, but in fact balsamic vinegar complements ripe strawberries beautifully. It is a popular dessert all over Italy — and nonfat to boot.

Preparation Time: 10 MINUTES
(pour balsamic vinegar over strawberries at last minute)
Cooking Time: NONE

1 pint ripe strawberries, hulled, washed and sliced in half vertically
1/3 cup of balsamic vinegar (or to taste)
4 teaspoons sugar

1. Place the strawberries in a tall stem glass, like a red wine goblet. Drizzle balsamic vinegar over them. Sprinkle with sugar.

Yield: Serves 4

Brandied Cherries over Vanilla Ice Cream

We love these sweet, heady cherries over vanilla ice cream (or no-fat frozen yogurt). Make a batch of brandied cherries and put them in mason jars. Wrap with ribbon and give them away as gifts.

Preparation Time: 10 MINUTES
Cooking Time: 25 MINUTES

1/2 cup water
1/4 cup sugar
2 cups pitted cherries — Bing cherries work well
1 1/4 cup brandy or Cognac

1. In a large, shallow pan (or a big fry pan), combine the water and sugar. Bring to a boil, lower the heat to simmer, and add the cherries.
2. Simmer for about 15 minutes. Add the brandy. Serve over vanilla ice cream or frozen yogurt. Brandied cherries should last several weeks, refrigerated, before getting too soft.

Yield: 1 pound of cherries

Brenda's Cold Apricot and Cinnamon Soup

This is a delightfully refreshing soup that can be served as an appetizer or a dessert. It was contributed by Brenda Sachs, our friend from Red Hook, N.Y., who is the restaurant critic for *The Poughkeepsie Journal* newspaper.

Brenda also gave us her recipe for Chilled Cantaloupe Soup with Ginger (see recipe page 71).

LOW FAT · PREPARE IN ADVANCE

Preparation Time: 15 MINUTES
Cooking Time: 20 MINUTES

¾ cup water
¾ cup sugar
2 pounds fresh ripe apricots, peeled, and pits removed (cut into 8 pieces)
2 cinnamon sticks
6 cloves
Juice of 1 orange
Juice of 1 lime
¾ cup dry white wine

1. In a deep saucepan over medium heat, combine the water and sugar and cook, stirring occasionally, until the sugar dissolves. Add the apricots, cinnamon, cloves, and wine. Simmer for 15 minutes, stirring occasionally.
2. Remove the cinnamon sticks and the cloves. Add the orange and lime juices. In a blender or a food processor, purée the mixture. Refrigerate to chill thoroughly. Serve with lime slices as garnish, and perhaps several mint leaves.

Yield: Serves 4

Brenda Sachs at her home in Red Hook, New York.

What are the different types of chocolate?

Here is a rundown of the types of chocolate usually called for in dessert making.

- **Unsweetened Chocolate** – This is also called baking chocolate or bitter chocolate. It is essentially pure chocolate with no sugar added. This is not an eating chocolate — it is too bitter. Unsweetened chocolate is mostly used in baking.
- **Semisweet (also called Bittersweet)** – This is probably the most widely used chocolate in dessert making. Although semisweet and bittersweet are in the same category, semisweet has slightly more sugar in it. If you come across a European chocolate that says "dark chocolate," it is usually equivalent to American bittersweet.

Smooth Chocolate Mousse

This is probably the all-time favorite American dessert, and it is surprisingly easy to make.

PREPARE IN ADVANCE

4 ounces semisweet chocolate, broken into pieces
¼ pound butter, cut into small pieces, room temperature
3 eggs, separated
¼ cup sugar

1. Place a 2 quart metal mixing bowl atop a pot so that the two fit snugly. Remove the mixing bowl and add boiling water to the saucepan. Set the bowl over it. Bring the water to a simmer. Add the chocolate to the mixing bowl and stir.
2. When the chocolate starts to melt, add the butter. Continue stirring until well blended, then remove the bowl from the heat. Add the egg yolks and stir until thoroughly blended.
3. Place the bowl briefly in the refrigerator until the mixture is slightly cooler than lukewarm. If it becomes too chilled, it will harden.
4. Meanwhile, beat the egg whites until they form soft peaks. Gradually add sugar, beating briskly. Continue beating until the whites are stiff. Fold the whites into the chocolate mixture. Spoon the mousse into four serving dishes. Chill until ready to serve. If desired, top with minimally sweetened whipped cream.

Yield: 4 servings.

Crème Brûlée

This has become one of the best-selling restaurant desserts in America. The French term crème brûlée means "burnt cream." That refers to the last-minute broiling that caramelizes the sugar on top of the custard. This recipe comes from Sirio Maccione, owner of Le Cirque 2000 restaurant in Manhattan.

Preparation Time: 10 MINUTES
Cooking Time: 50 MINUTES

PREPARE IN ADVANCE

4½ cups cream
1 vanilla bean, split, or 1 teaspoon vanilla extract
Pinch of salt
¾ cups sugar
8 egg yolks
½ teaspoon grated lemon zest
8 tablespoons brown sugar

1. Preheat the oven to 300 degrees.
2. In a pot, heat the cream, vanilla, and salt. Stir — do not let the milk boil. Remove from the heat immediately and let cool for 10 minutes.
3. In a bowl, whisk together the sugar, egg yolks and lemon zest.
4. Slowly drizzle the hot milk into the egg yolk mixture while whisking. Transfer to a pitcher and skim bubbles from surface.
5. Pour the mixture into 8 ovenproof ramekins, each about ¾-cup capacity, or any kind of shallow cups. (You may have to improvise here.) Place the ramekins in a shallow baking dish that is filled with 1 inch of water. Bake for about 1¼ hours or until it is slightly firm to the touch. Remove from the oven and let the custards cool for 30 minutes. Refrigerate for at least 2 hours.
6. Sprinkle the custards evenly with shifted brown sugar. Turn on the broiler. The custards should be as close as possible to the heating element. Broil the tops of the custards very quickly, just until golden brown — be careful, once they start to brown it goes very quickly and they can burn. Serve.

Yield: Serves 8

Here is a little trick when you are using a grater to remove the zest of lemons or limes. Place a sheet of plastic wrap over the tiny holes before you grate. When you are done grating, pull off the plastic wrap and the grater is clean!

- **Milk Chocolate –** This designation must have about 12% milk solids and about 3.5% butterfat. It is sweet and creamy and generally an eating chocolate.
- **White Chocolate –** This is a very confusing category. The real thing is not manufactured in this country, so labels should not say "white chocolate." Typically, the mixture sold in America combines sugar, cocoa butter, milk solids, lecithin and vanilla. It has very little chocolate flavor and is commonly used as a coating or icing.
- **Cocoa Powder –** This is the product left over from the chocolate extracting process. It is a concentrated, unsweetened powder, and very chocolately. It is used primarily in cakes and cookies. (It has nothing to do with cocoa drink mixes, which are made of milk powder, sugar, cocoa and other flavorings.)

What is tapioca?

Tapioca, which is usually used in desserts in this country, is made from the yucca plant, a starchy tuber also known as cassava and manioc. In some countries tapioca is used to thicken soups, stews and sauces. The type of tapioca used in our pudding is called large pearl, or fish eye. It is precooked, so it needs very little cooking. Raw tapioca must be soaked for hours to soften before using.

Orange Tapioca Pudding

Preparation Time: ABOUT 10 MINUTES
Cooking Time: 20 MINUTES

PREPARE IN ADVANCE

¼ cup instant pearl tapioca
3½ cups non-fat milk
½ cup sugar
1 tablespoon grated orange zest (about 1 orange)
1 vanilla bean, split in half, or 2 teaspoons vanilla extract
3 eggs

1. Place the tapioca, 1 cup of milk, sugar, and orange zest in a saucepan. Let sit for 5 minutes. Over medium heat, bring the mixture to a boil, stirring constantly. Remove from the heat and add the vanilla. Let cool.
2. Simmer the tapioca mixture for 5 minutes. Add the remaining milk. Return the mixture to a boil, reduce the heat, and simmer, stirring constantly, for 5 to 9 minutes. The tapioca will become translucent.
3. While the mixture is simmering, beat the eggs in a large bowl. Slowly add a cup of the tapioca mixture into the beaten eggs, whisking constantly so the eggs do not scramble. Then slowly whisk the egg mixture into the simmering tapioca pot. Cook the tapioca for a minute longer, stirring constantly.
4. Pour the hot pudding into a decorative serving bowl. Remove the vanilla bean and let the pudding cool completely before refrigerating. Chill and serve with fresh orange slices and whipped cream.

Yield: 6 to 8 servings

Gloria Holomakoff and Delia Nunez have been at Stew's a combination of more than 20 years. They know how to make customers happy.

Here's a great healthful dessert ... grilled pineapple!

After peeling and coring a pineapple, cut it into 1-inch-thick rings. Place the rings on a hot grill. Grill until golden brown on each side. Serve with a dollop of vanilla ice cream or frozen yogurt.

Heavenly Angel Hair Pudding

A creation of Chef George Llorens, this is an extremely popular dessert at Stew Leonard's, especially around the Jewish holidays. The recipe is almost identical to the bread pudding that follows it, only pasta replaces the bread.

Preparation Time: 10 MINUTES
Cooking Time: ABOUT 1 HOUR

PREPARE IN ADVANCE

½ pound angel hair pasta
3 tablespoons raisins
1½ cups sugar
4 eggs
2 egg whites
1½ teaspoons vanilla extract
1½ cups sugar

1. Heat the oven to 375 degrees.
2. Bring a large pot of salted water to a boil and cook the pasta until barely al dente. Drain well and place in a 2-quart ovenproof casserole.
3. Sprinkle the raisins over the pasta. Dust with a little sugar.
4. In a large bowl, whisk together the eggs, egg whites, vanilla and sugar until they turn yellow. In a pot bring the milk to a boil. Very gradually whisk the hot milk into the egg mixture.
5. Ladle the egg mixture over the pasta. Sprinkle with cinnamon.
6. Place the casserole dish in a water bath (a larger dish filled with several inches of water). Bake for 20 minutes at 375 degrees, lower heat to 350 and cook another 25 minutes. The custard should be firm to the touch.

Yield: Serves 6 to 8

What is the difference between Valencia and Navel oranges?

Valencia oranges, also known as "summer" oranges, are available from February through October. They are great for juicing, have few seeds, and have thin, loose skins. A navel orange is also very popular, available from November through May. Navels are considered the best eating oranges. They have no seeds and a thicker skin.

Another orange that is gaining in popularity is the blood orange. Popular in Europe, this is very sweet and seedless, with red flesh.

Stew's TIP

A *bain marie,* also called a double boiler, is a pot or pan of simmering water that gently heats the pot immersed in it. It promotes more even cooking all around for the ingredients in it, like sauces, custards, and other fragile ingredients.

Chef George's Knockout Bread Pudding

This is so easy a child could make it. It gets rave reviews from our customers!

Preparation Time: 30 MINUTES
Cooking Time: 45 MINUTES

PREPARE IN ADVANCE

3 tablespoons raisins
12 thin slices of French bread, like a baguette, buttered (or another type of bread)
4 eggs
2 egg whites
1½ teaspoons vanilla extract
½ cup sugar

1. Preheat the oven to 375 degrees.
2 Sprinkle the raisins over the bottom of a 1½- to 2-quart ovenproof casserole. Arrange the bread slices over the raisins, slightly overlapping (if you need more bread slices add them). Dust with sugar.
3. In a large bowl, whisk together the eggs, egg whites, vanilla, and sugar until they turn yellow. In a medium-sized pot, bring the milk to a boil. Very gradually whisk the milk into the egg mixture.
4. Ladle the egg mixture over the bread slices. Let it sit for 10 minutes. Sprinkle with cinnamon.
7. Place the casserole dish in a water bath (a larger dish filled with several inches of water. Bake for 20 minutes at 375 degrees, lower heat to 350 and cook another 25 minutes. The pudding should be firm to the touch.

Yield: Serves 6 to 8

Vanilla Custard with Fresh Blueberries

When sweet blueberries are in season this is a fabulous and easy-to-make dessert that looks great on the table.

Preparation Time: 15 MINUTES
Cooking Time: 45 MINUTES

SUPER FAST

PREPARE IN ADVANCE

6 egg yolks
¾ cups sugar
1½ cup milk
1 vanilla bean, split down the middle to expose the tiny seeds within (or 2 teaspoons vanilla extract)
1 pint blueberries, washed and stemmed
Powdered sugar for garnish

1. Preheat the oven to 375 degrees.
2. In a large bowl, whisk together the egg yolks and sugar for 45 seconds.
3. In a pot, combine the milk and the vanilla bean. Bring the milk to a boil; remove vanilla bean and take the milk off the heat.
4. Very slowly drizzle the milk into the egg mixture while whisking vigorously.
5. Pour the mixture into an ovenproof casserole (1- to 1½-quarts capacity). Place the casserole into a high-sided roasting pan holding 1 inch of water. Place in the oven and cook for about 45 minutes, or until the custard is firm to the touch (Another test is to pierce the custard with a thin skewer and see if it comes out clean). Remove and refrigerate.
6. When the custard is cool, run a large knife around the perimeter. Take a flat serving dish and place it firmly over casserole. Invert the custard so it transfers to the serving tray.
7. Cover the top of the custard with blueberries. Dust with powdered sugar.

Yield: Serves 6 to 8

Stew's TIP

Save the paper wrappers from butter or margarine to grease cookie sheets, cake pans, and so on. Fold them in half and store them in a plastic bag and freeze until needed.

Stew's TIP

Lemon is a critical ingredient in many dishes. Lemon zest — the highly aromatic yellow skin, without the bitter white pith — adds a cleansing, sharp sensation to rich foods. To remove the zest, scrape a lemon over the small holes of a kitchen grater.

Remember that most storebought lemons have a waxy coating for protection during shipping. Wash the lemons with warm water and a little soap before extracting lemon zest.

If you leave a lemon uncovered after removing the zest, it will lose much of its flavor in just a few days. Peeled or cut lemons will keep for two weeks or longer if stored in an airtight plastic bag or jar.

Panna Cotta (Italian Dessert Cream)

Panna cotta means "cooked cream" in Italian. This subtly sweet dessert is essentially an eggless custard. Prepare it in spring or late summer when ripe berries and fruits are at their glorious peak.

Preparation Time: 5 MINUTES
Cooking Time: 10 MINUTES (plus overnight chilling)

SUPER FAST
PREPARE IN ADVANCE

2 cups half-and-half
Pinch of cinnamon
1 tablespoon lemon zest (about 1 medium lemon)
⅓ cup sugar
1 envelope gelatin dissolved in ¼ cup cold water (in a medium-size bowl)

1. In a stainless steel pot, bring the half-and-half to a boil then add the cinnamon and lemon zest. Remove the pot from the heat.
2. Slowly beat 1 cup of the hot cream mixture into the dissolved gelatin. Add the mixture to the rest of the cooked cream and stir until completely blended.
3. Pour the mixture into 6 ramekins (8-ounce capacity) or a single 6-cup serving bowl. Allow the mixture to cool completely, then cover and refrigerate for 6 hours or overnight.
4. If you like, unmold before serving, and garnish with fresh raspberries, sliced fresh strawberries, or any ripe fruit. To unmold, run hot tap water over the bottom of the ramekin. Run a thin knife around the perimeter of the custard. Place the ramekin upside down on the serving plate and tap the bottom.

Yield: 6 servings

Mocha Walnut Tart

This irresistible tart never lasts long when we make it. The coffee flavor cuts the sweetness and gives it a faint sharp edge. If you don't want to make the crust, buy an 9- or 11-inch frozen pie shell. If you have leftover filling you can bake it like brownies.

Preparation Time: ABOUT 40 MINUTES
Cooking Time: ABOUT 35 MINUTES

PREPARE IN ADVANCE

The crust:

1 cup all-purpose flour
Pinch of salt
4 ounces cream cheese, cut into 1-inch cubes
2 tablespoons butter, cut into 1-inch cubes

The filling:

2 tablespoon instant coffee
2 tablespoons rum or vanilla extract
3 ounces unsweetened chocolate
2 tablespoons butter
3 eggs
¾ cup brown sugar
½ cup light corn syrup
2 cups chopped walnuts
Pinch of salt

1. Preheat the oven to 350 degrees.
2. Blend the flour and salt in a mixing bowl. With your hands or a pastry cutter, blend the cream cheese and butter into the flour to make a smooth, soft dough. Shape the dough into a ball, cover with plastic wrap, and refrigerate until needed.
3. To roll out the crust, place the cool dough on a floured sheet of waxed paper. With a well-floured rolling pin, roll it into a ¼-inch-thick round about 12 to 13 inches in diameter. Line an 11-inch tart pan or a 9-inch pie dish with the dough. Trim the excess dough and crimp the edges to form a decorative border. Refrigerate until ready to bake.
4. To make the filling, dissolve the instant coffee in the rum or vanilla extract in the top of a bain marie (double boiler) or a pot filled with 2 inches simmering water and with a mixing bowl on top. Add the chocolate and remaining butter. The mixture will have a grainy, mud-like consistency, but don't worry. When the chocolate is melted, set aside in a warm spot.
5. Place the eggs and brown sugar in a bowl and mix with an electric blender or mixer at high speed. When the mixture doubles in volume, add the corn syrup, then the melted chocolate. Stir in the nuts and salt.
6. Pour the filling into the pastry-lined pan. Bake on the center rack of the oven for 30 to 35 minutes or until the center puffs slightly.
7. Cool the tart on a wire rack. Serve with a sprinkling of powdered sugar and a large dollop of whipped cream.

Yield: 8 to 10 servings

Stew's TIP

Mocha is the combined flavors of chocolate and coffee. The proportions of each really depends on your taste. We used two tablespoons of coffee to 3 ounces of bittersweet chocolate, which yields a predominantly chocolate flavor with a sharp coffee edge.

Chocolate-Chunk Banana Bread

Whoever discovered the combination of bananas and chocolate deserves a plaque in the Dessert Hall of Fame. This delicious creation combines the ease of a quick banana bread enhanced with the bittersweet taste of chocolate. Kids love it. Serve the banana bread warm, perhaps with a scoop of ice cream.

Preparation Time: 20 MINUTES
Cooking Time: ABOUT 1 HOUR AND 15 MINUTES

½ cup unsalted butter or margarine at room temperature (1 stick)
½ cup dark brown sugar
½ cup granulated sugar
1 teaspoon vanilla extract
2 eggs, beaten
¼ teaspoon salt
1½ teaspoons baking powder
½ teaspoon baking soda
½ cup yogurt
1 cup of mashed banana (2 ripe bananas)
2 cups of all-purpose flour
1 cup semisweet chocolate chips

1. Preheat the oven to 350 degrees.
2. Grease a loaf pan measuring 9 x 5 inches, and 3 inches deep (approximately). Set aside.
3. In the bowl of an electric mixer, beat the butter at high speed with both sugars until light and creamy (about 2 minutes). Add the vanilla, eggs, and salt. Beat for 1 more minute. Scrape down the bowl with a rubber spatula. Beat briefly.
4. While the butter mixture is beating, stir the baking powder and baking soda into the yogurt. Add to the butter mixture. Beat together.
5. Add bananas to the mixture, then the flour. Scrape the bowl. Stir in chocolate chips.
6. Pour the batter into the prepared loaf pan and bake on the center rack of the oven for 1 hour. Lower the heat to 325 degrees and bake for an additional 10 to 15 minutes, or until a toothpick inserted in the center of the cake comes out clean.
7. Place the pan on a wire rack for 20 minutes, then remove the bread from the pan. Serve warm. This bread keeps for 1 week in the refrigerator or up to 1 month in the freezer.

Yield: 12 servings

Carmine Vartolone has been making bread for more than 25 years. He grew up in Palermo, Italy, and is one of our master bakers at Stew's.

Coffee Crumble Parfait

Everyone has a set of flea-market treasures or forgotten wedding gifts that never get used. Here is a no-fuss dessert that can be served in those mixed stem glasses gathering dust in the cabinet. Assemble these layered parfaits in the afternoon and keep them frozen until a half-hour before serving.

Preparation Time: 10 MINUTES
Cooking Time: 15 MINUTES

SUPER FAST

PREPARE IN ADVANCE

6 whole Graham crackers
1 pint cappuccino or coffee-flavored frozen yogurt
6 tablespoons chopped peanuts
1 pint chocolate frozen yogurt
6 tablespoons rum
6 teaspoons honey
½ cup plain yogurt or whipped cream
1 ounce bittersweet chocolate

1. Crumble half a Graham cracker into each of six 8-ounce stem glasses. Add a few spoonfuls of cappuccino frozen yogurt, a tablespoon of peanuts, and some chocolate frozen yogurt. Drizzle each with rum and repeat the process until the glasses are full. Top each with a teaspoon of honey.
2. Place the filled glasses in the freezer. Half an hour before serving, transfer the parfaits to the refrigerator to soften the yogurt slightly.
3. Top each parfait with a spoon of whipped cream and a grating of semisweet chocolate.

Yield: 6 servings

Stew's TIP

You can have fun playing with different fruit flavors in these parfaits. Try fresh raspberries layered with honey vanilla frozen yogurt, raspberry jam and raspberry liqueur.

Another might be crushed chocolate wafers layered with strawberry ice cream, mint liqueur, and chocolate chips. Go for it!

Crunchy Peanut Butter Cookies

The pure taste of unsweetened, unadulterated peanut butter (like Smucker's) makes the best cookie. These cookies are especially crisp because butter and vegetable shortening are used. Add your favorite chips or nuts to add crunch.

Preparation Time: 15 to 20 MINUTES
Cooking Time: ABOUT 20 MINUTES

SUPER FAST · PREPARE IN ADVANCE

4 ounces unsalted butter or margarine, at room temperature (1 stick of butter)
¼ cup vegetable shortening
1 cup peanut butter
1 cup sugar
1 egg
1 cup raw oatmeal
1½ cups all-purpose flour
½ teaspoon salt
½ teaspoon baking soda
½ cup chocolate chips
Granulated sugar for garnish

1. Preheat the oven to 350 degrees. Grease a cookie sheet.
2. Beat the butter or margarine, vegetable shortening, peanut butter, and sugar in an electric mixer for 2 to 3 minutes until light and creamy. Add the egg and beat just to combine.
3. In a separate bowl, combine the oatmeal, flour, salt, and baking soda. With the mixer set at low speed, blend the dry ingredients into the butter mixture. Stir in the nuts or chips.
4. Form the dough into 2-inch balls placed 2 inches apart on a cookie sheet. Press the cookies with the back of a fork to flatten slightly. Sprinkle with sugar. Bake on the center rack of the oven for 18 to 24 minutes. Cool the cookies on a wire rack.

Yield: 3 dozen 3-inch cookies

Debbie Fields and my dad love to talk about baking and how to make great cookies. They are good friends and entrepreneurs, too!

Reverse Chocolate Chip Cookies

Here is a winsome twist on a favorite sweet: these are chocolate cookies with white chocolate chips. They also contain ground coriander, which gives them a zesty edge.

Preparation Time: 15 MINUTES
Cooking Time: 15 MINUTES (per batch)

PREPARE IN ADVANCE

1 stick of softened butter
1 cup firmly packed dark-brown sugar
1 teaspoon vanilla extract
1 large egg
1 cup all-purpose flour
⅓ cup cocoa powder
1 teaspoons salt
½ teaspoon double-acting baking powder
1 tablespoon ground coriander
1 cup of macadamia nuts, sliced almonds, walnuts, or other nuts
1½ cups of white chocolate chips

1. Preheat oven to 375 degrees.
2. Grease two cookie sheets.
3. In a bowl, cream the butter with an electric mixer. Beat in the sugar a little at a time until the mixture is lightened. Add the vanilla, then beat in the egg. With the mixer set to low, stir in the flour, cocoa powder, salt, baking powder, and coriander. Then stir in the nuts and chocolate chips.
4. Form the cookies by scooping up ⅓ cup of the batter and dropping it on the greased cookie sheet. Repeat, making rows of cookies roughly 3 inches apart. Bake the cookies on the middle rack of the oven for 12 to 15 minutes, or until lightly browned.

Yield: 20 3-inch cookies

Stew's TIP

History took a great leap forward when Central American and Mexican Indians discovered chocolate, which they used mainly in drinks. In the 16th century Spanish conquistadors took the cocoa plant back to Europe — the Greek botanical name for it, *theobroma*, translates as "Food of the Gods." After refinements were made in preparing chocolate it was brought back to the American continent.

By the mid-1600s much of Europe was in the habit of drinking chocolate beverages. In the 1700s the Austrians discovered that chocolate had wider uses, specifically as an ingredient in cakes. In the 1840s the first chocolate candies appeared in England, and diets have never been the same since.

My sister Beth started Bethy's Bakery from scratch. She now sells more than 250,000 cookies a week, 50,000 muffins, and more than 20,000 loaves of bread! What a sister!

Stew's TIP

When you are whipping egg whites, be sure that the bowl you use is absolutely clean. Any little bit of grease or dirt will prevent the egg whites from fluffing up. Also, if you have trouble getting egg whites to foam add a pinch of cream of tartar.

The Amazing Leonard Brownies

These moist, intense brownies can be made in about 45 minutes, including cooking. You won't be able to eat just one.

Preparation Time: 10 MINUTES
Cooking Time: ABOUT 35 MINUTES

PREPARE IN ADVANCE

½-inch pat of butter, for greasing the baking dish
8 ounces bittersweet dark chocolate, chopped into dime-size pieces
¾ cup butter (1½ sticks)
4 eggs
2 cups sugar
1 vanilla bean, split lengthwise, or 1 teaspoon vanilla extract
½ teaspoon salt
1½ cups flour
1½ cups shelled walnuts or pecans, chopped

1. Preheat the oven to 350 degrees. Grease a 9 x 12-inch baking dish.
2. Set aside ⅓ of the chocolate pieces and place the rest and all the butter into a metal bowl. Place the metal bowl over another bowl of very hot tap water to melt it. Set aside and keep warm.
3. Place the eggs, sugar, vanilla, and salt in a mixing bowl and beat until frothy.
4. Stir in the melted chocolate mixture and then gently fold in the flour, nuts and remaining chocolate pieces until well blended.
5. Pour the mixture into a baking dish and spread the top evenly. Bake for 30 to 40 minutes. The center should still be a little soft.
6. Remove the brownies from the oven and let cool for 1 hour. Cut into 3 x 3-inch pieces.

Yield: 12 portions

Bob Wesley, Sales Director, fills the egg display at Stew's. We get our eggs from local farms. Organic eggs are getting more and more popular with our customers," Bob says.

"Pucker up!"

Aunt Helen Clark's Lemon Pie

This old-fashioned lemon pie has been a staple at Leonard family gatherings for years.

Preparation Time: 15 MINUTES
Cooking Time: ABOUT 20 MINUTES

PREPARE IN ADVANCE

1¼ cup sugar
6 tablespoons cornstarch
½ teaspoon salt
2 cups cold milk
3 eggs, separated
2 tablespoons unsalted butter
2 teaspoons grated lemon zest
½ cup lemon juice
1 baked 9-inch frozen pie crust

1. In the top of a double boiler (see definition of double boiler page 326), combine 1 cup of the sugar with the cornstarch, salt, and milk. Cook for 2 minutes, stirring constantly. Beat in the egg yolks and cook for 3 to 4 minutes, until thickened and bubbling slightly.
2. Remove the pot from the heat and stir in the butter, lemon rind, and juice. Let mixture cool completely. The custard may be prepared up to this point as much as 2 days in advance and kept covered in the refrigerator.
3. Before serving, preheat the oven to 350 degrees. Spoon the cold filling into the pie shell. Refrigerate while you make the meringue. Beat the egg whites at high speed with an electric mixer until they become stiff but not dry (about 5 minutes). Add the remaining ¼ cup of sugar and beat until stiff.
4. Spoon the meringue on top of the custard. Bake the pie until the meringue is golden brown (about 7 minutes). Serve immediately. If not used immediately, keep in a cool place.

Yield: 8 servings

Stew's TIP

You will notice that in some recipes we call for cake flour. Widely available, cake flour has less gluten than regular flour and yields a lighter result.

Bret Cherry and Loretta Miller check on some hot pies coming out of the oven. We sell more than 40,000 pies just during the week of Thanksgiving!

Stew's TIP

You may substitute whatever pitted fruit — peaches, pears, cherries and the like — for the plums in this spoon bread. Traditional spoon breads are made with cornmeal, either white or yellow. Our unconventional dessert spoon bread is made with flour, which is more compatible with the fresh fruit.

Plum Spoon Bread

In Colonial New England, breads and corn cakes were often cooked in a cast-iron pan over an open fire of burning thin timbers, called spoons. Today, any soft bread or cake served in the pan in which it is baked is called spoon bread in memory of this tradition.

Preparation Time: 20 MINUTES
Cooking Time: 40 MINUTES

PREPARE IN ADVANCE

8 tablespoons unsalted butter or margarine, room temperature
1½ cups granulated sugar
1 pound plums, about 6
2 cups cake flour or all-purpose flour
2 eggs, beaten
1 cup plain yogurt
1 teaspoon grated lemon zest
1 tablespoon baking powder
1 teaspoon ground cinnamon
½ teaspoon salt
Powdered sugar for decoration

1. Preheat the oven to 350 degrees. Grease a shallow two-quart glass or ceramic casserole and sprinkle with 2 tablespoons of the sugar.
2. Cut the plums in half, remove the pits, and cut into ¼-inch slices. Toss with 3 tablespoons of the flour. Set aside.
3. Using an electric mixer, beat butter or margarine and remainder of the sugar until creamy. Add the eggs, yogurt and lemon zest and stir well.
4. In separate bowl, combine remaining flour, baking powder, cinnamon, and salt. Stir into the egg mixture and beat for a few seconds to blend. Fold in the plums. Pour the batter into the prepared casserole, smoothing the surface with a spatula.
5. Bake for 35 to 45 minutes or until a toothpick inserted in the center of the cake comes out clean.
6. Serve with a sprinkle of powdered sugar and a dollop of whipped cream, ice cream or sour cream. This spoon bread keeps for one week in the refrigerator.

Yield: 10 to 12 servings

"A family winner!"

Aunt Bernetta's Rhubarb Pie

Aunt Bernetta's sweet-sour torte has always been a treat at family summer gatherings. When buying fresh rhubarb, choose stalks that are crisp and straight, not limp.

Preparation Time: ABOUT 10 MINUTES
Cooking Time: 45 MINUTES

PREPARE IN ADVANCE

For the crust *(or buy one frozen 9-inch pie crust):*
2½ cups flour
¾ cup vegetable shortening
3 tablespoons sugar
Pinch of salt

For the filling:
2 pounds rhubarb, cut into ½-inch pieces
2 cups sugar
½ cup buttermilk
4 eggs, separated
3 tablespoons flour
¼ teaspoon cream of tartar
Pinch of salt

1. Preheat oven to 350 degrees.
2. To make the crust, place the flour, shortening, sugar, and salt in a bowl and crumble with your fingers to blend (or put in a food processor with the plastic dough blade). Pat this mixture into the bottom of a 9-inch pie pan. Bake the crust for 15 to 20 minutes in the preheated oven until golden brown.
3. While the crust is baking, combine the rhubarb, 1 cup of the sugar, and the buttermilk in a pot over high heat. Bring the mixture to a boil, reduce the heat to medium, and cover. Simmer for 5 minutes until the rhubarb is soft. Set aside.
4. While the rhubarb is cooking, whisk the egg yolks and 1 cup of the sugar until light and foamy. Whisk a little of the hot rhubarb mixture into the egg mixture. Stir to blend, then pour that mixture back into the saucepan of cooked rhubarb. Cook the rhubarb for 2 more minutes, stirring constantly so the egg yolks do not curdle. Pour the filling into the hot crust.
5. In a clean mixing bowl, beat with a mixer or a whisk the egg whites, salt, and cream of tartar until stiff. Beat in the remaining ¾ cup sugar. Spoon this meringue on top of the hot filling. Place the pan in the oven and bake for 12 to 15 minutes, or until the meringue is golden brown. Let the pie cool completely.

Yield: 8 to 10 servings

How do I make meringue?

Meringue is really quite simple — all you need is a good strong arm or a mixing machine. The one in this recipe is called French meringue, in which you fold sugar into the egg whites *after* they have been whipped stiff. This is the meringue you find on baked Alaska, in layer cakes, and mousses. If you are having trouble getting the meringue to form peaks, add a pinch of cream of tartar; that helps bubbles form and makes the mixture rise. Also, egg whites are best beaten at room temperature. Lastly, your workbowl must be immaculately clean. Any grease, dirt or fat inhibits the formation of air bubbles. Copper bowls are best for making meringue — there is something about the chemical composition of copper that enhances the foaming of egg whites.

Index

R

S